OFFICIAL HISTORY OF
THE INDIAN ARMED FORCES
IN THE SECOND WORLD WAR
1939–45

ATLAS

CAMPAIGNS IN THE WESTERN THEATRE

OFFICIAL HISTORY OF THE INDIAN ARMED FORCES IN THE SECOND WORLD WAR 1939–45

ATLAS

CAMPAIGNS IN THE WESTERN THEATRE

THE CAMPAIGN IN ITALY
1943–45

THE NORTH AFRICAN CAMPAIGN
1940–43

CAMPAIGNS IN WESTERN ASIA

EAST AFRICA CAMPAIGN
1940–41

The Naval & Military Press Ltd

Published by

The Naval & Military Press Ltd

Unit 5 Riverside, Brambleside
Bellbrook Industrial Estate
Uckfield, East Sussex
TN22 1QQ England

Tel: +44 (0)1825 749494

www.naval-military-press.com
www.nmarchive.com

In reprinting in facsimile from the original, any imperfections are inevitably reproduced and the quality may fall short of modern type and cartographic standards.

OFFICIAL HISTORY OF THE INDIAN ARMED FORCES
IN THE SECOND WORLD WAR
1939-45

THE CAMPAIGN IN ITALY
1943-45

Maps and Sketches

The Campaign in Italy 1942–45
List of maps

1. Map of Italy
2. Crossing of the Biferno & the Trigno (October-November 1942)
3. 8 Indian Division's Advance to the River Sangro (6-19 November 1943)
4. The crossing of the Sangro by V Corps (27-30 November 1943)
5. 2nd New Zealand Division's thrust towards Orgogna (2-3 December 1943)
6. Cassino area
7. Monte Cassino and Cassino town
8. The Liri Valley Offensive (May 1944)
9. Dispositions of Rival Forces (11 May 1944)
10. Operation Honker (11-16 May 1944)
11. 8 Indian Division's advance to Guarcino (1-4 June 1944)
12. The Ortona-Orsogna Sector
13. Rome area
14. 17 Indian Infantry Brigade's attack on the Ripa ridge (18-19 June 1944)
15. 4 Indian Division's advance (8-12 June 1944).
16. Advance in the Tiber Valley (30 June-22 July 1944)
17. 10 Indian Division's advance to Citta di Castello (6-22 July 1944)
18. 10 Indian Infantry Brigade's attack on Trestina (9-12 July 1944)
19. 4 Indian Division's advance (9-17 July 1944)
20. 21 Indian Infantry Brigade's advance to Montespertoli (23-27 July 1944)
21. Empoli area
22. 21 Indian Infantry Brigade's advance to the river Arno (27 July-4 August 1944)
23. Advance towards Bibbiena
24. Anghiari area
25. M. Castiglione area

26 Subbiano area
27 Alpe di Catenaia area
28 Allied and German Dispositions (25 August 1944)
29 4 Indian Division's advance to S. Marino (25 August-20 September 1944)
30 4 Indian Division's advance to Urbino (25-28 August 1944)
31 4 Indian Division's advance to Tavoleto–S. Giovanni (29 August-6 September 1944)
32 Piano di Castello–Coriano area
33 4 Indian Division's·advance to M.S.Colomba
34 43 Indian Infantry Brigade's advance: to river Marano (1-15 September 1944)
35 Fifth Army breaks through the Gothic Line (13-22 September 1944)
36 8 Indian Division's advance to M. Calvana (1-3 September 1944)
37 8 Indian Division's advance to Femmina Morta (12-18 September l944)
38 Bibbiena area
39 11 Indian Infantry Brigade's attack· on the: Monte-bello-Scorticata ridge (22-23 September 1944)
40 43 Indian Infantry Brigade's bridge-head on the river Marecchia (23-24 September 1944)
41 S. Martino Sogliano area
42 M. Farneto area
43 20 Indian Infantry Brigade's attack on M. Cavallo (21-23 October 1944)
44 10 Indian Infantry Division's bridge-heads on the river Ronco (23-30 October 1944)
45 Marradi area
46 M. Cavallara area
47 M. Pianoereno area
48 21 Indian Infantry Brigade's attack M. Pianoereno and M. Romano (17-22 October 1944)
49 Dispositions of 10 Indian Infantry Brigade (20 November 1944)
50 10 Indian Division's advance to the river Lamone (24 November-2 December 1944)

51	V Corps plan for the December Offensive
52	Pideura–Olmatello area (10 Indian Division's advance, 14-15 December 1944)
53	10 Indian Division's advance to the river Senio (10-20 December 1944)
54	Faenza area (43 Indian Infantry Brigade's advance, 17-20 December 1944)
55	17 Indian Infantry Brigade's advance to M.S. Bartolo (3-14 November 1944)
56	Dispositions of 8 Indian Division in the Serchio Valley
57	Dispositions of 10 Indian Division in S. Clemente area (February 1945)
58	Monte Grande area (dispositions of 25 Indian Infantry Brigade, March 1945)
59	43 Indian Infantry Brigade's attack on Senio river defences (February–March 1945)
60	Allied and German dispositions (9 April 1945)
61	V Corps dispositions (9 April 1945)
62	Dispositions of 8 Indian Division (7-9 April 1945)
63	8 Indian Division's advance to Scolo Tratturo (9-10 April 1945)
64	Medicina area
65	43 Indian Infantry Brigade's advance to Medicina
66	10 Indian Division's advance to the river Idice (17-21 April 1945)
67	25 Indian Infantry Brigade's advance to the river Reno (21-23 April 1945)
68	8 Indian Division's advance to the river Po (21-25 April 1945)
69	8 Indian Division's bridge-head over the river Po (25-26 April 1945)
70	17 Indian Infantry Brigade's advance to Vescovana (26-28 April 1945)

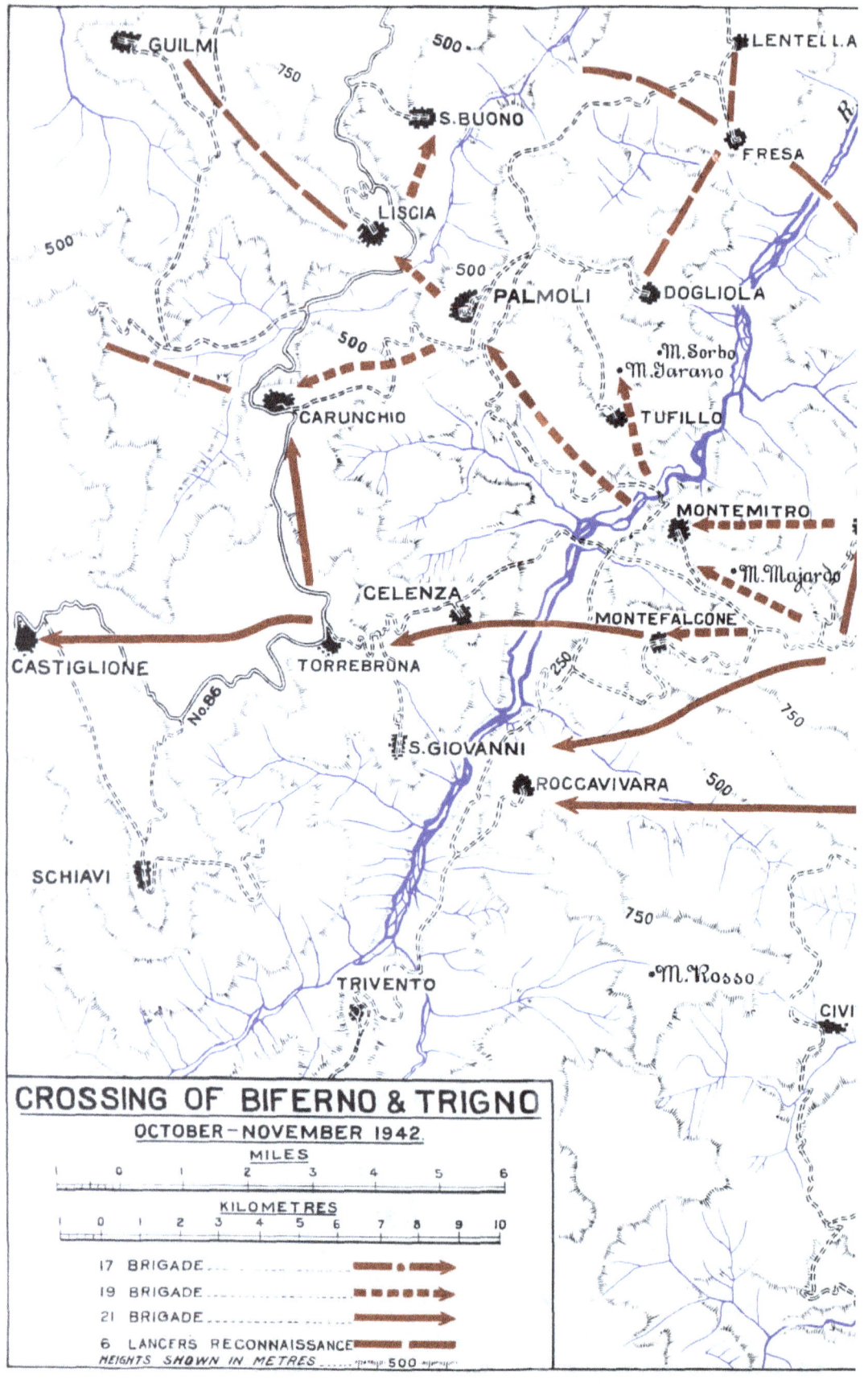

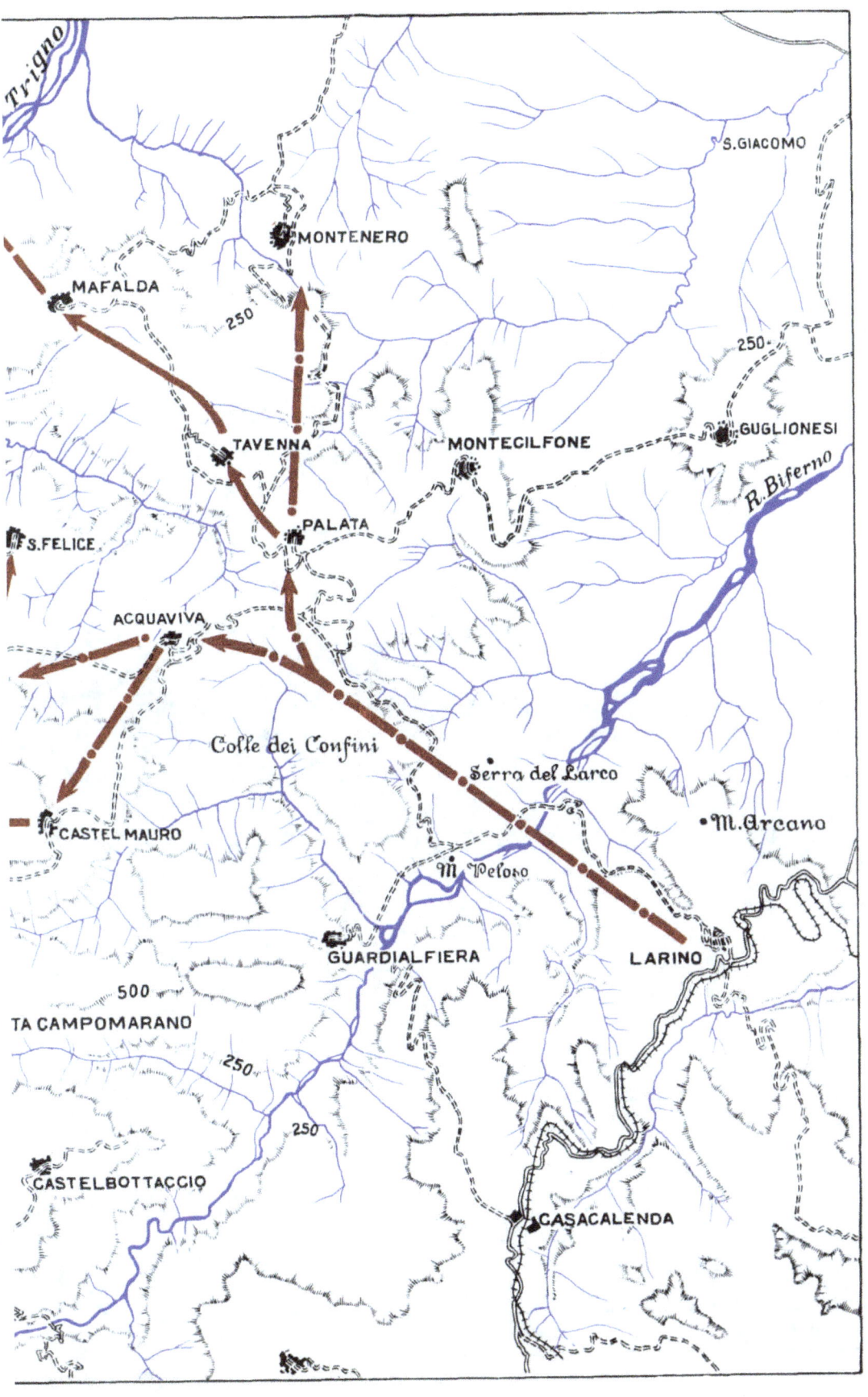

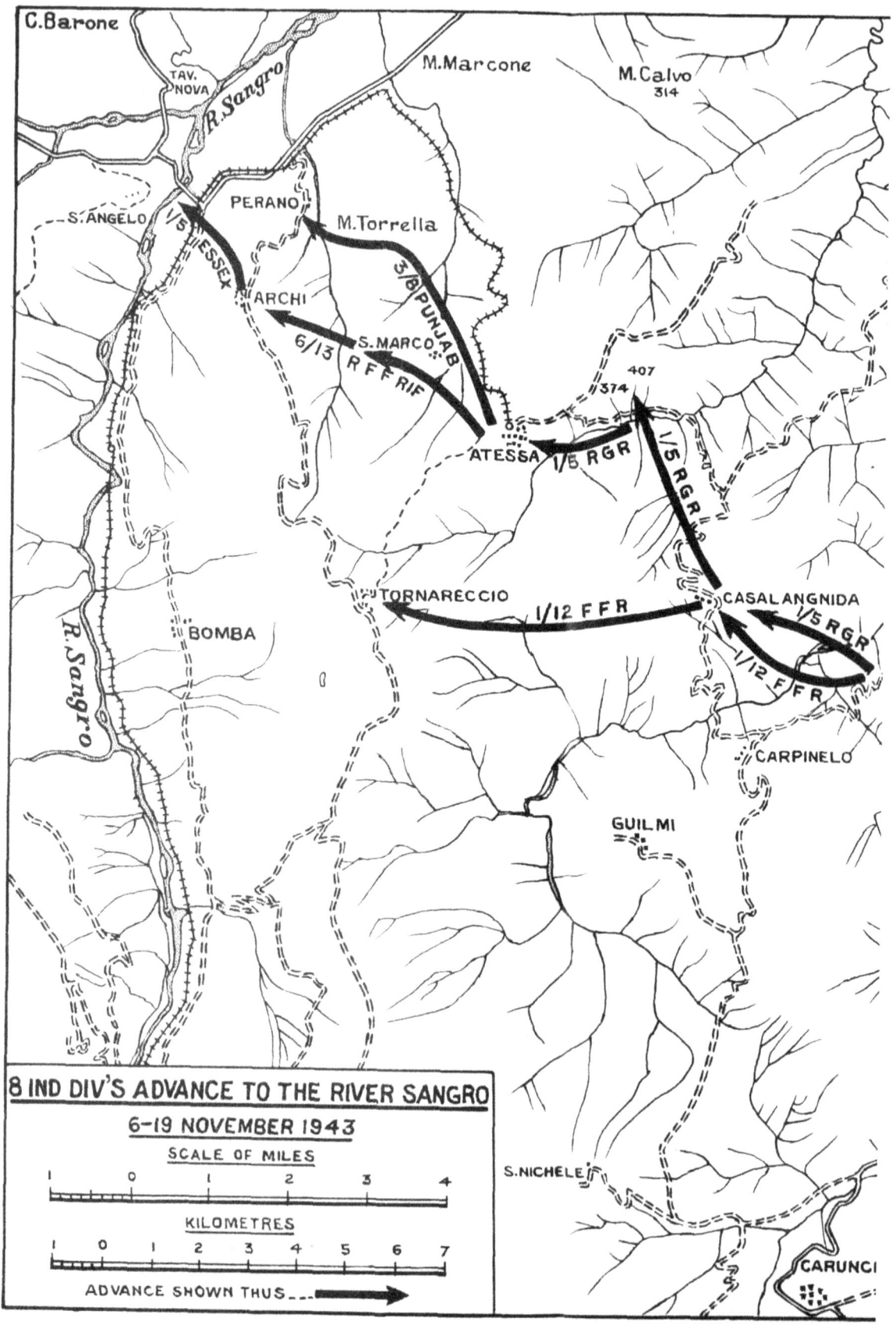

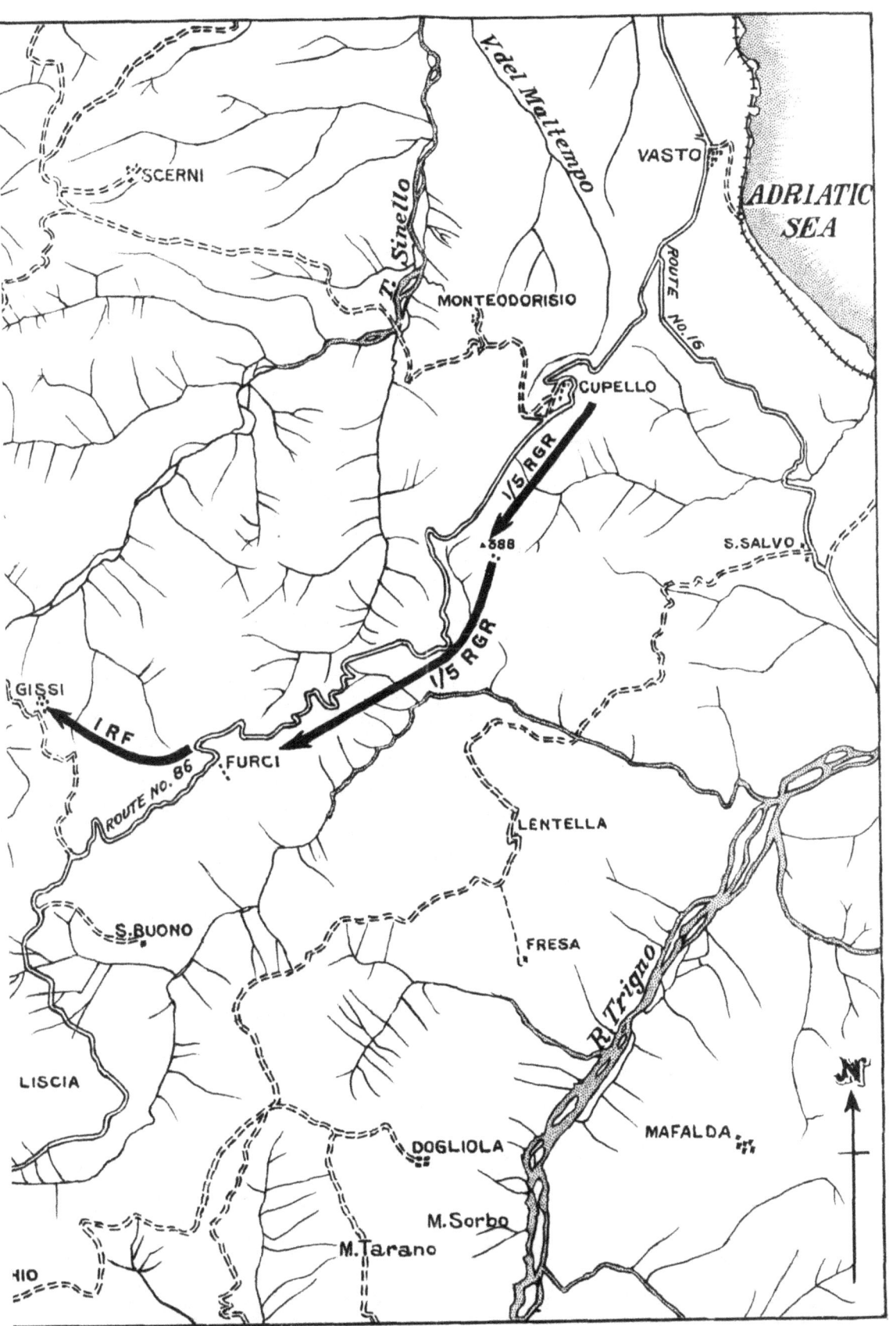

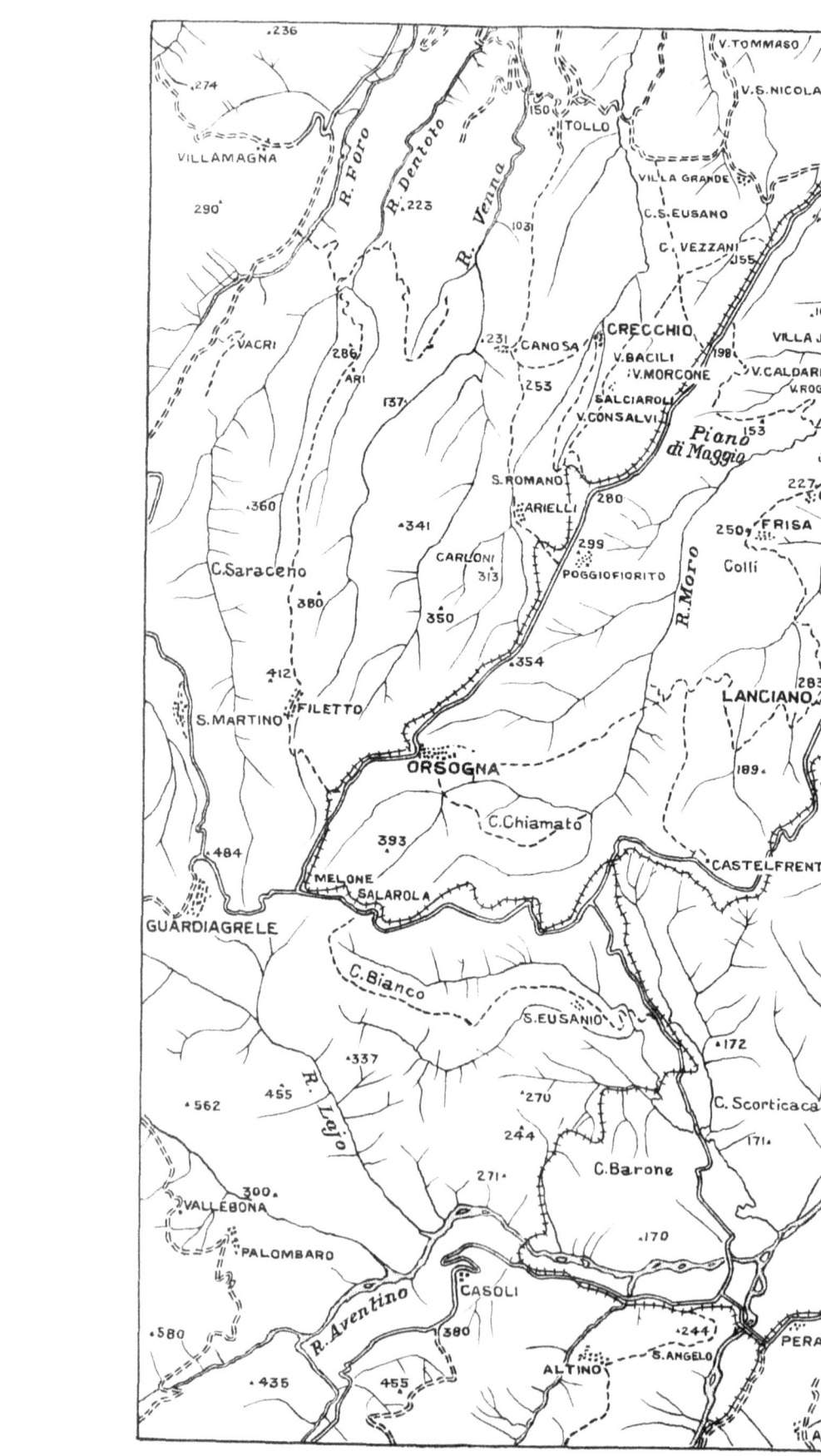

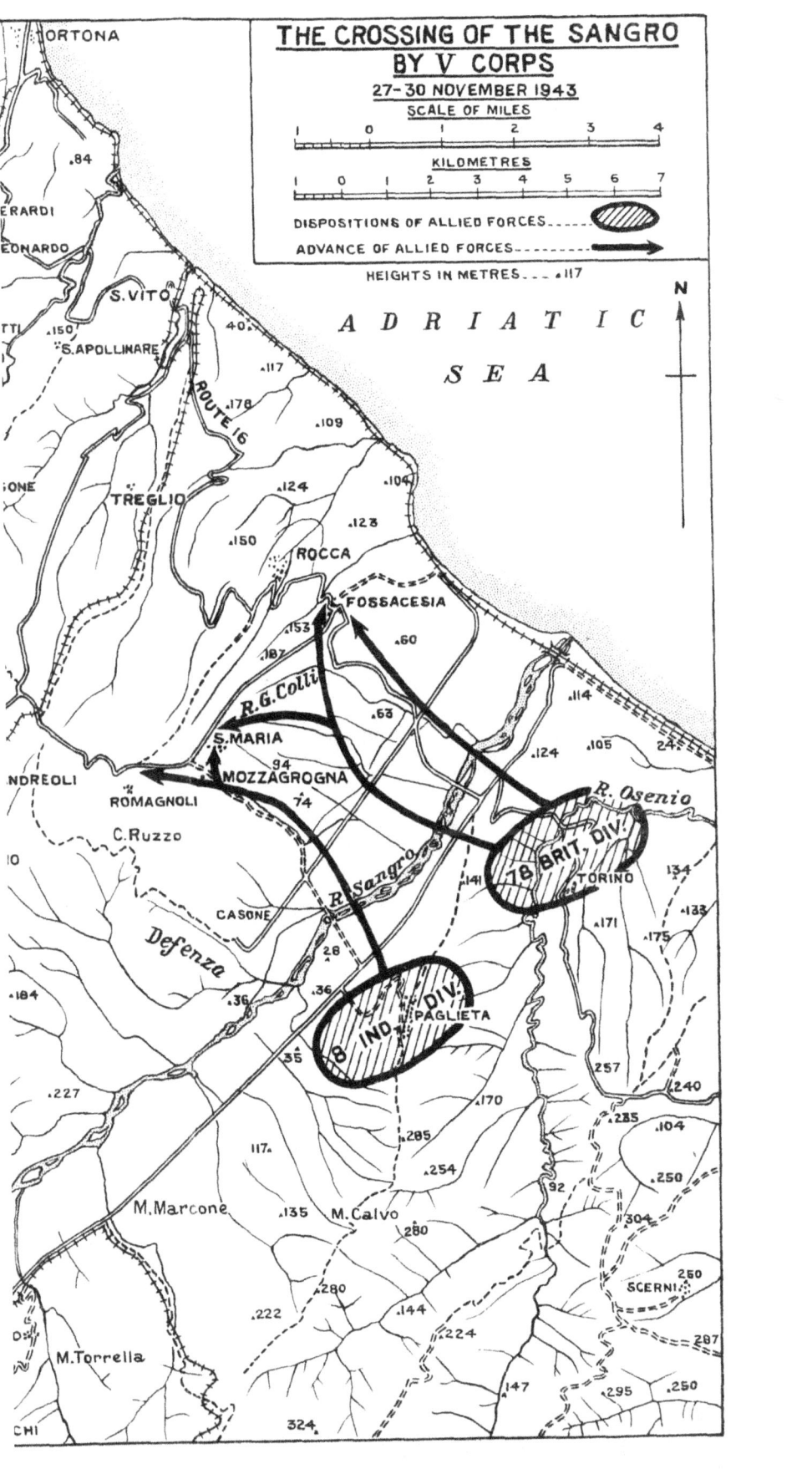

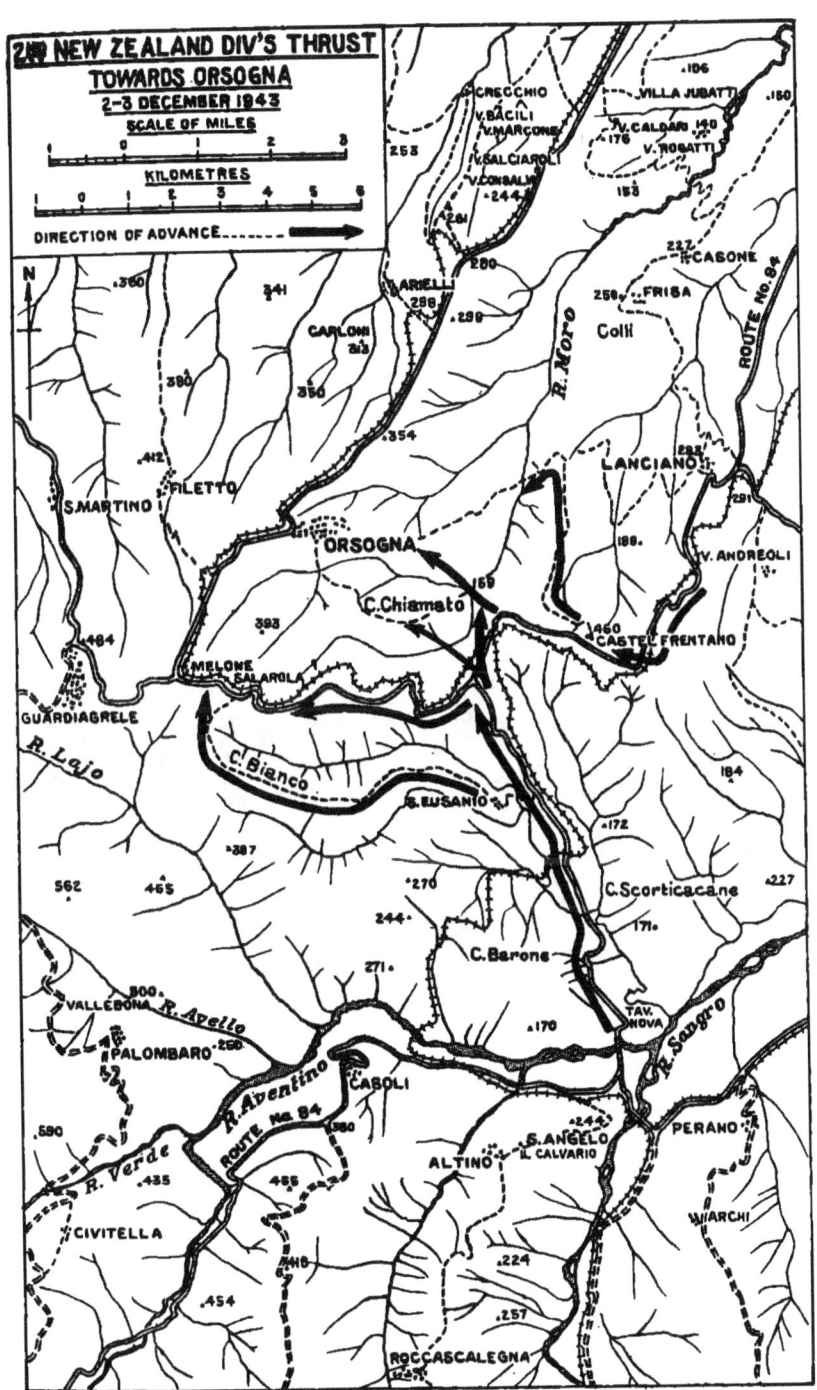

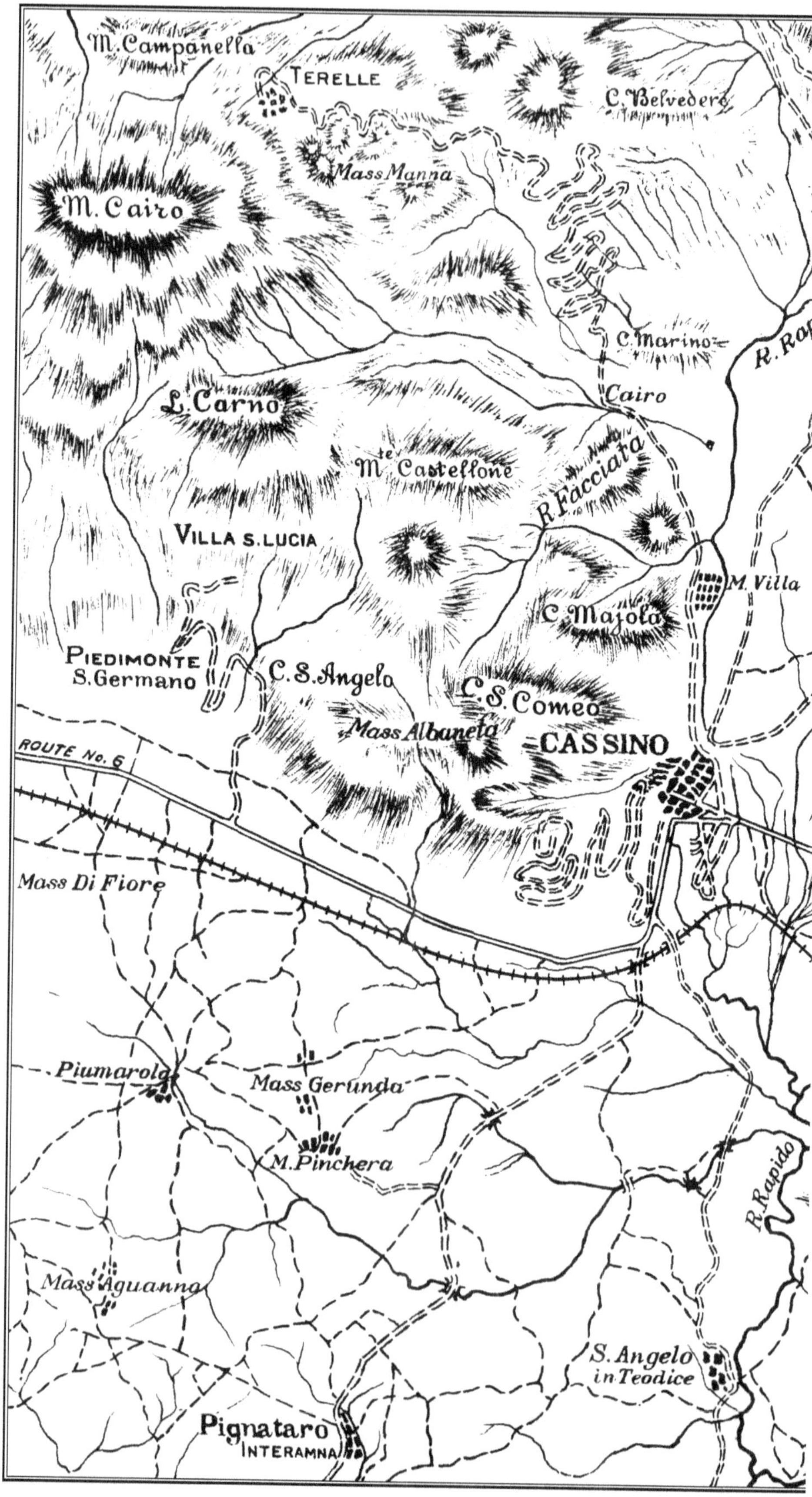
M. Campanella
TERELLE
C. Belvedere
Mass Manna
M. Cairo
C. Marino
R. Rapi
Cairo
L. Carno
Mte Castellone
R. Facciata
VILLA S. LUCIA
M. Villa
C. Majola
PIEDIMONTE
S. Germano
C. S. Angelo
C. S. Comeo
Mass Albaneta
CASSINO
ROUTE No. 6
Mass Di Fiore
Piumarola
Mass Gerunda
M. Pinchera
R. Rapido
Mass Aguanna
S. Angelo
in Teodice
Pignataro
INTERAMNA

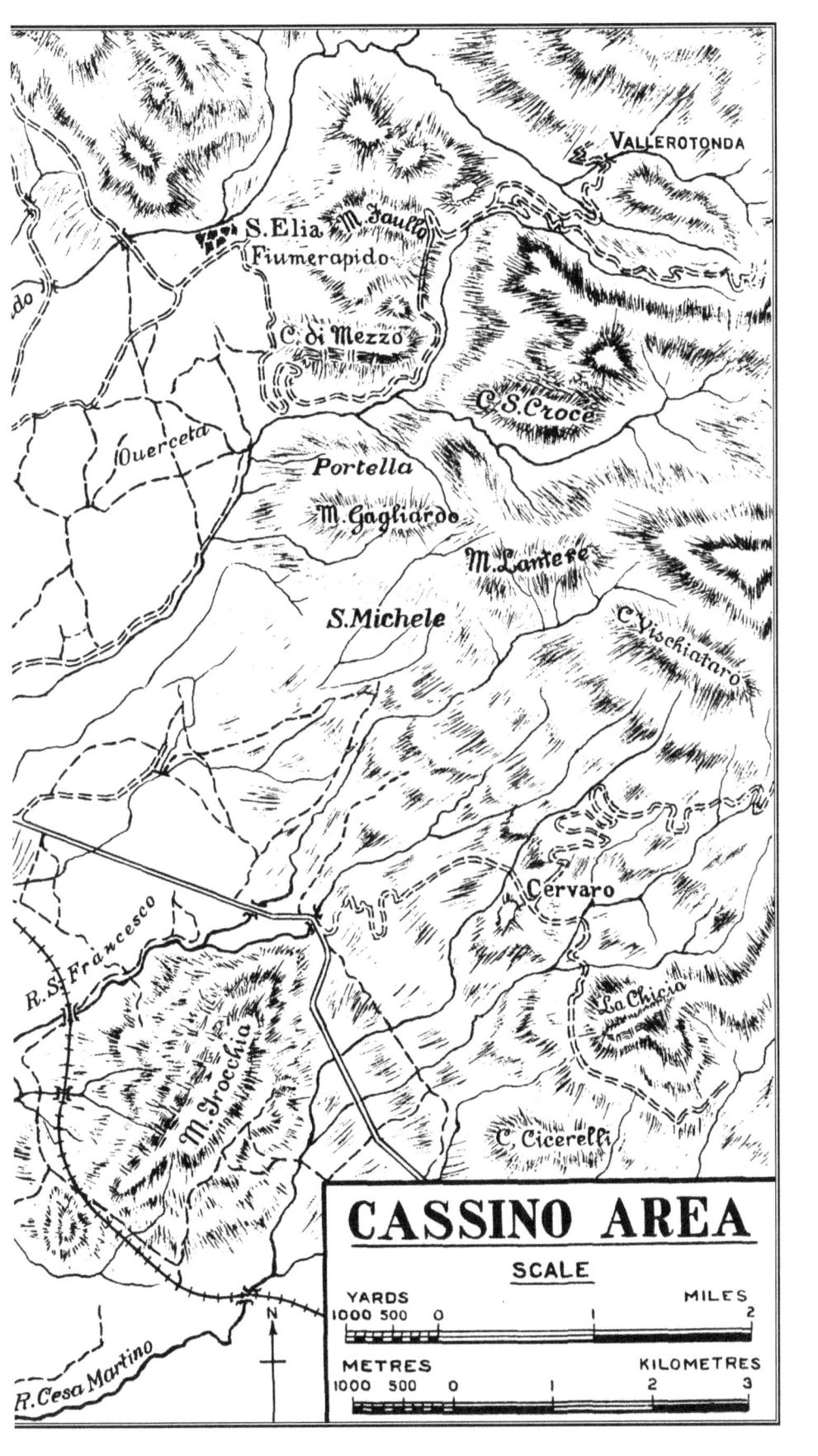

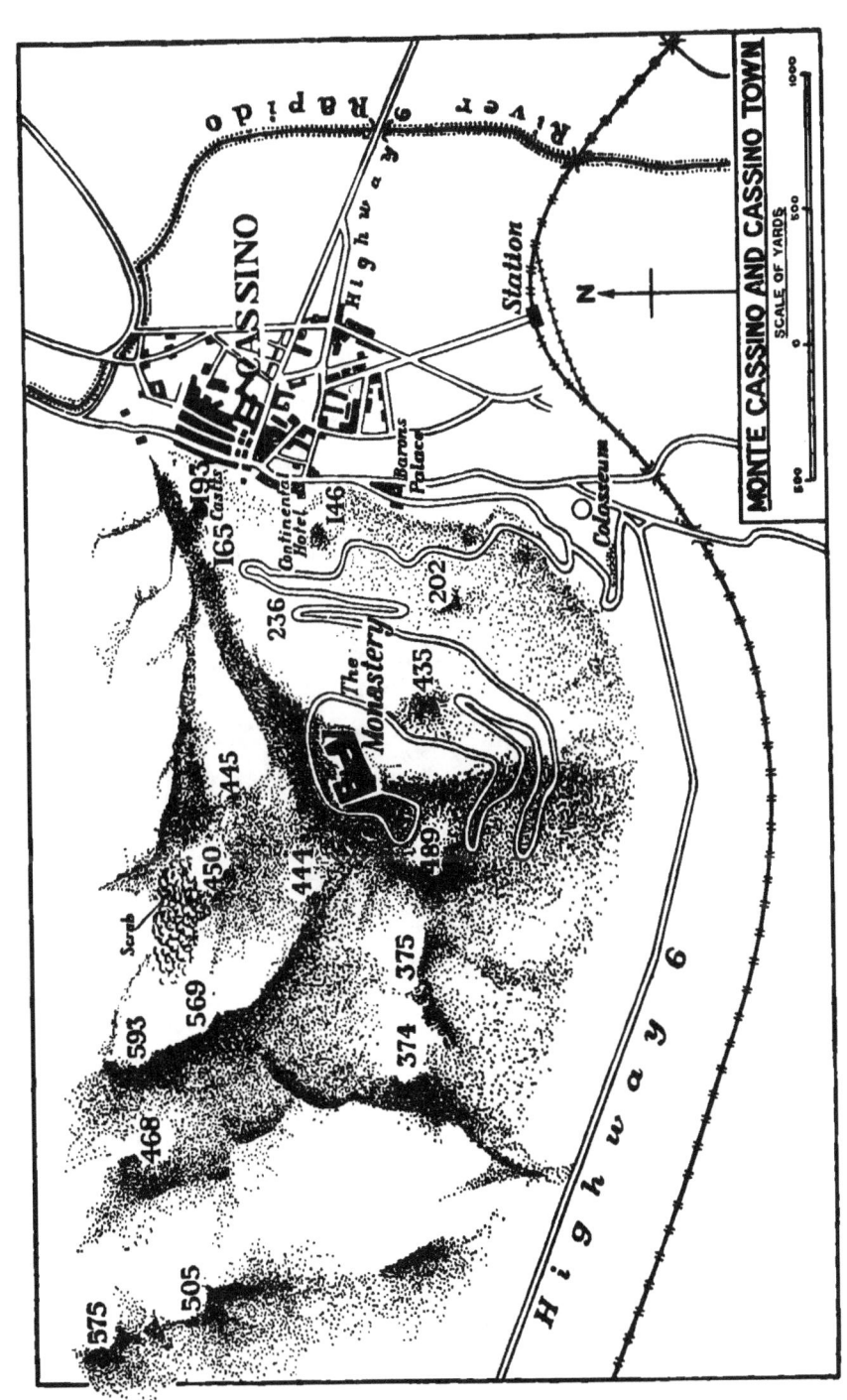

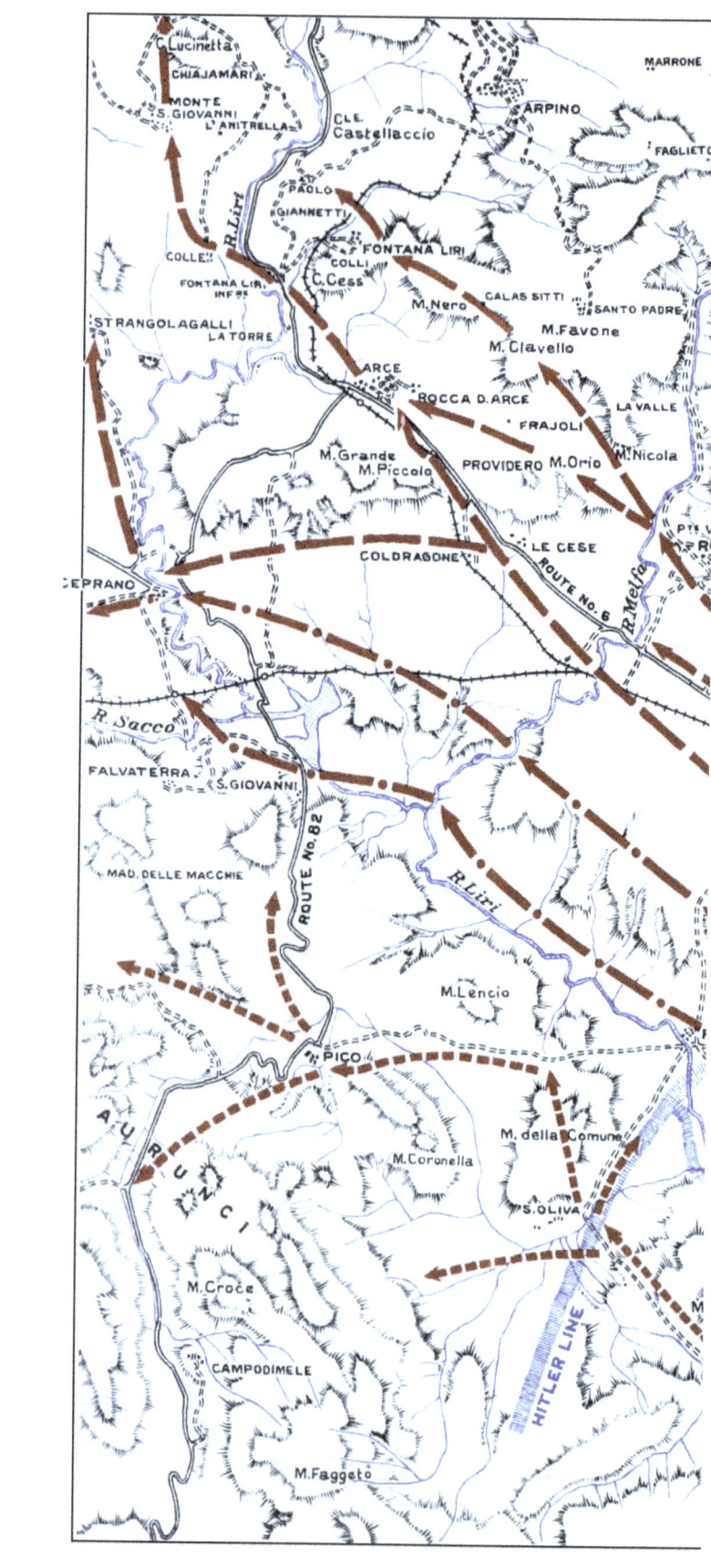

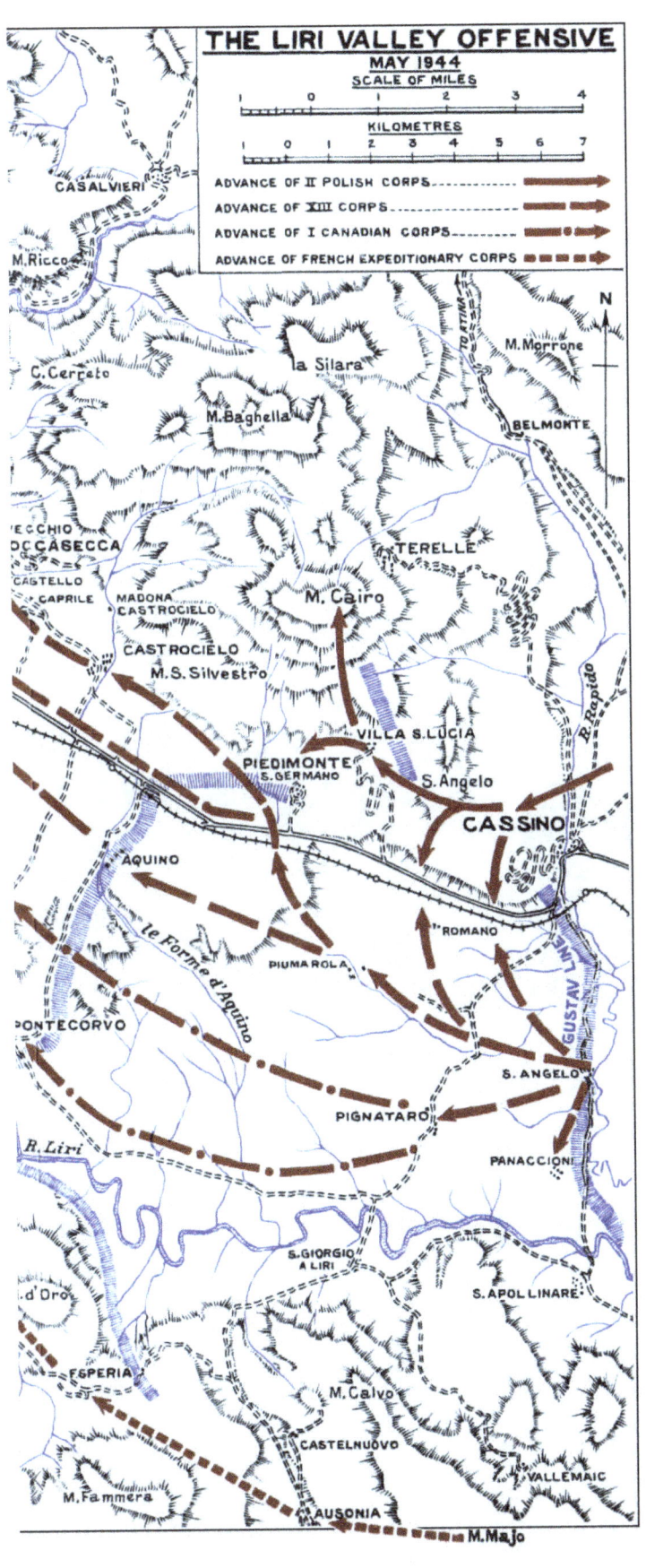

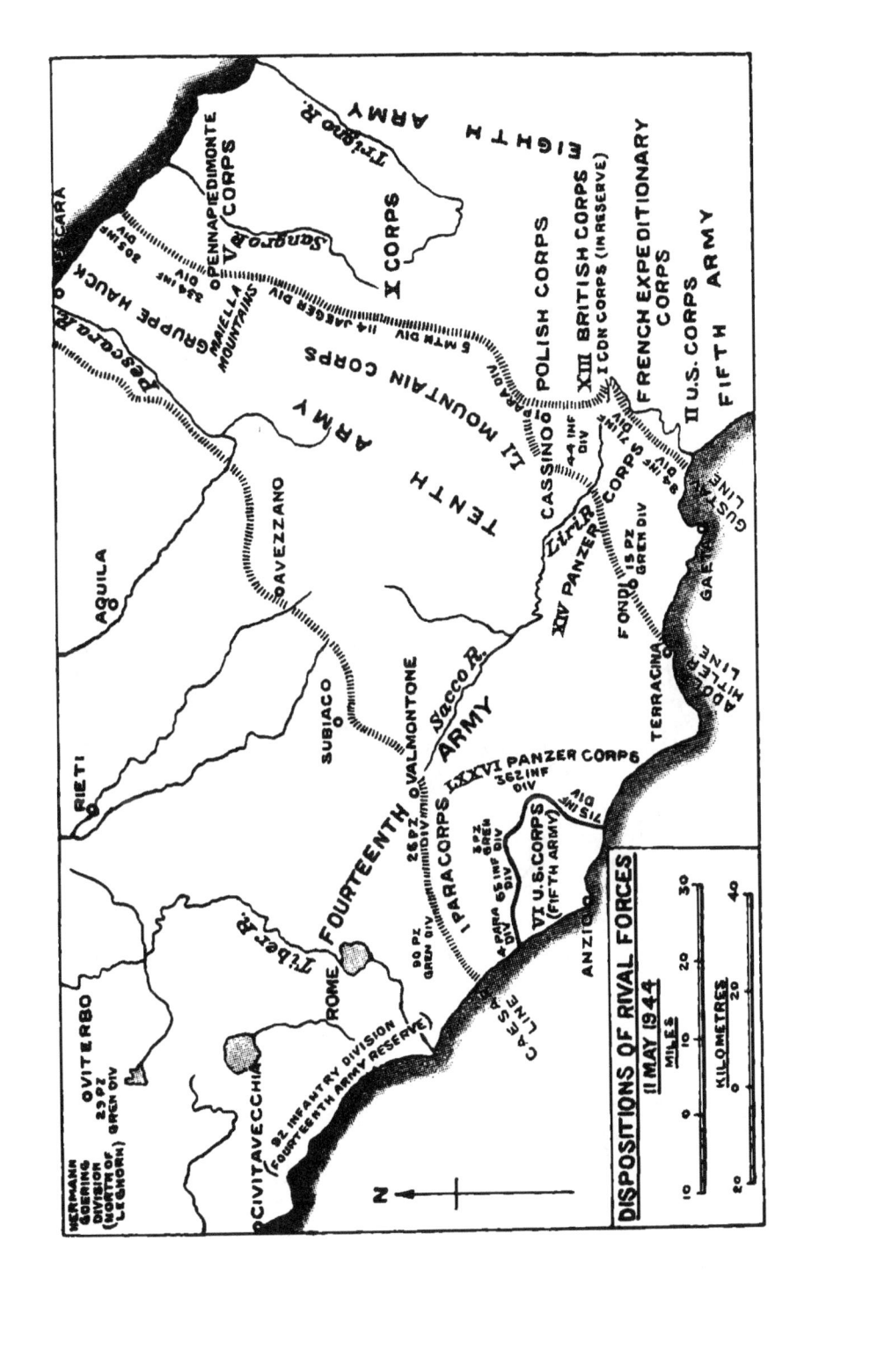

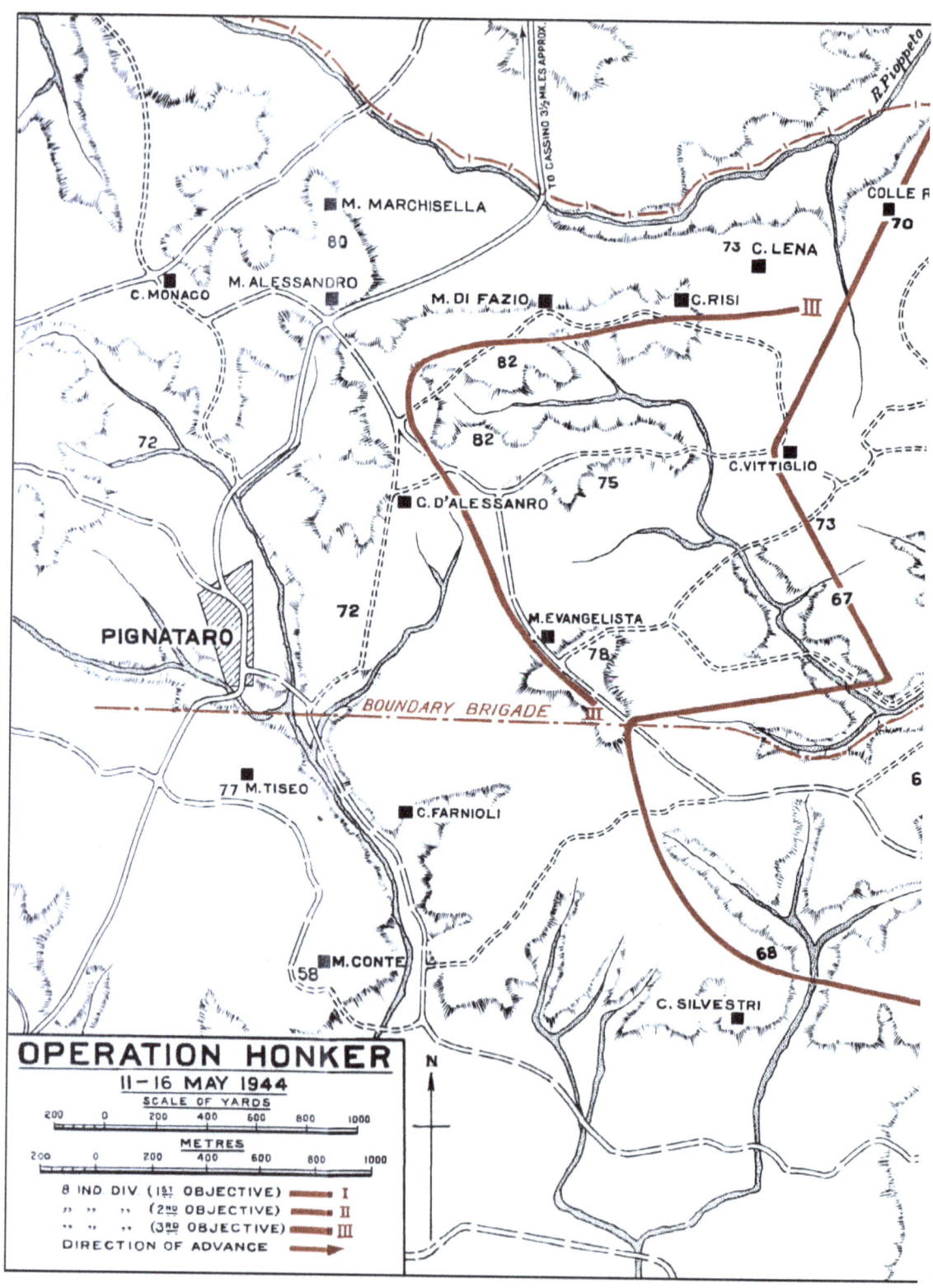

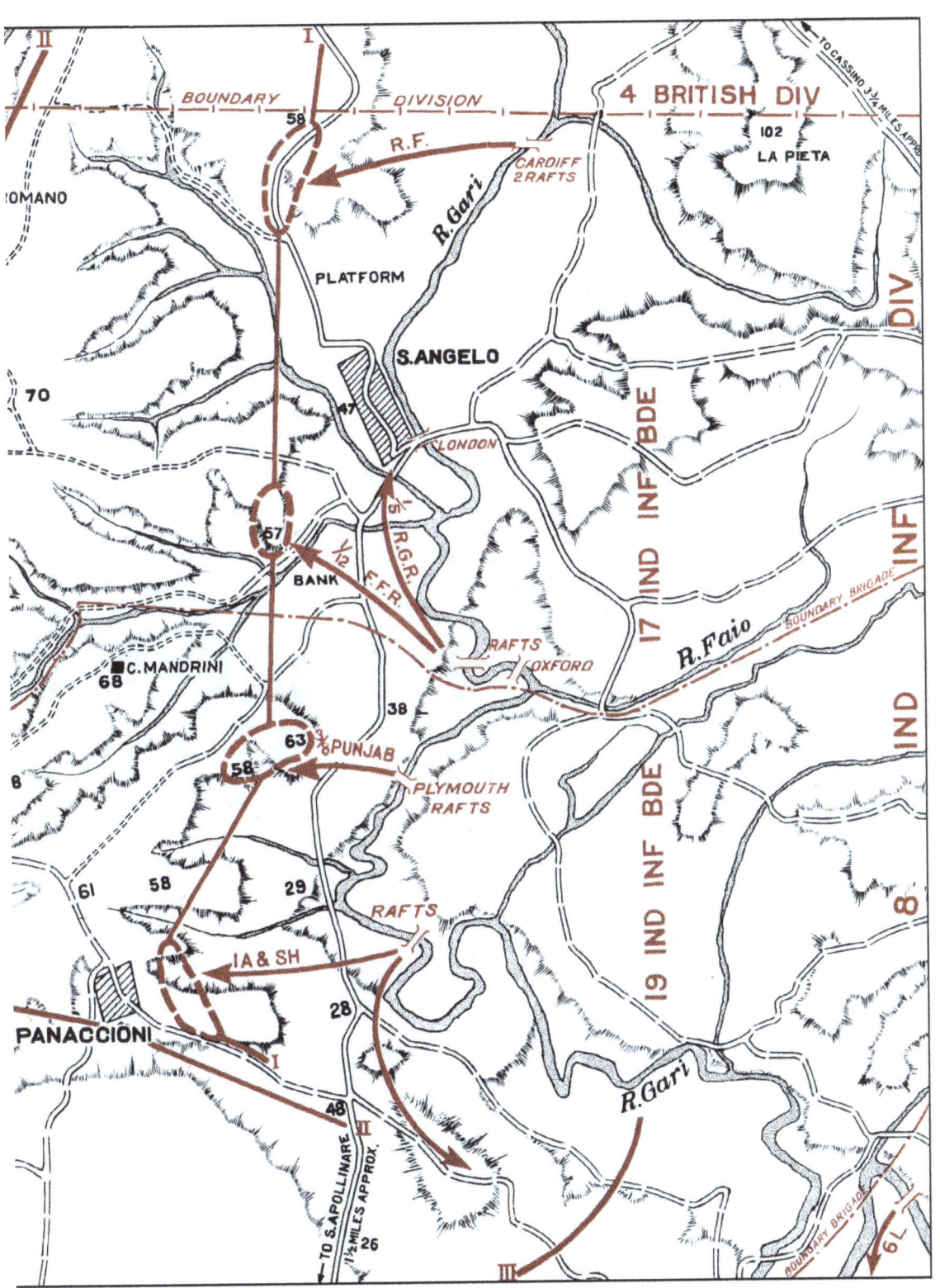

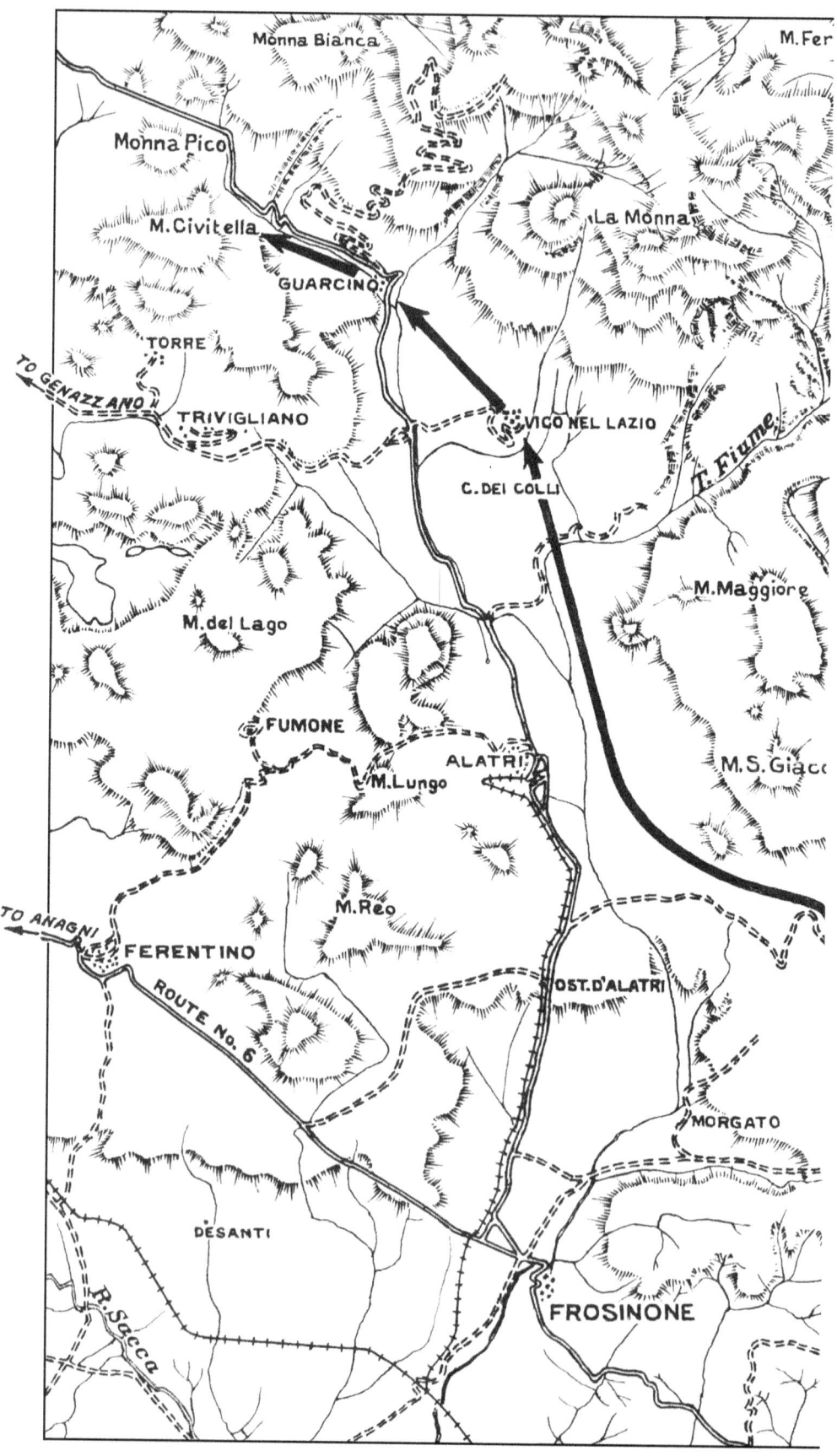

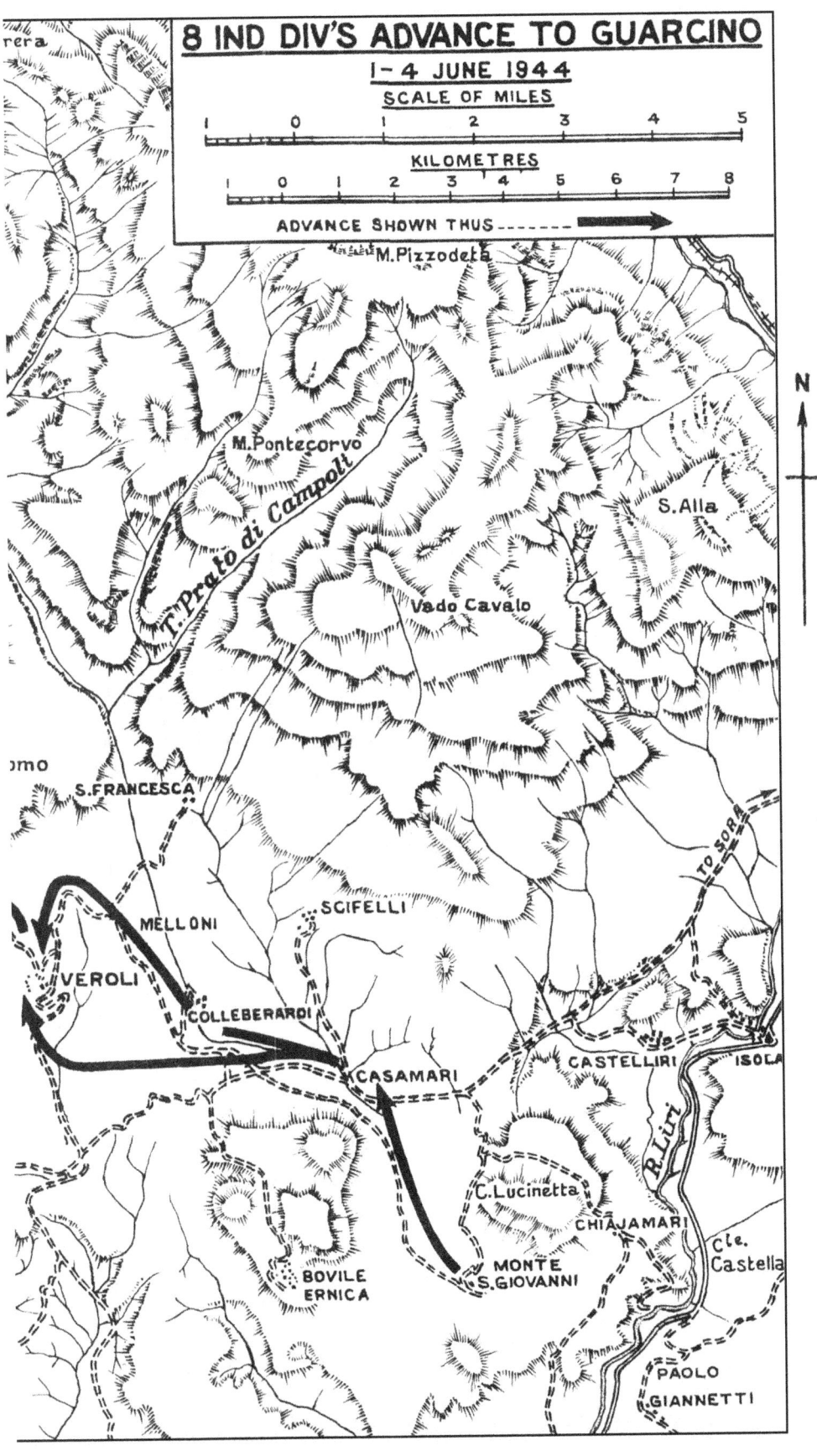

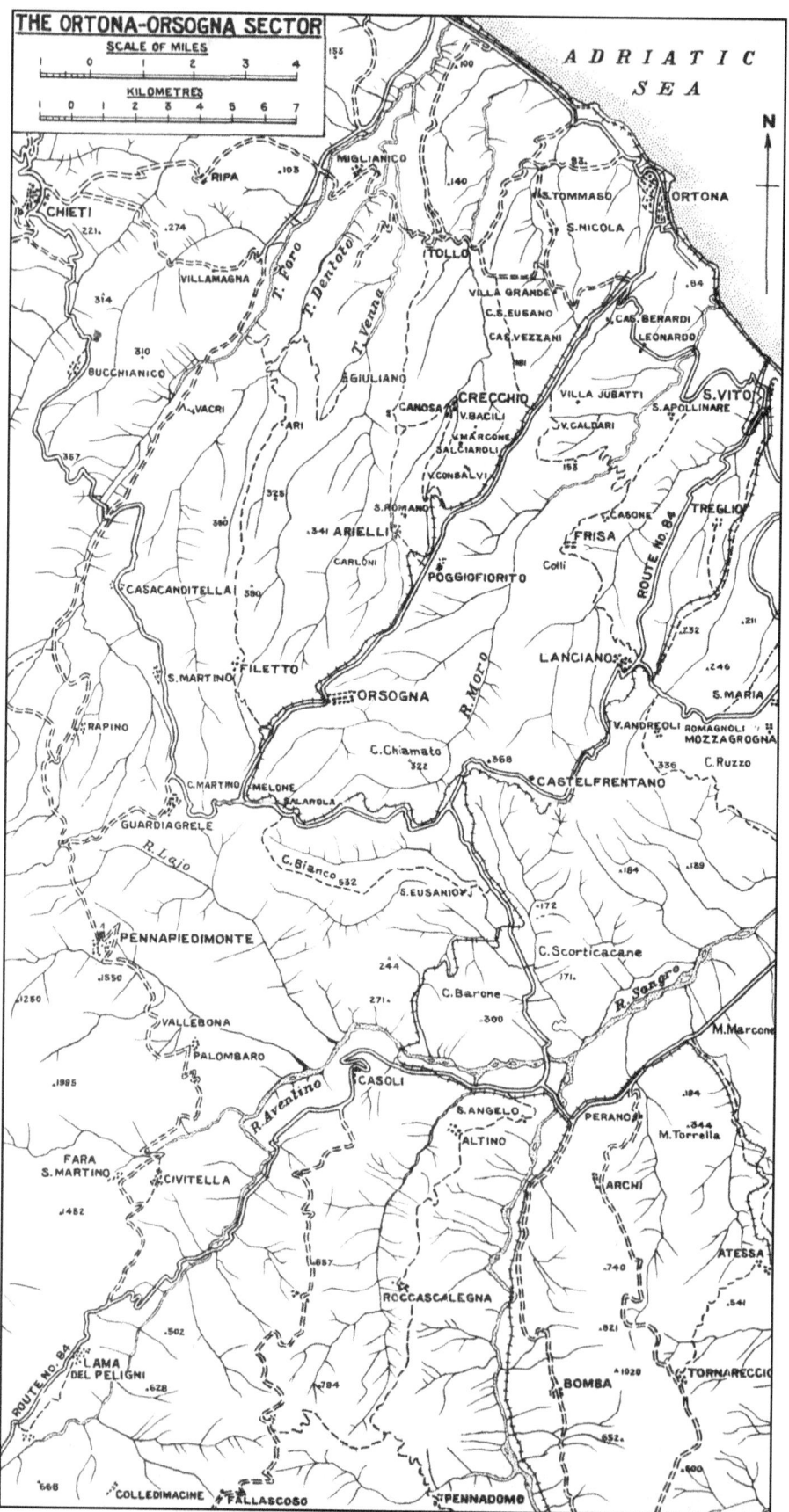

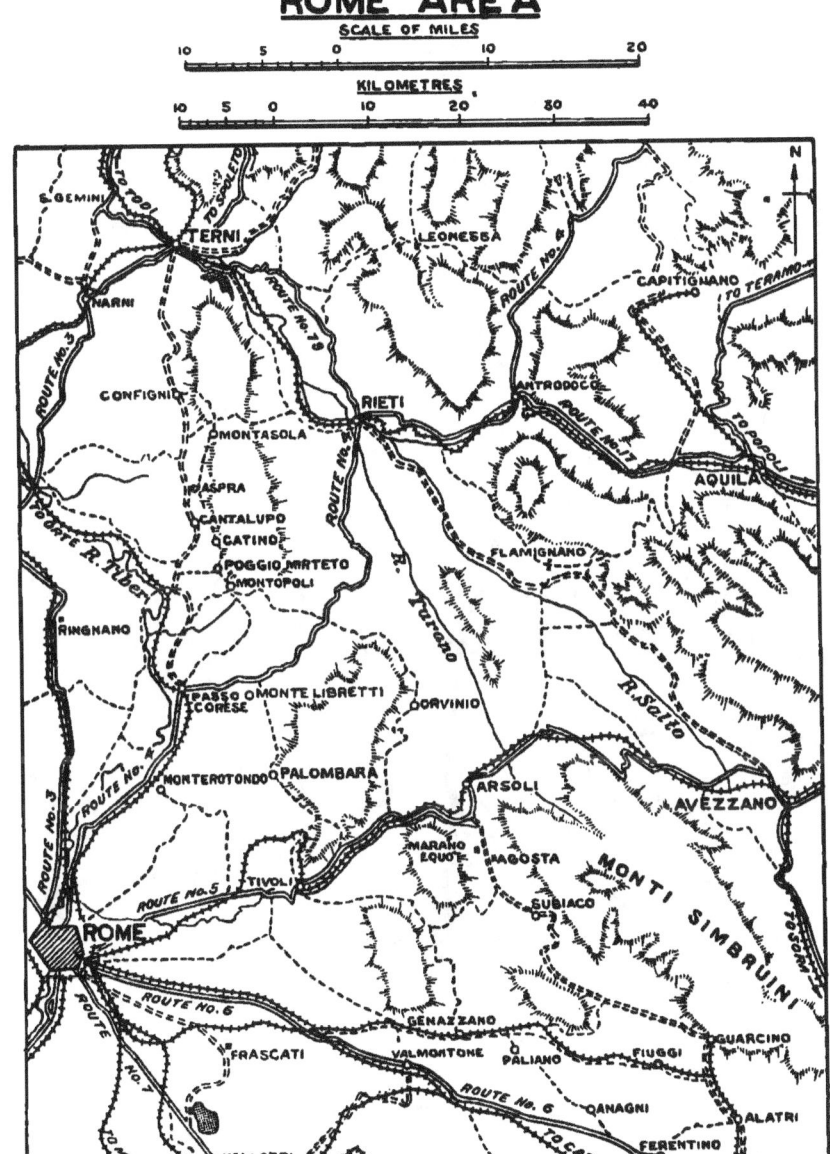

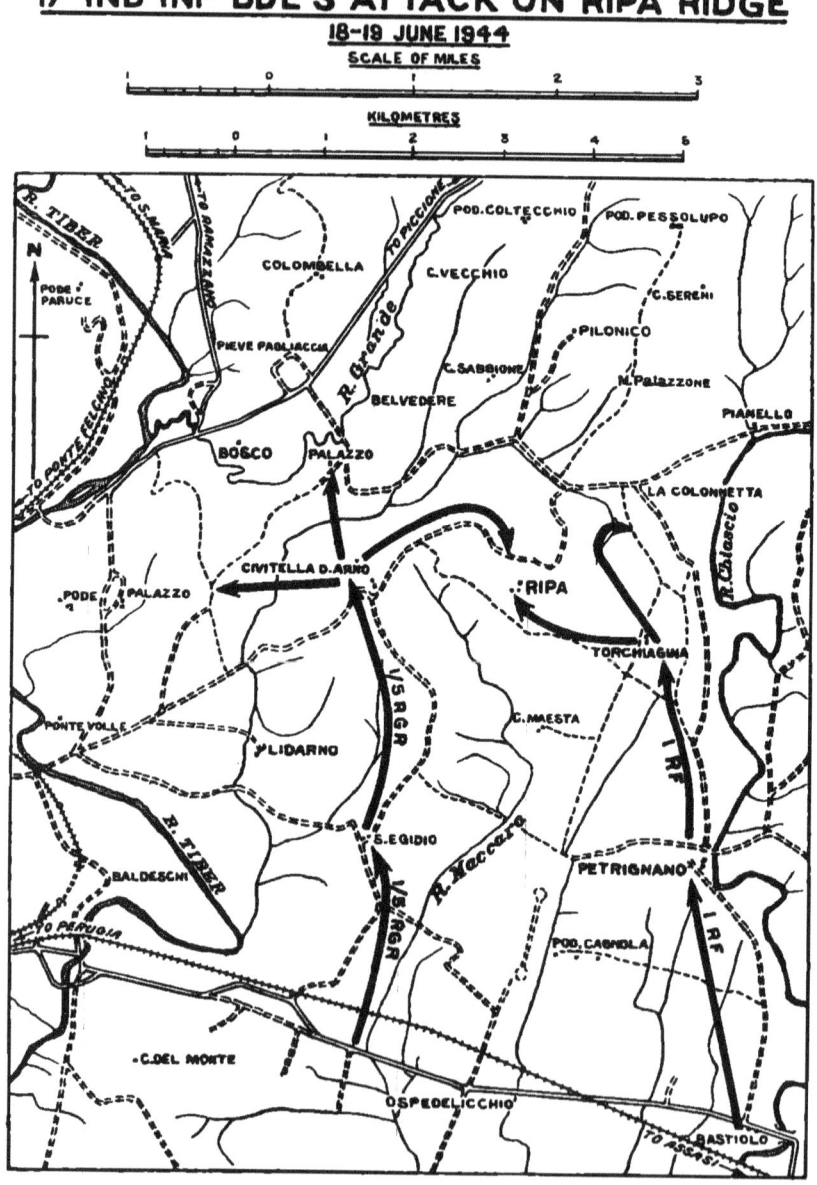

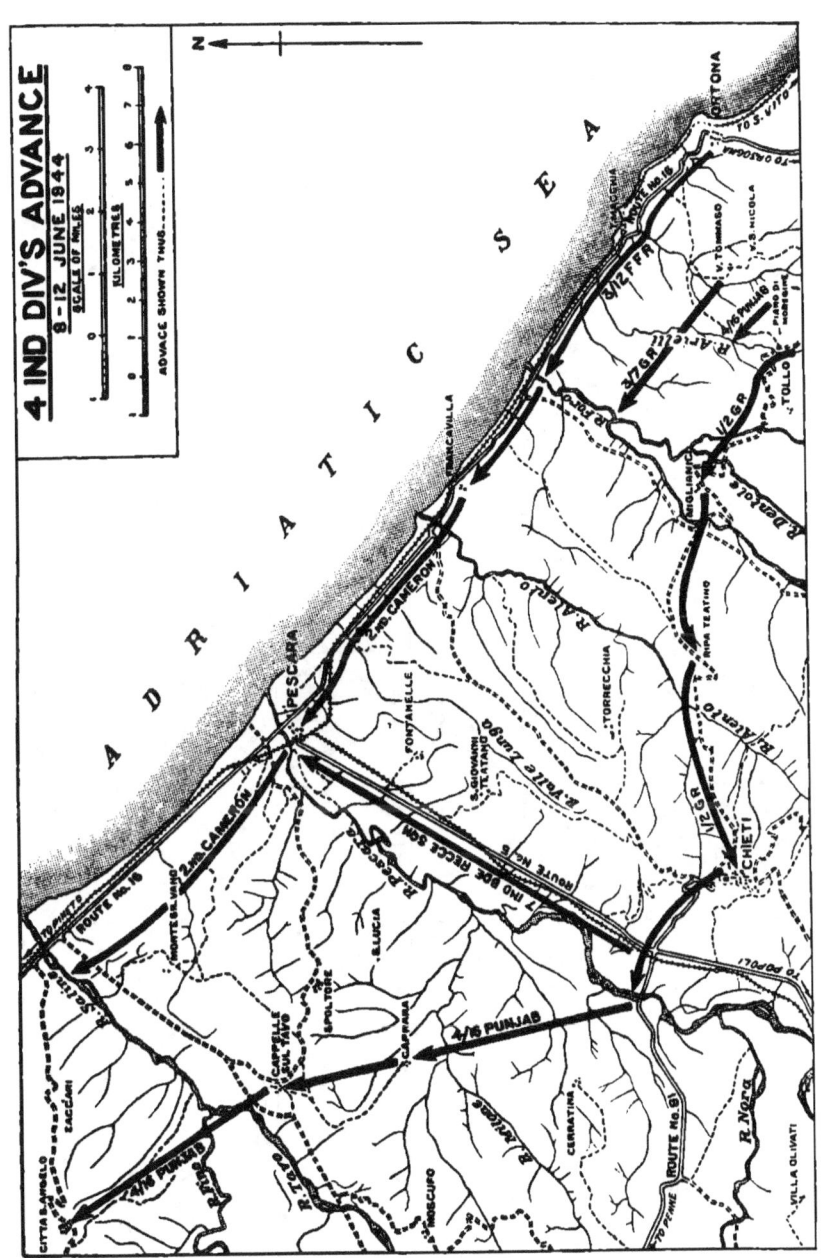

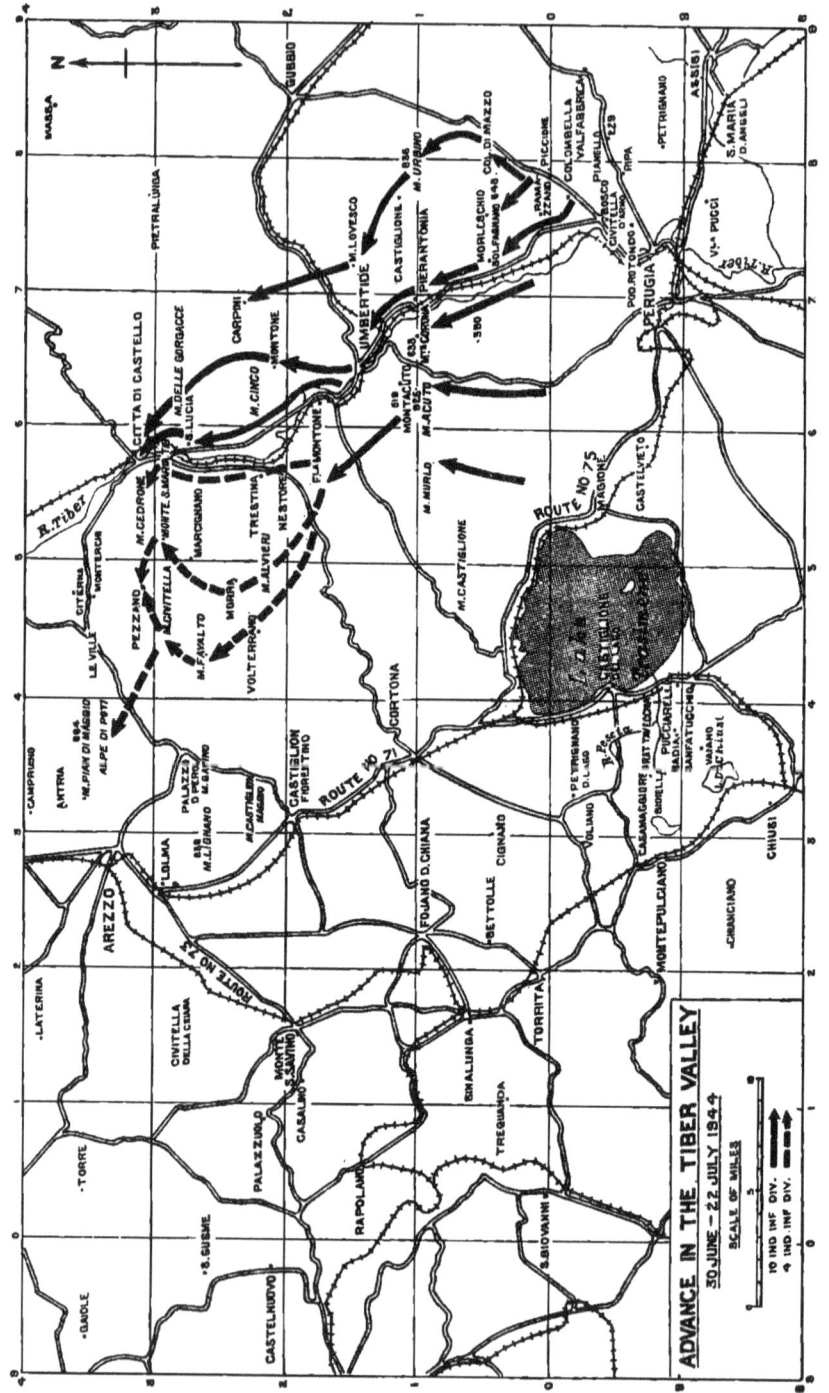

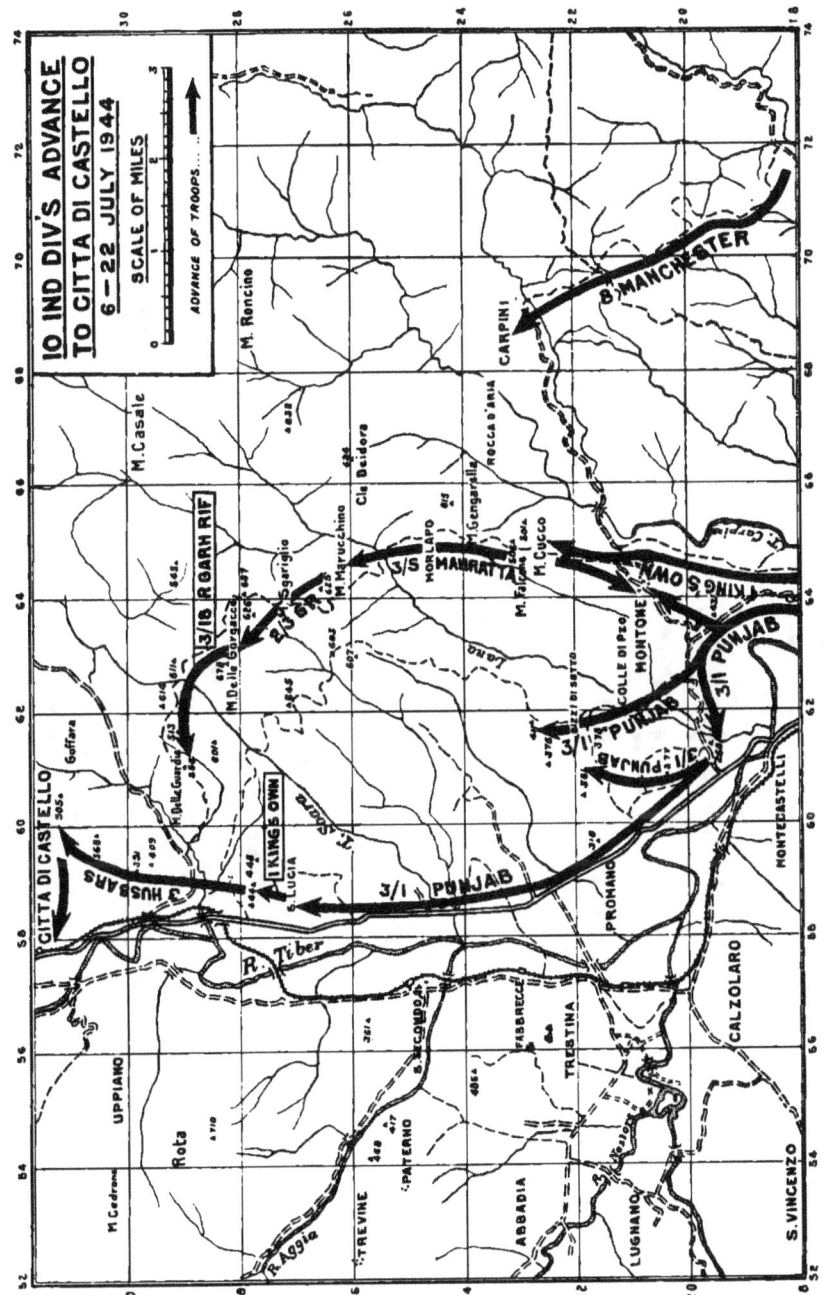

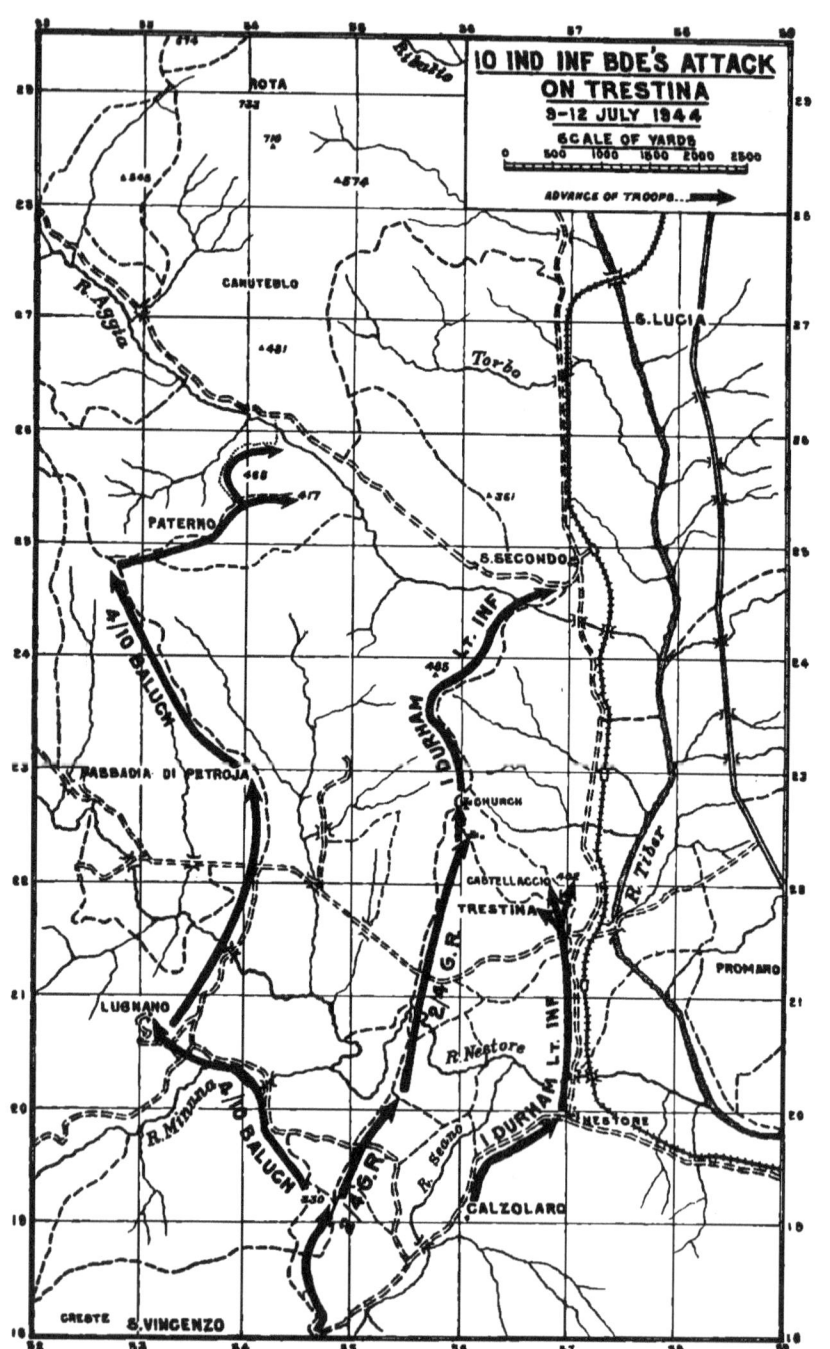

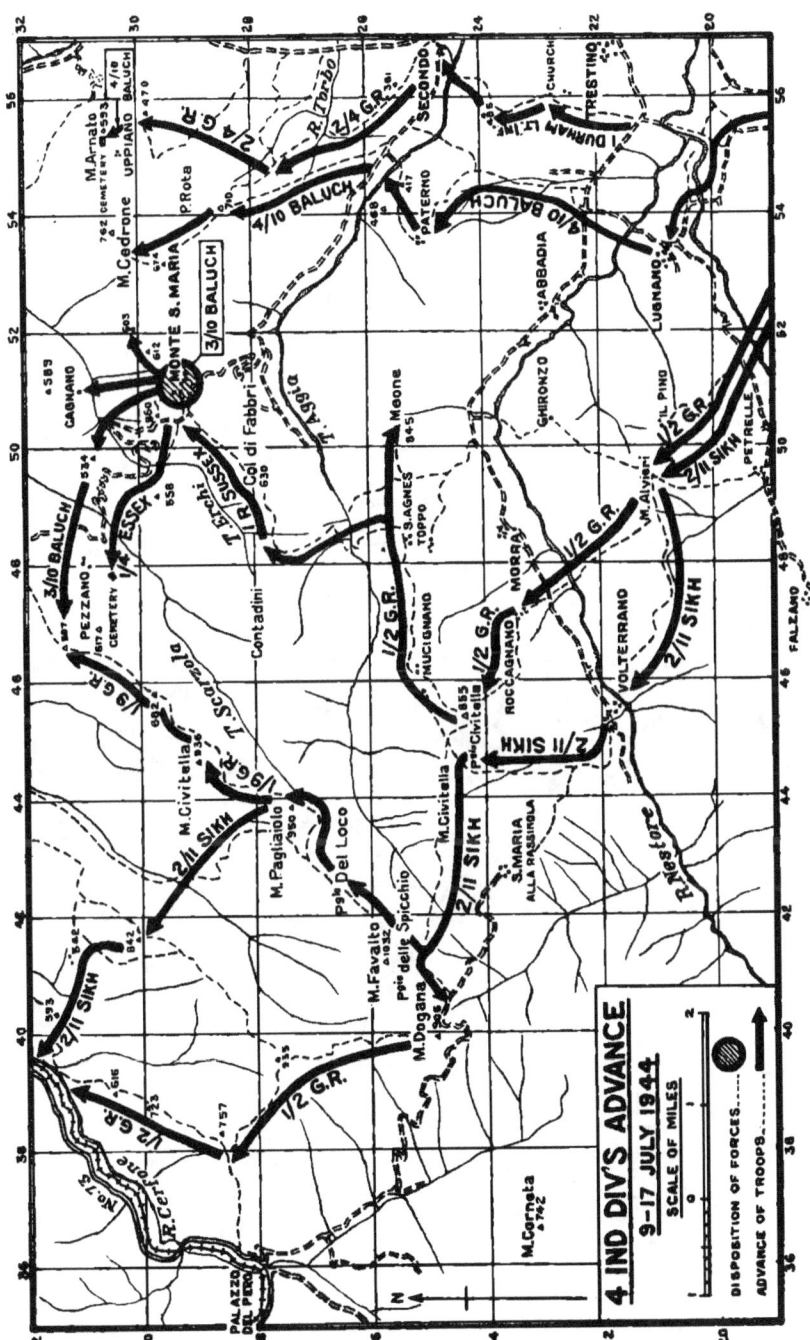

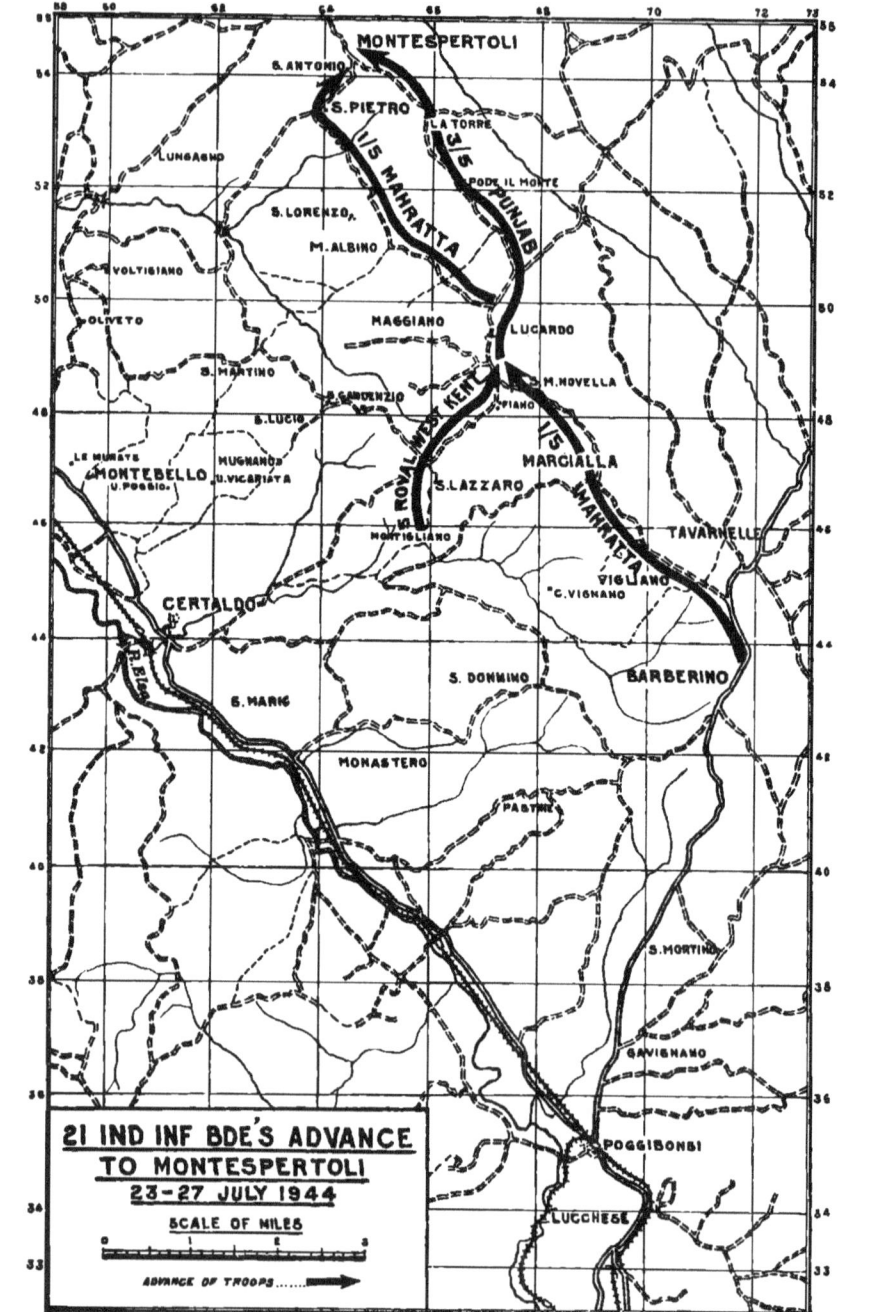

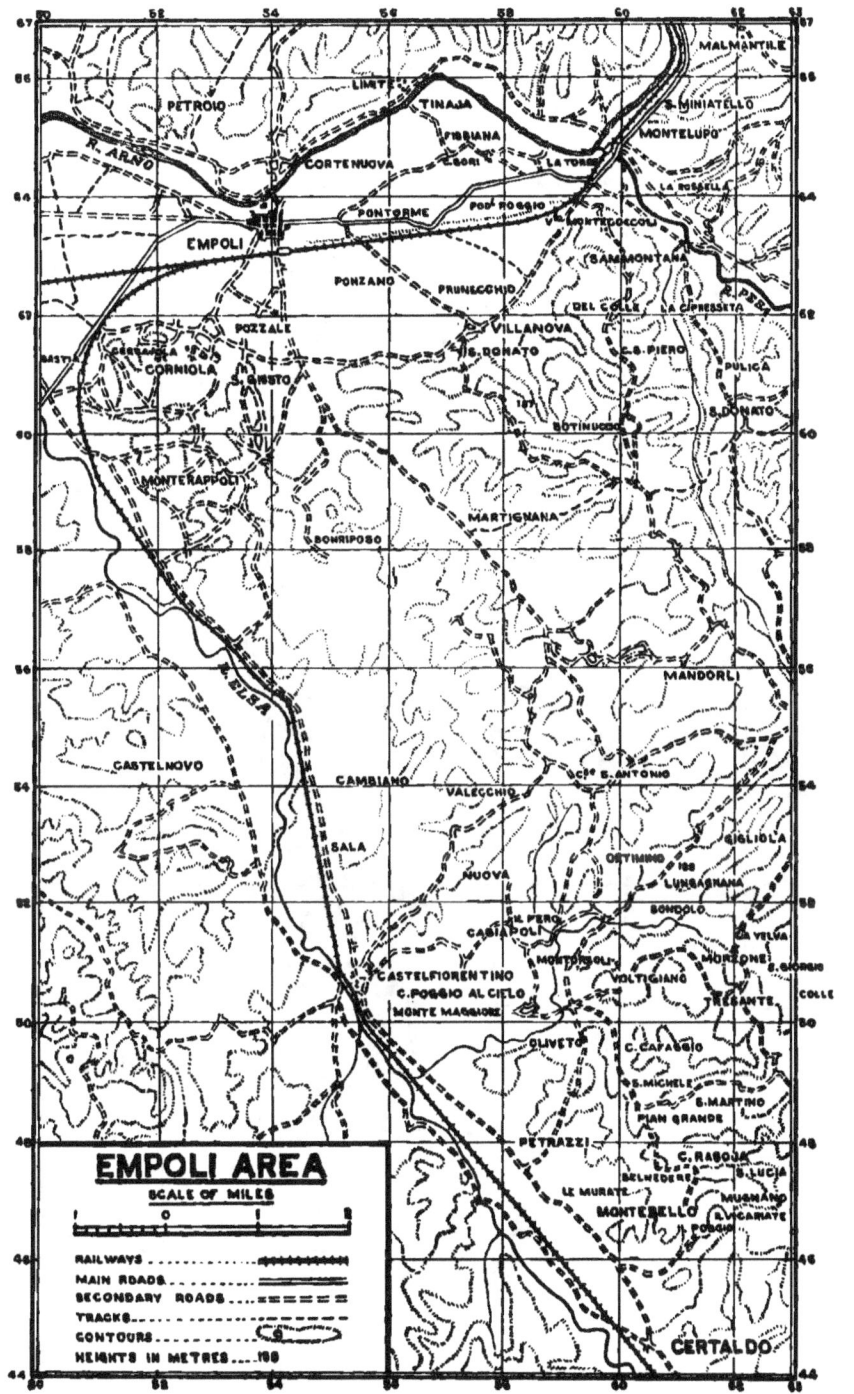

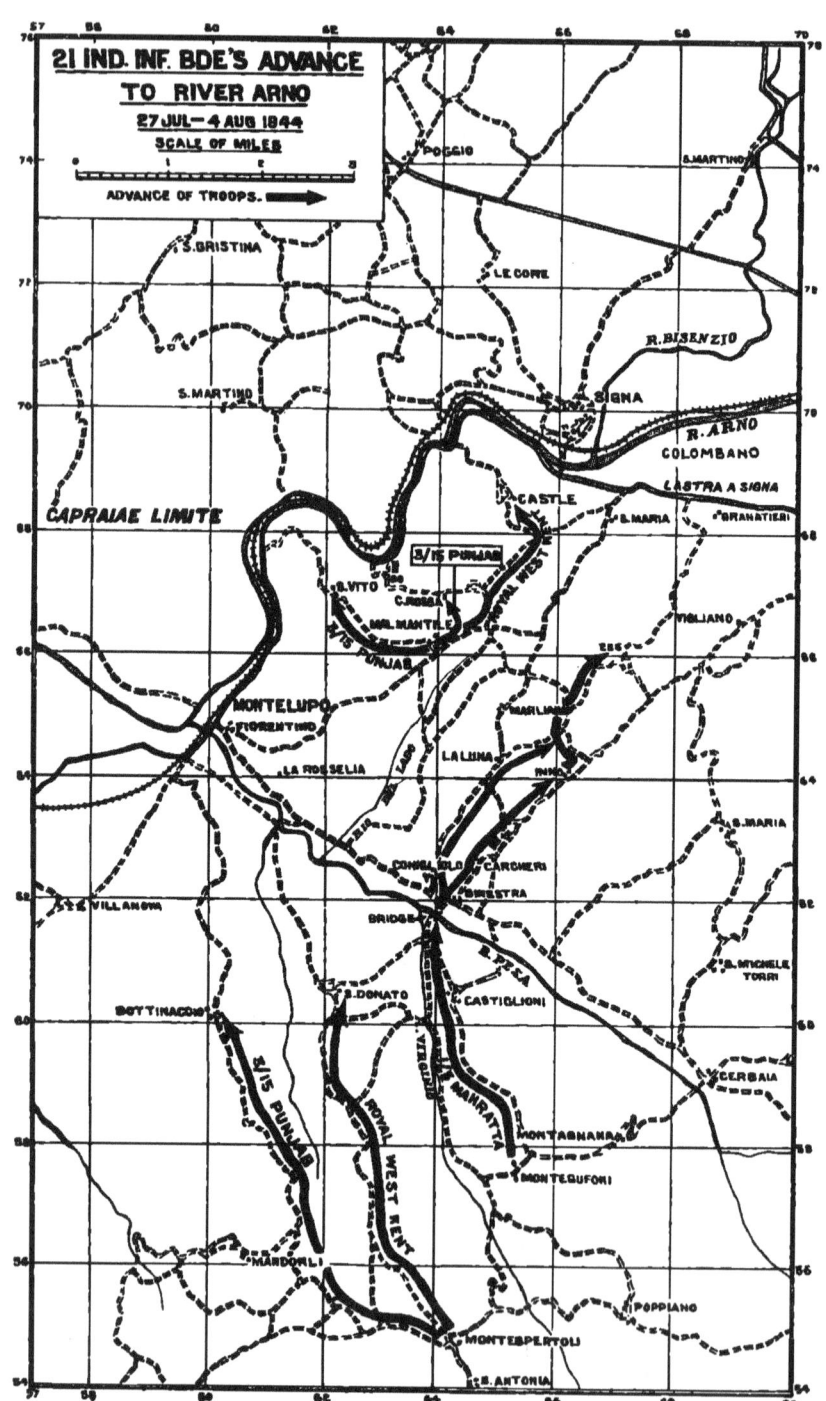

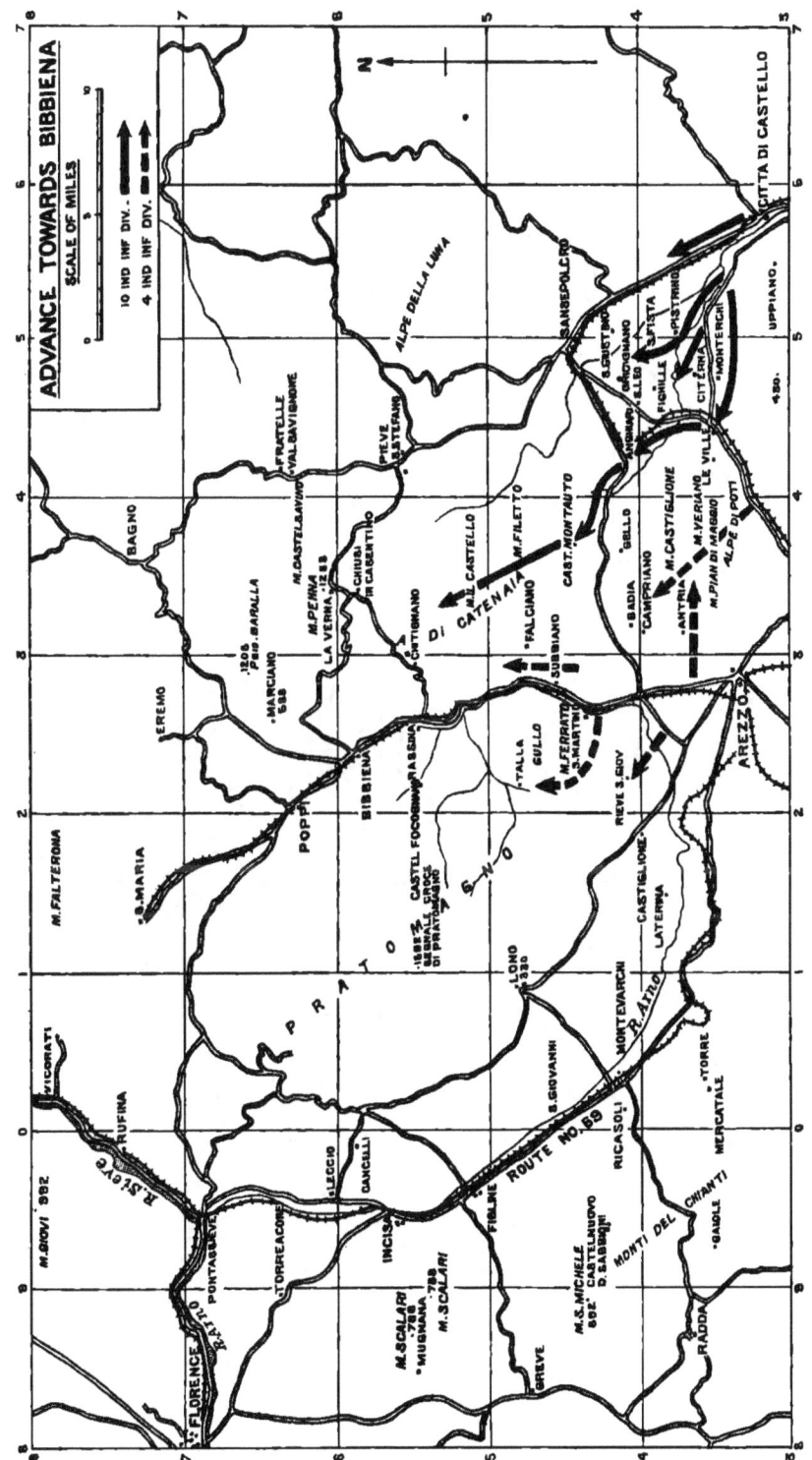

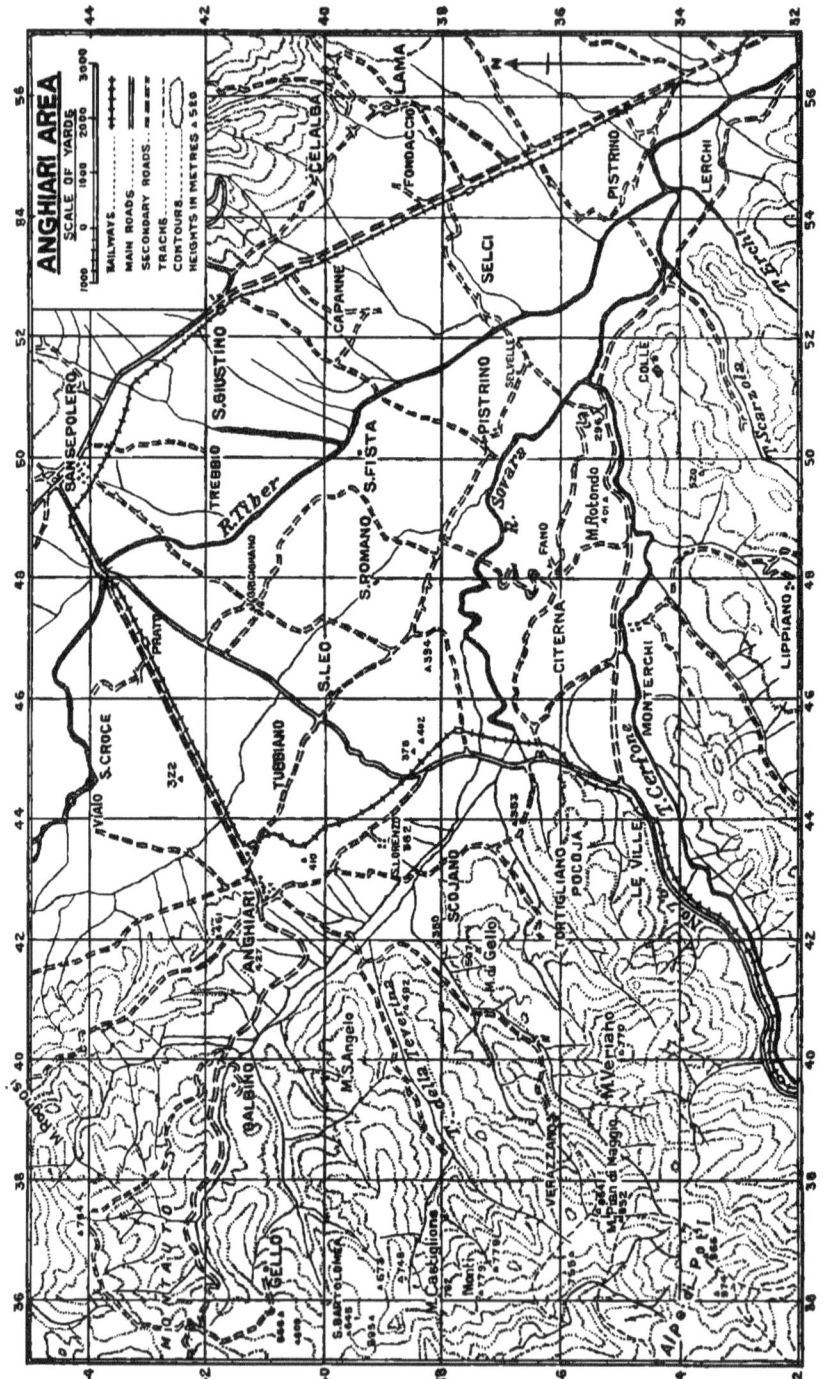

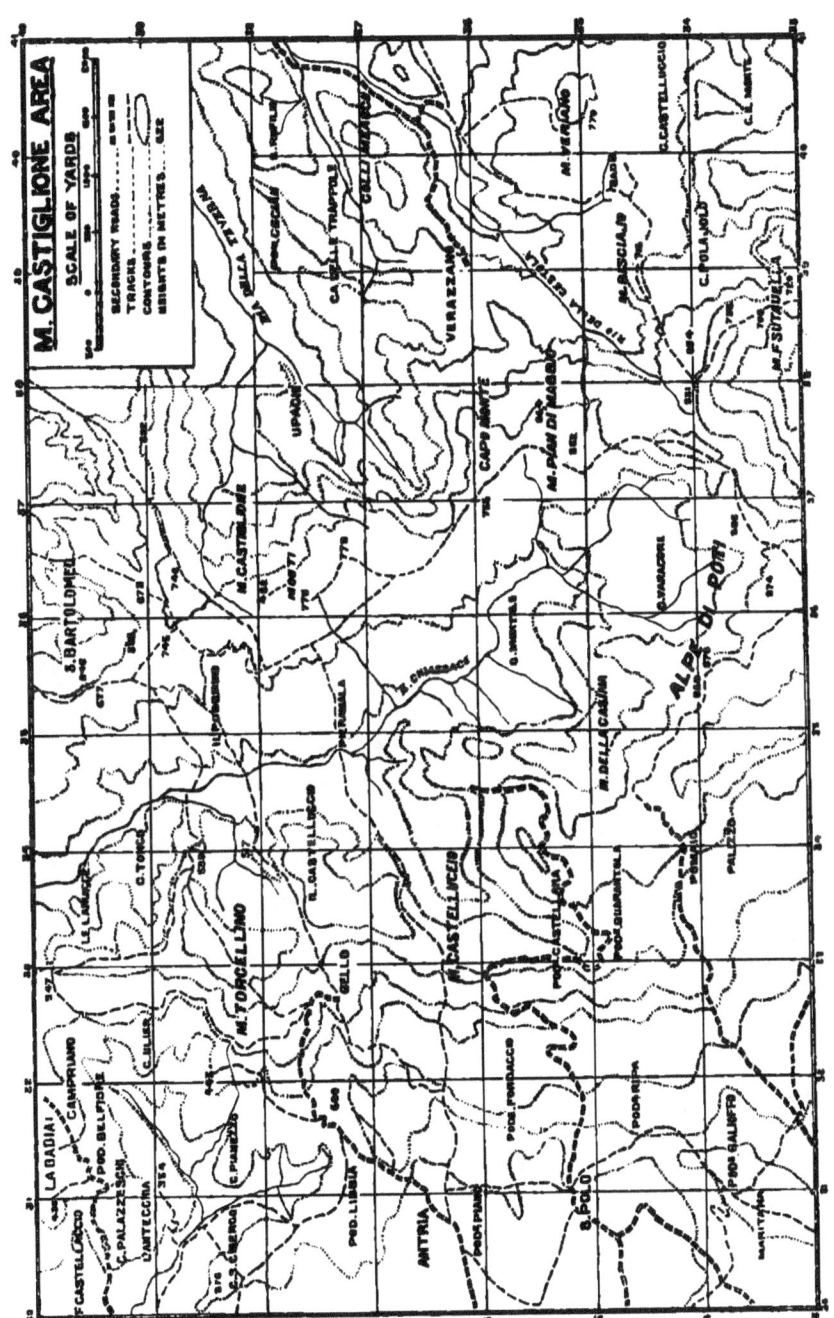

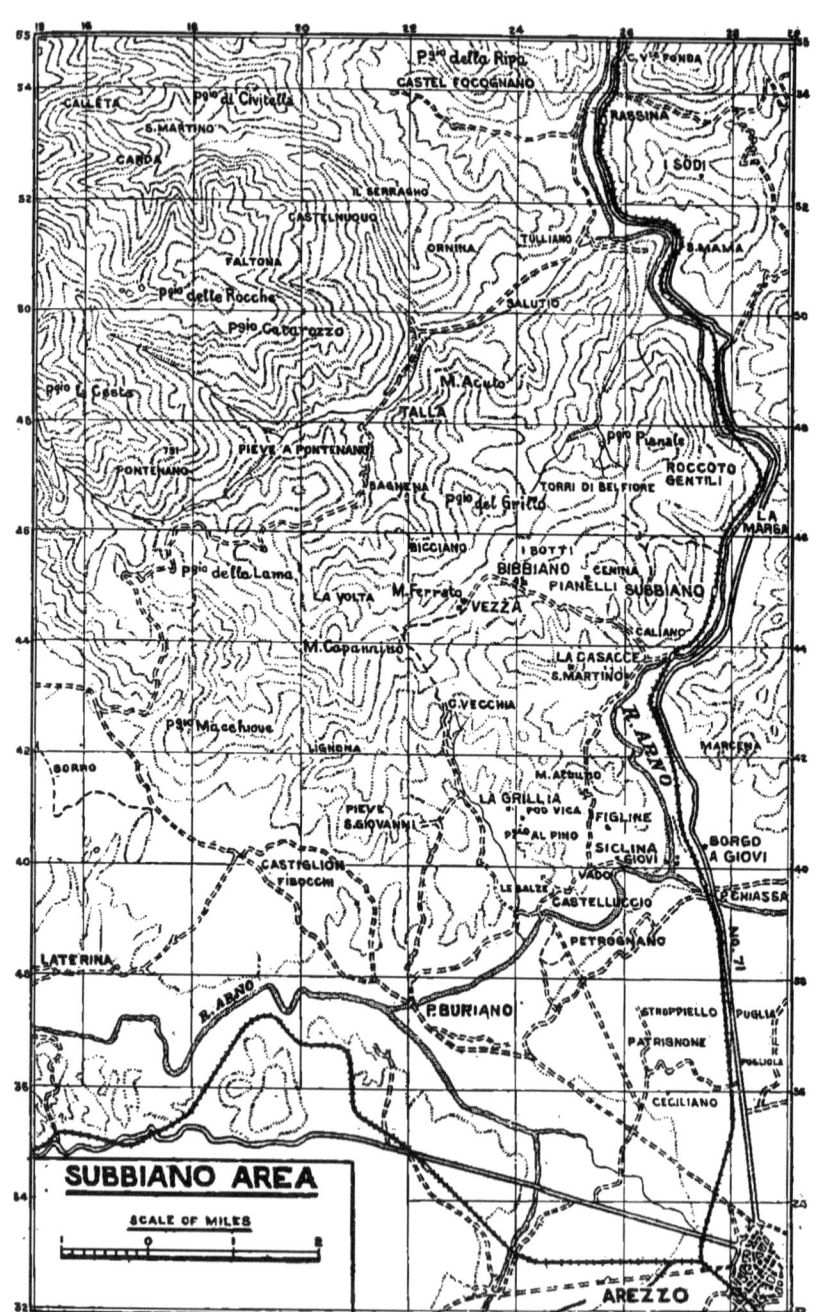

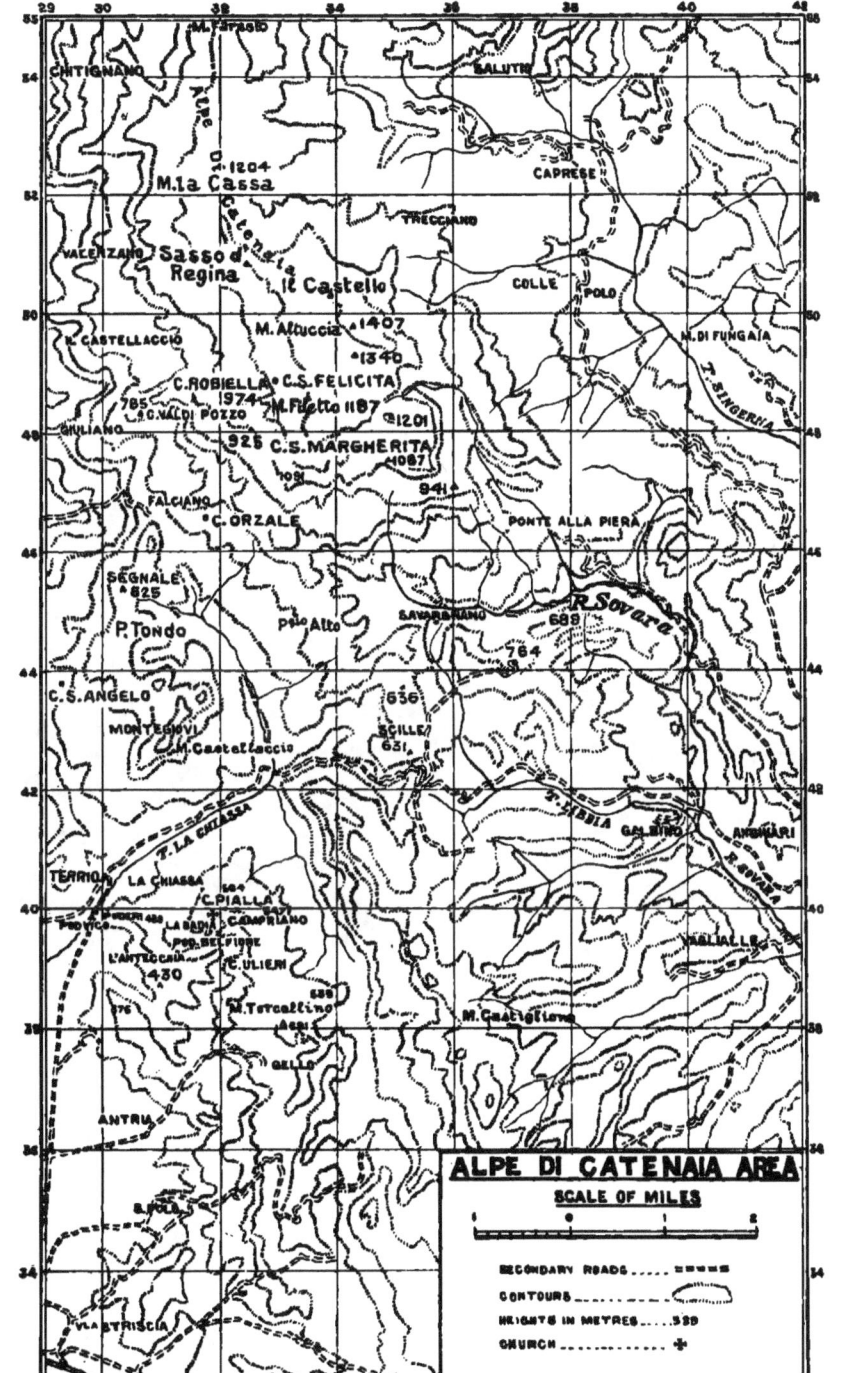

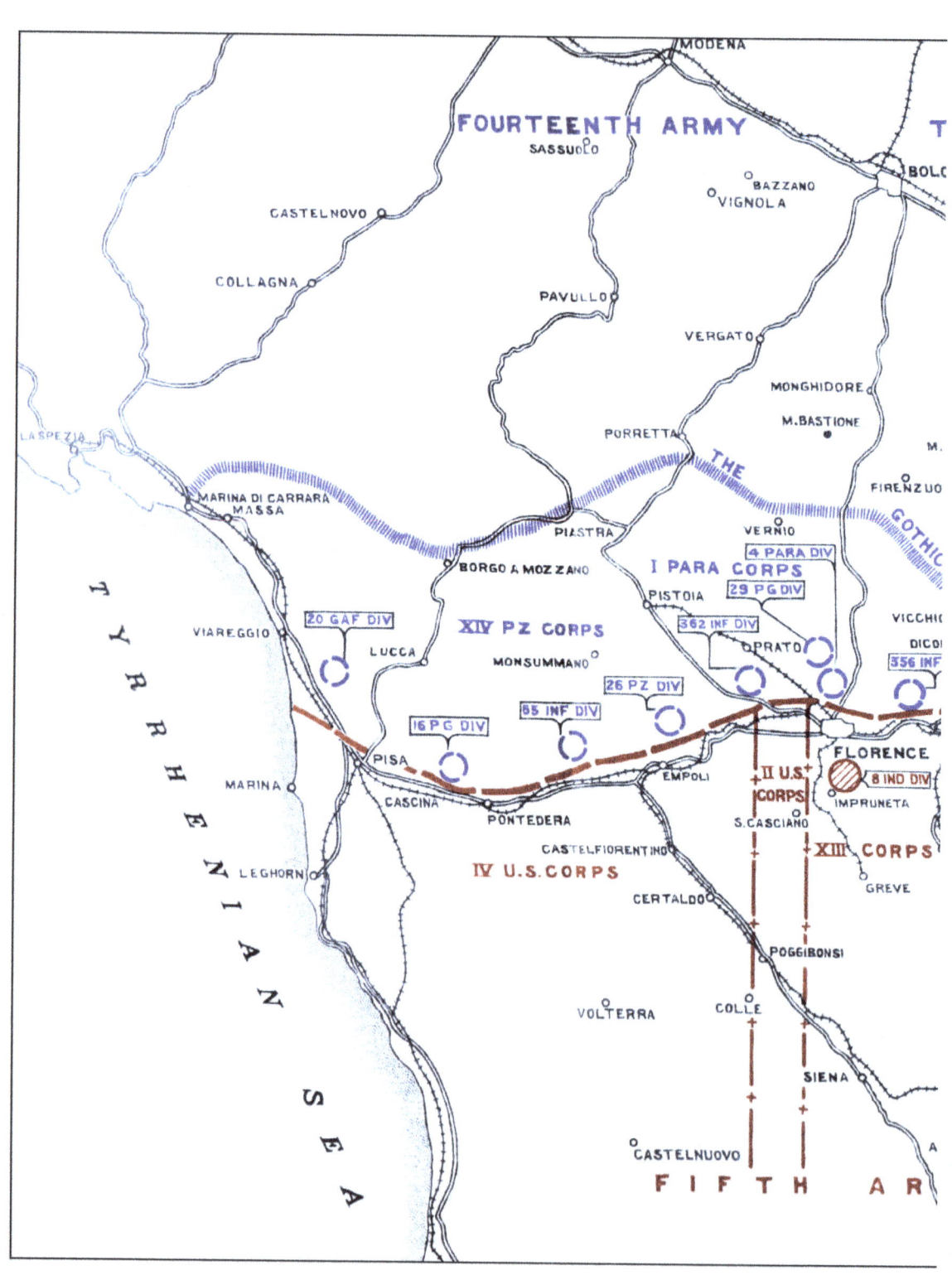

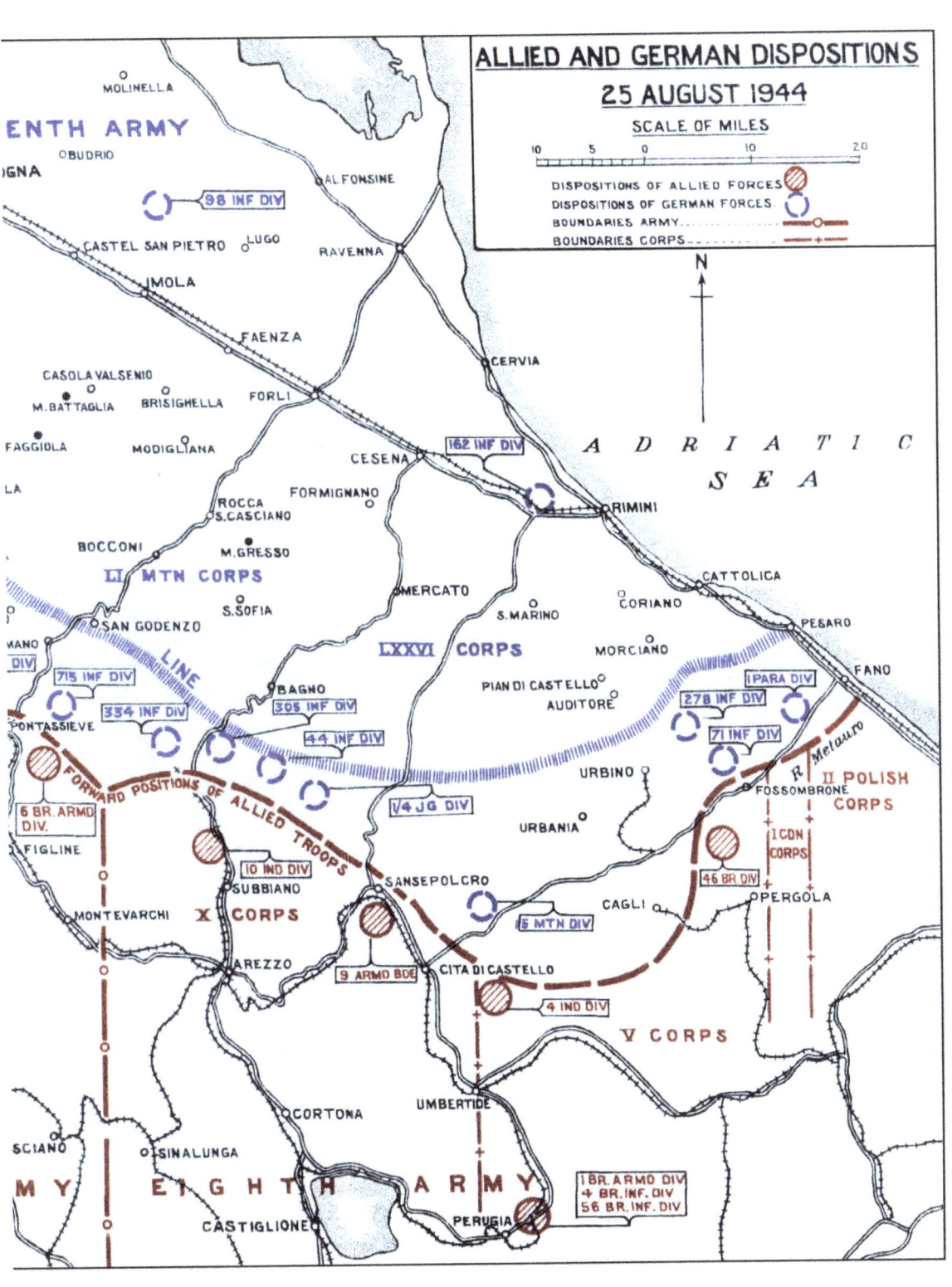

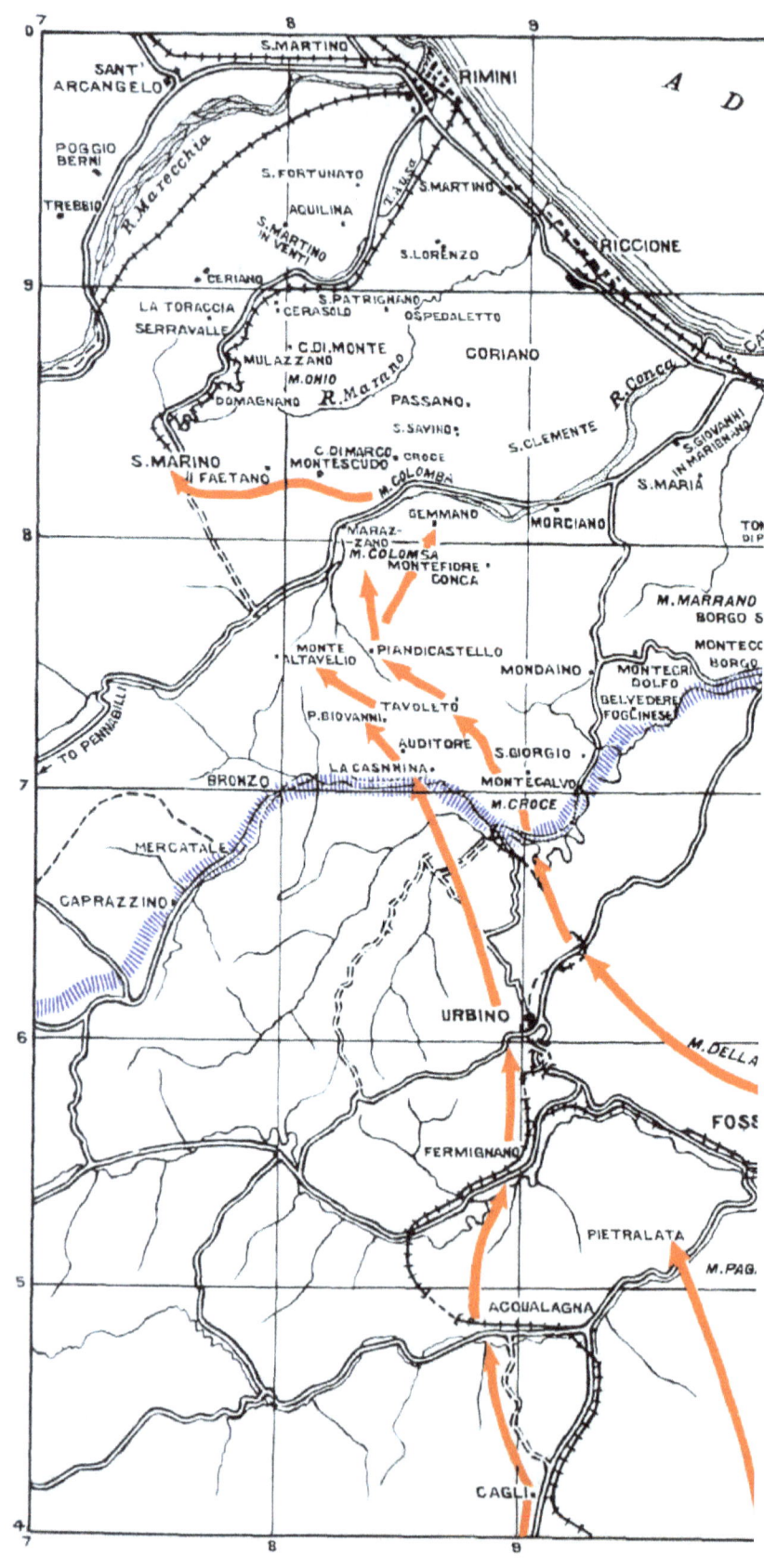

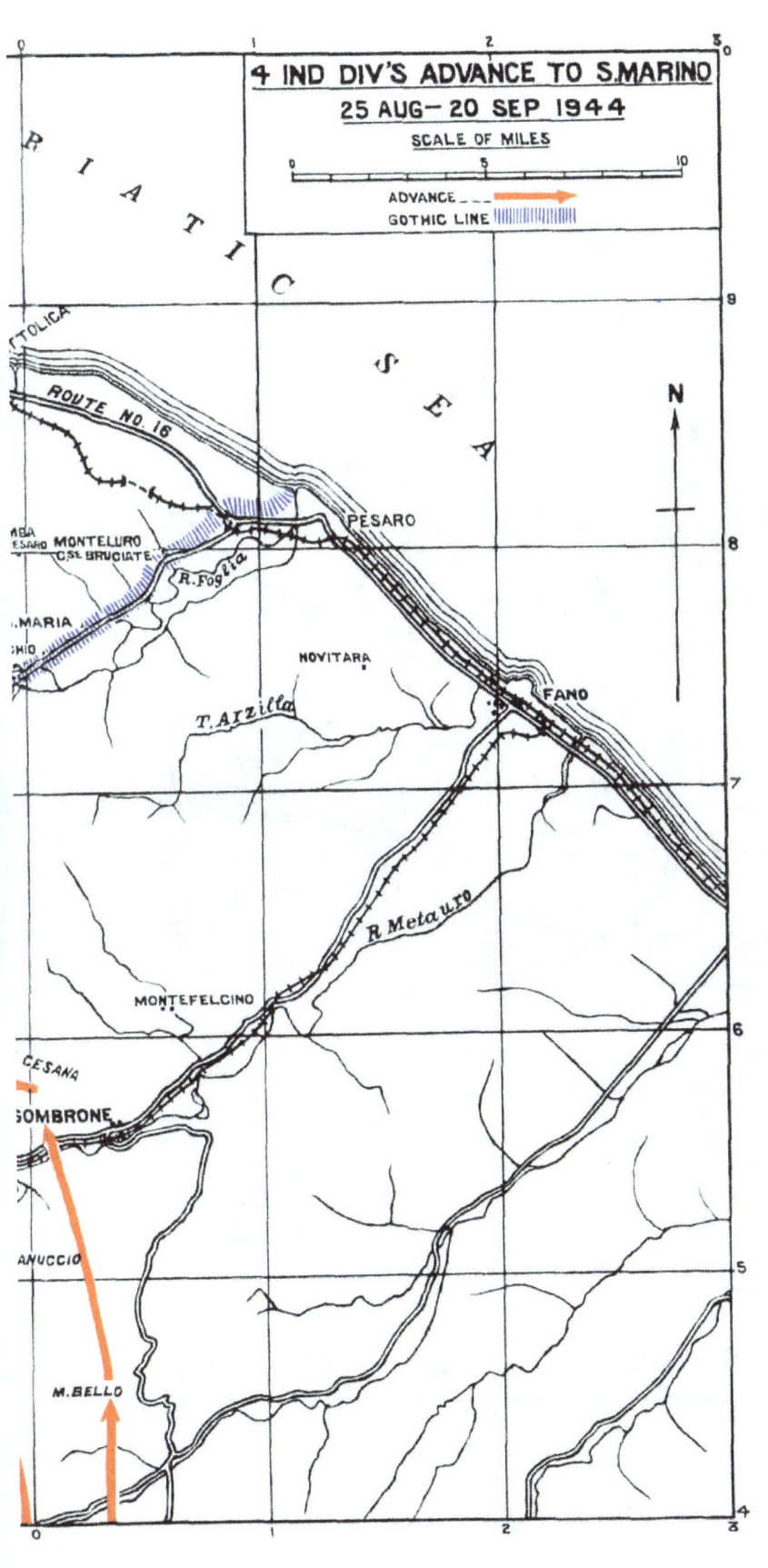

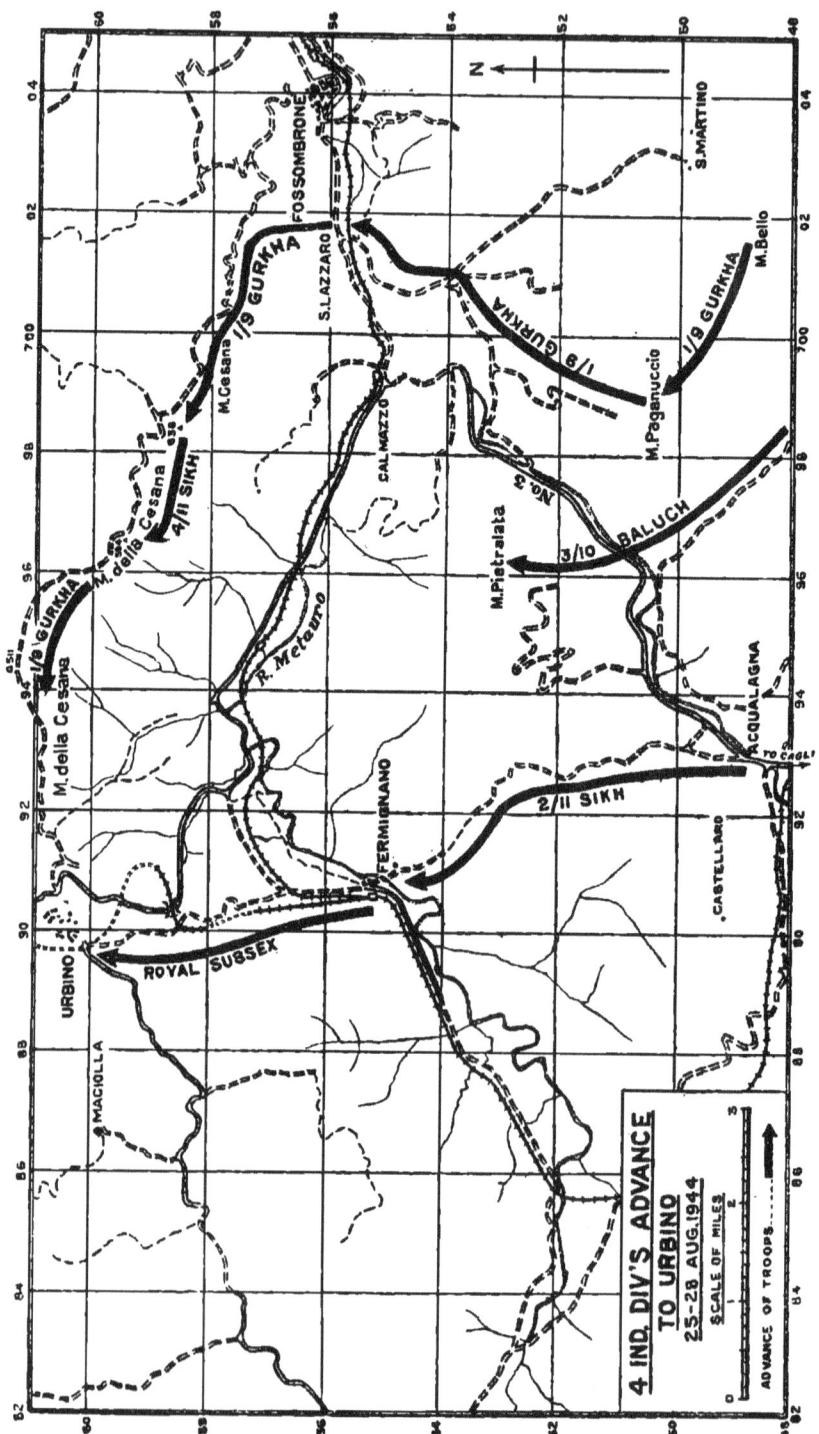

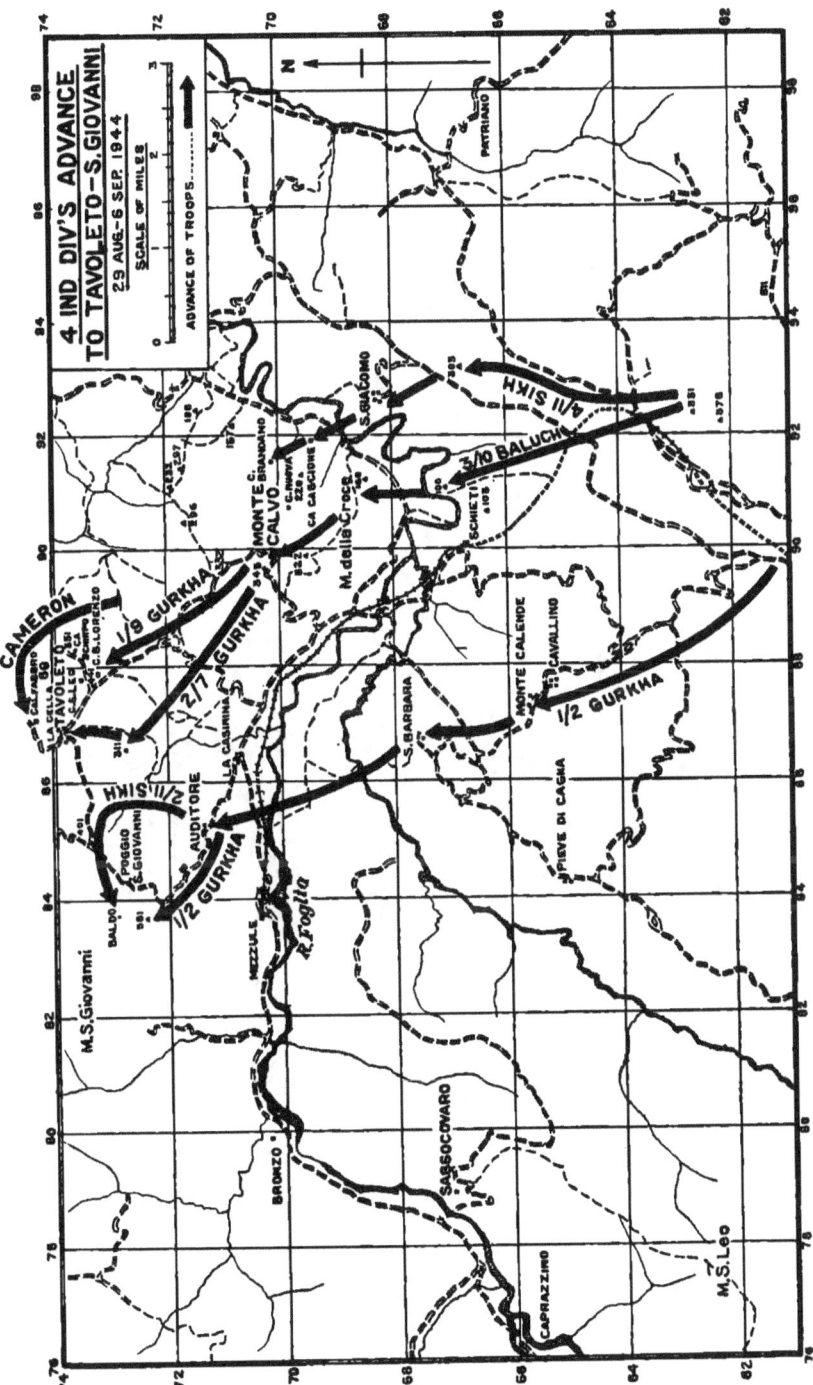

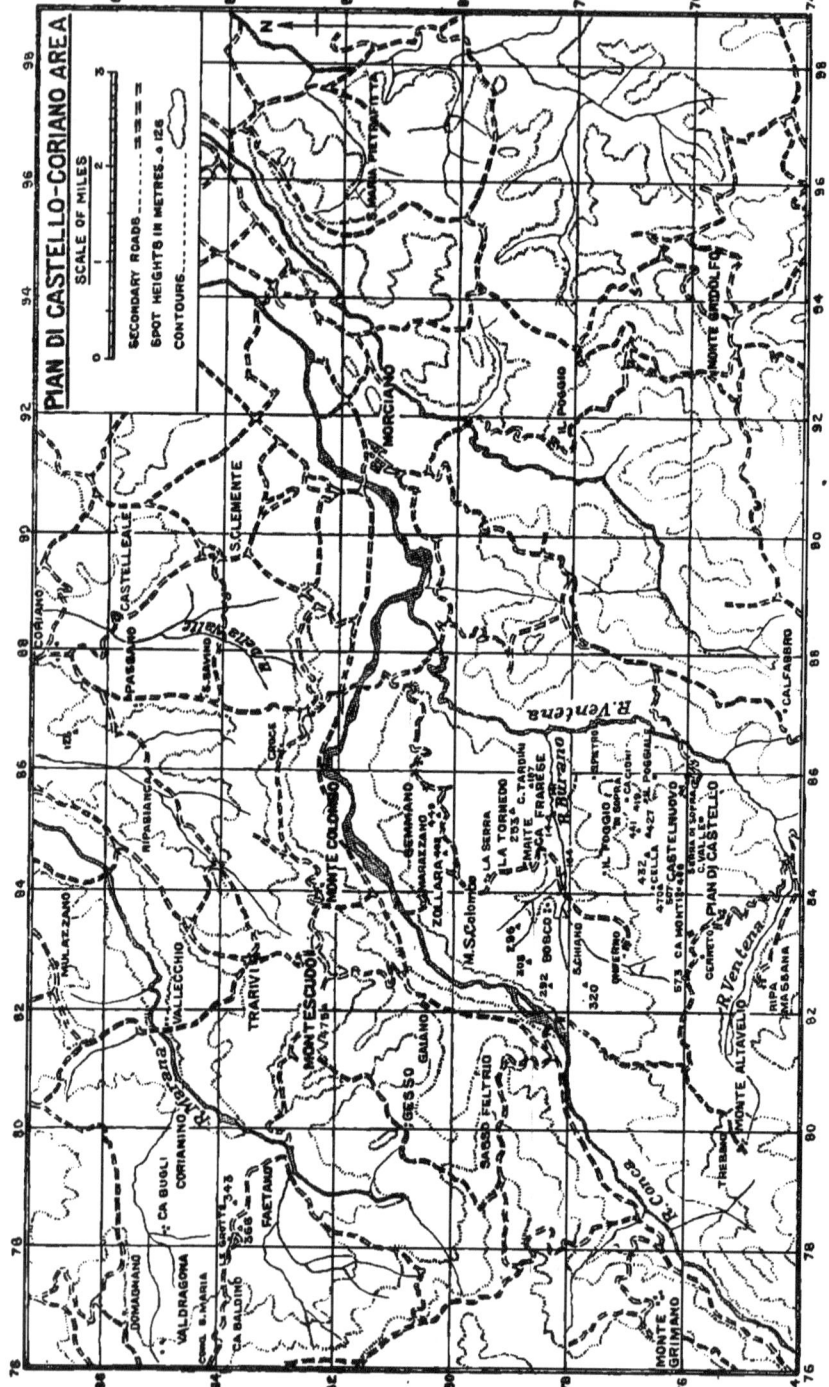

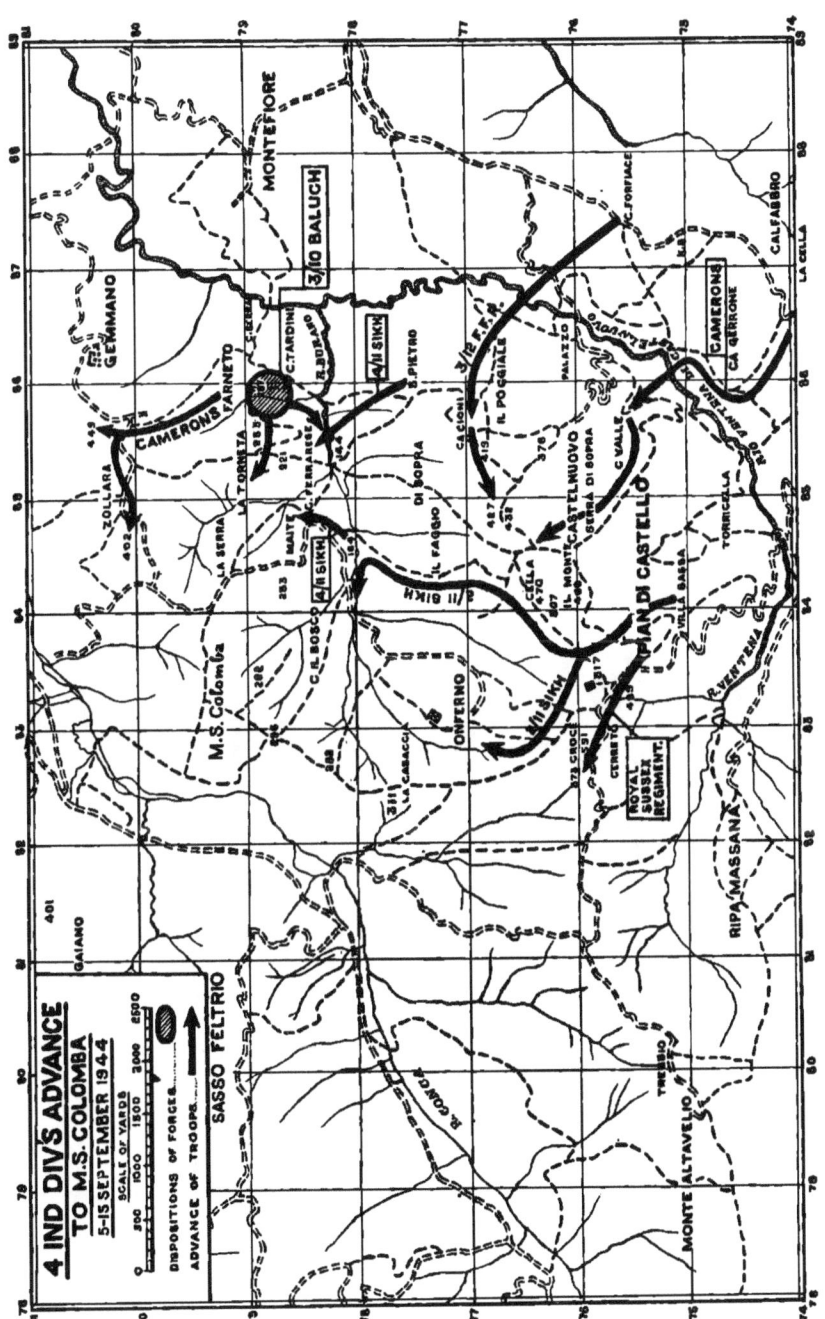

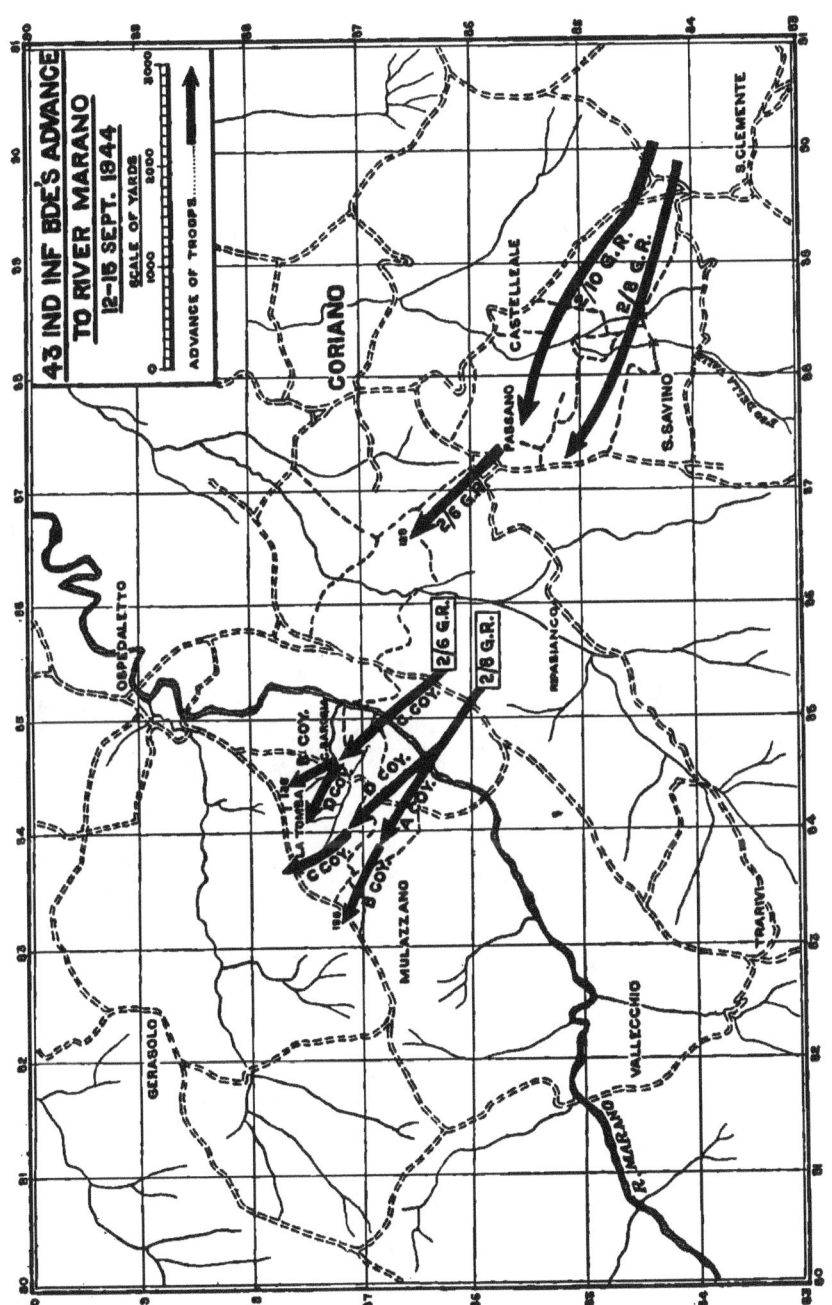

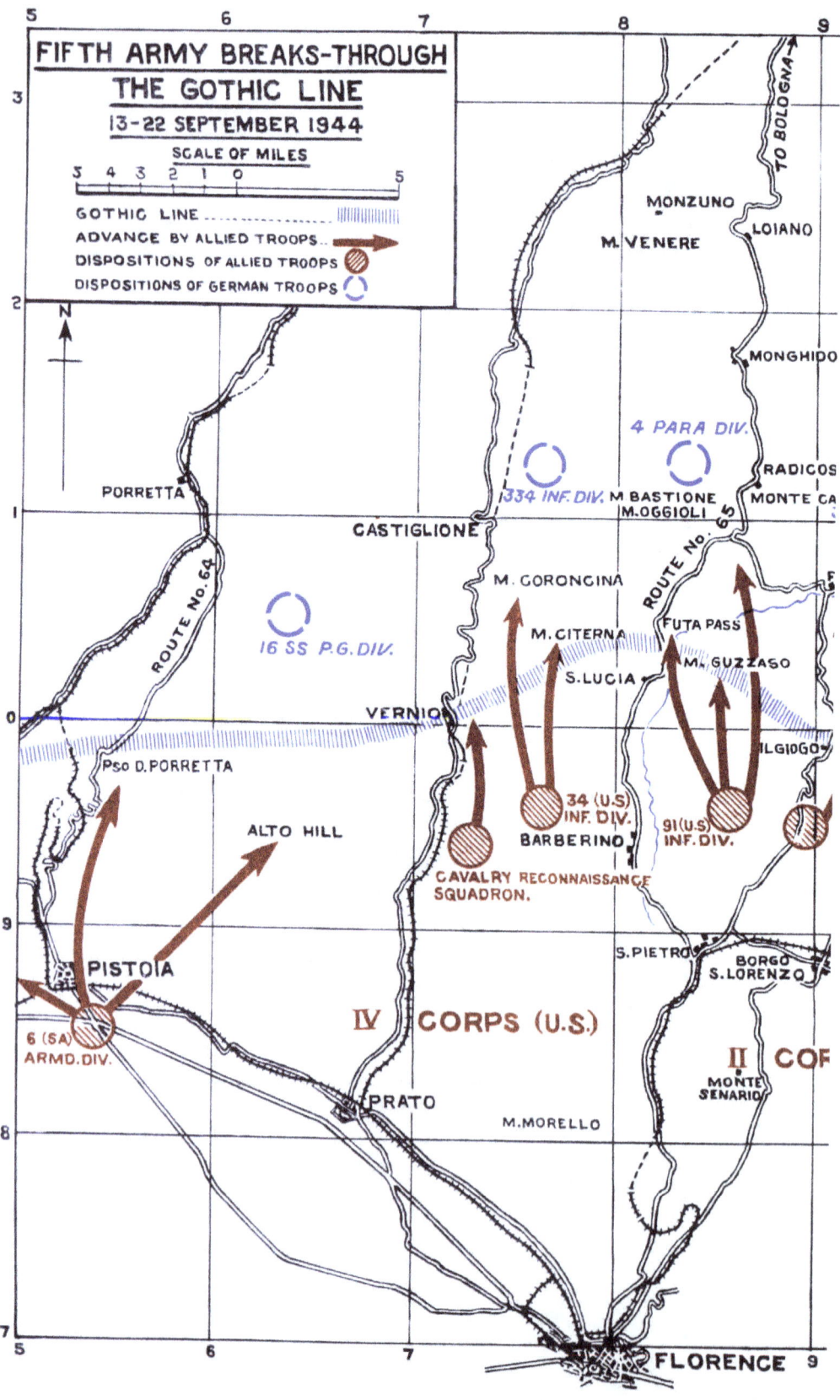

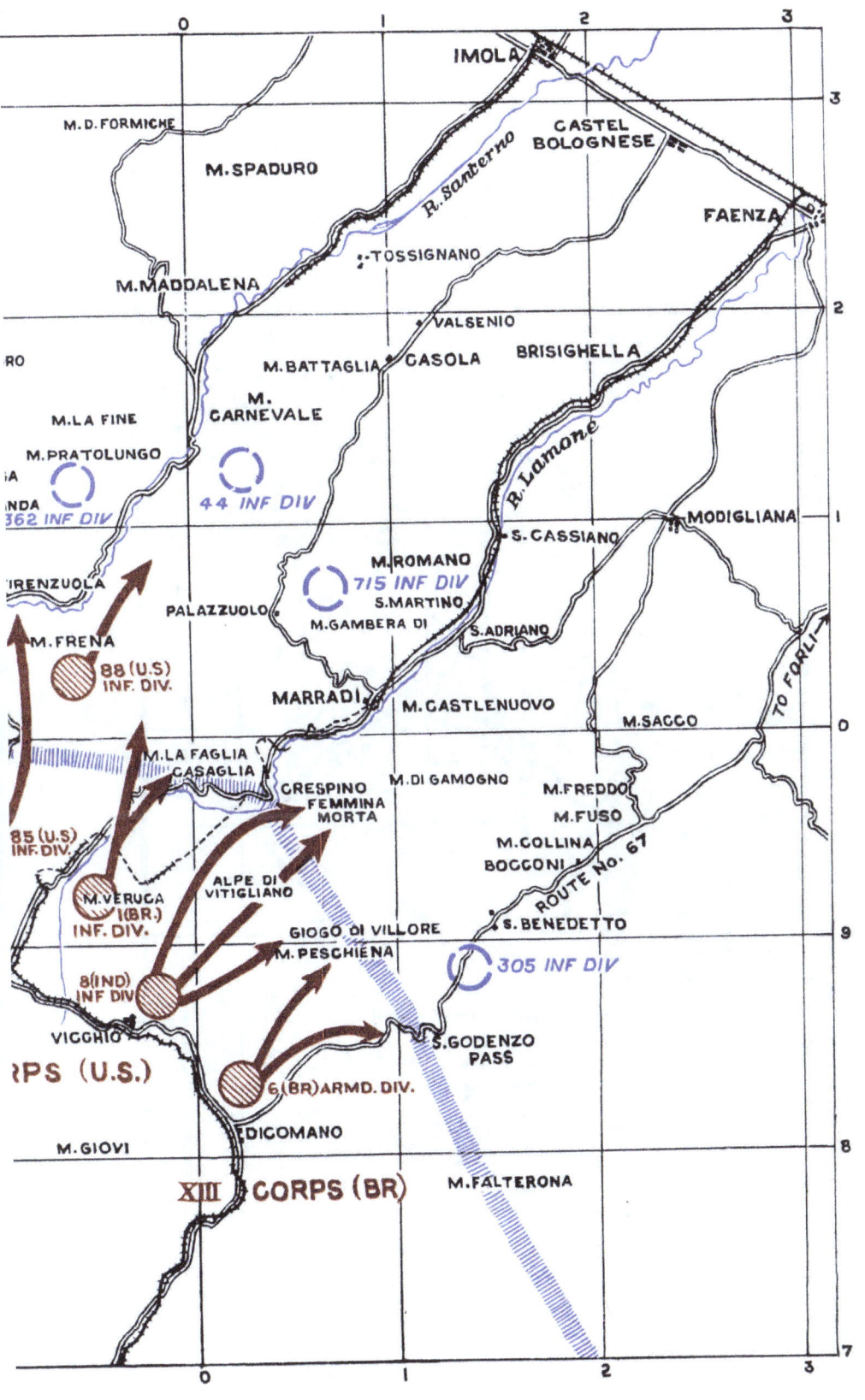

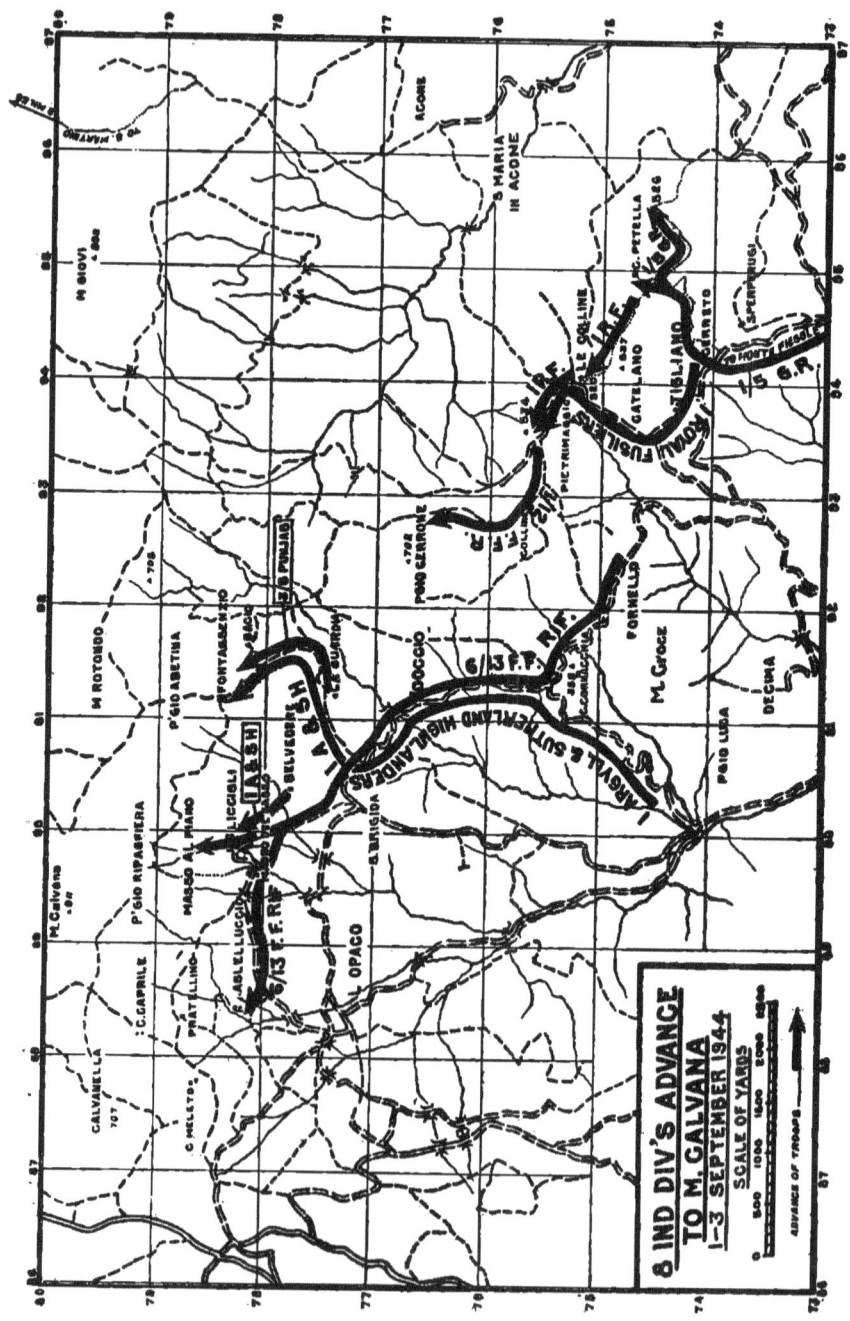

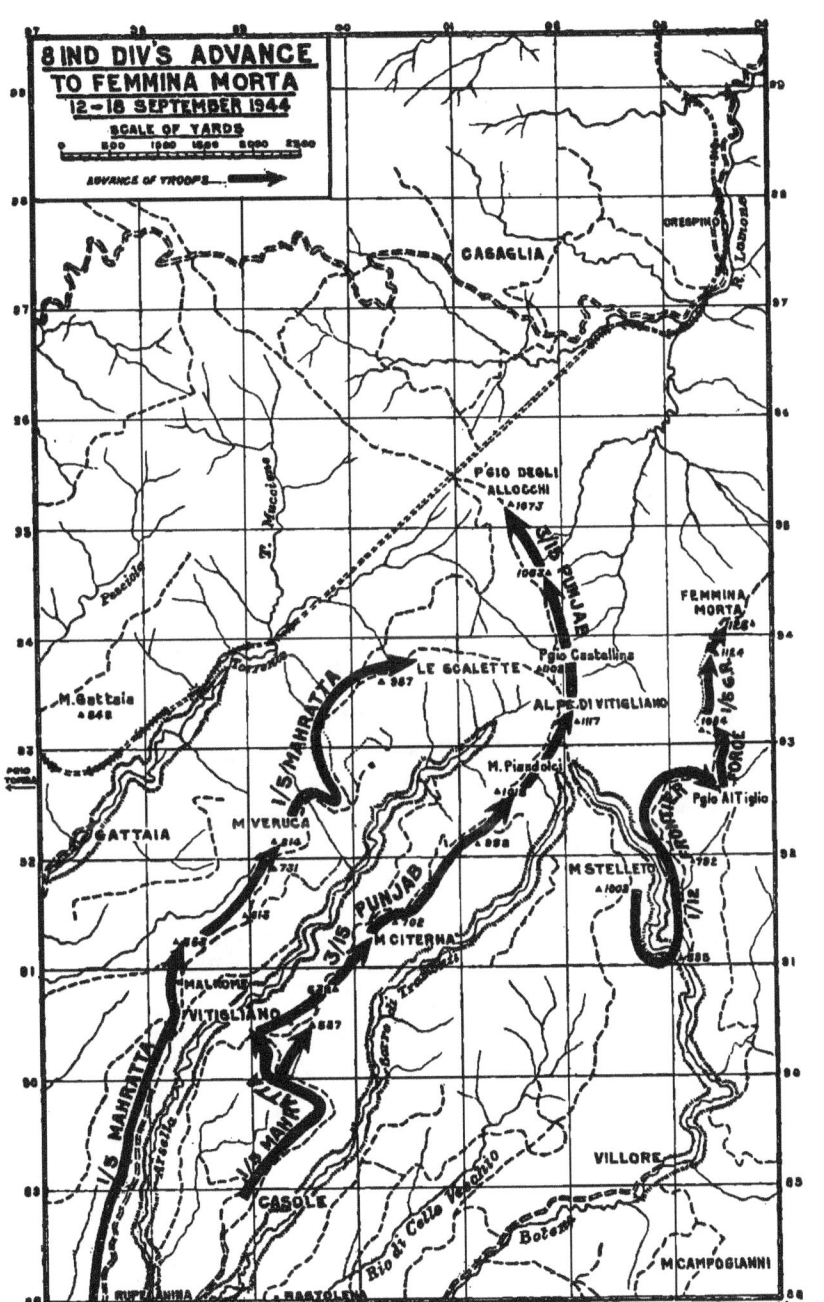

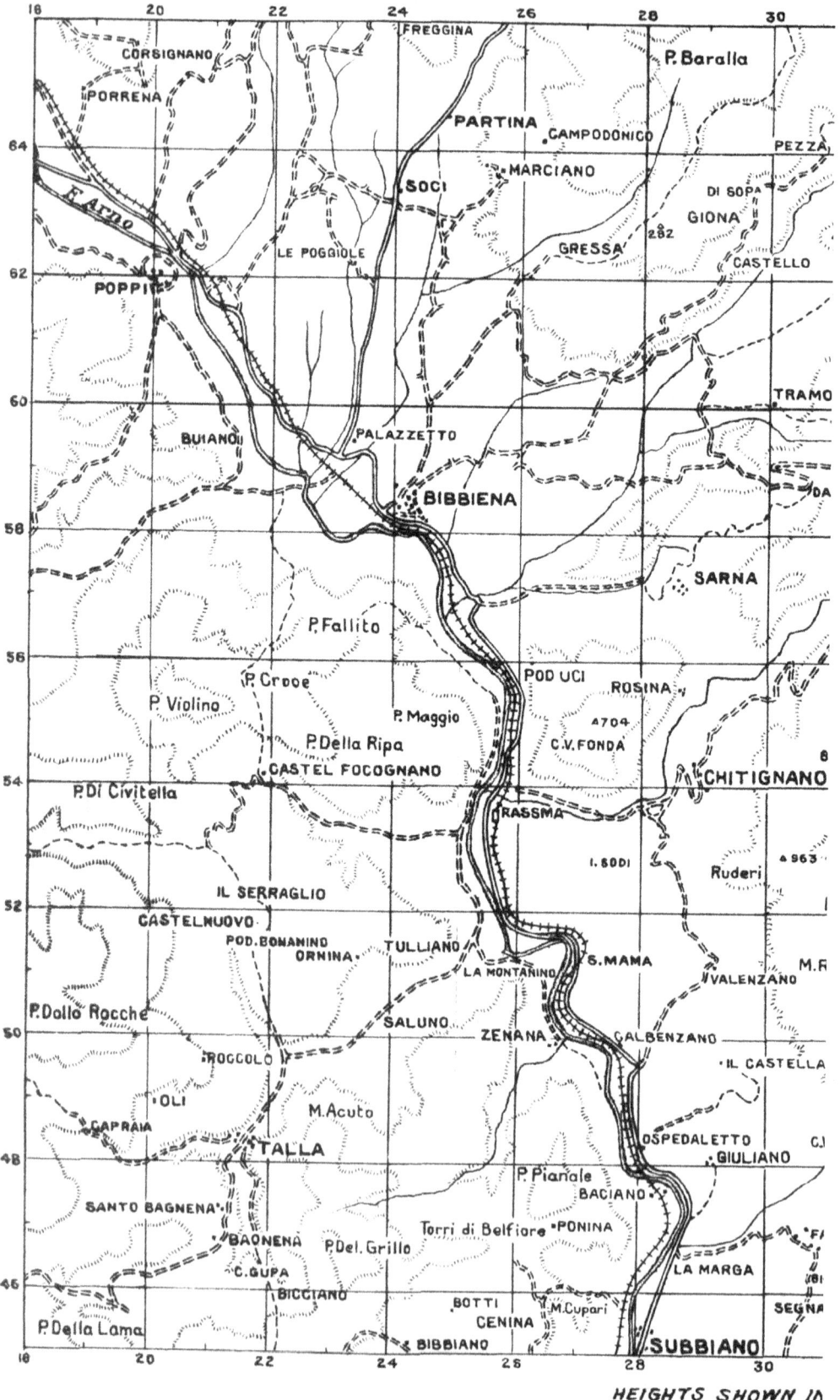

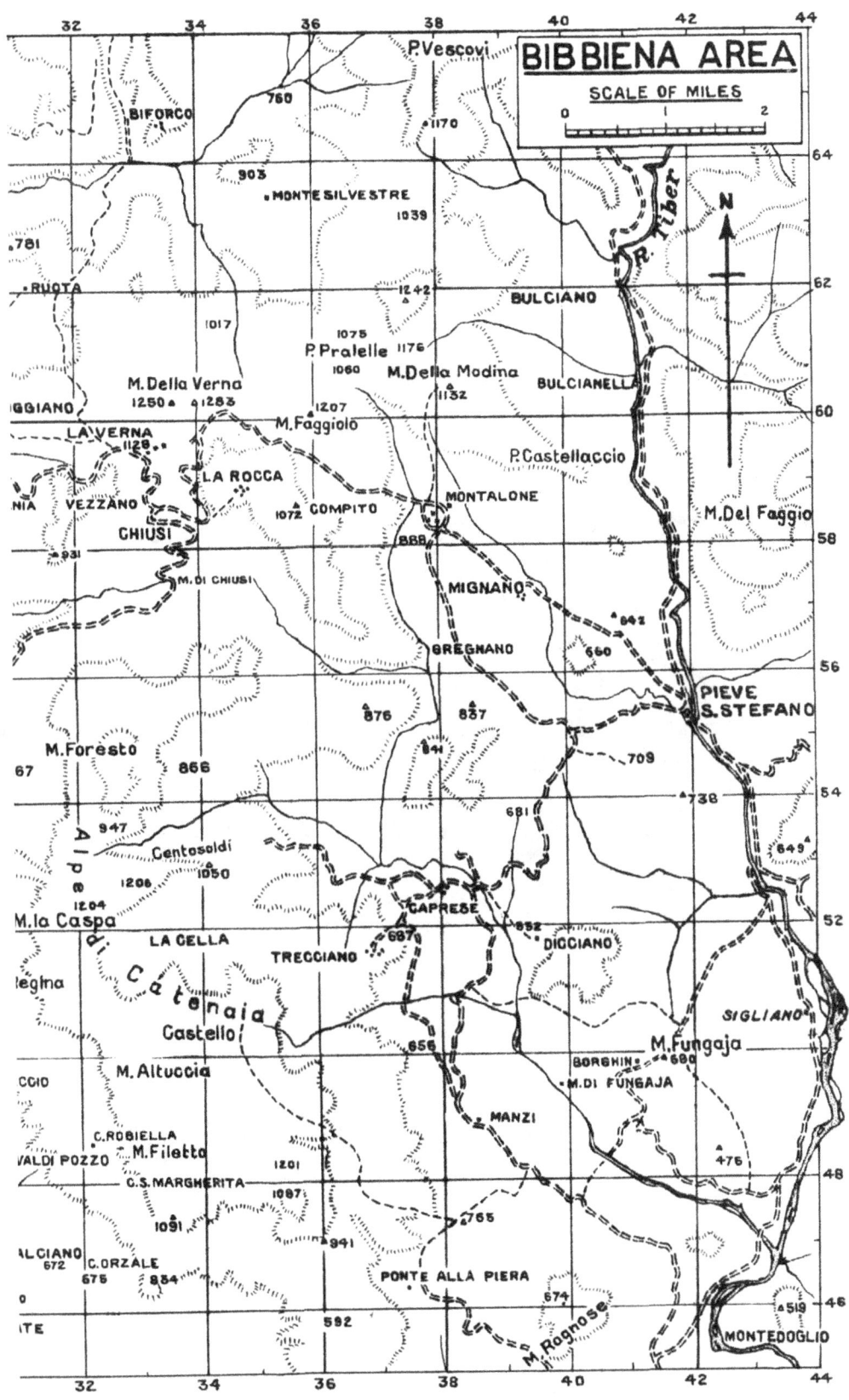

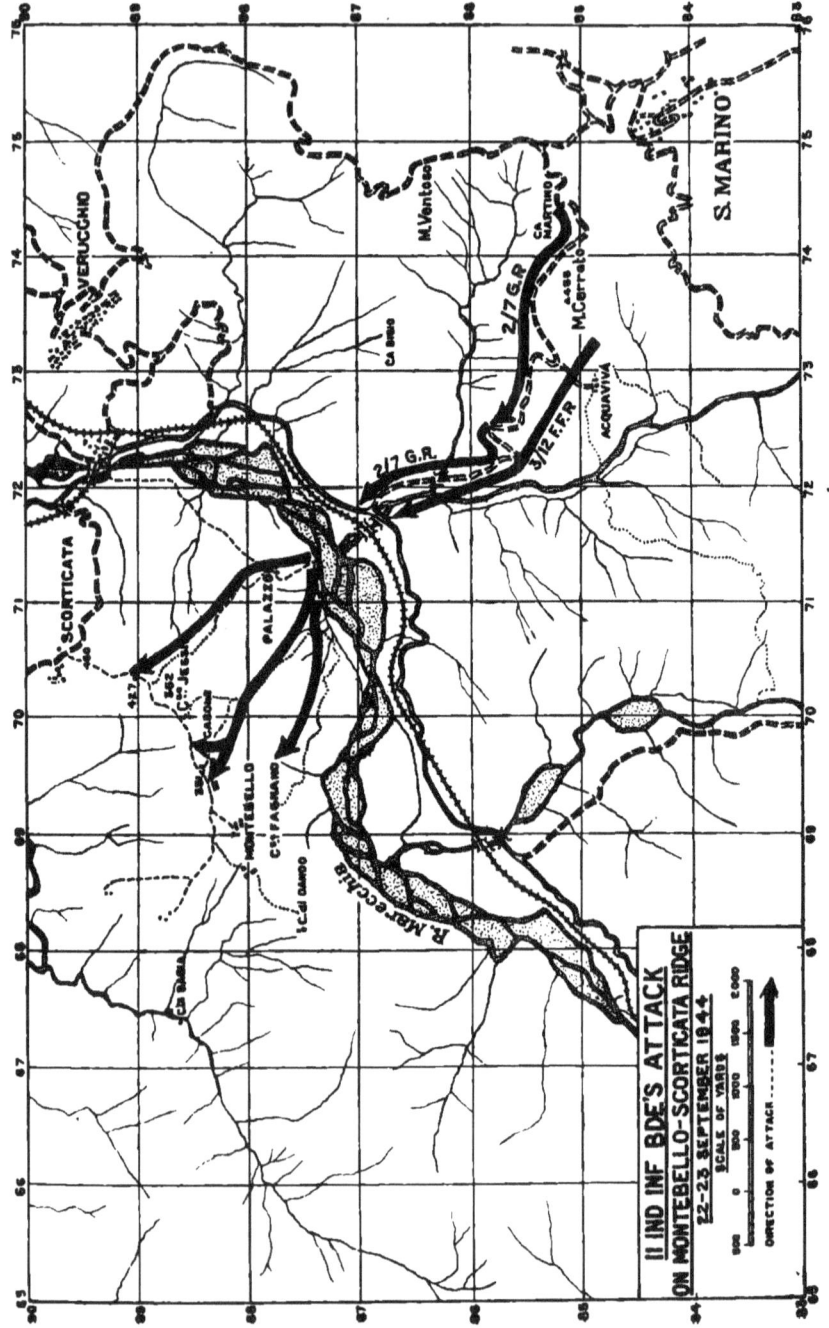

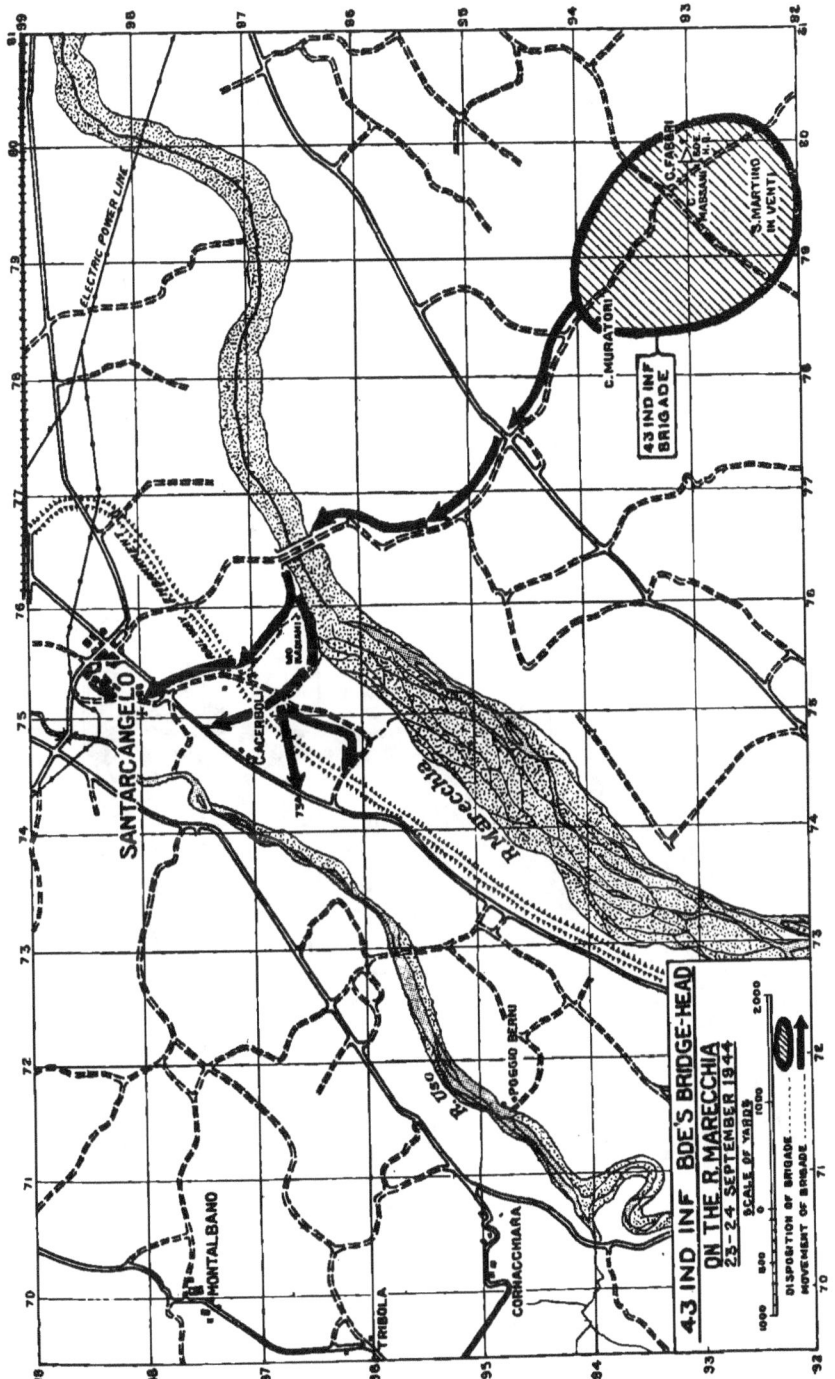

S MARTINO-SOGLIANO AREA

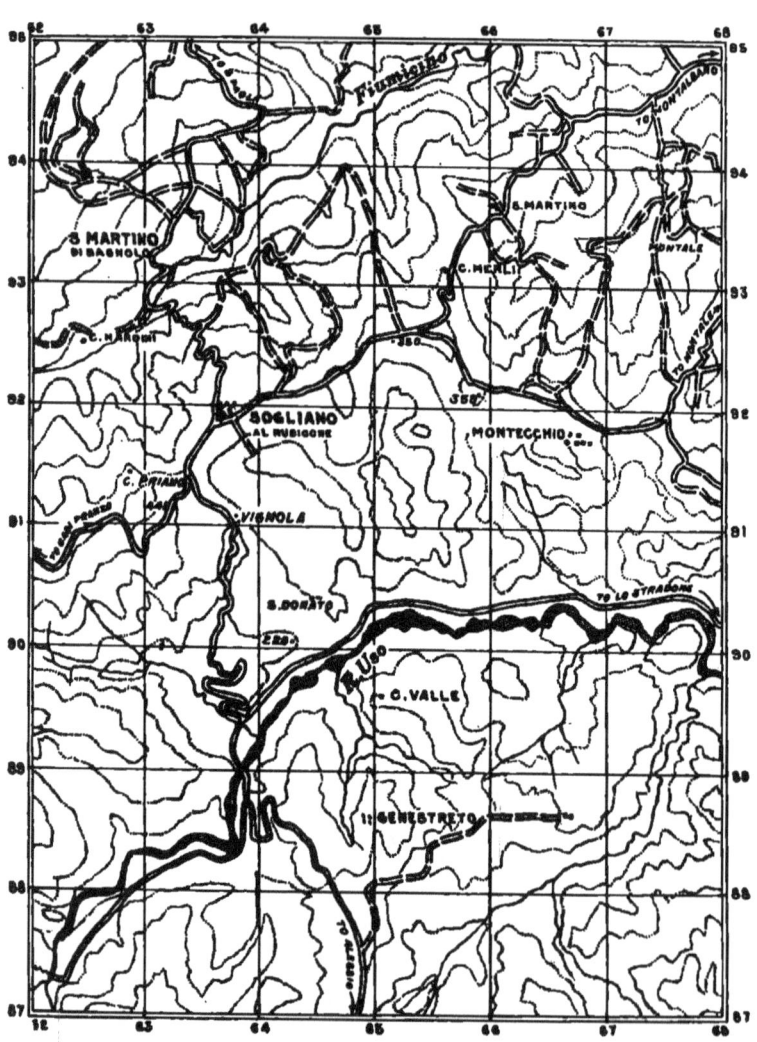

M FARNETO AREA

SCALE OF YARDS

500 0 500 1000 1500 2000 2500

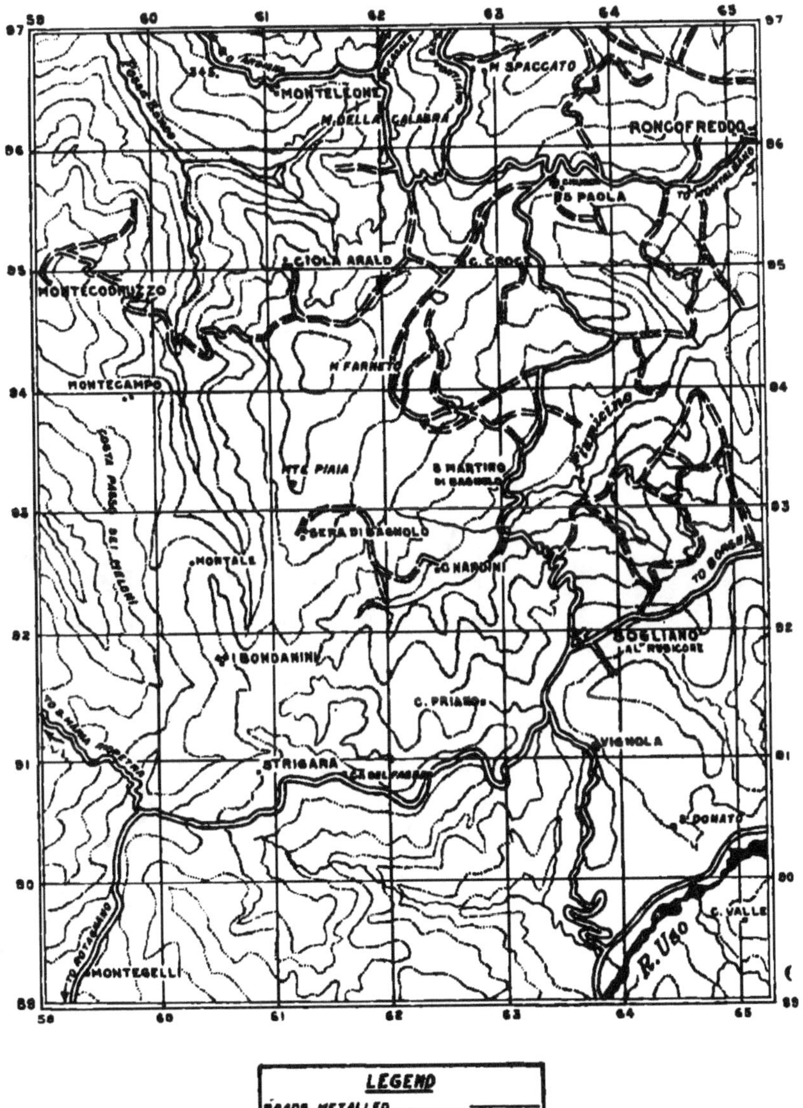

LEGEND

ROADS, METALLED ....

ROADS, GENERALLY UNMETALLED

CONTOURS ....

SPOT HEIGHTS IN METERS 328

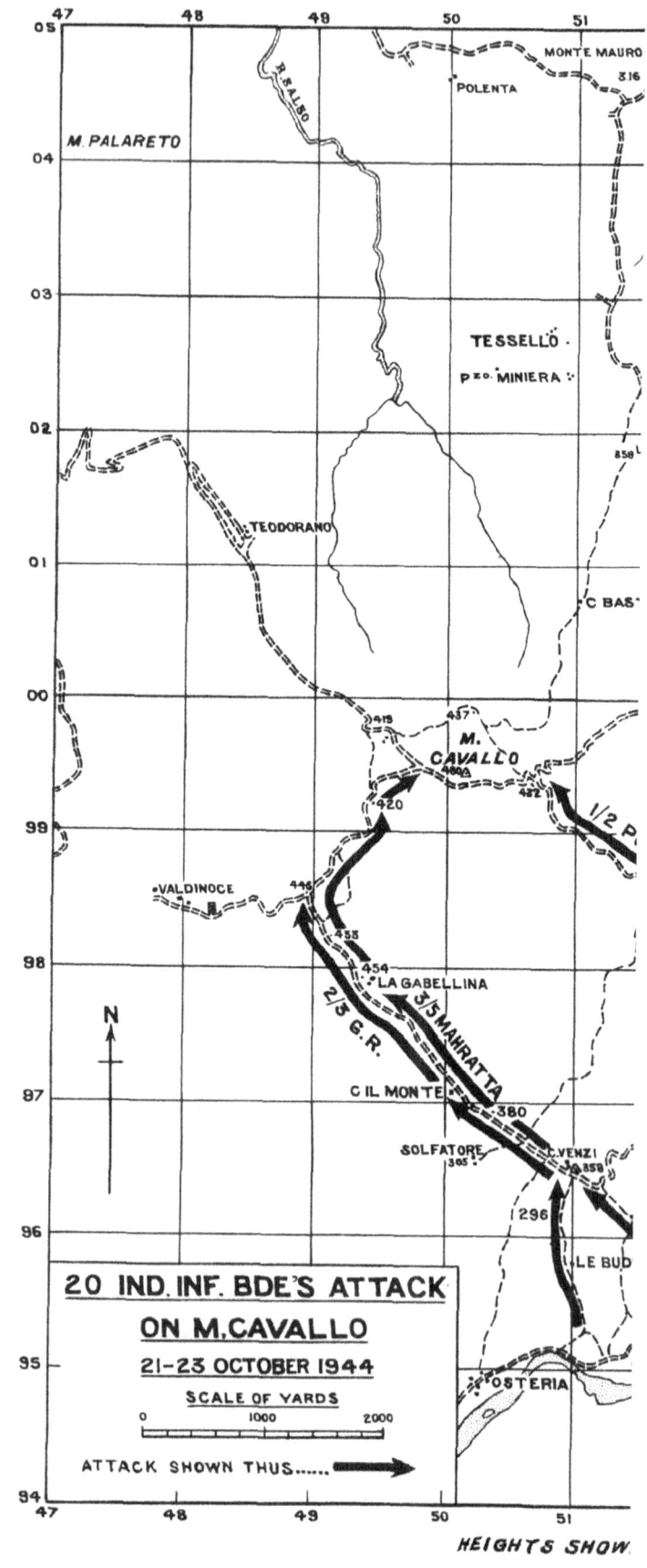

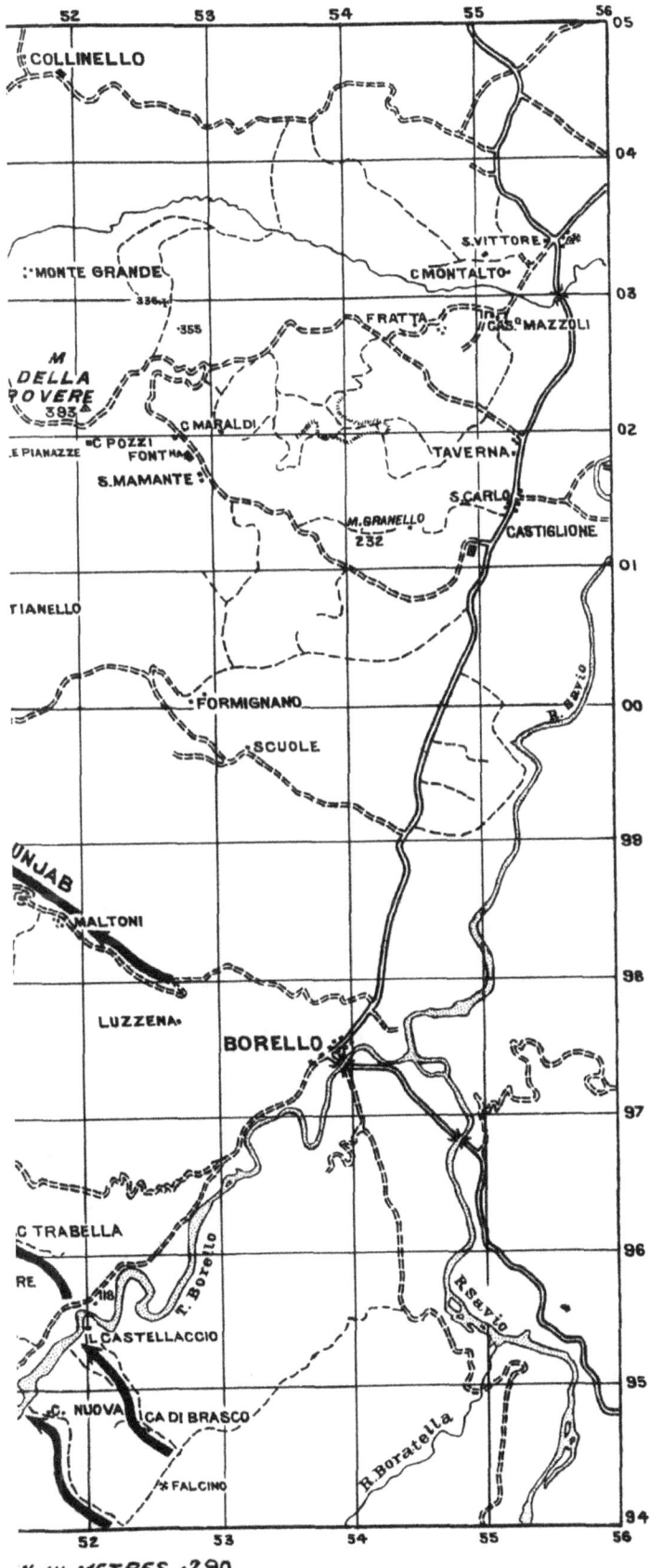

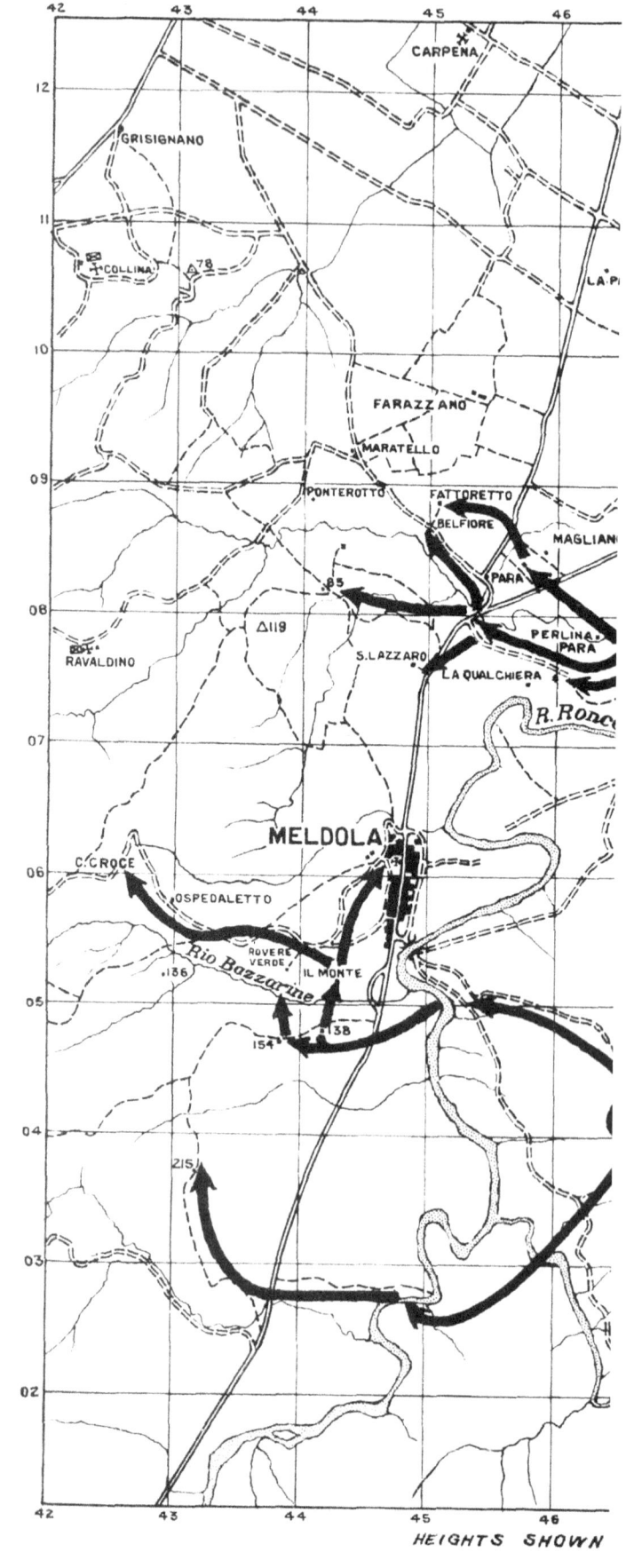

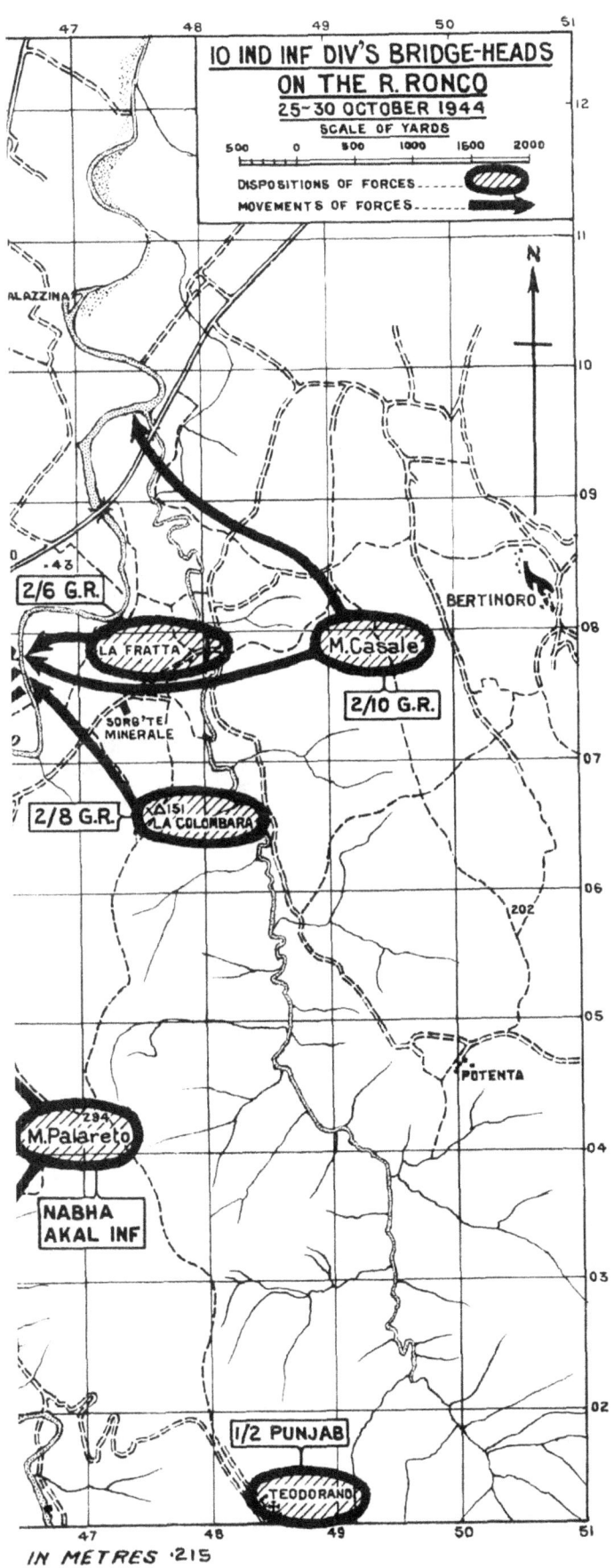

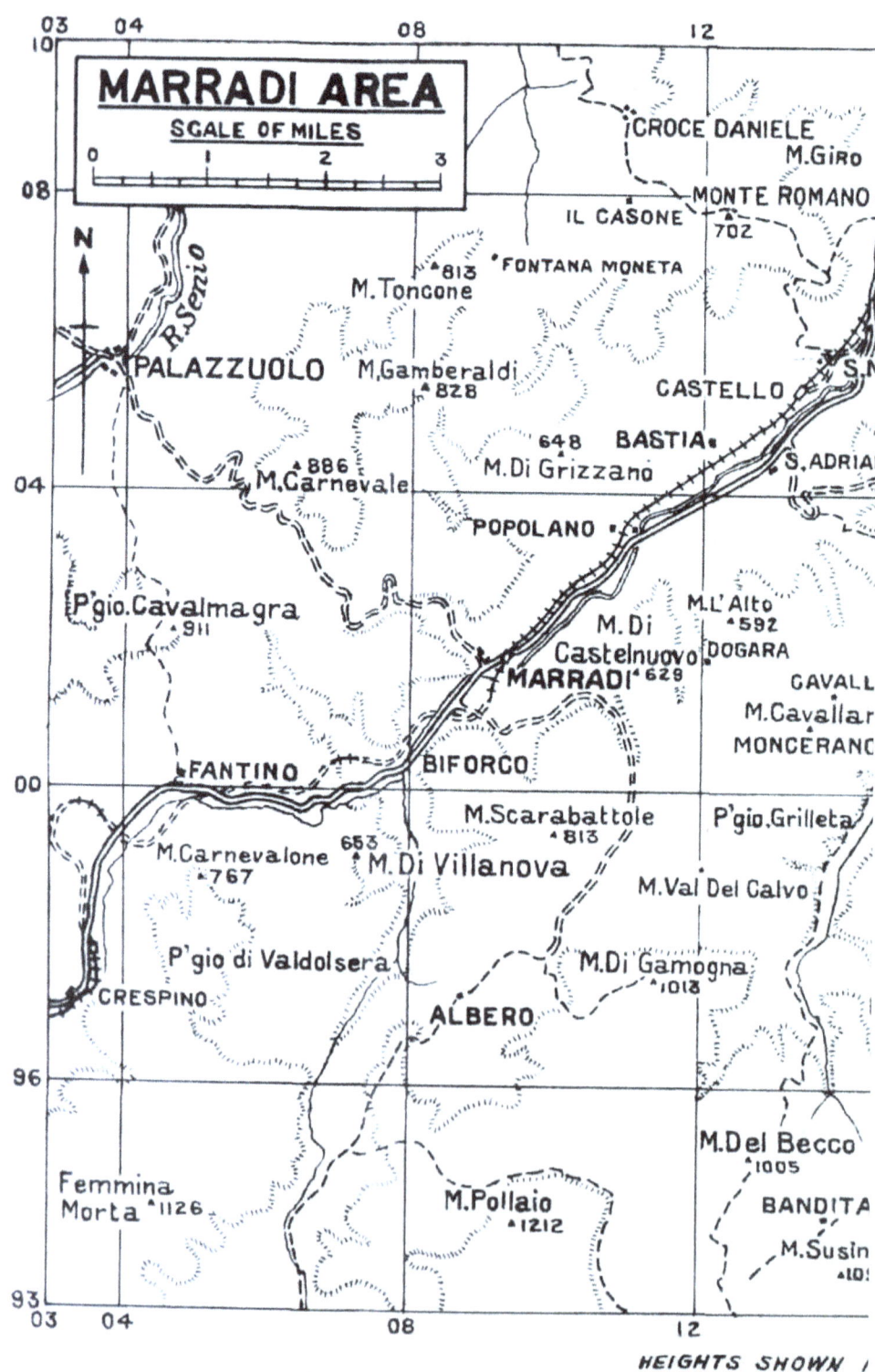

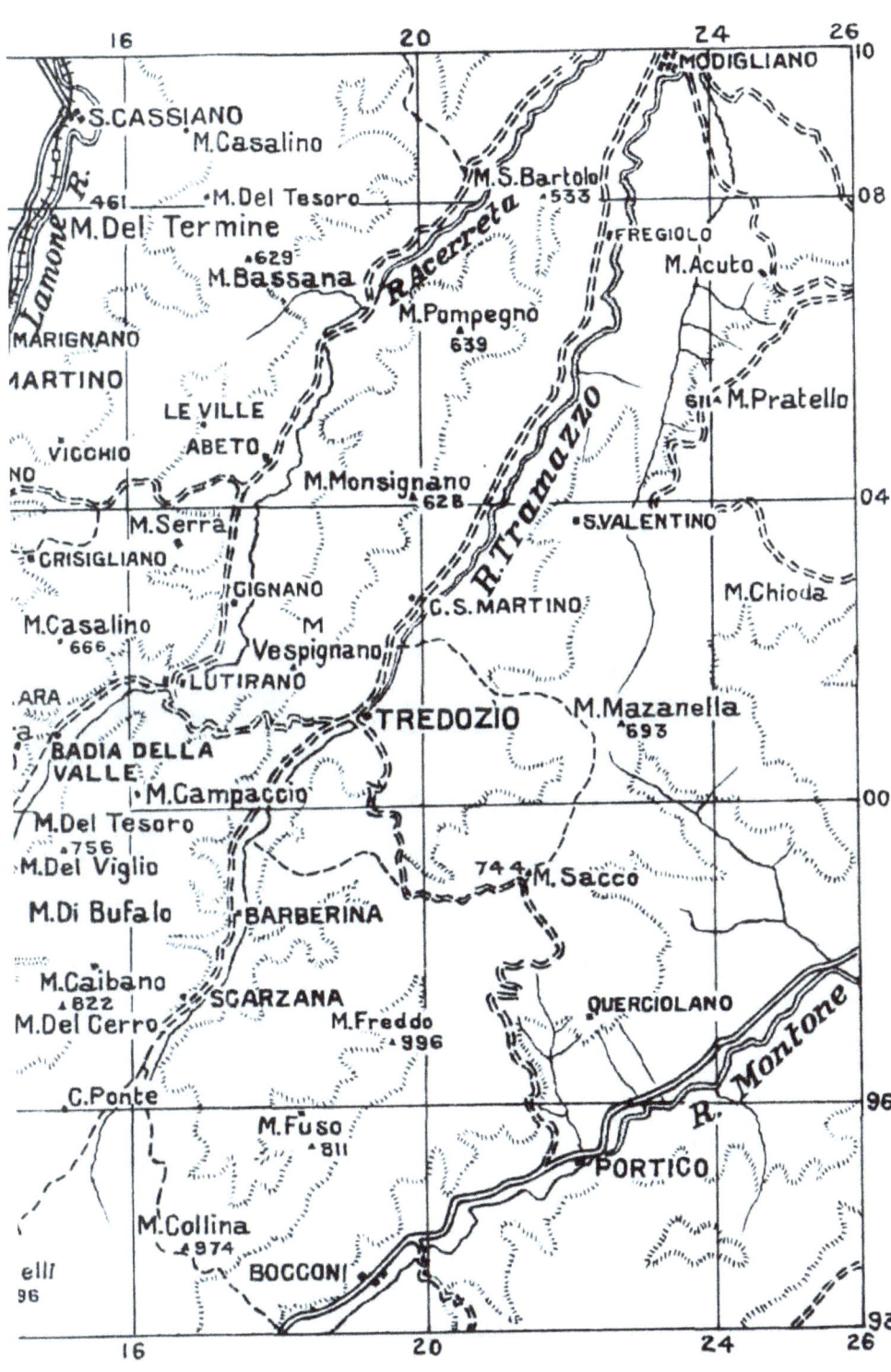

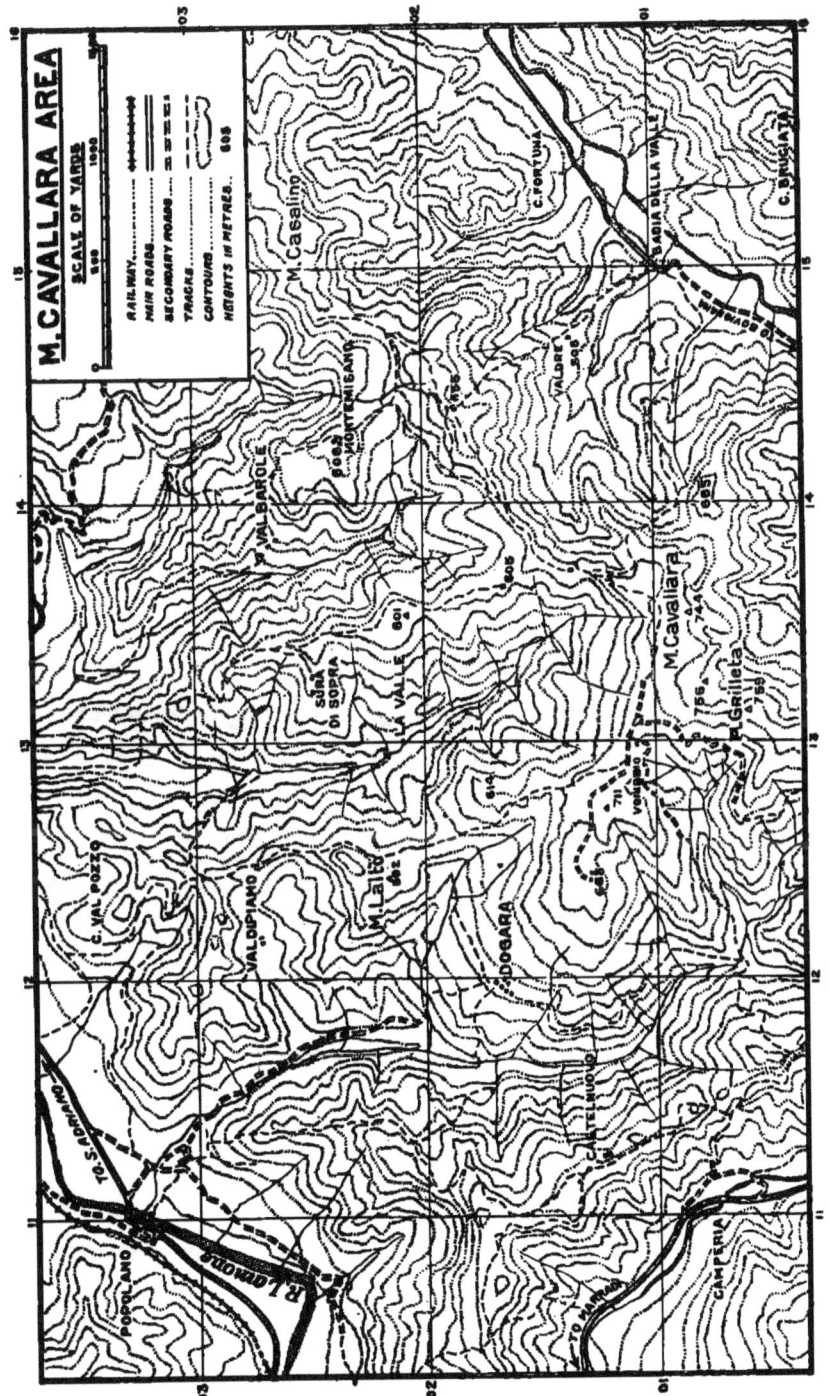

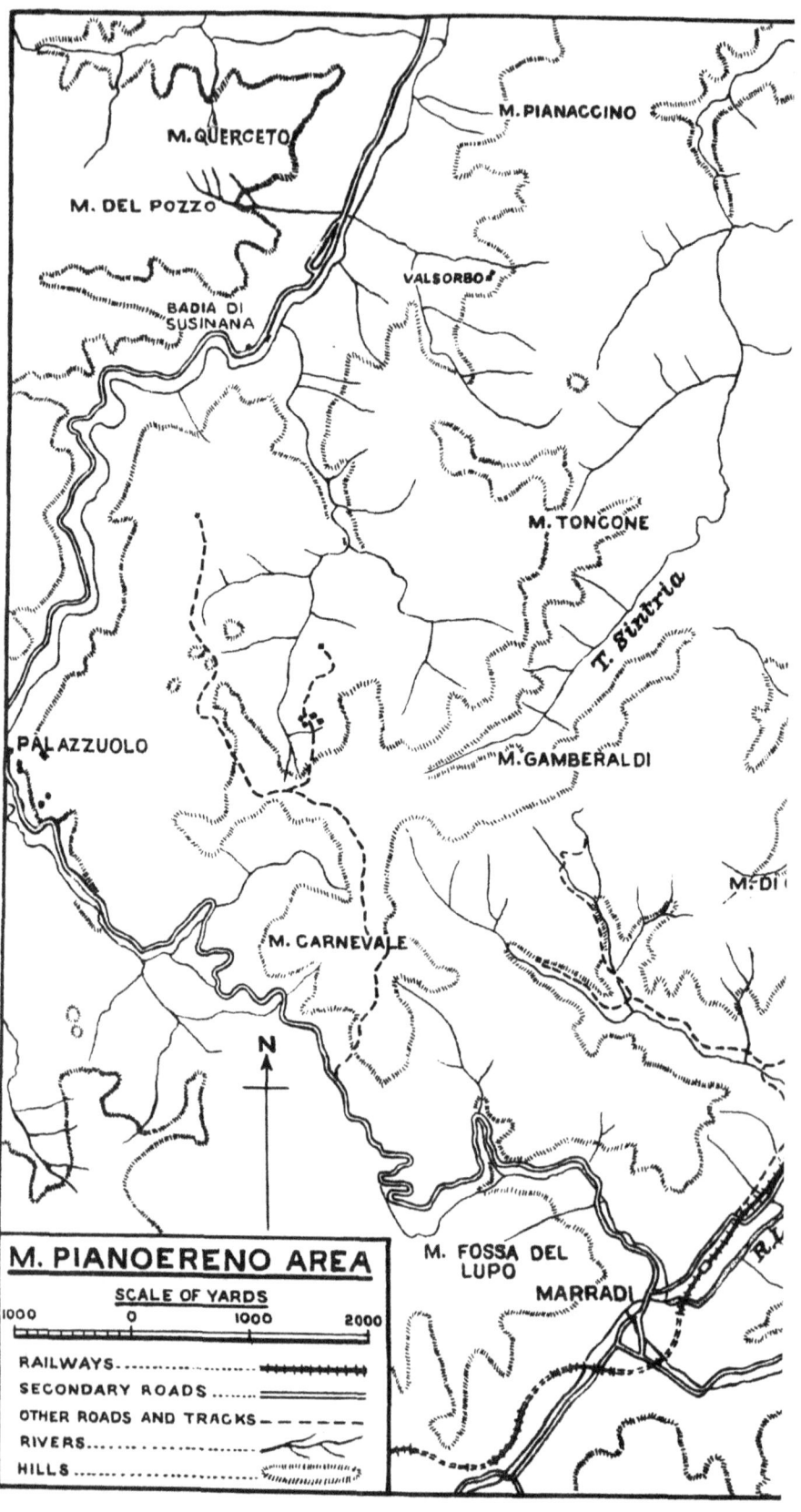

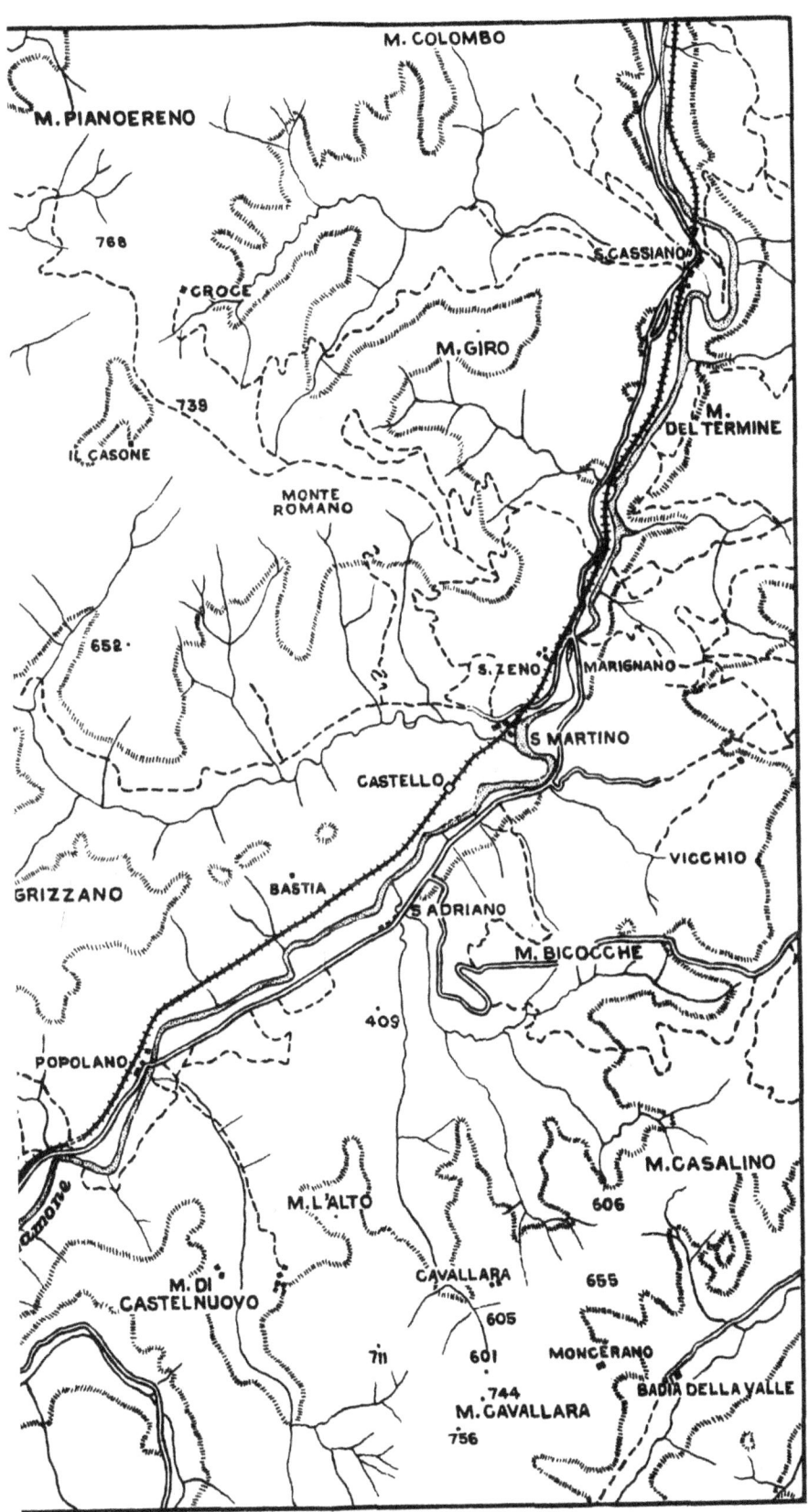

IN METRES ·711

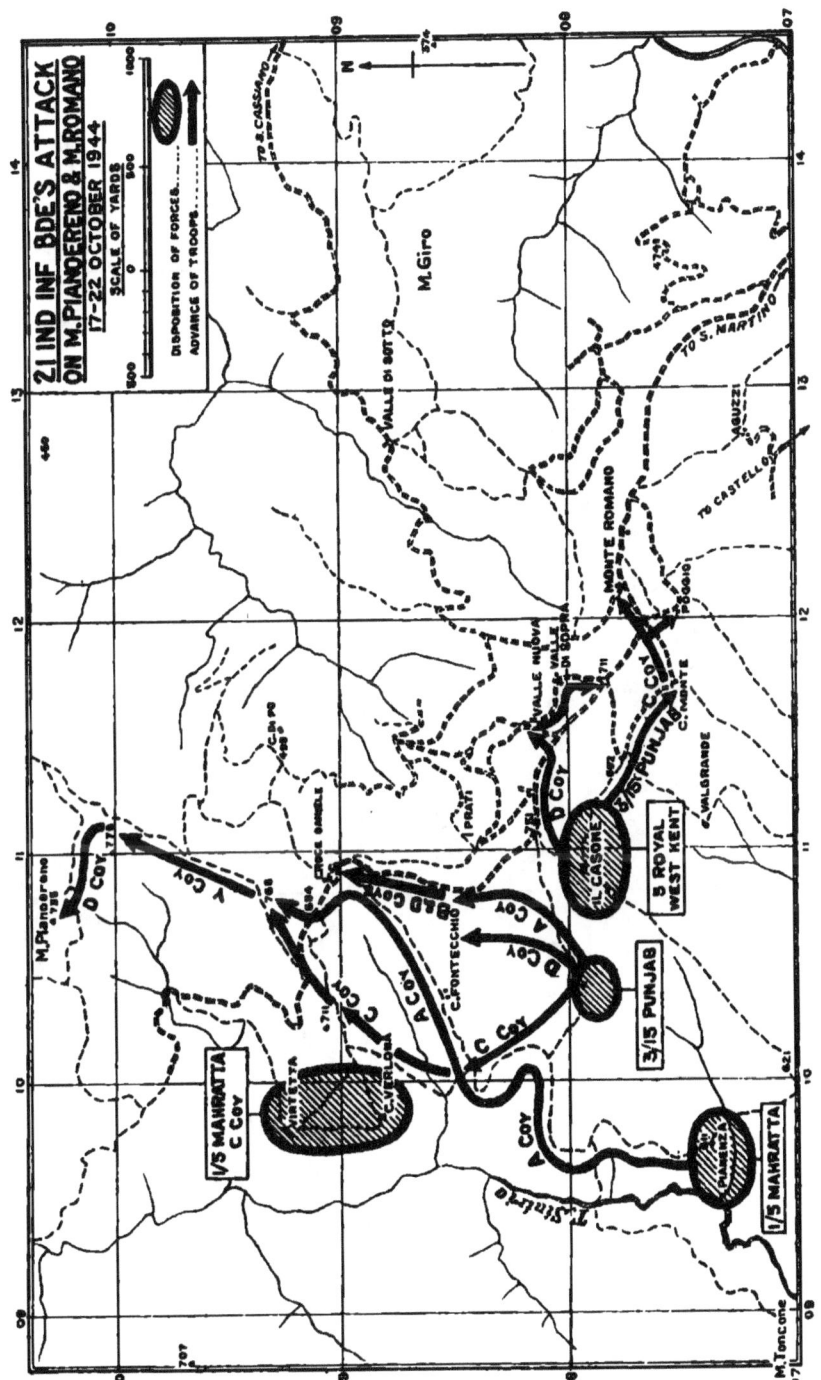

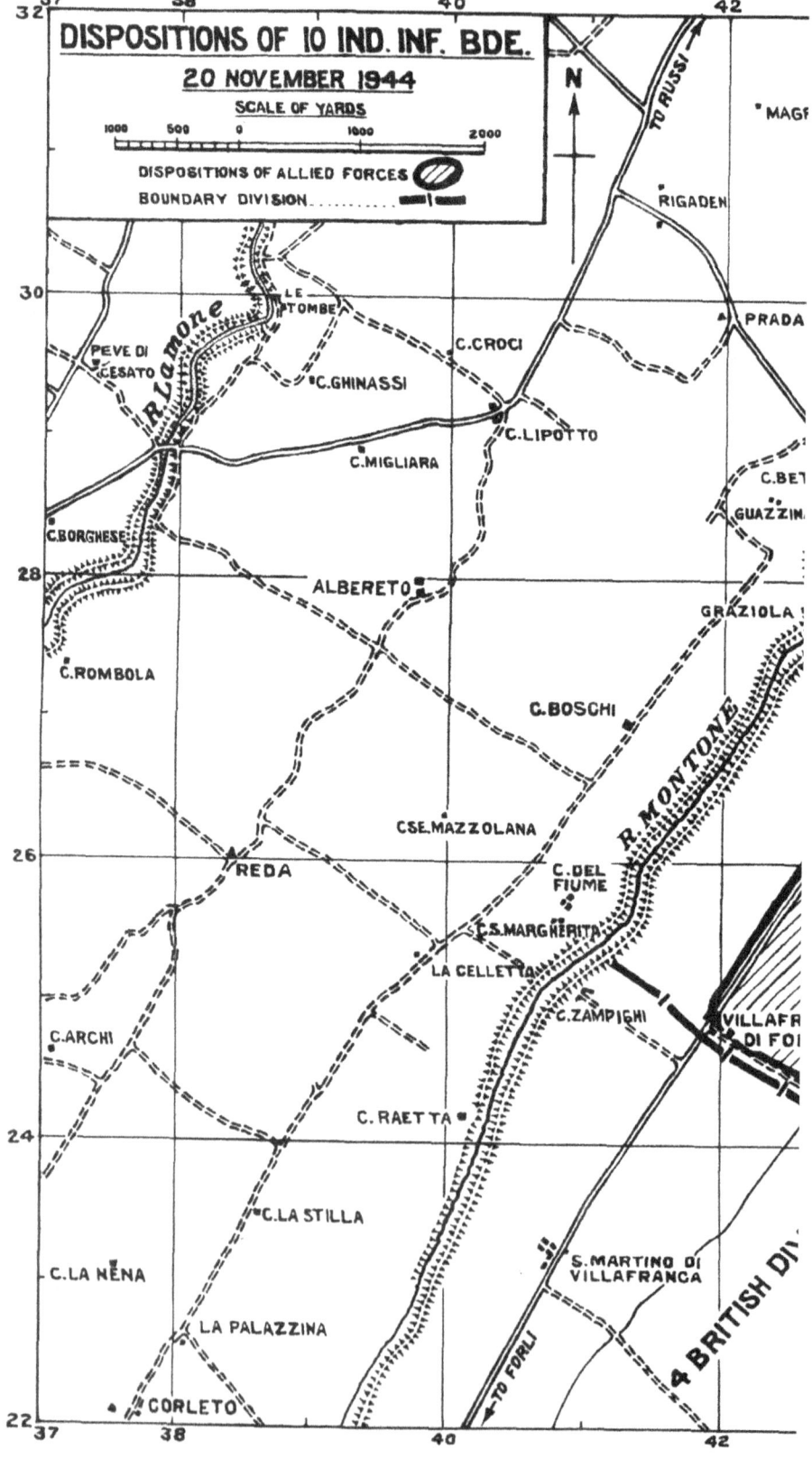

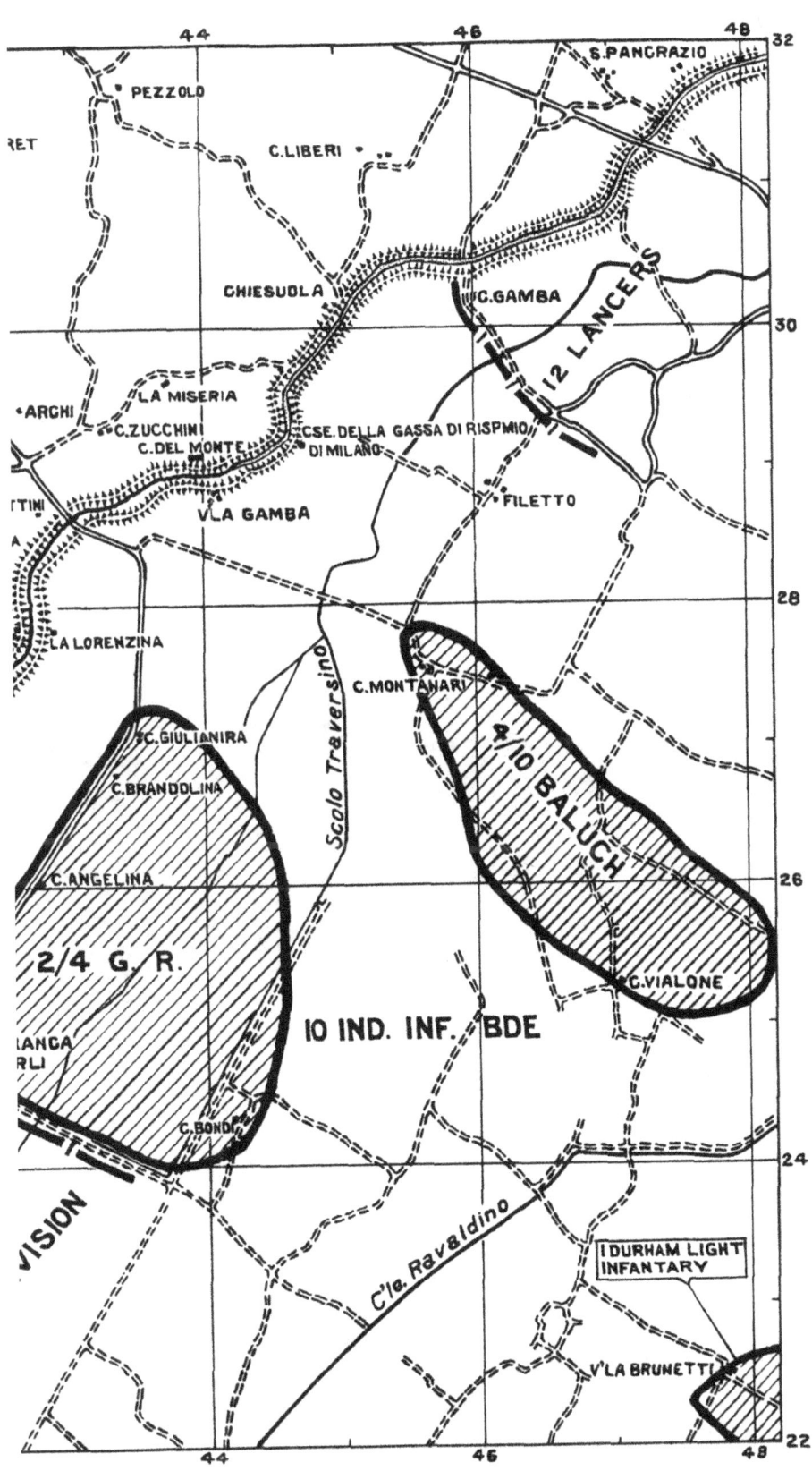

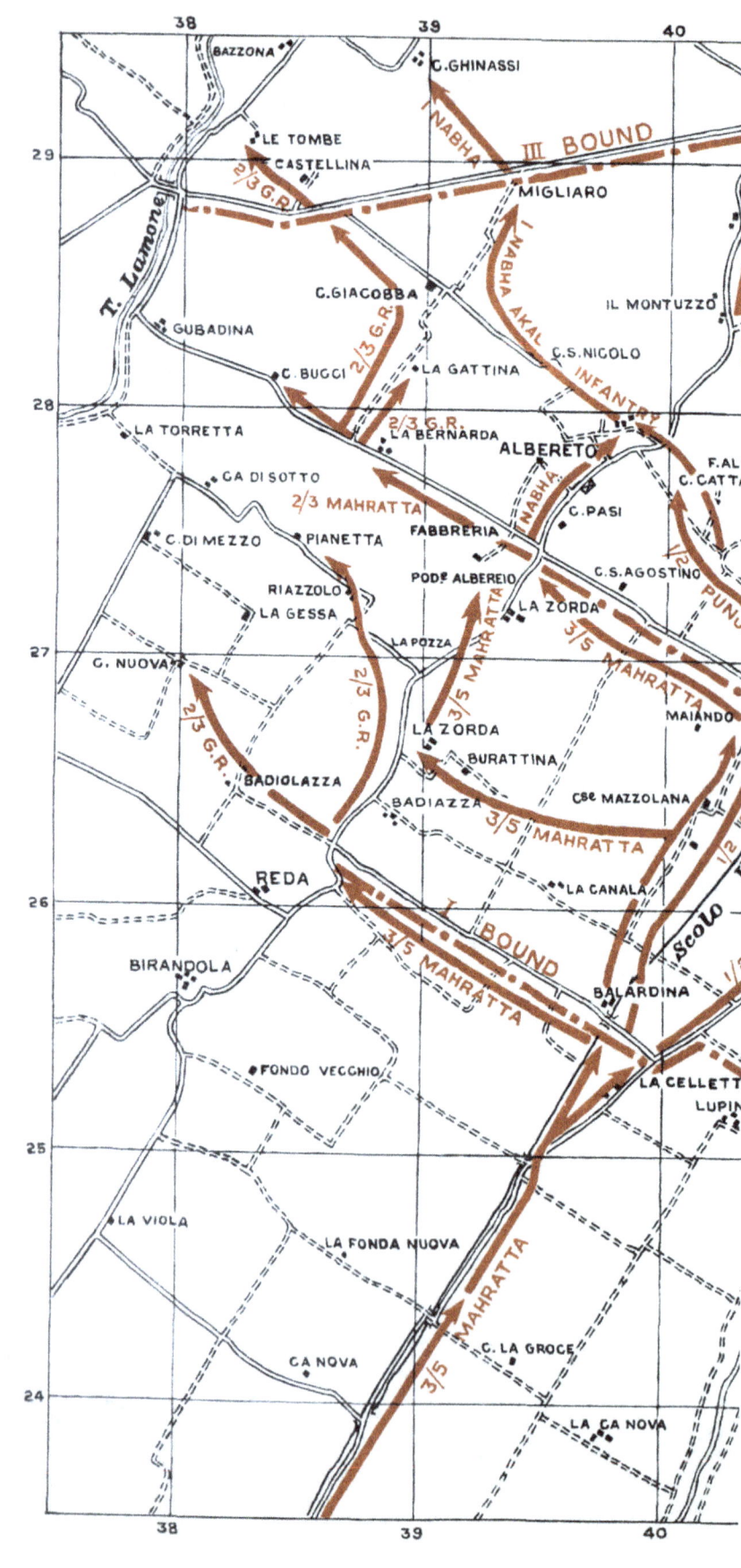

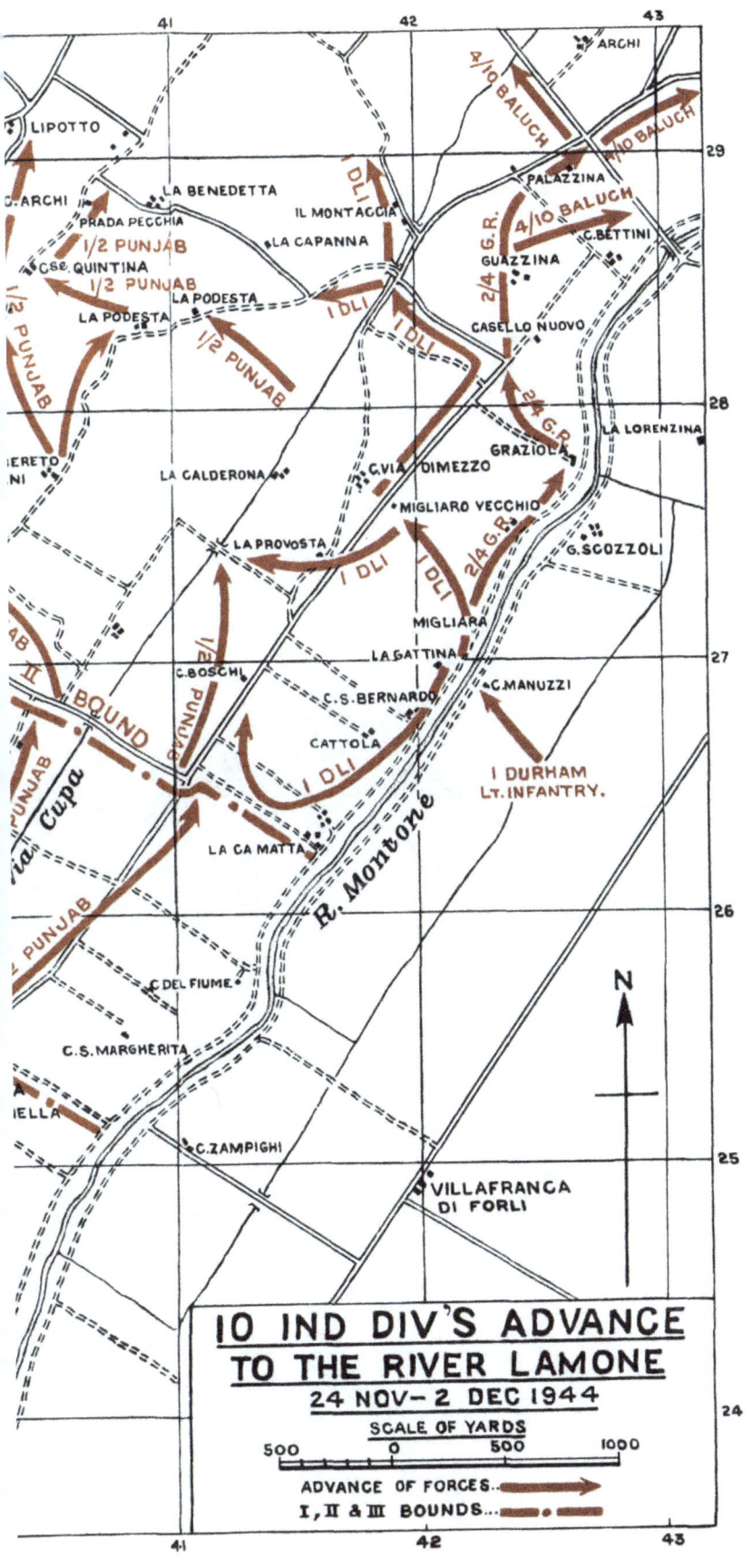

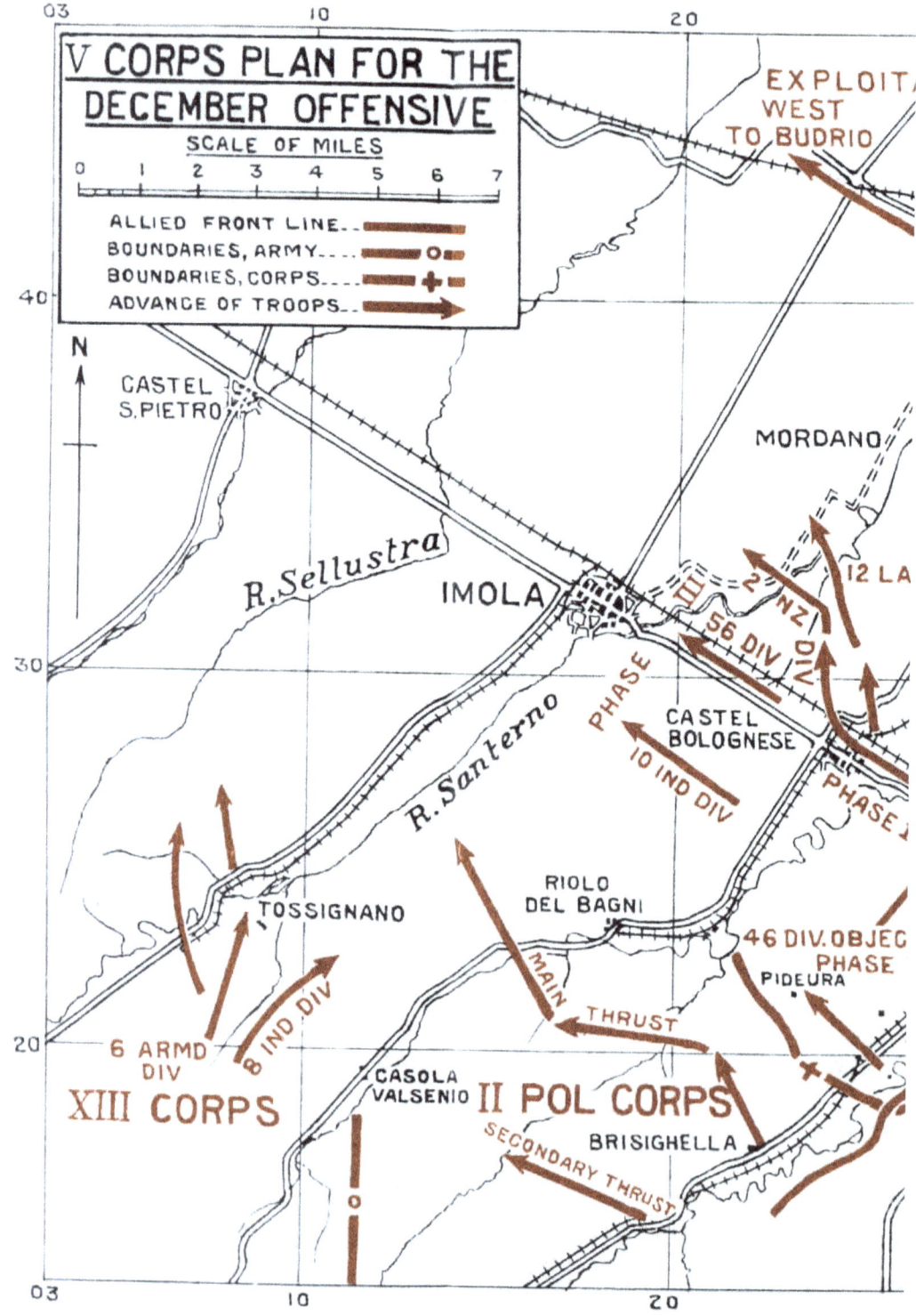

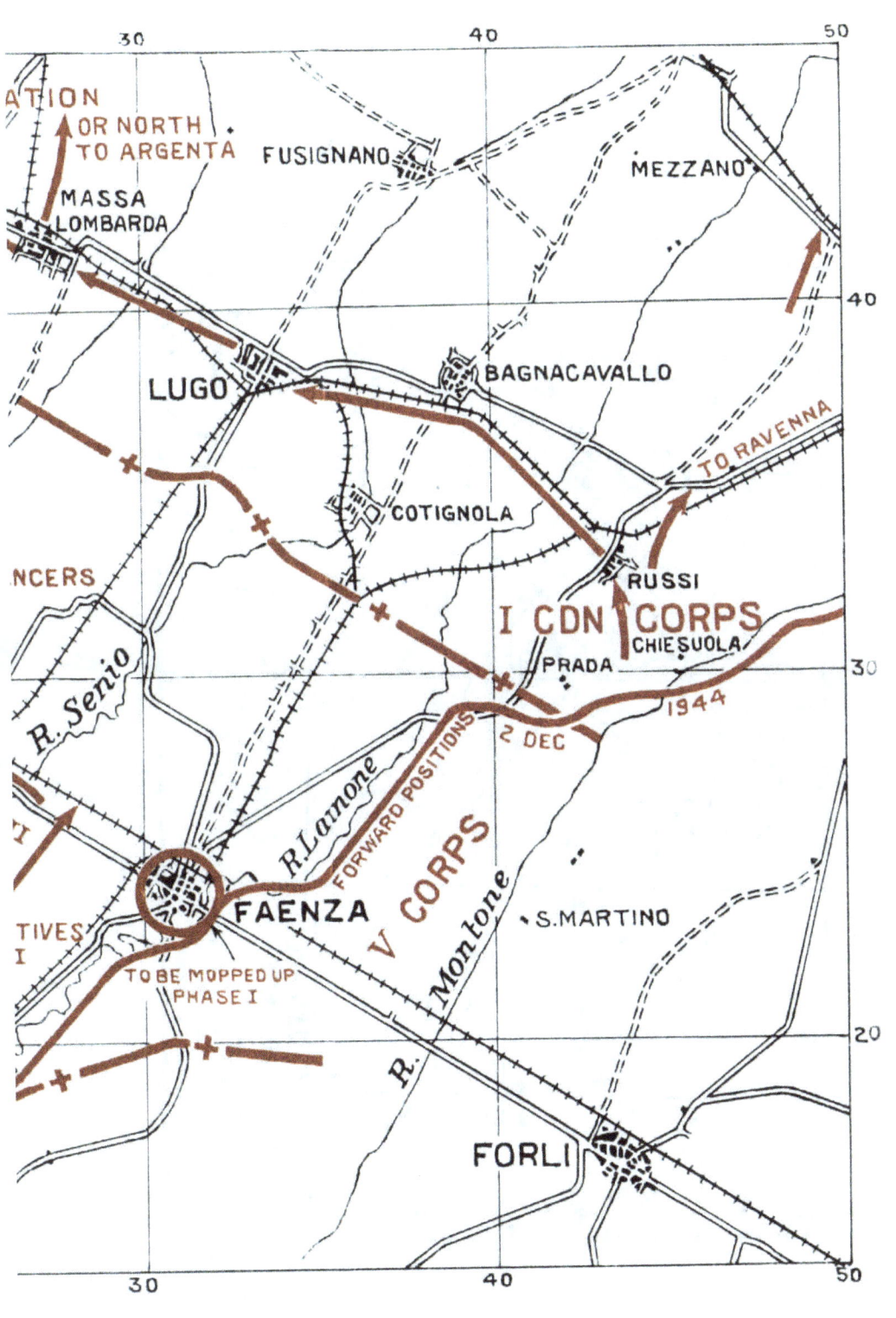

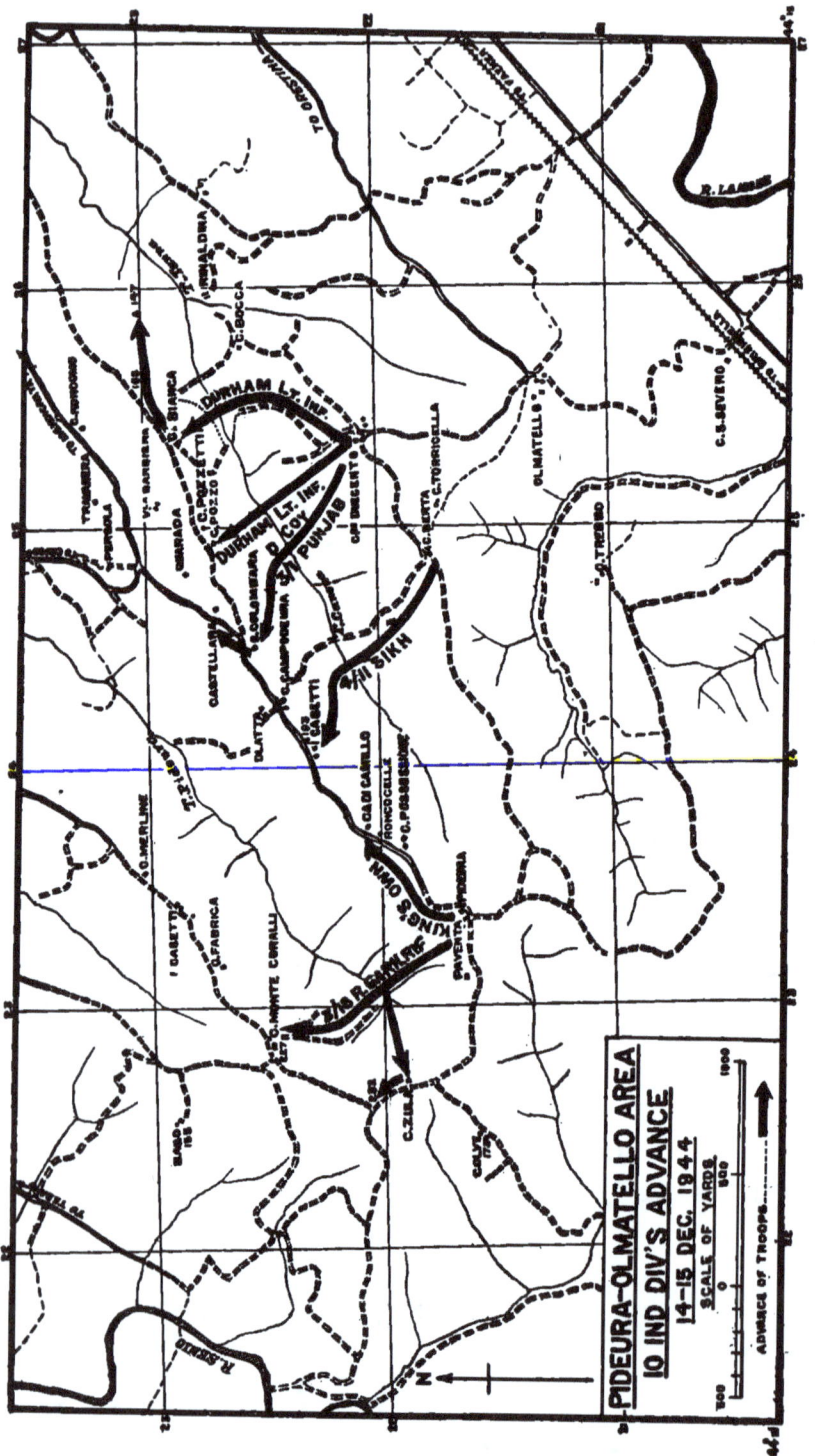

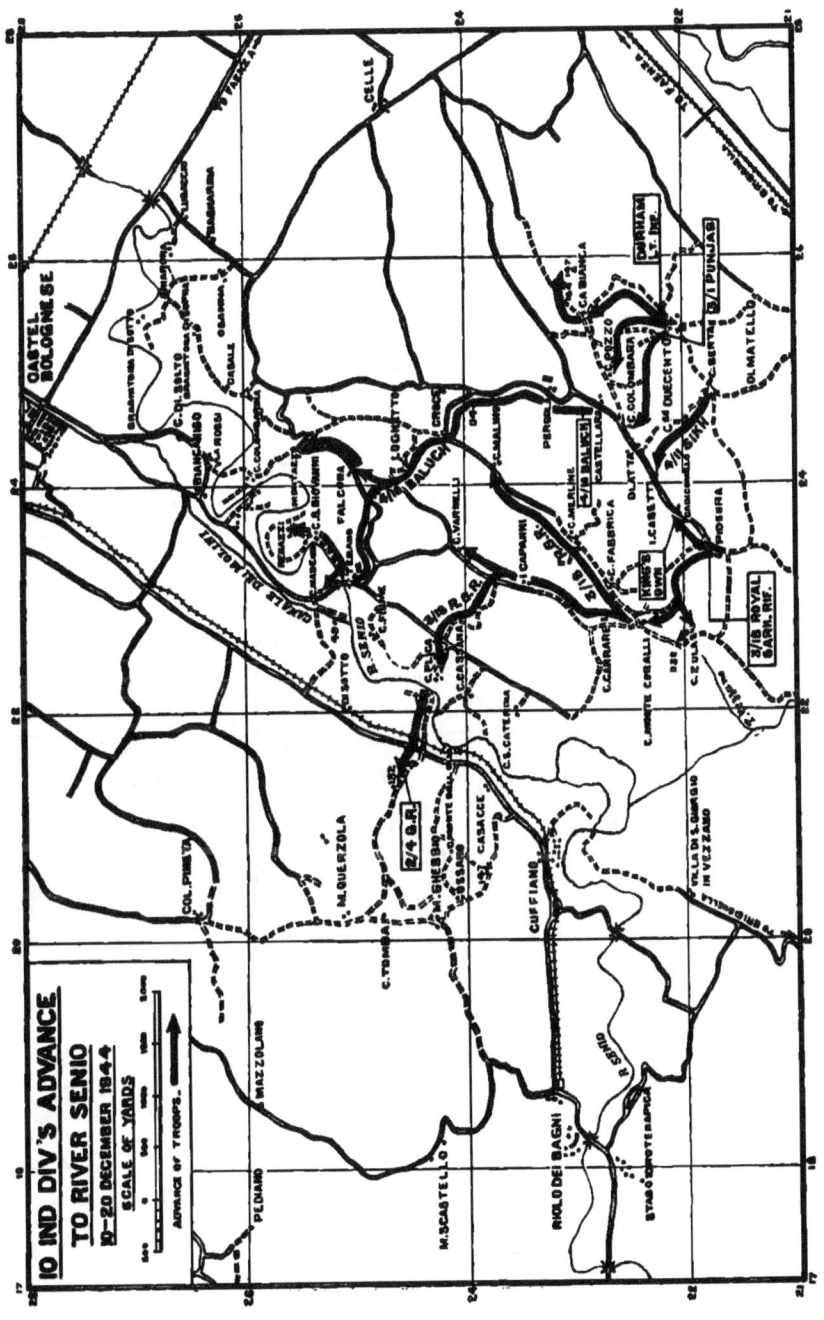

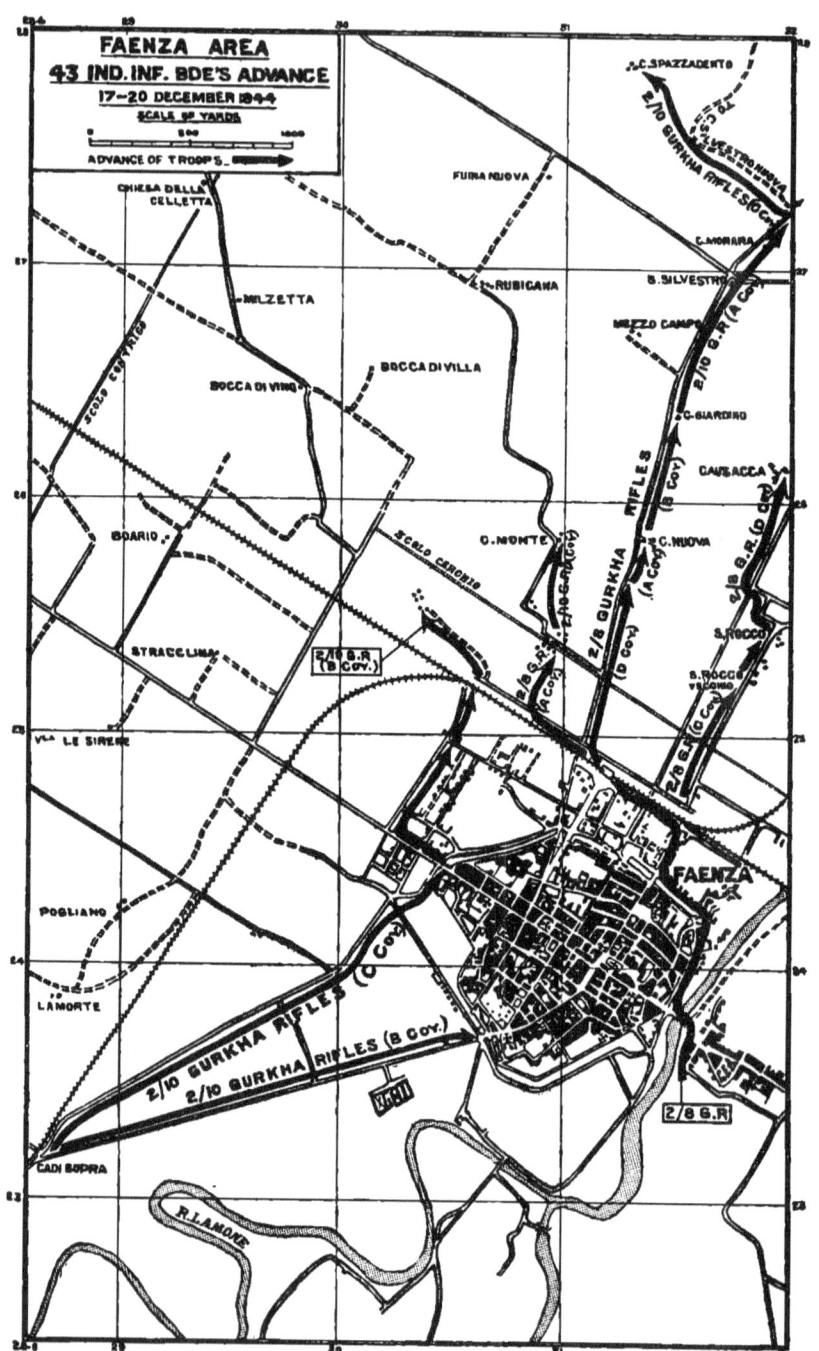

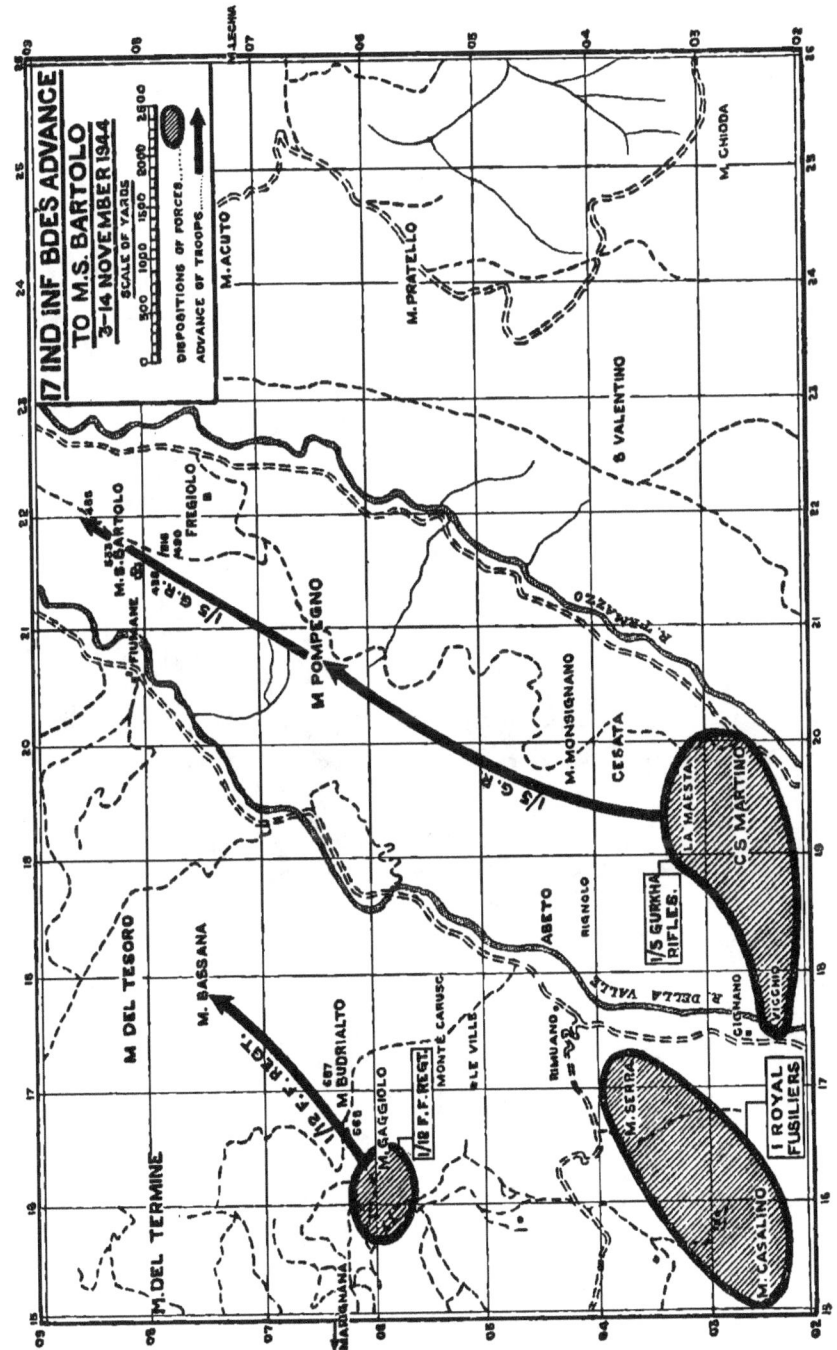

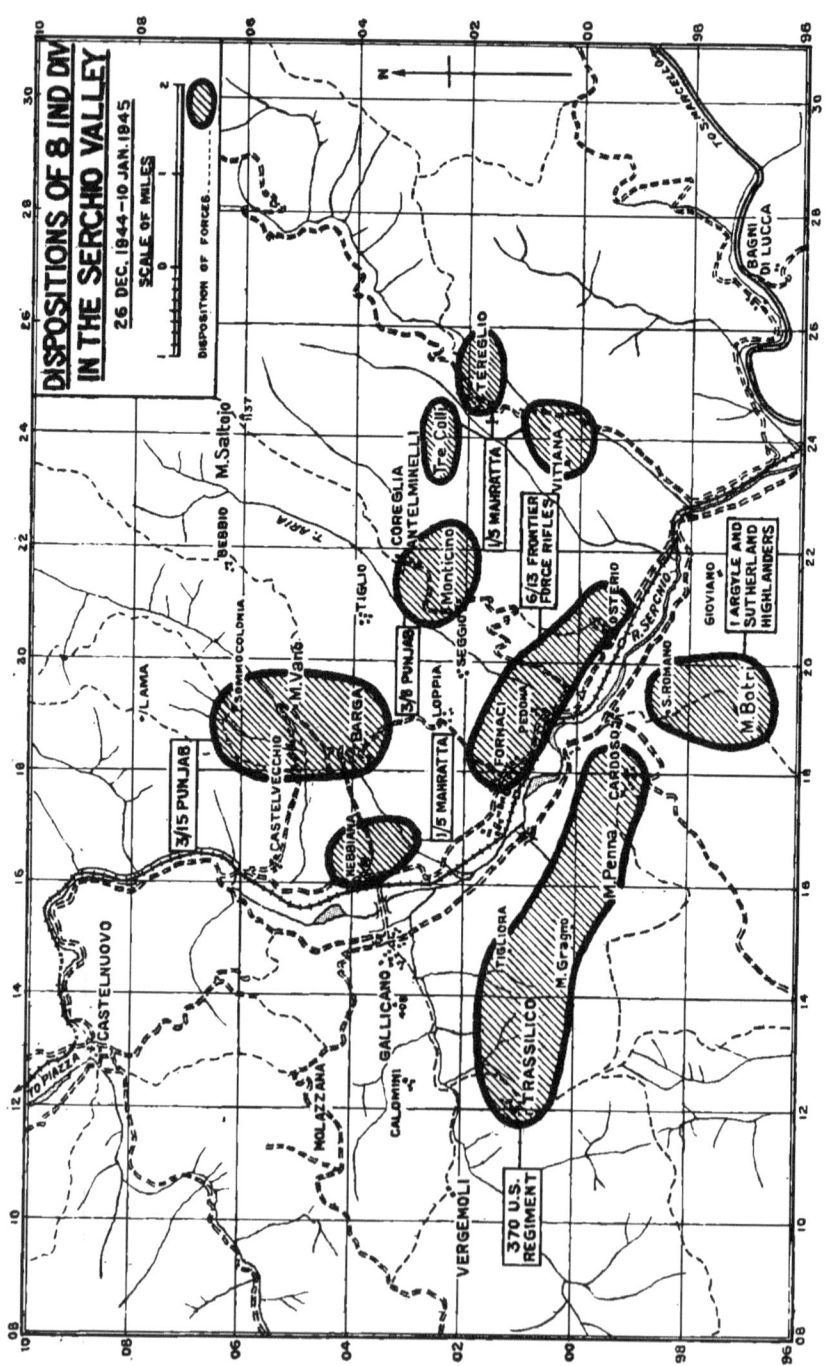

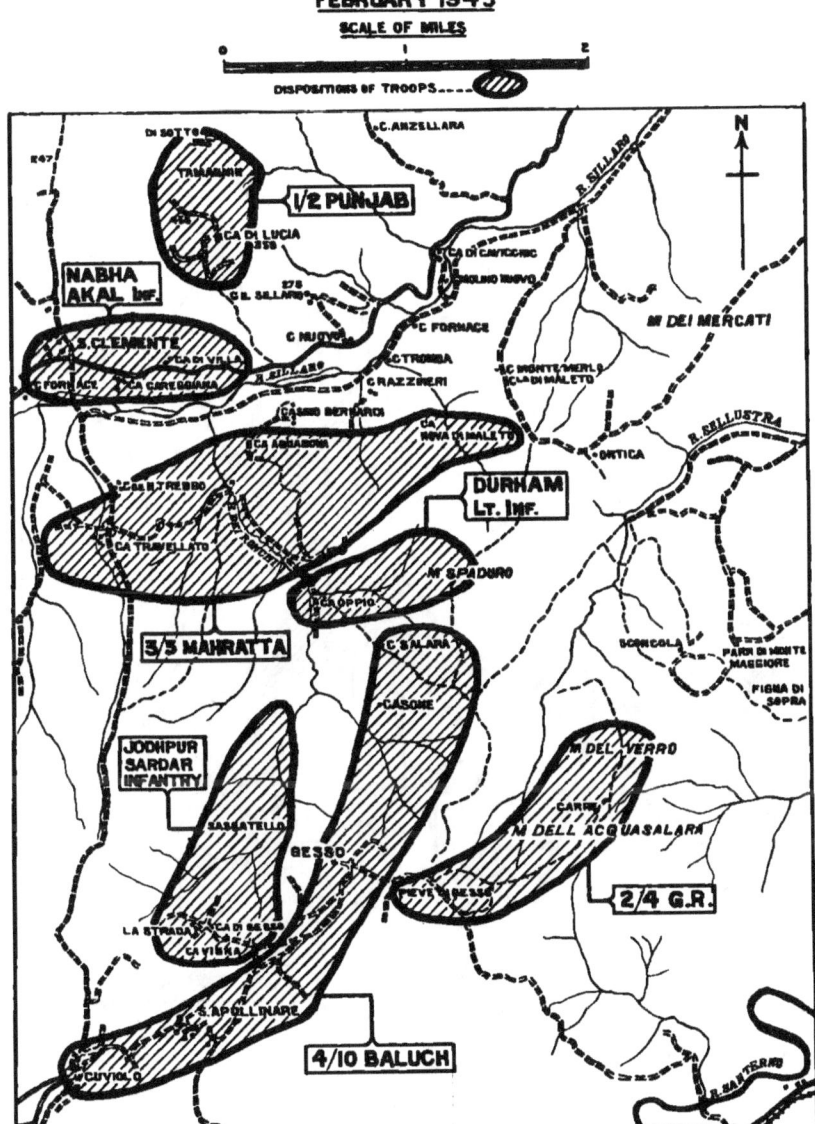

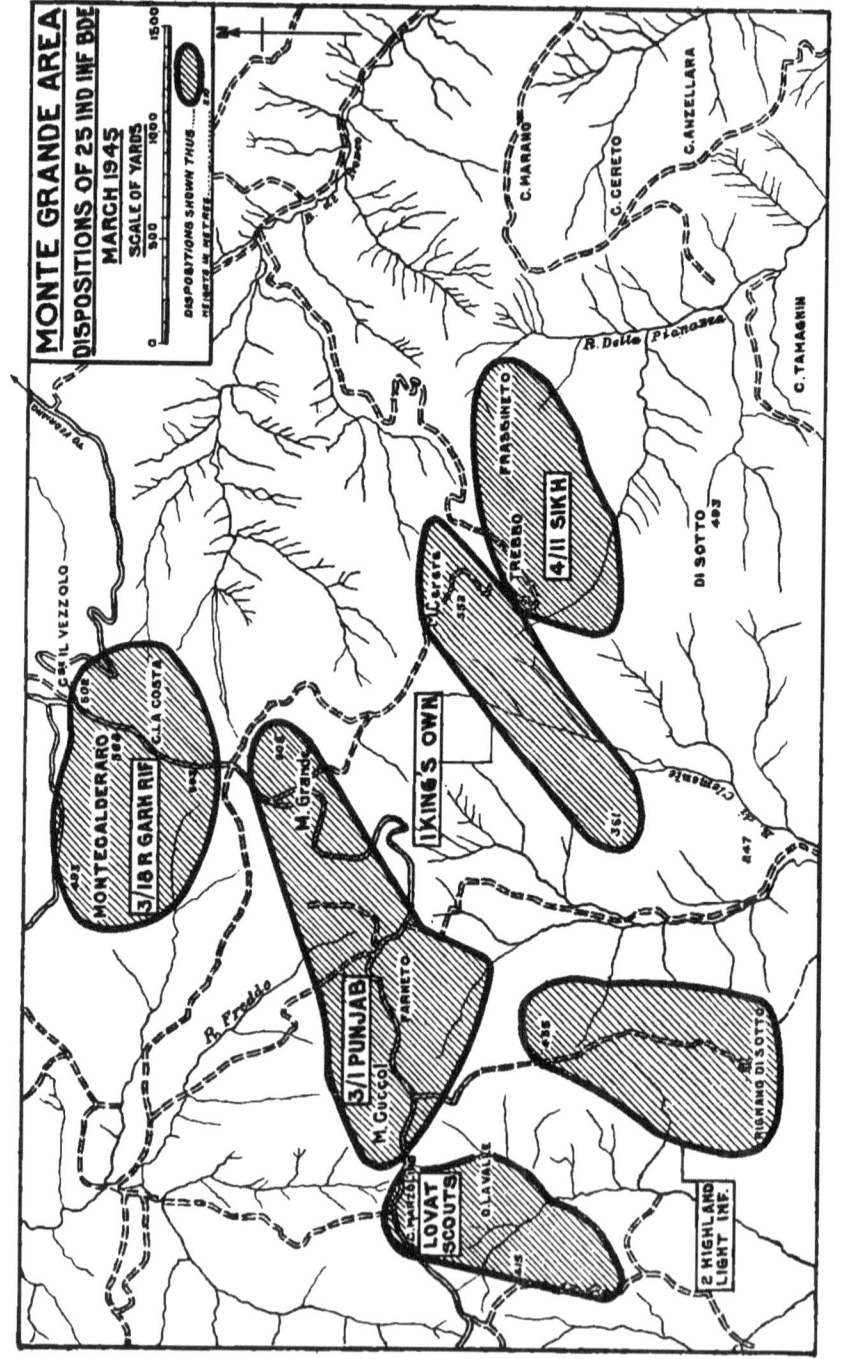

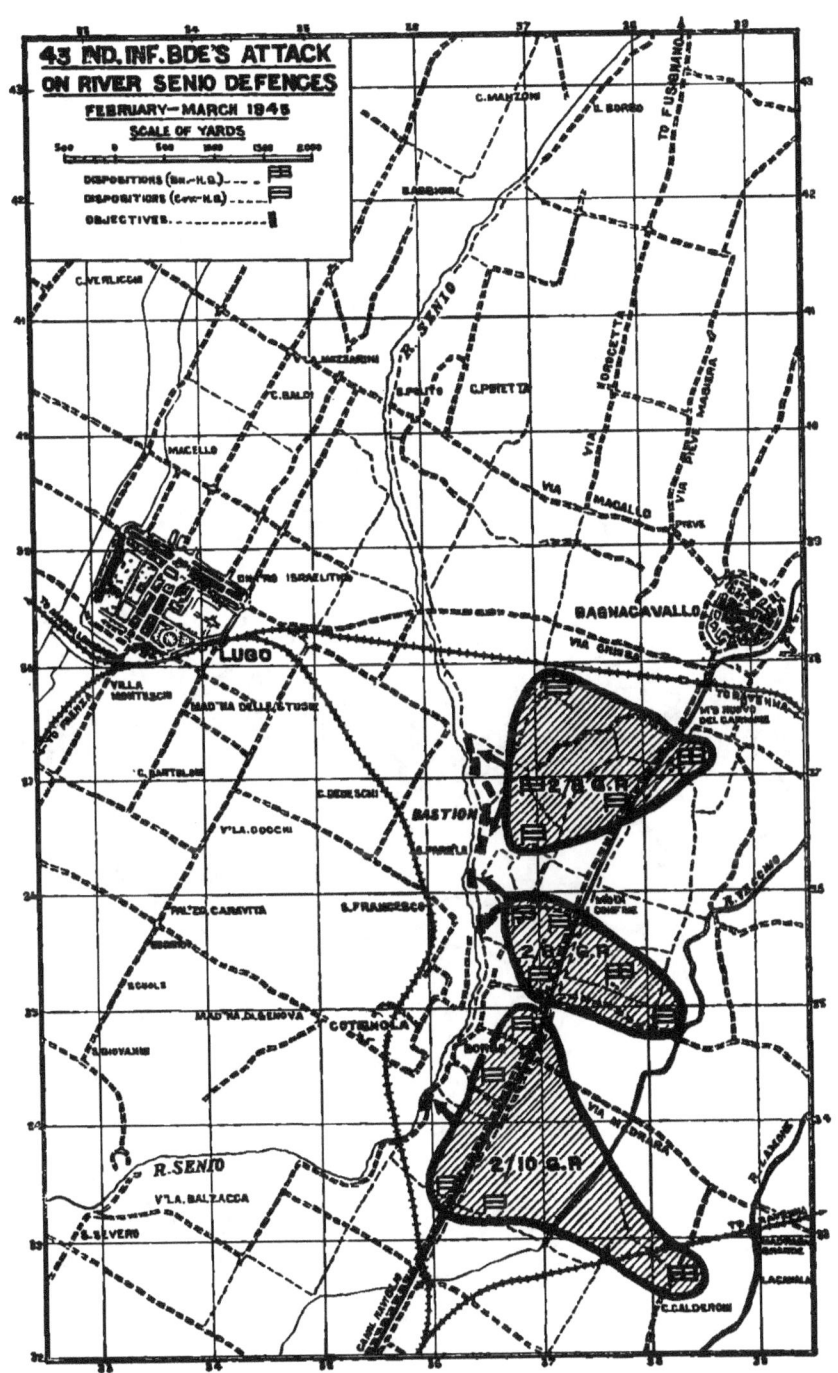

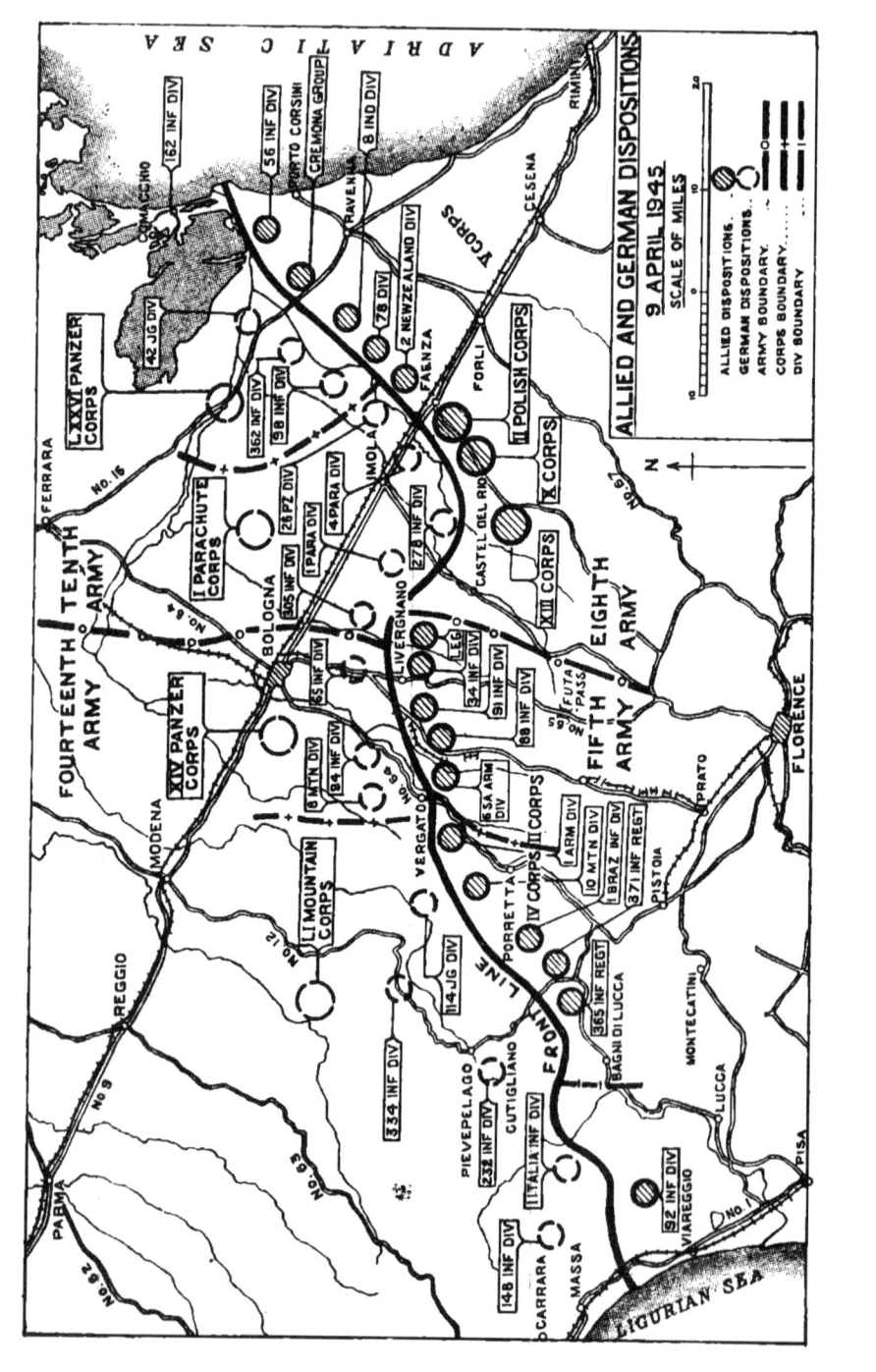

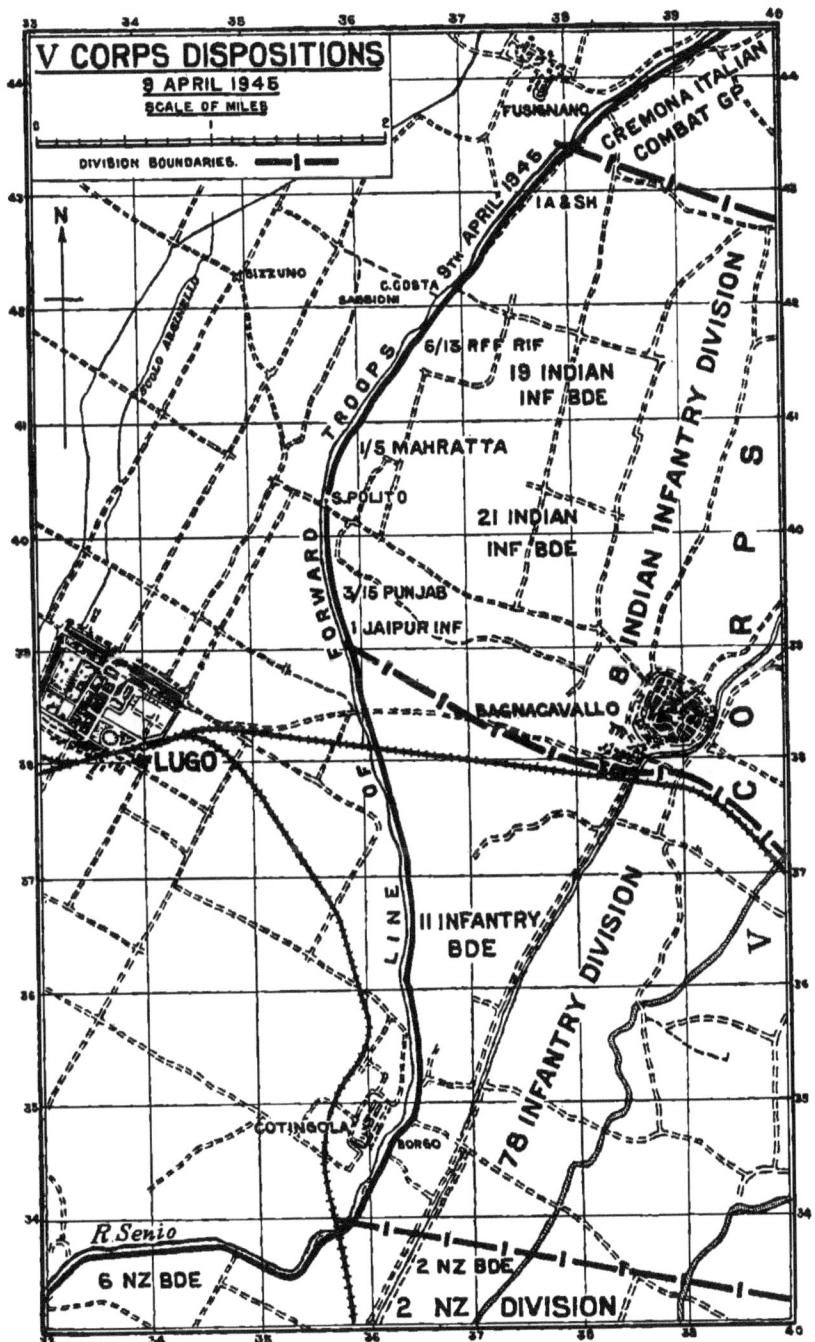

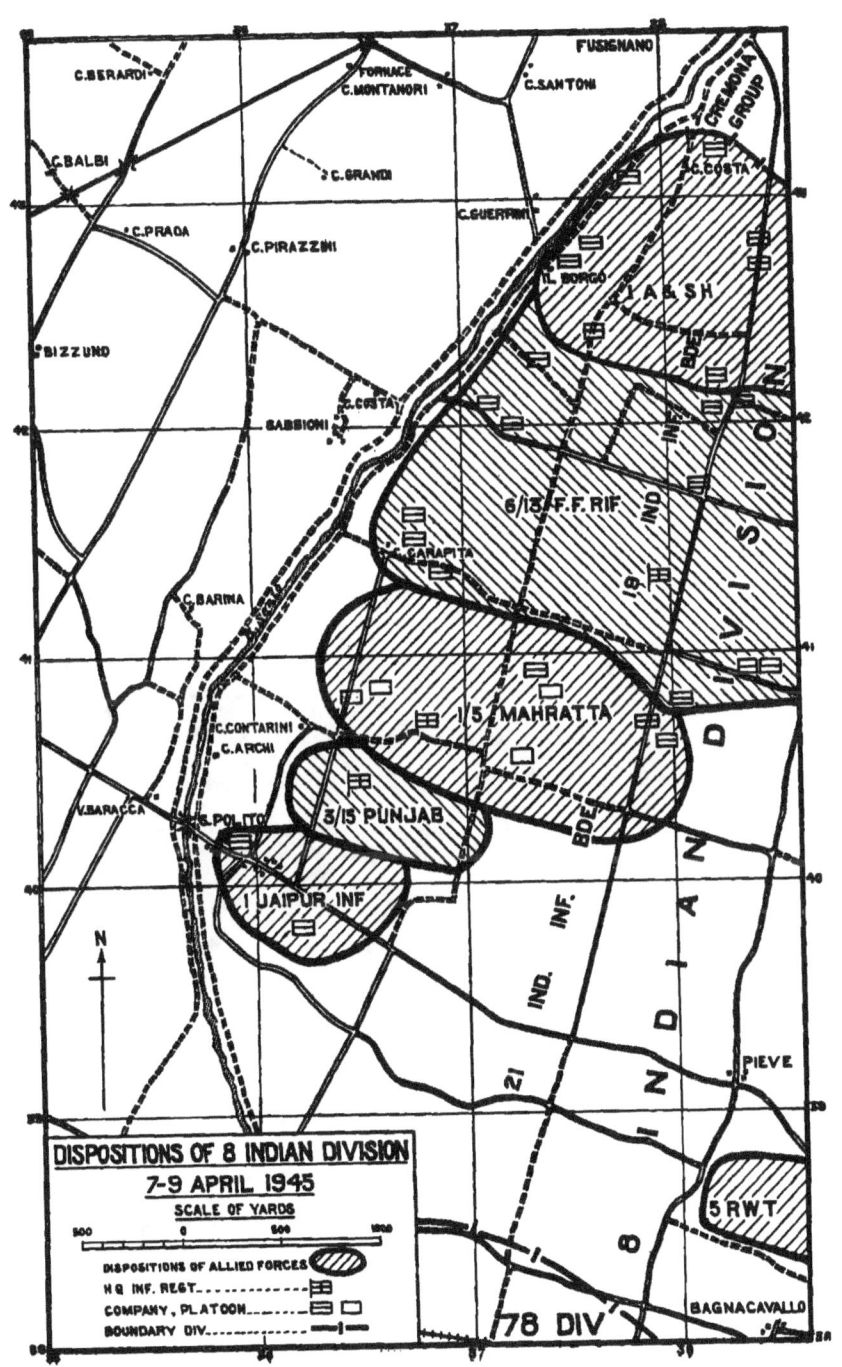

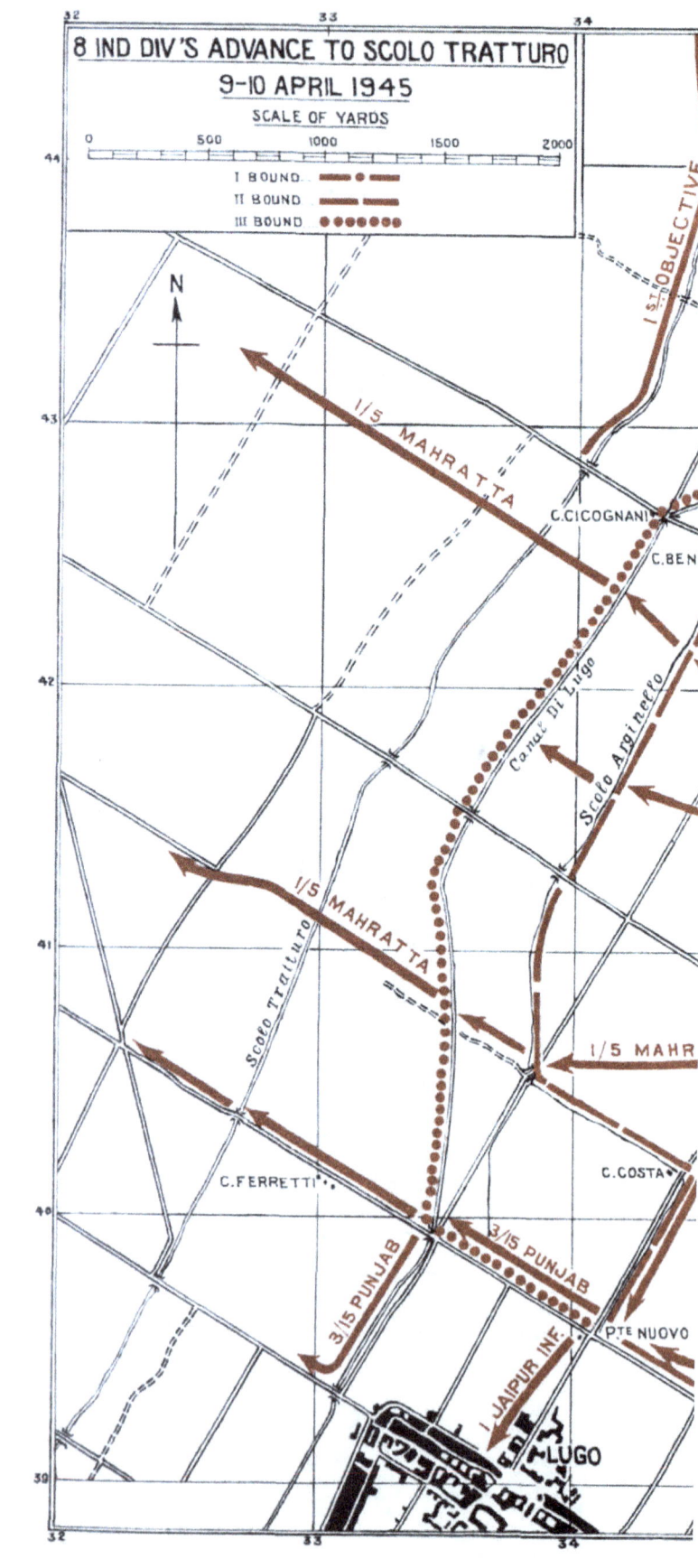

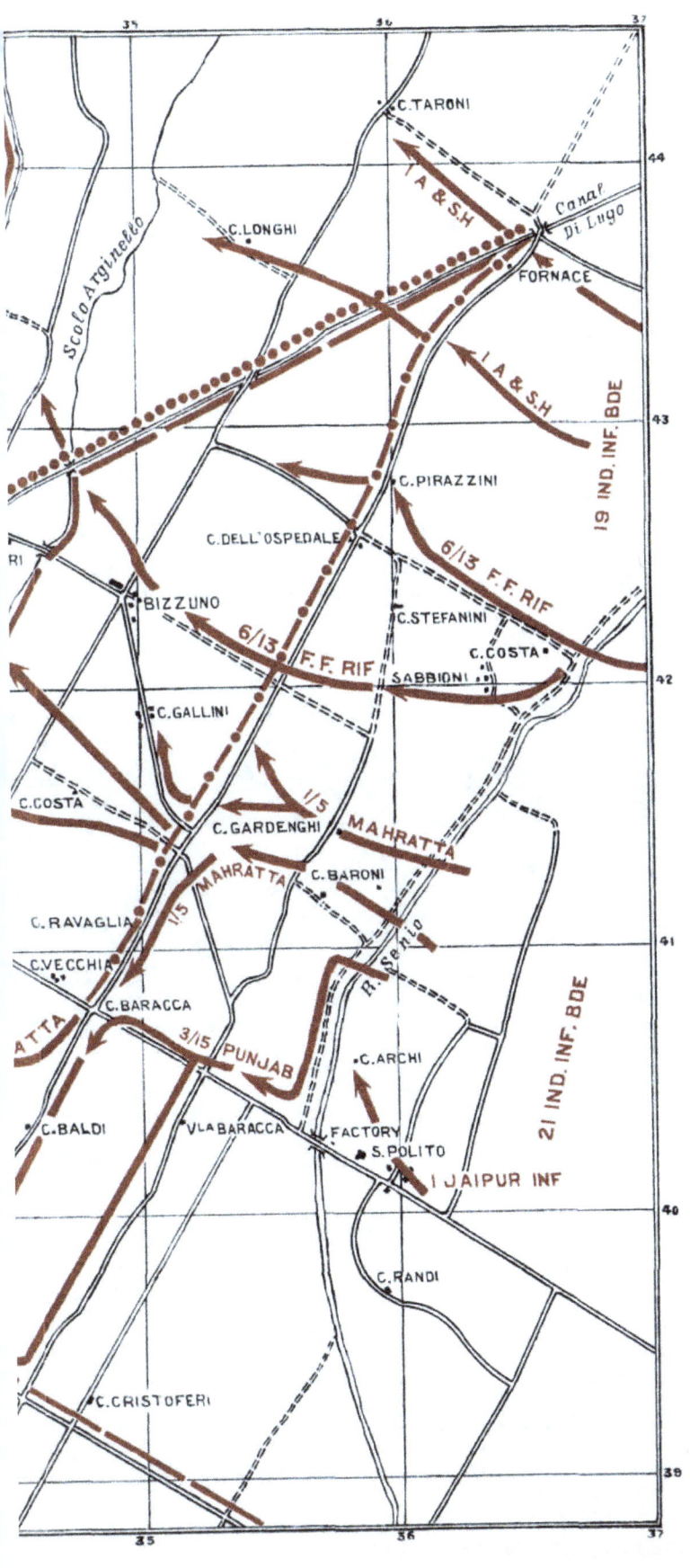

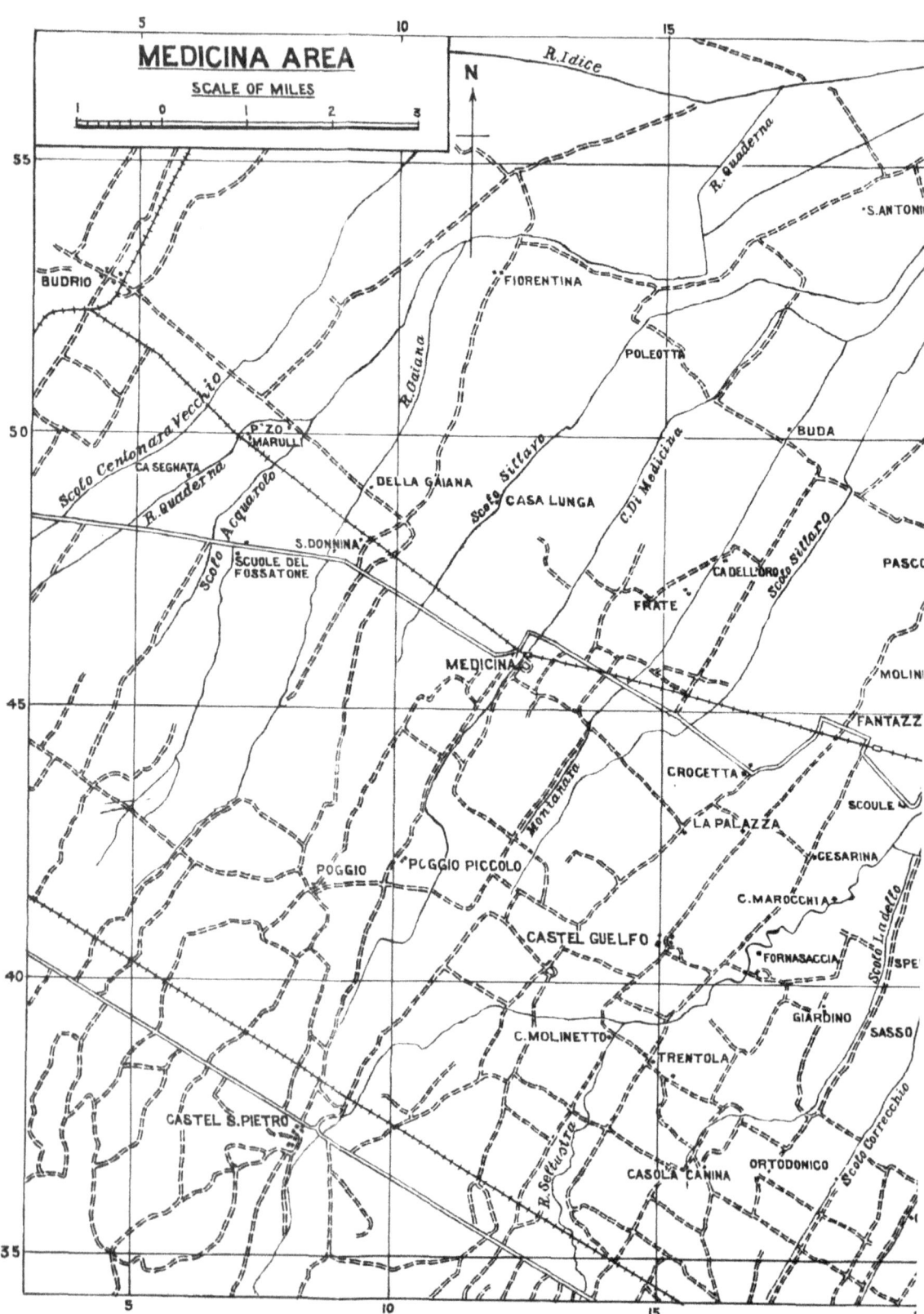

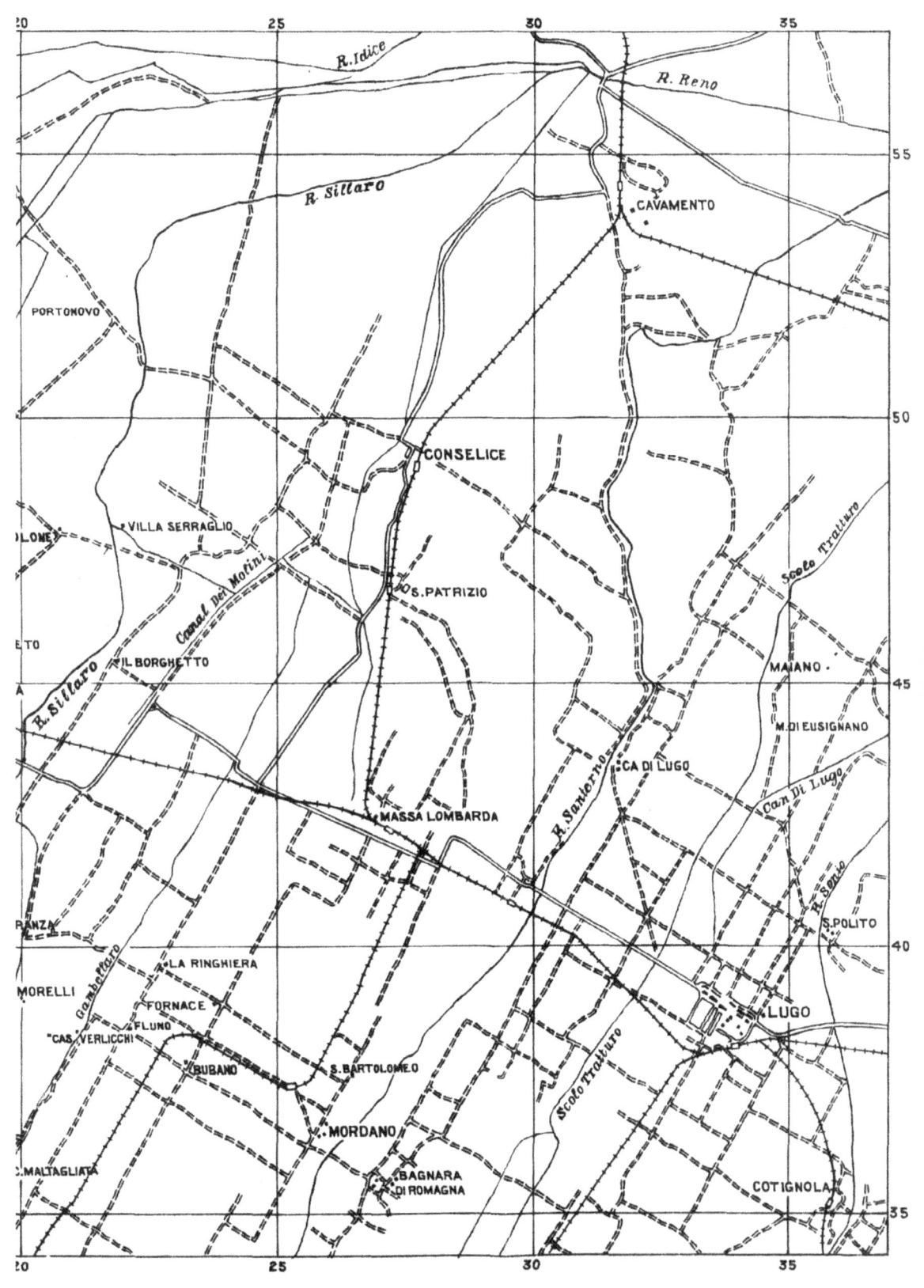

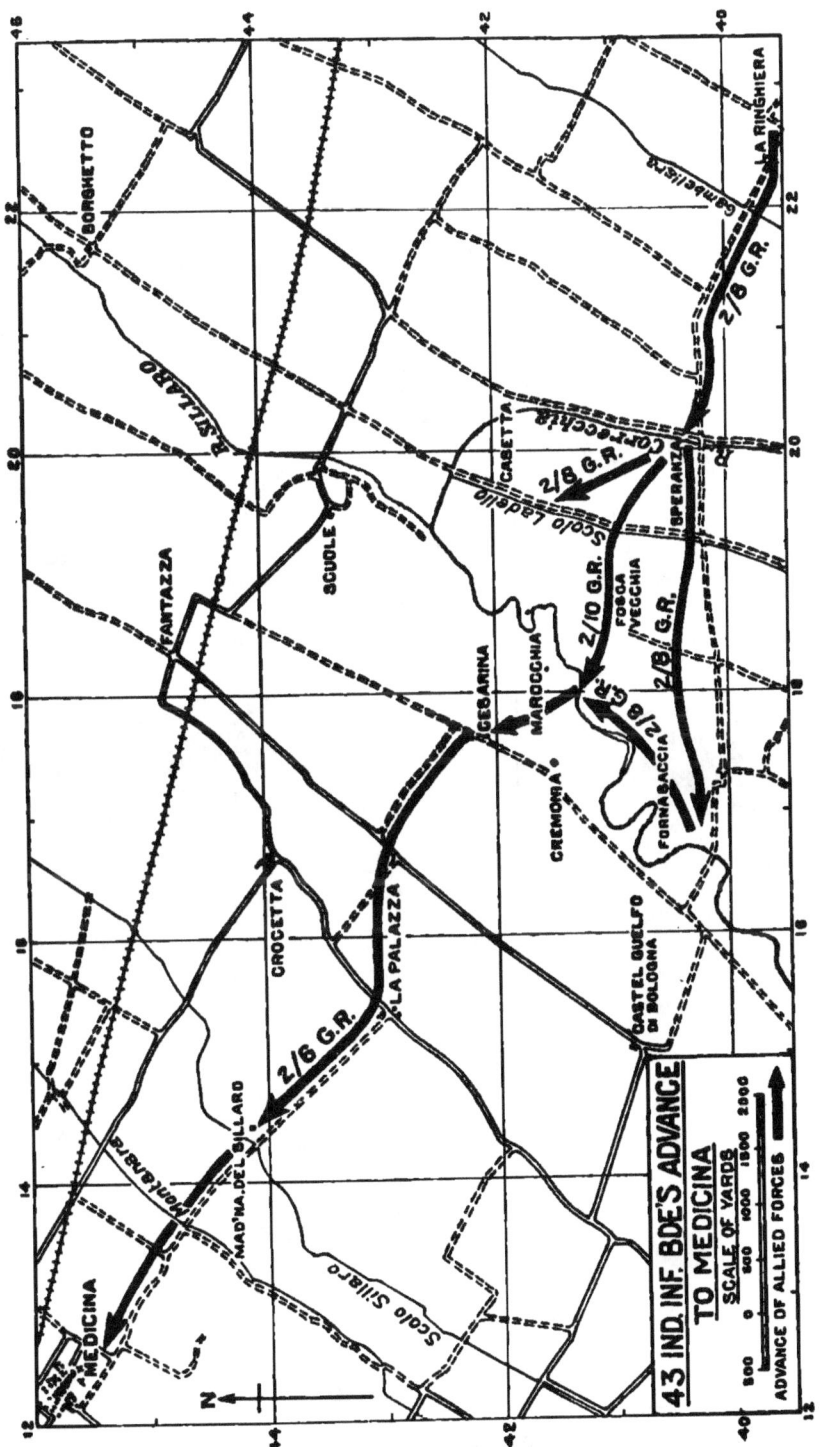

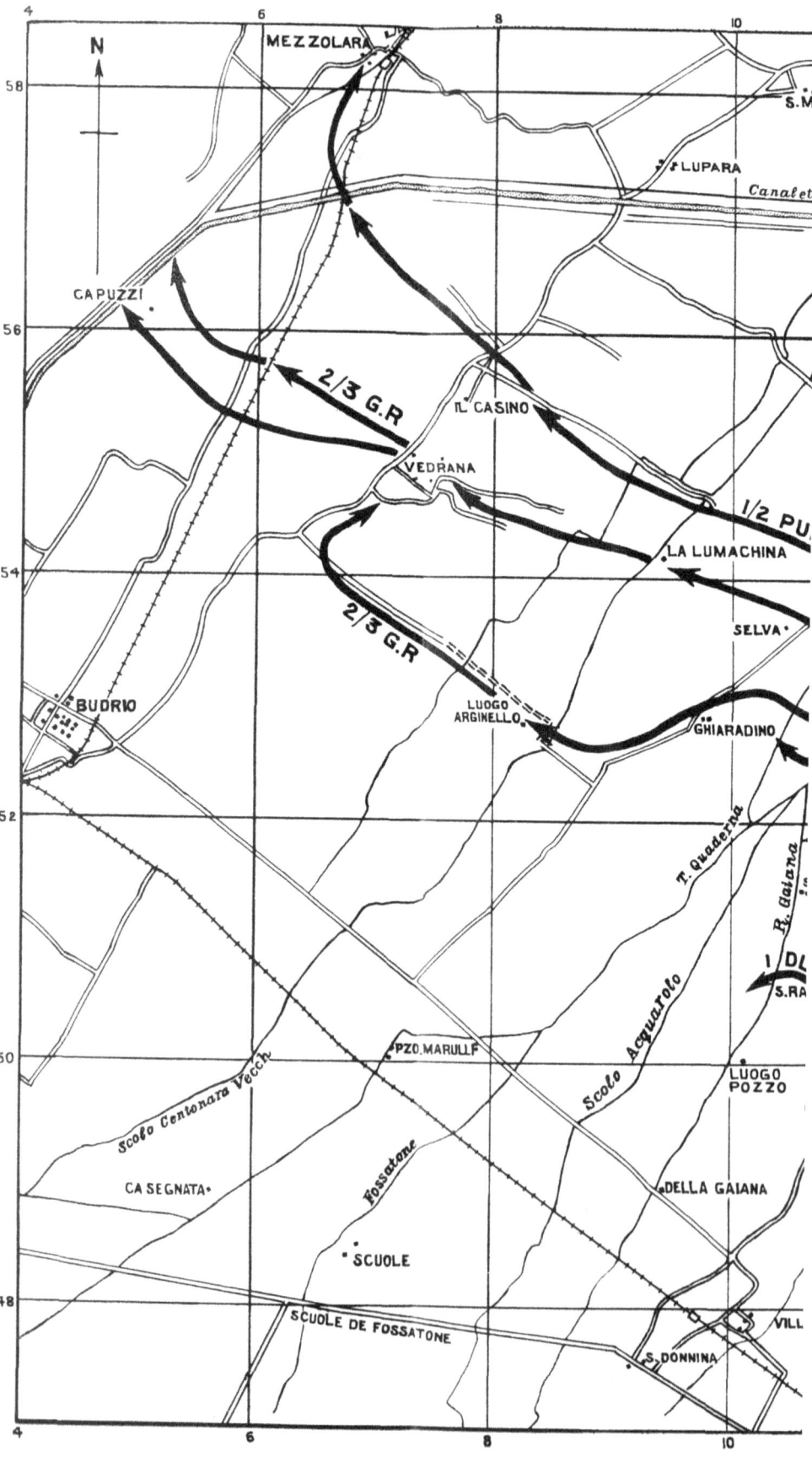

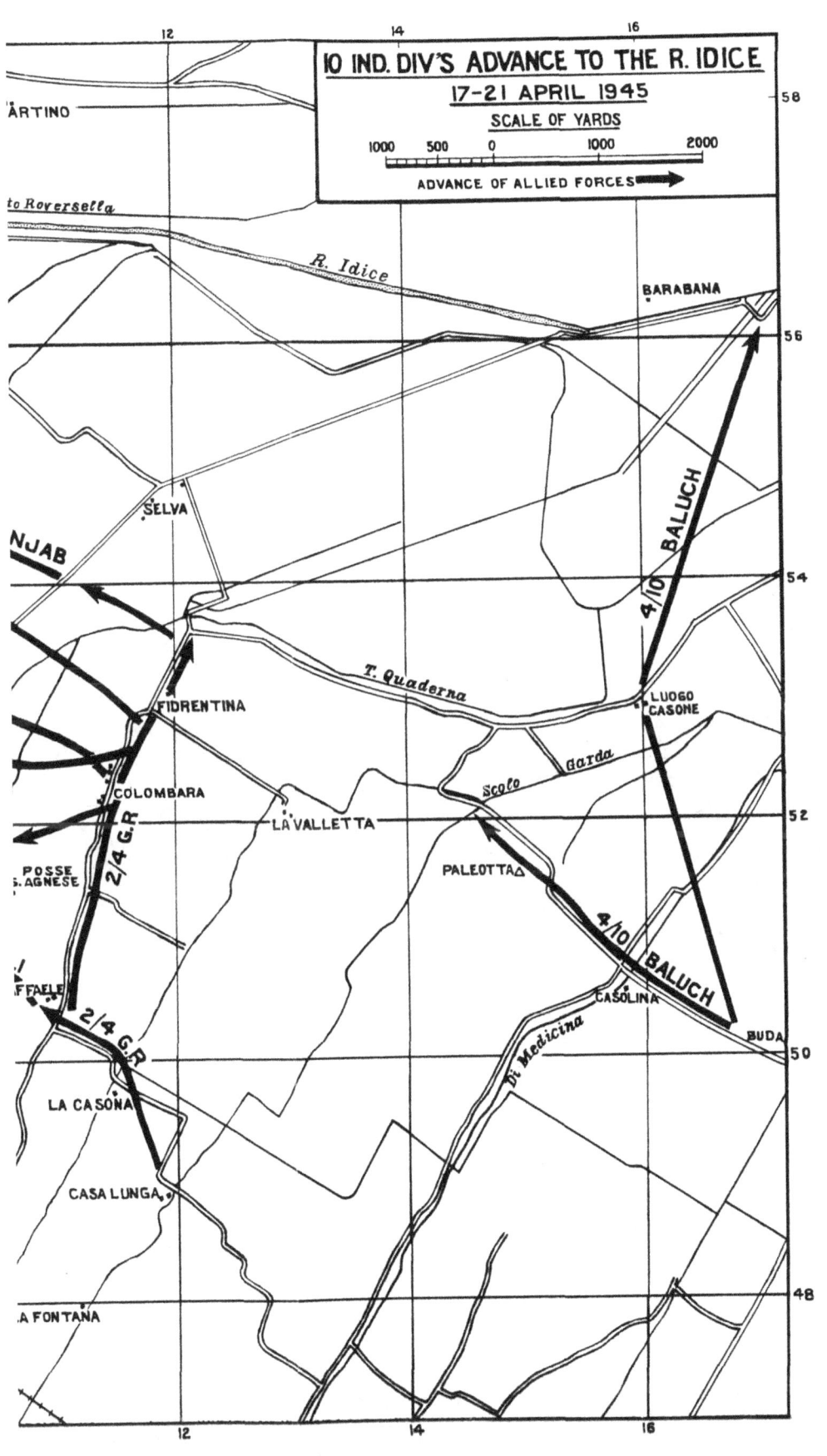

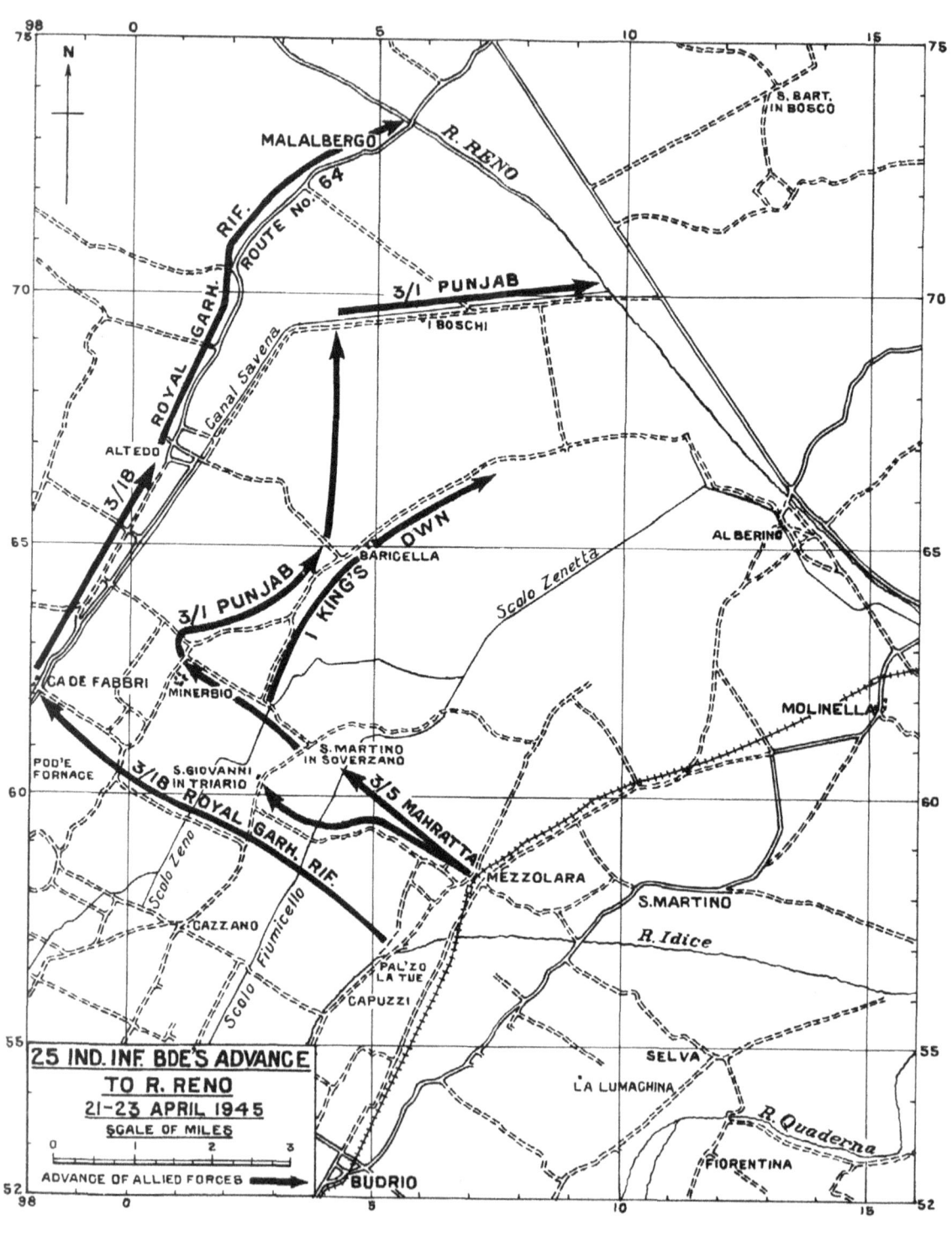

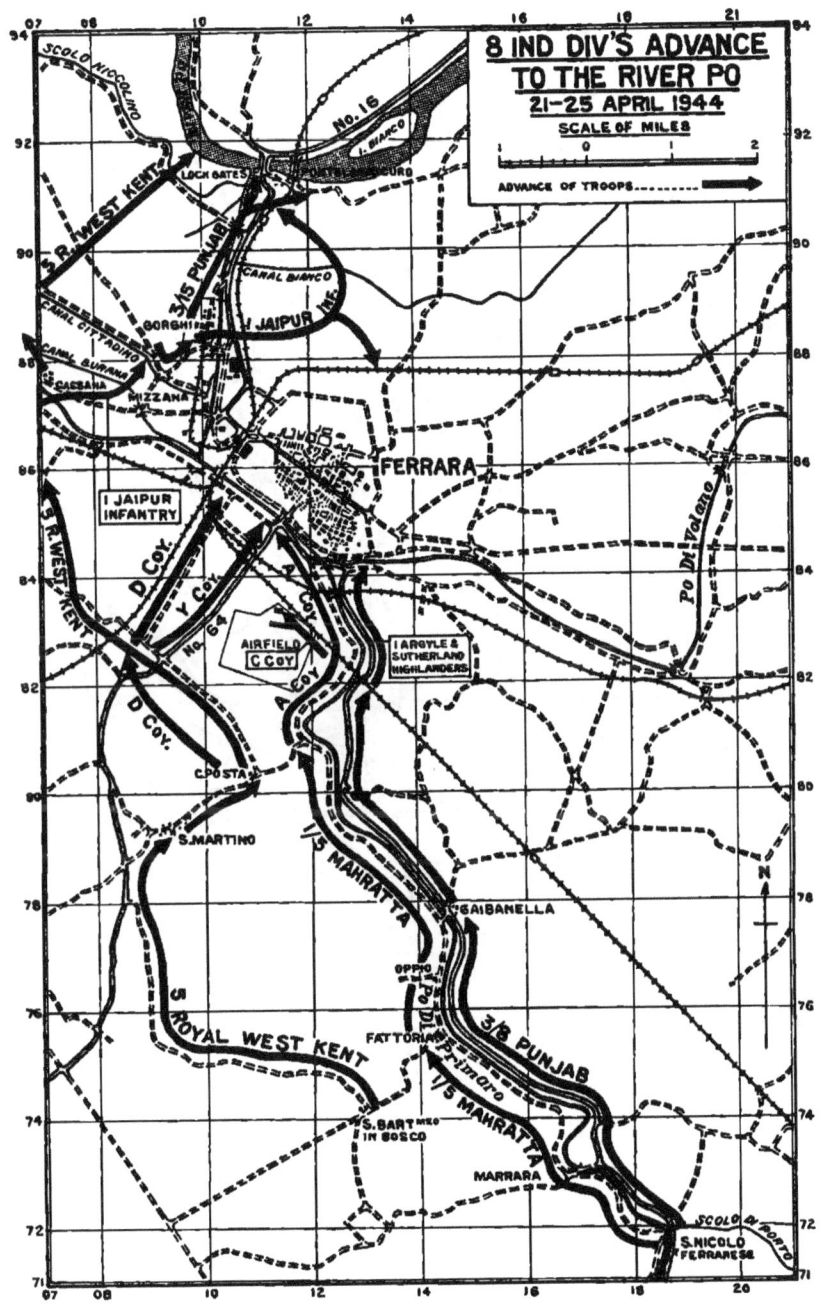

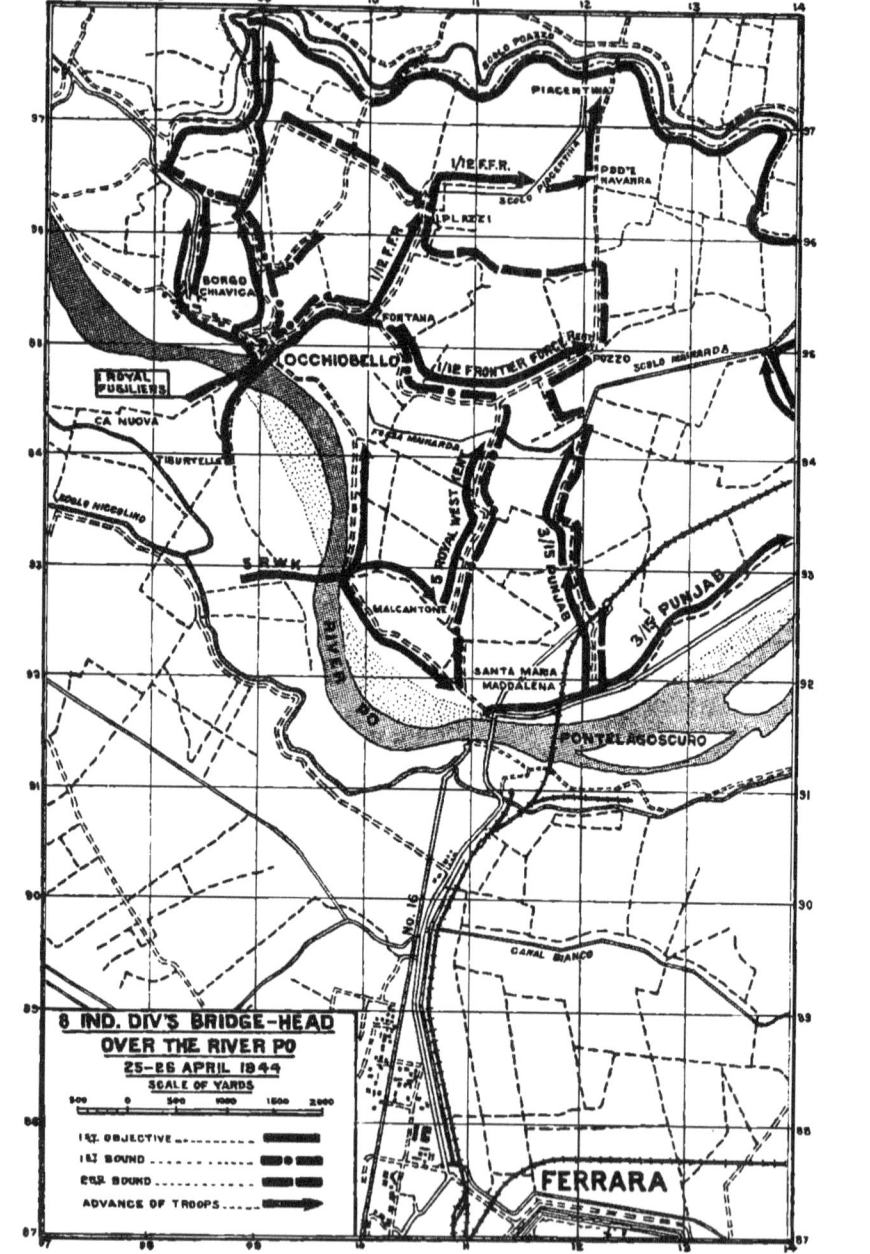

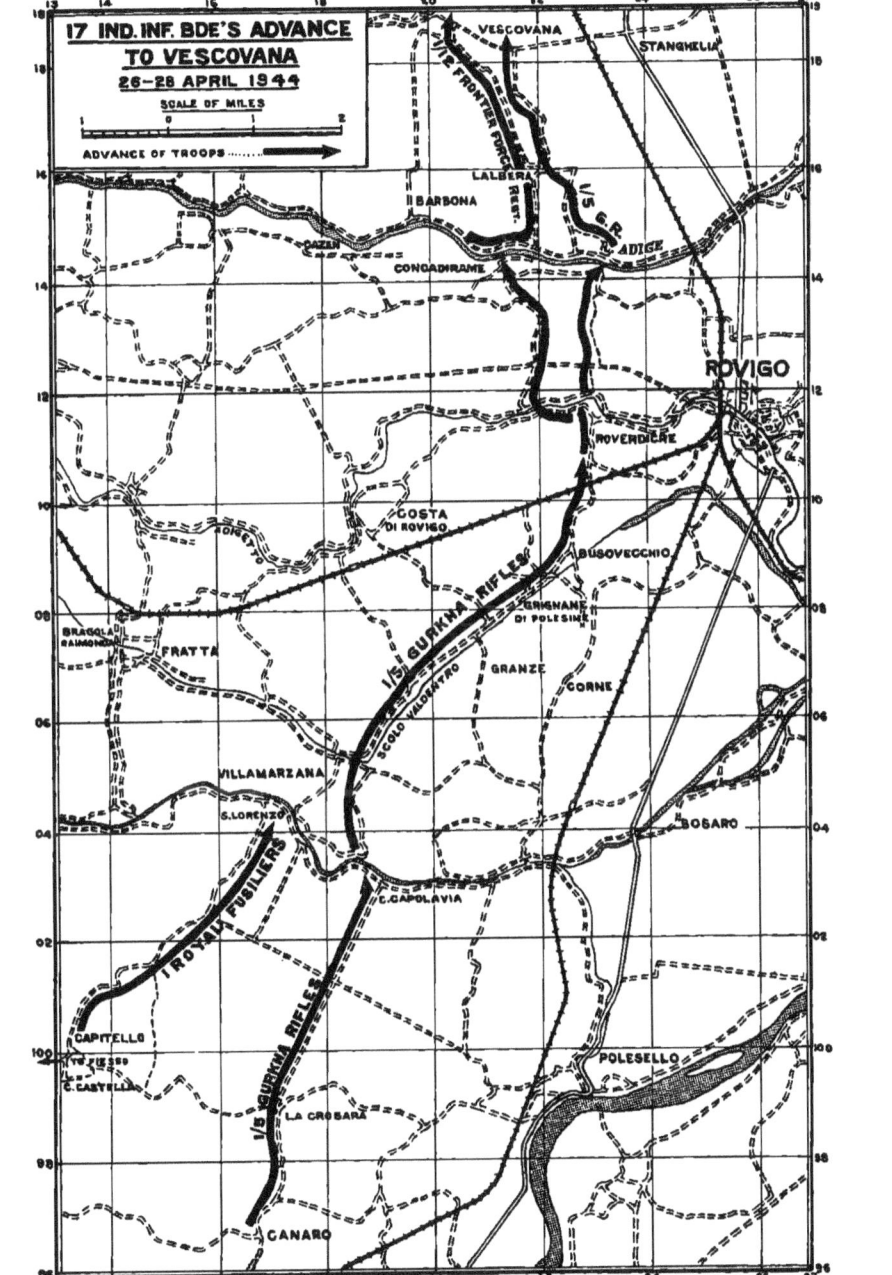

OFFICIAL HISTORY OF THE INDIAN ARMED FORCES
IN THE SECOND WORLD WAR
1939-45

Campaigns in the Western Theatre

THE NORTH AFRICAN CAMPAIGN
1940-43

Maps and Sketches

The North African Campaign 1940–43
List of Maps

1. Example of a desert formation for an Infantry Brigade
2. Example of a desert formation for an Infantry Battalion
3. Mena-Garawla-Naghamish Area. Move of the 4th Indian Division, 19-21 August 1940
4. Movement of the 4th Indian Division from Mena to Naghamish, 19-21 August 1940
5. Egypt-Libya. The Egyptian frontier showing the Italian wire fence
6. Italian positions, August 1940
7. Sidi Barrani
8. Dumping Area, 10 November 1940
9. The Bardia Perimeter, August/September 1940, showing Italian fortifications
10. Allied attack on Bardia, 3-5 January 1941
11. Giarabub, Siwa and Kufra Oases
12. Area of Allied retreat, 31 March to 8 April 1941 (Benghazi-Tobruk)
13. 3rd Indian Motor Brigade's action at Mekili on 8 April 1941
14. Mekili Area, showing junction of desert tracks
15. Egypt and Cyrenaica (Tobruk area) showing coastal and desert communications
16. Jebel Akhdar
17. Axis offensive, January 1942, converging moves on Benghazi
18. Egypt and Cyrenaica (ZT Msus area) showing desert communications
19. Egypt and Cyrenaica (Antelat area) showing desert communications
20. Africa (Benghazi-Augila Area)
21. Egypt and Cyrenaica (Gazala area) showing coastal and desert communications
22. Southern end of the Gazala Line, 26-27 May 1942
23. 18th Indian Infantry Brigade at Deir el Shein

24	Benghazi-Tobruk Area
25	Misuraca Area
26	Tripoli Area
27	Gabes Area
28	Tunis Area
29	Operational Area (Alam Halfa)
30	The Mediterranean with Europe, Middle East and North Africa
31	The alternative route to Egypt via the Persian Gulf and Palestine
32	Battle of Sidi Barrani, 9-11 December 1940
33	Attack on Tobruk, 19-21 January 1941
34	Withdrawal of 4 Ind. Div. through the 10 Defensive Lines, January 1942
35	Tobruk: Axis Assault, 20-21 June 1942 (Sketch 1)
36	Tobruk: Axis Assault, 20-21 June 1942 (Sketch 2)
37	Tobruk: Axis Assault, 20-21 June 1942 (Sketch 3)
38	Africa (Alexandria-Tobruk Area) Communications–Coastal and Interior
39	Tobruk: Axis Assault, 20-21 June 1942 (Sketch 4)
40	Eye Sketch of 29th Ind. Inf. Bde. position at Fuka
41	5th Indian Division at Ruweisat Ridge, 18 July 1942
42	Dispositions on El Alamein front, 9 September 1942
43	North Africa (General Map)

EXAMPLE OF A DESERT FORMATION FOR INFANTRY BRIGADE

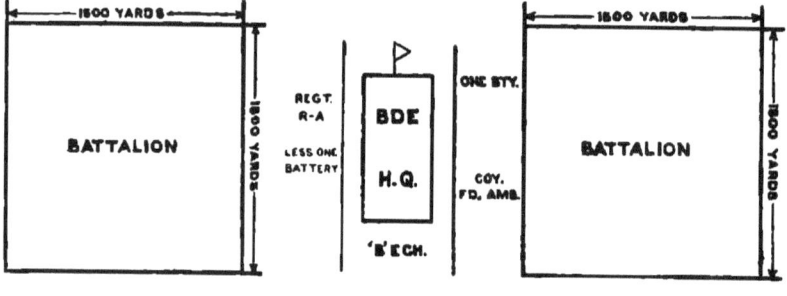

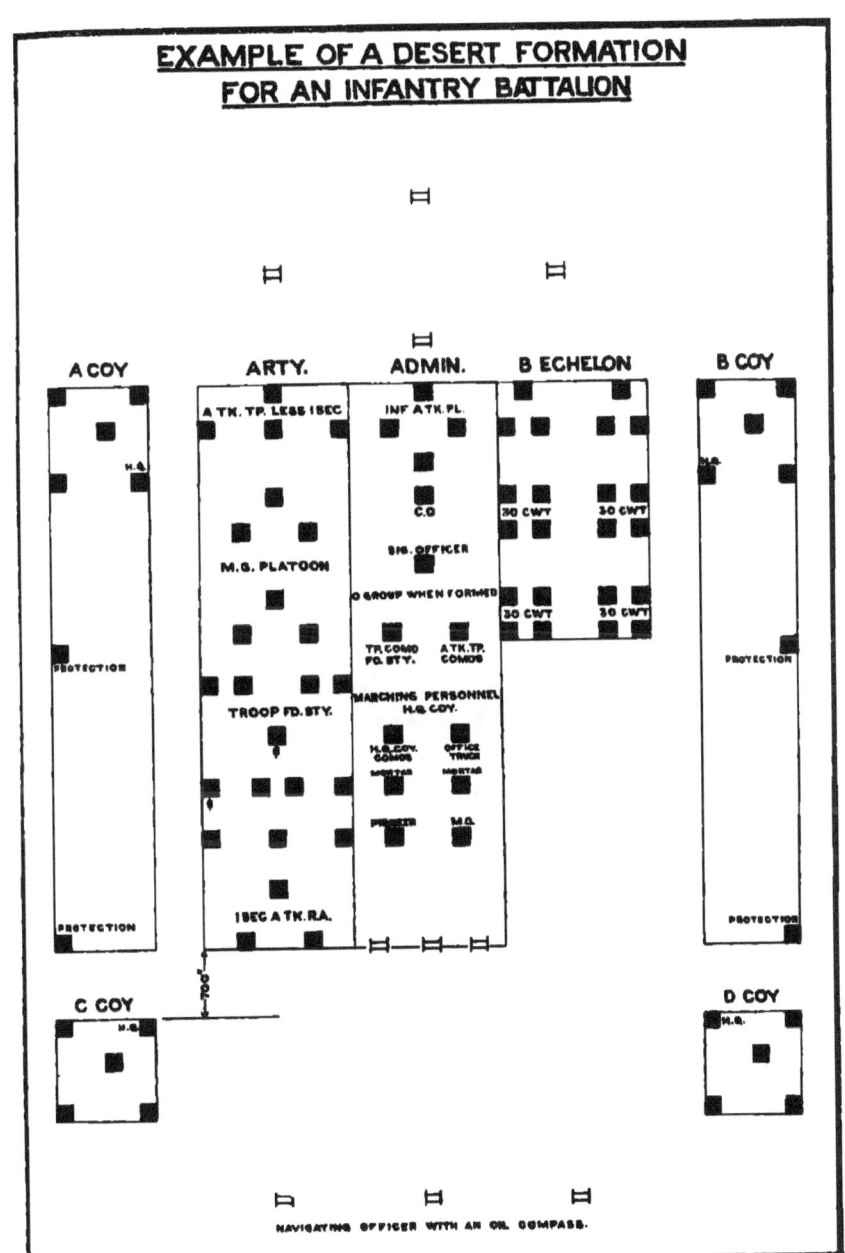

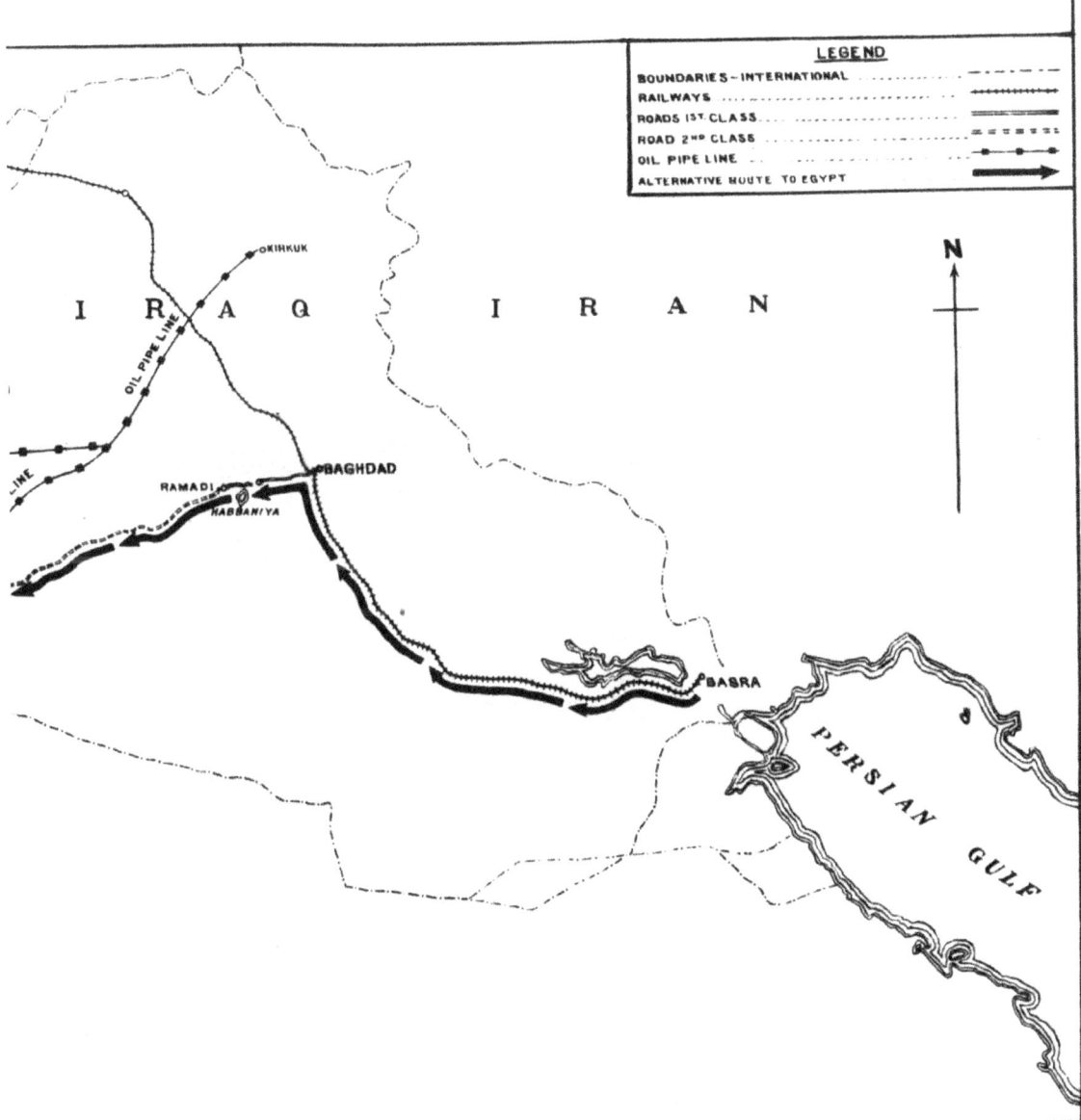

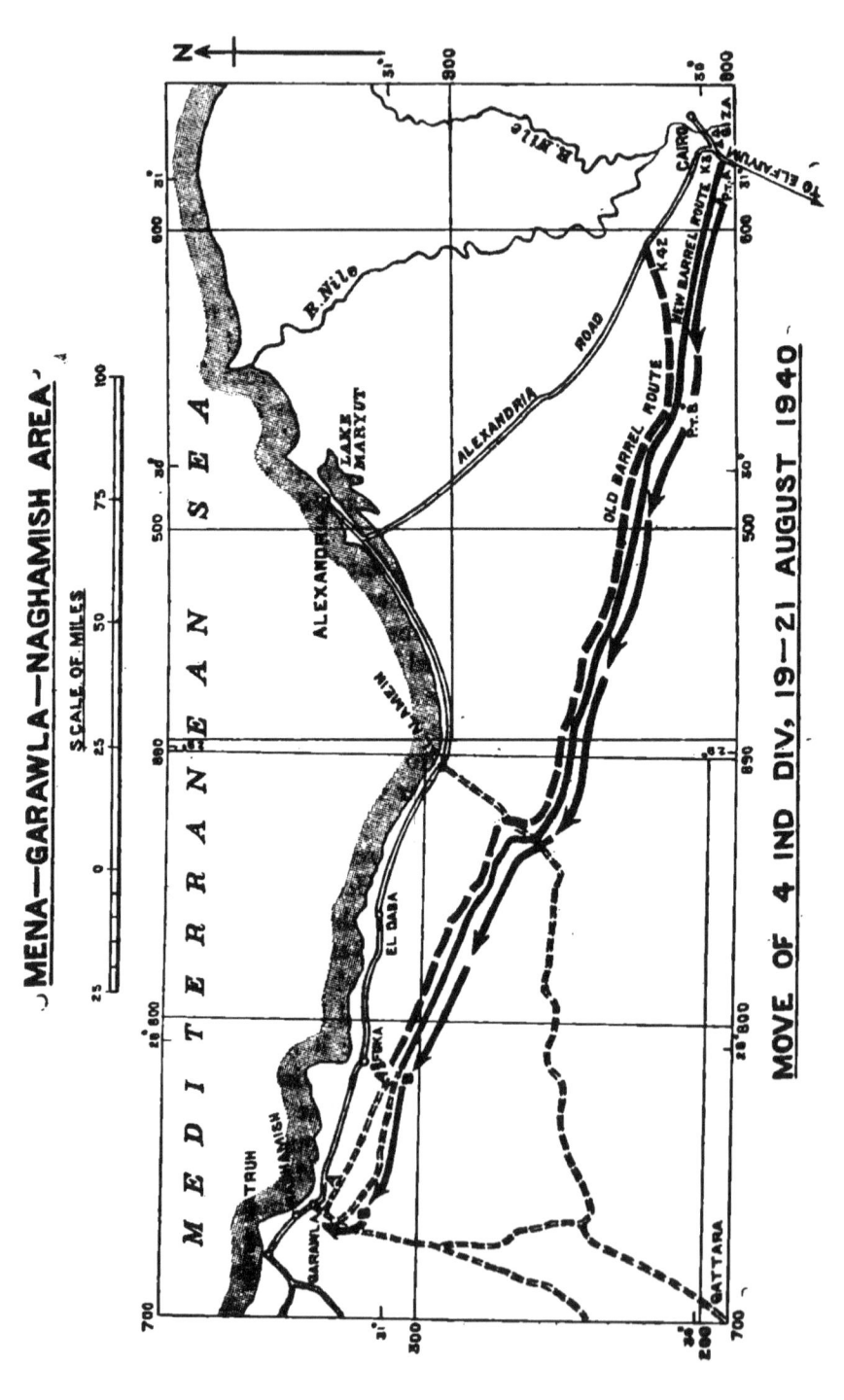

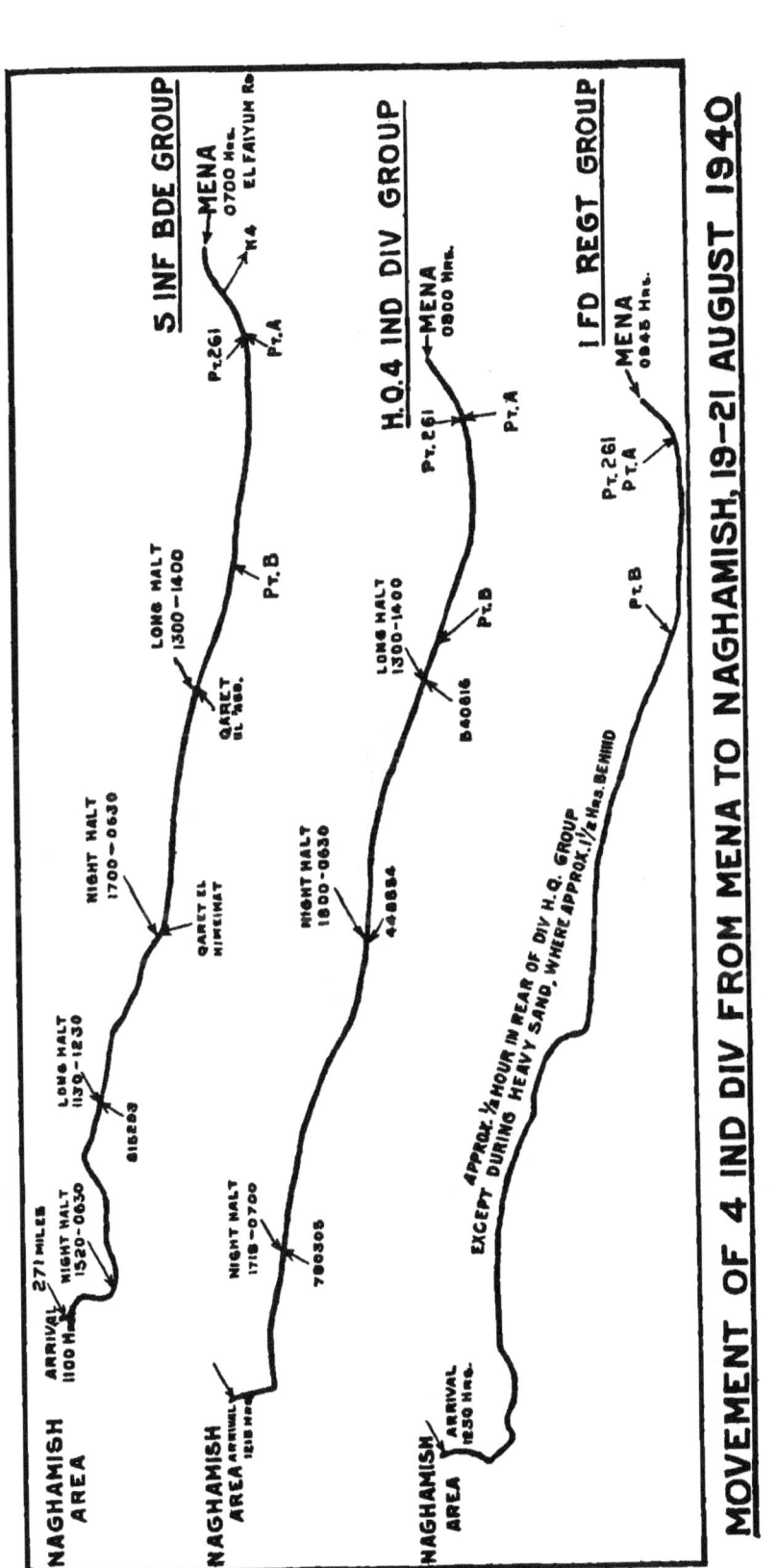

EGYPT–LIBYA

THE EGYPTIAN FRONTIER SHOWING THE ITALIAN WIRE FENCE
(FROM SOLLUM TO GIARABUB)

ITALIAN POSITIONS AUGUST 1940

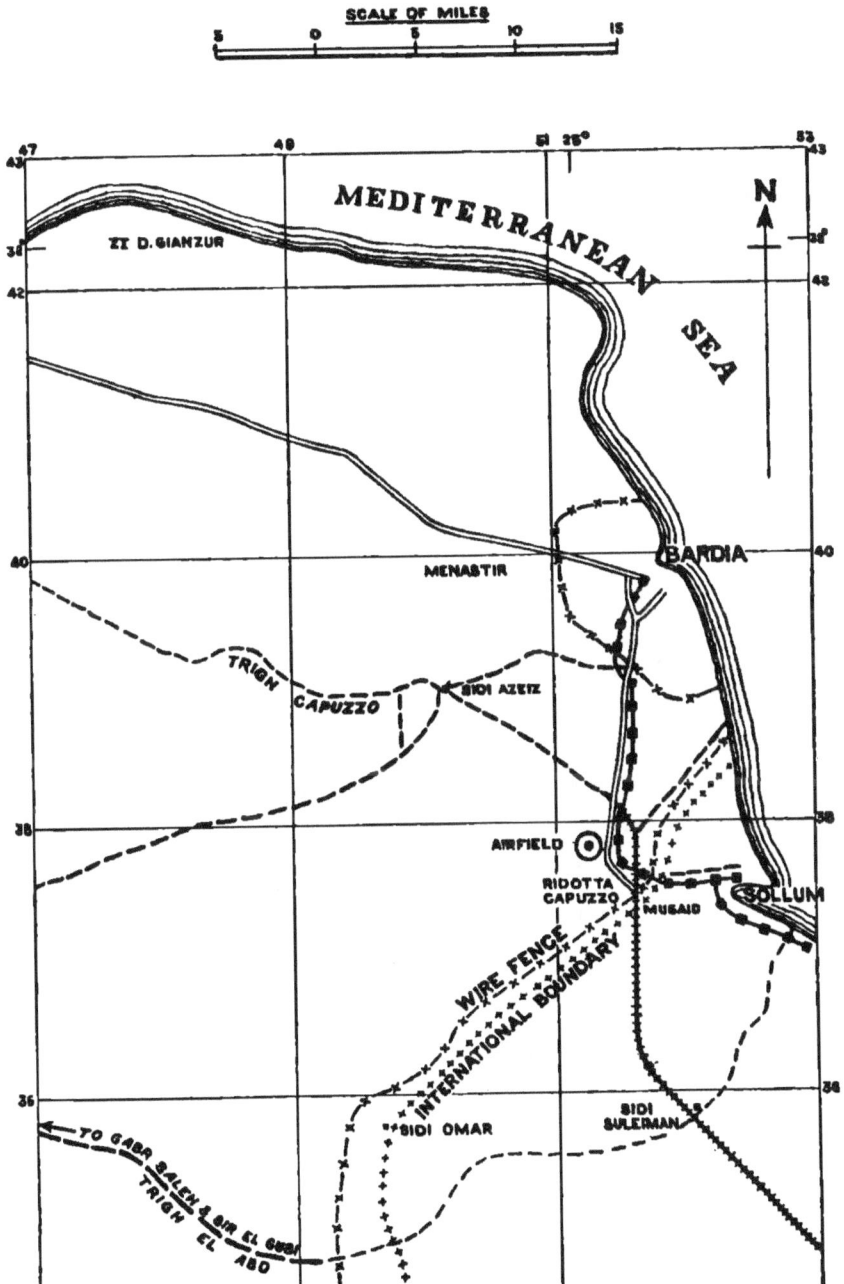

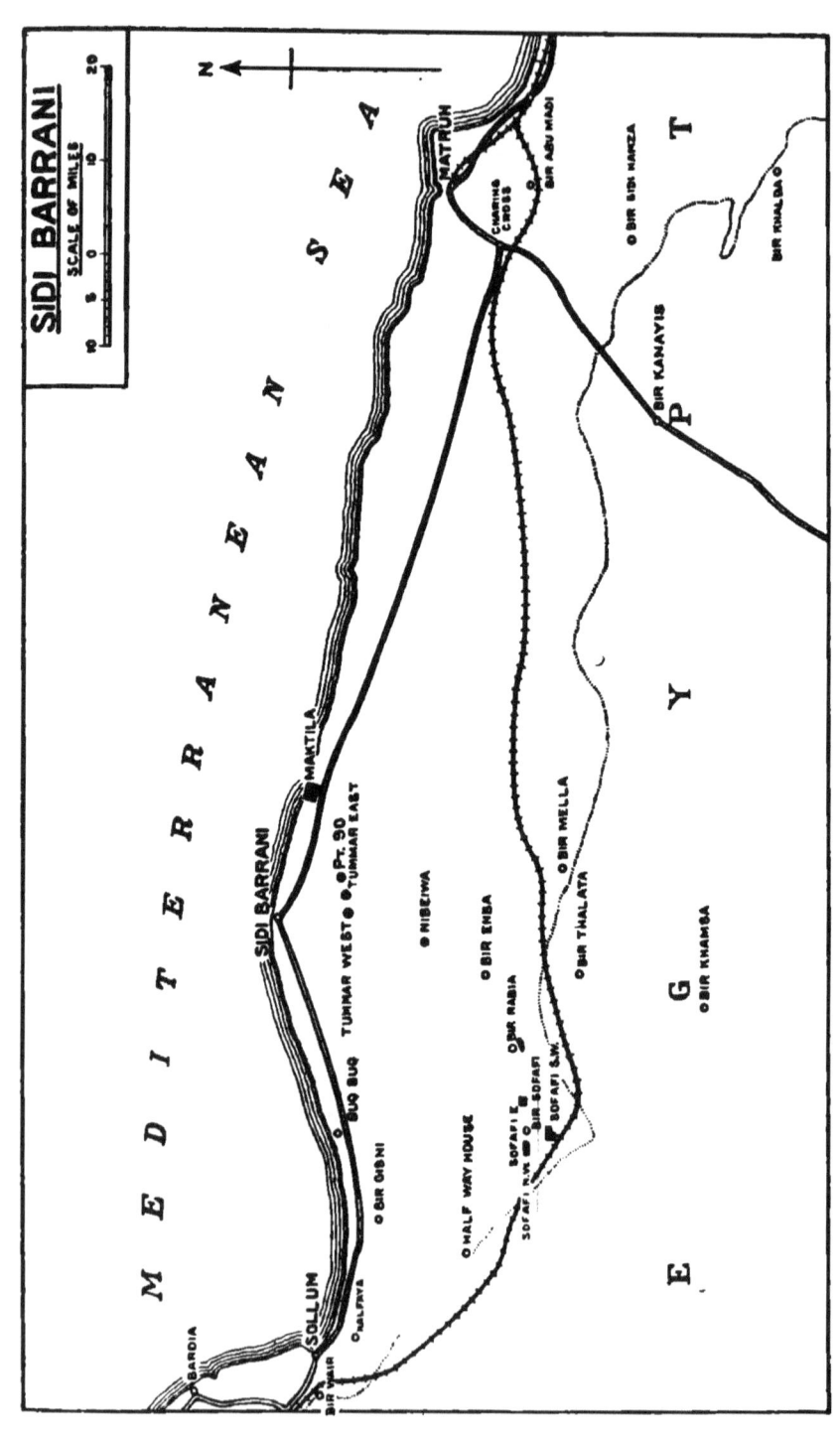

DUMPING AREA
10 NOVEMBER 1940
SCALE OF MILES

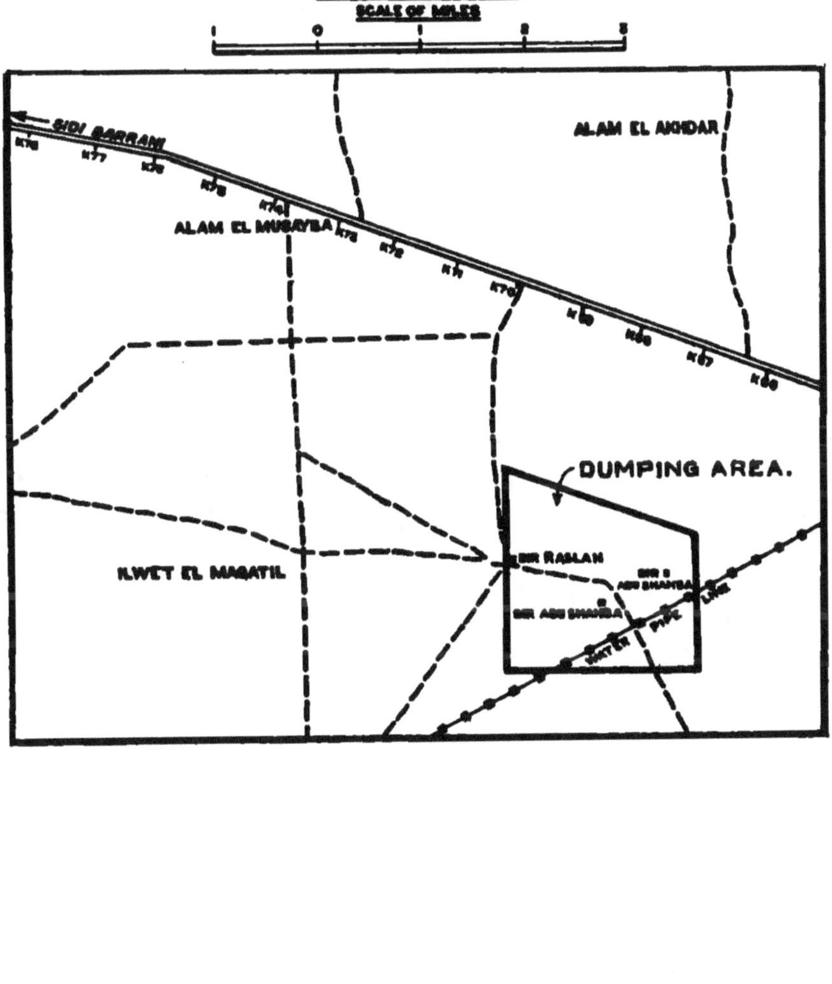

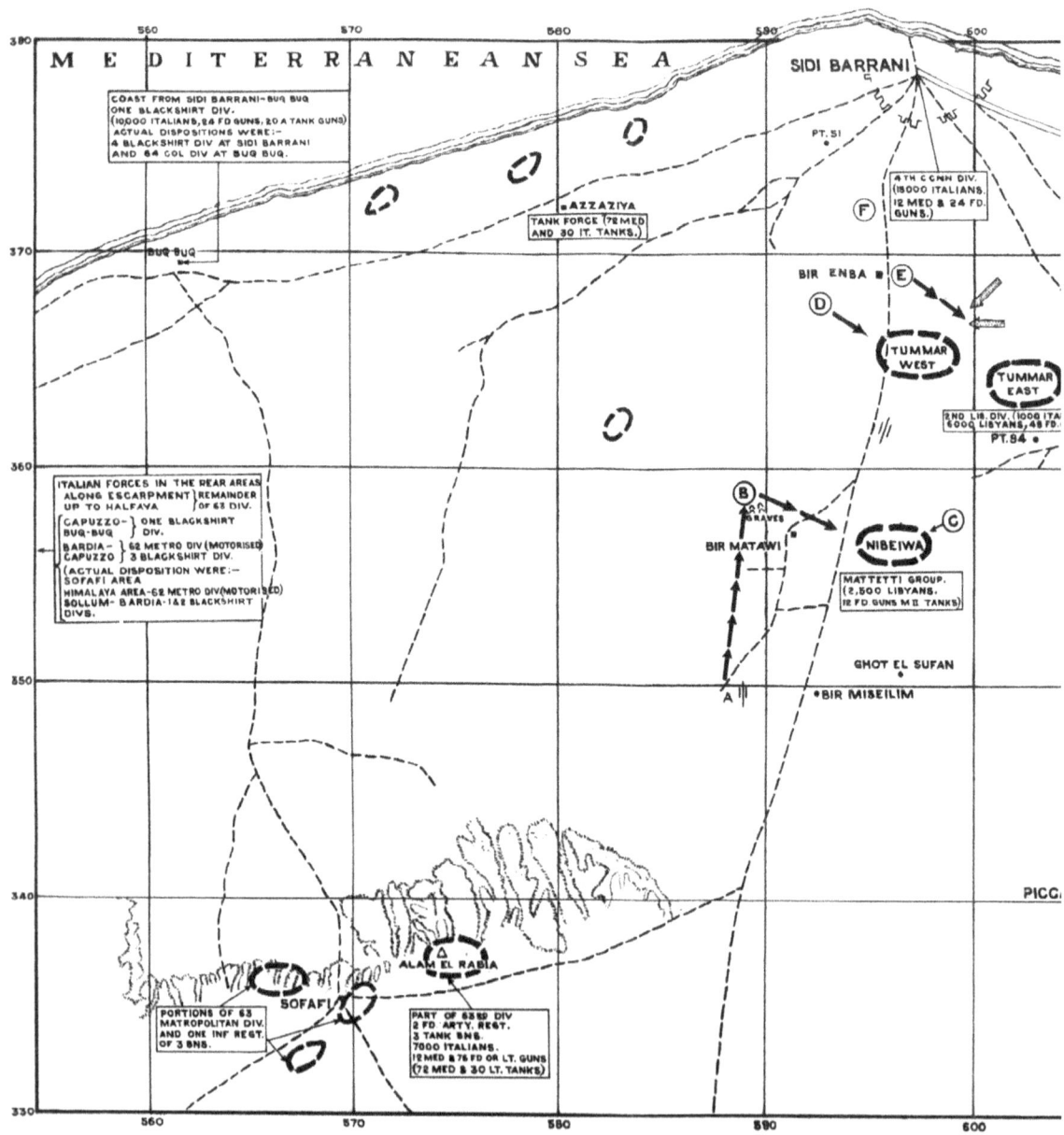

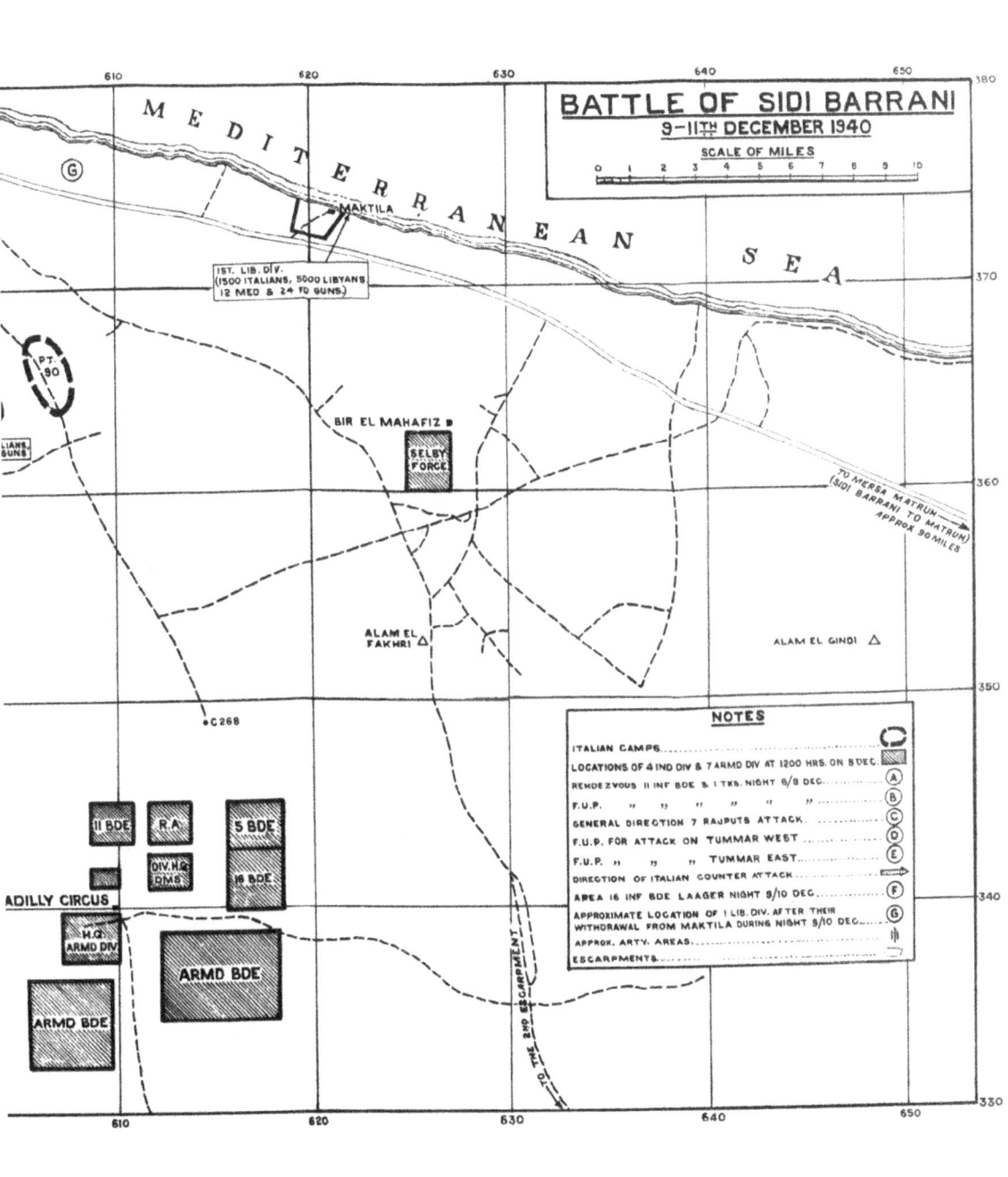

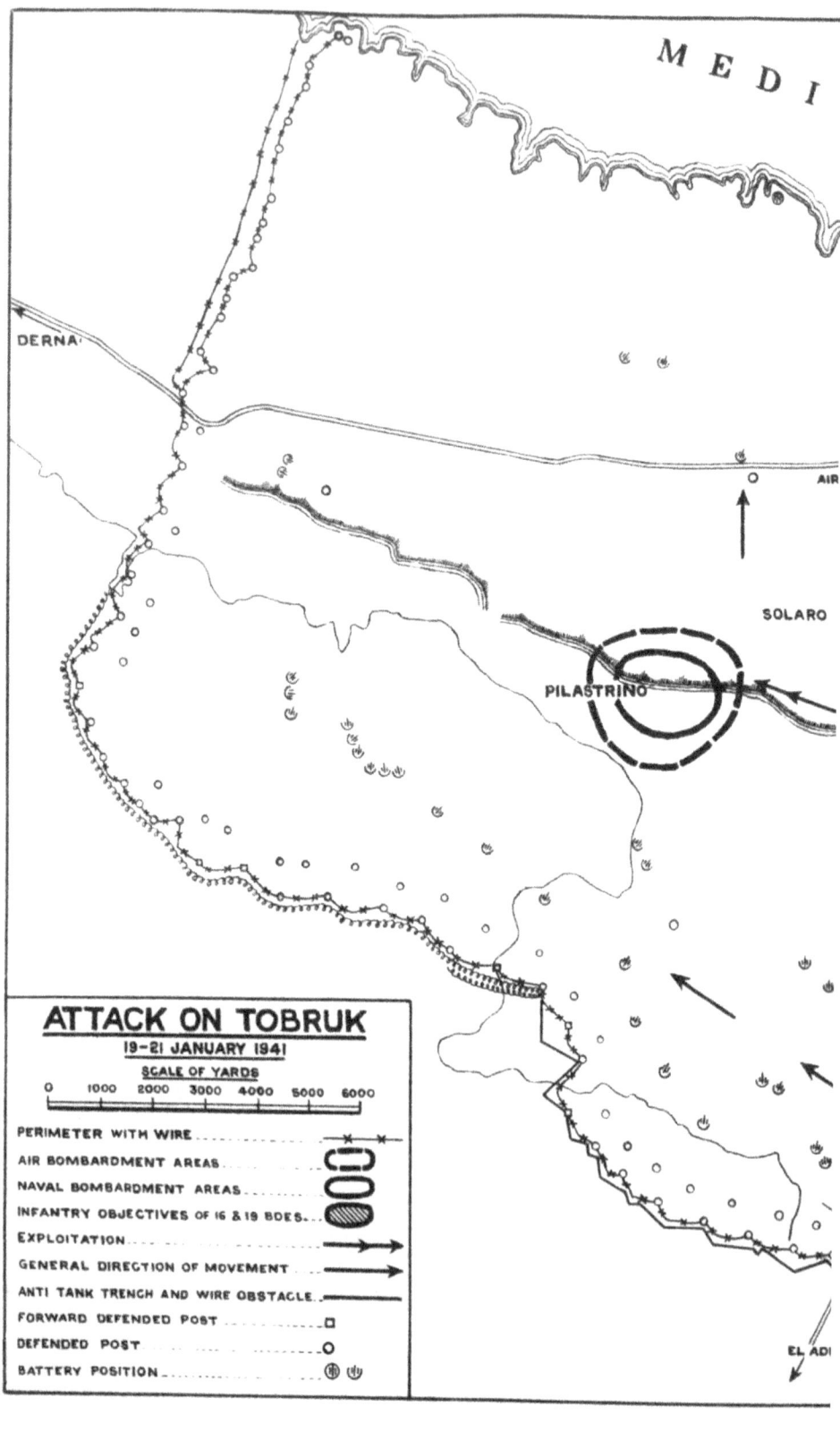

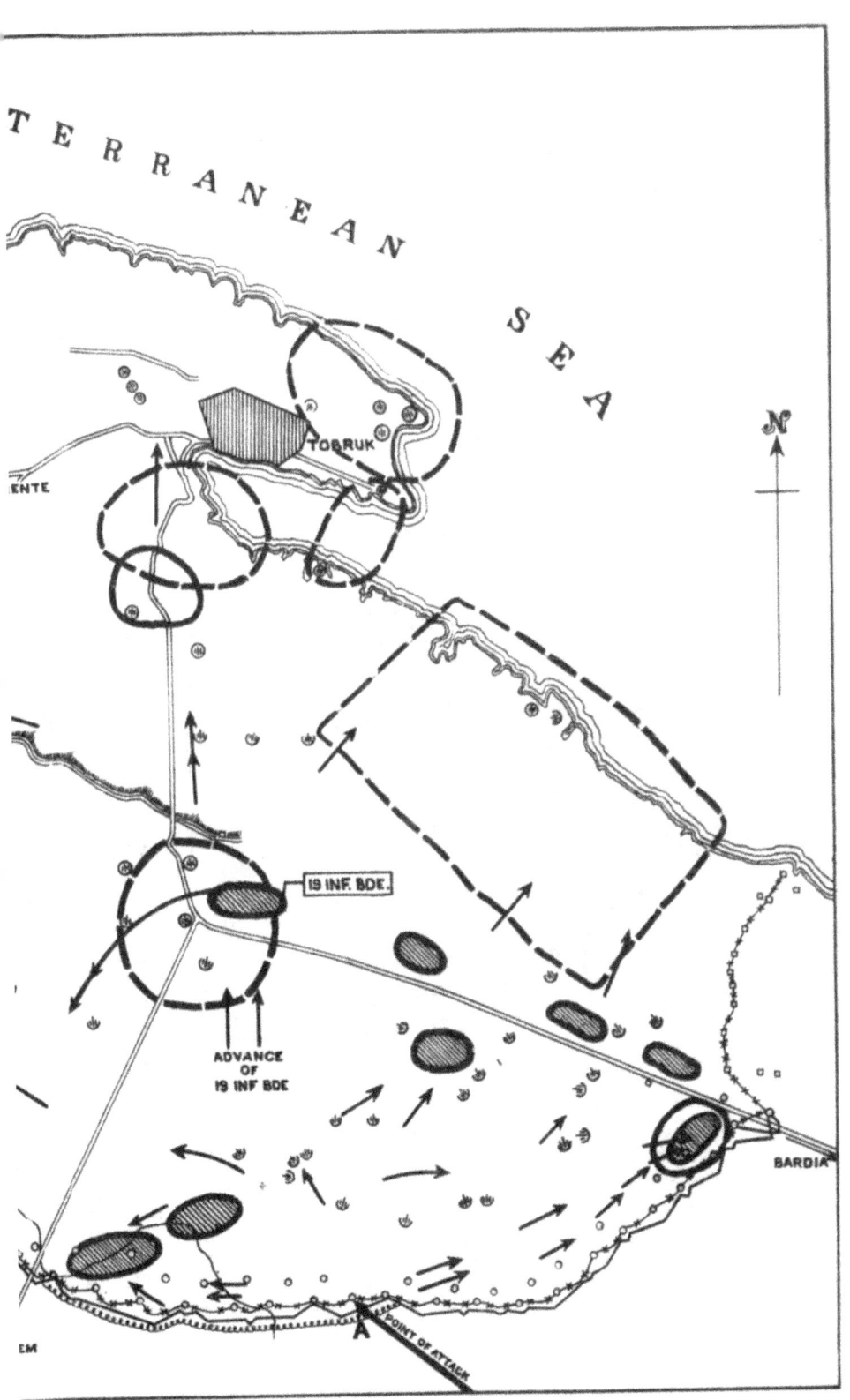

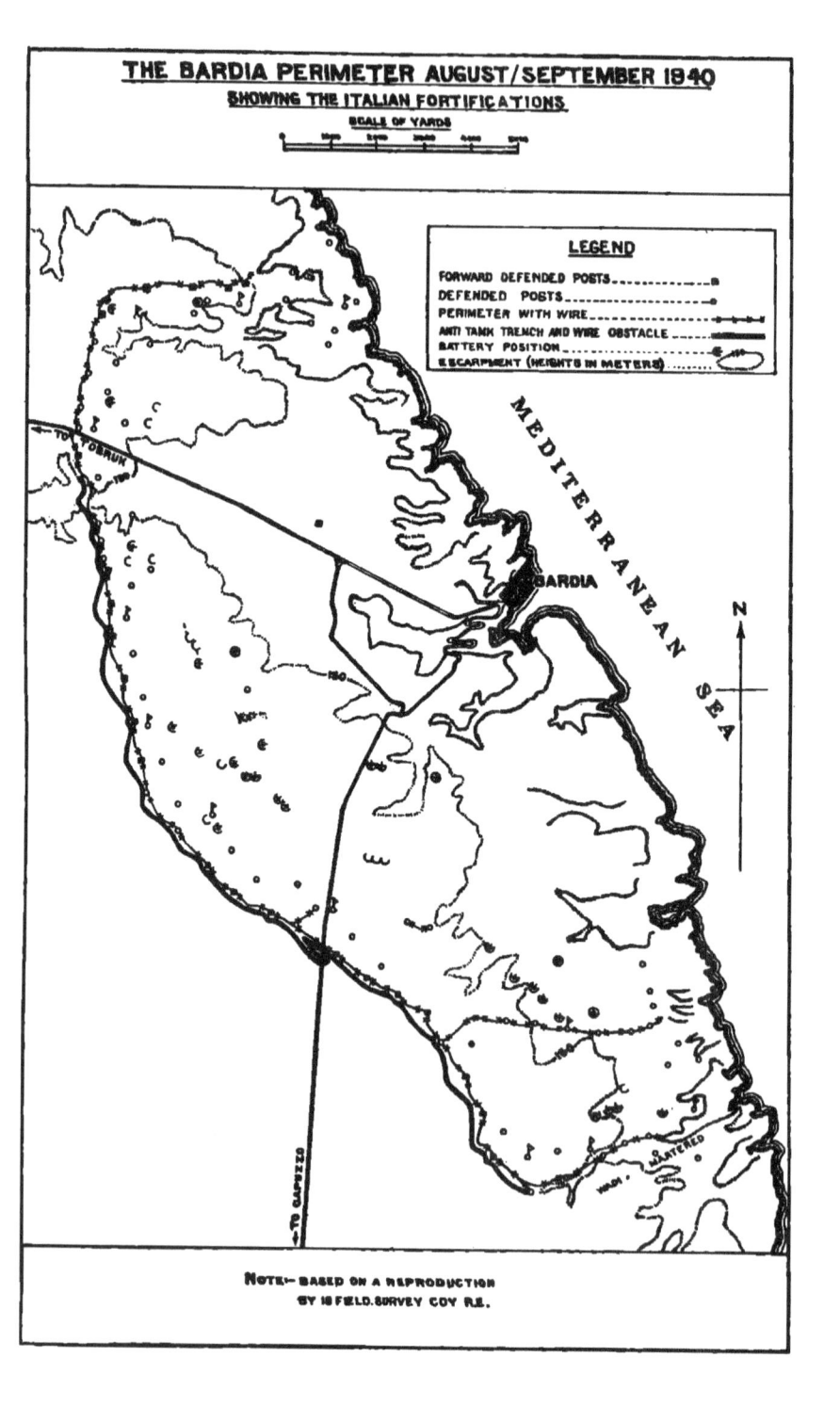

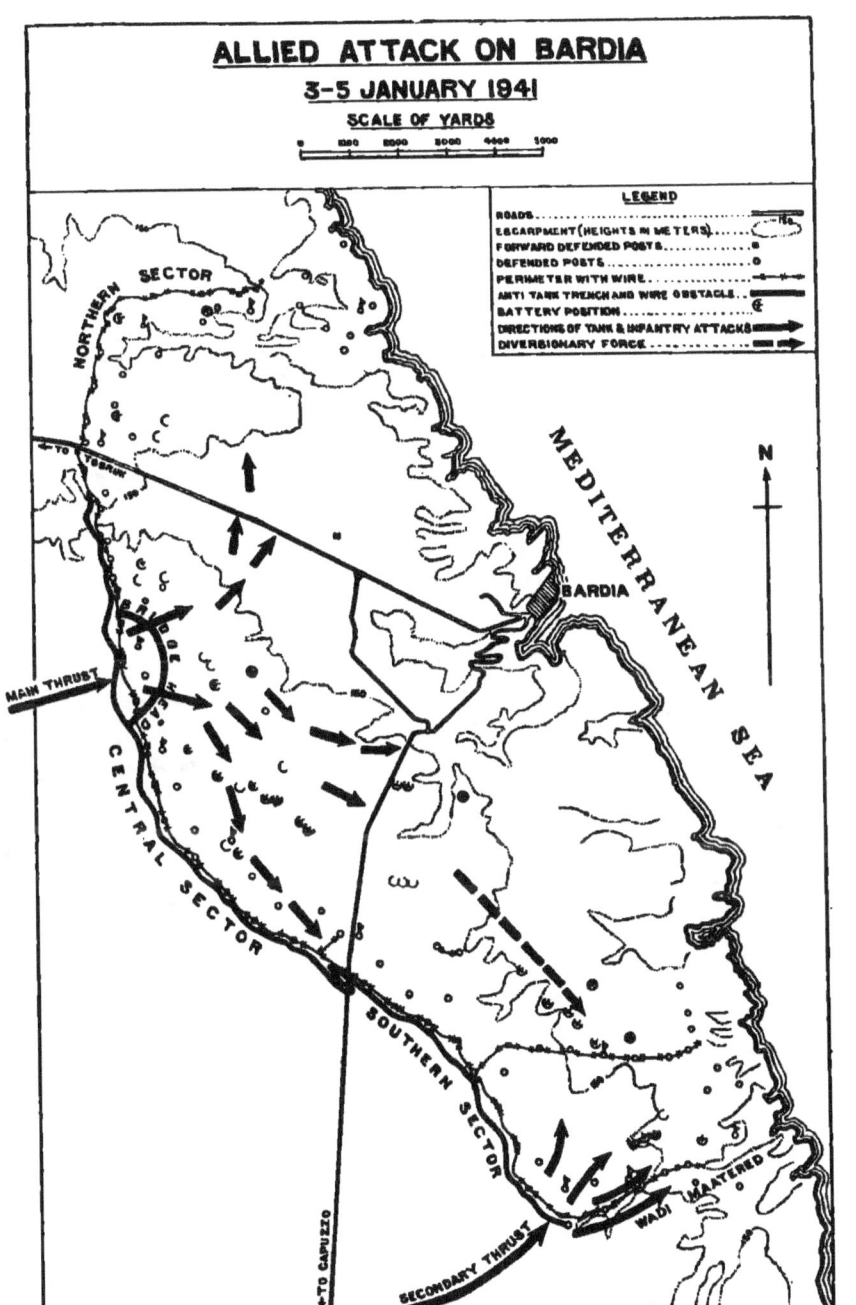

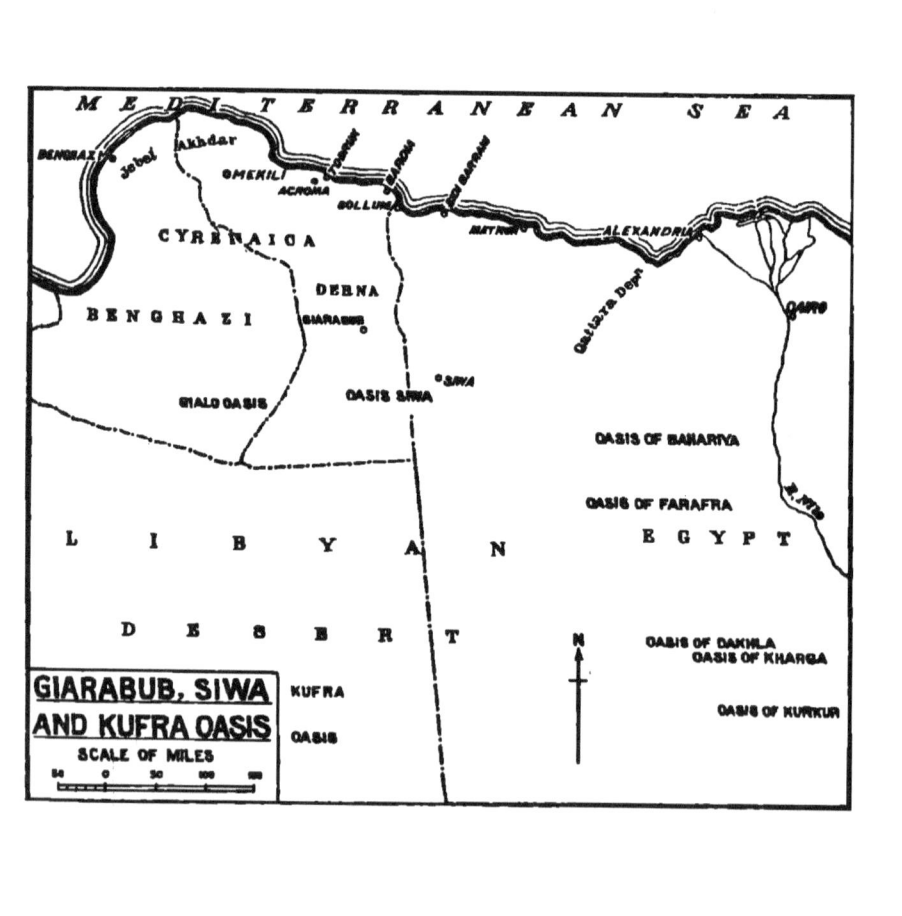

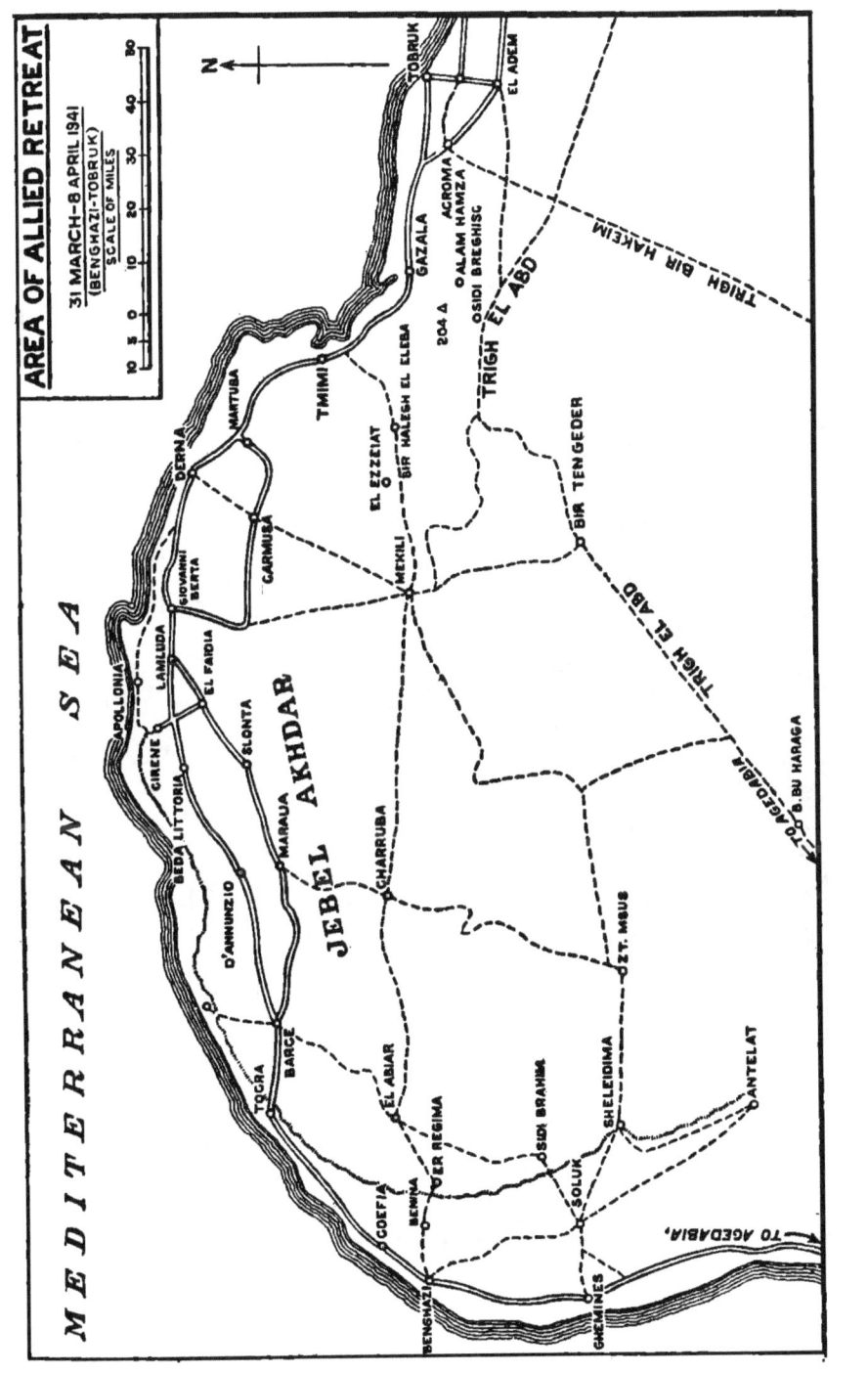

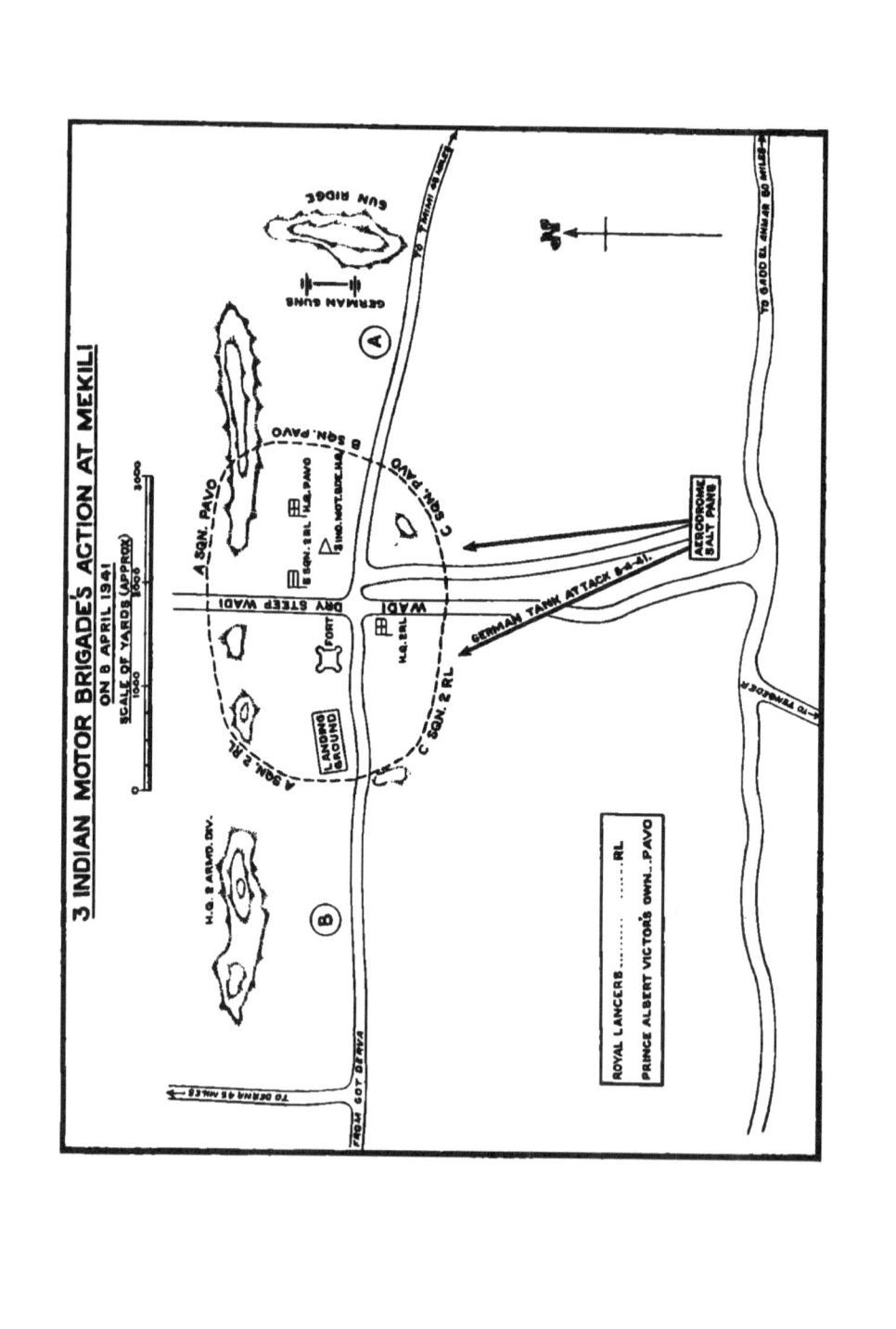

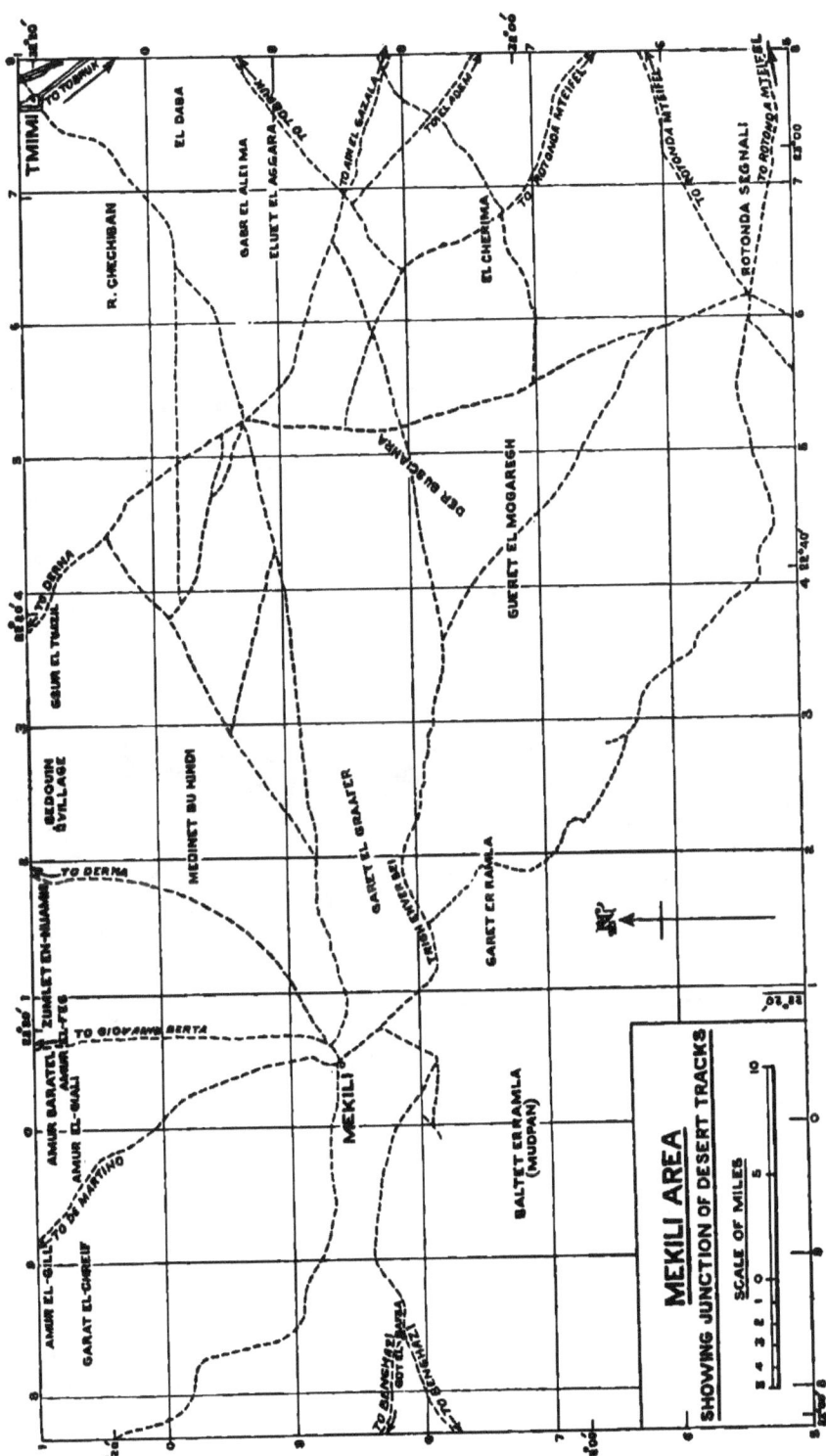

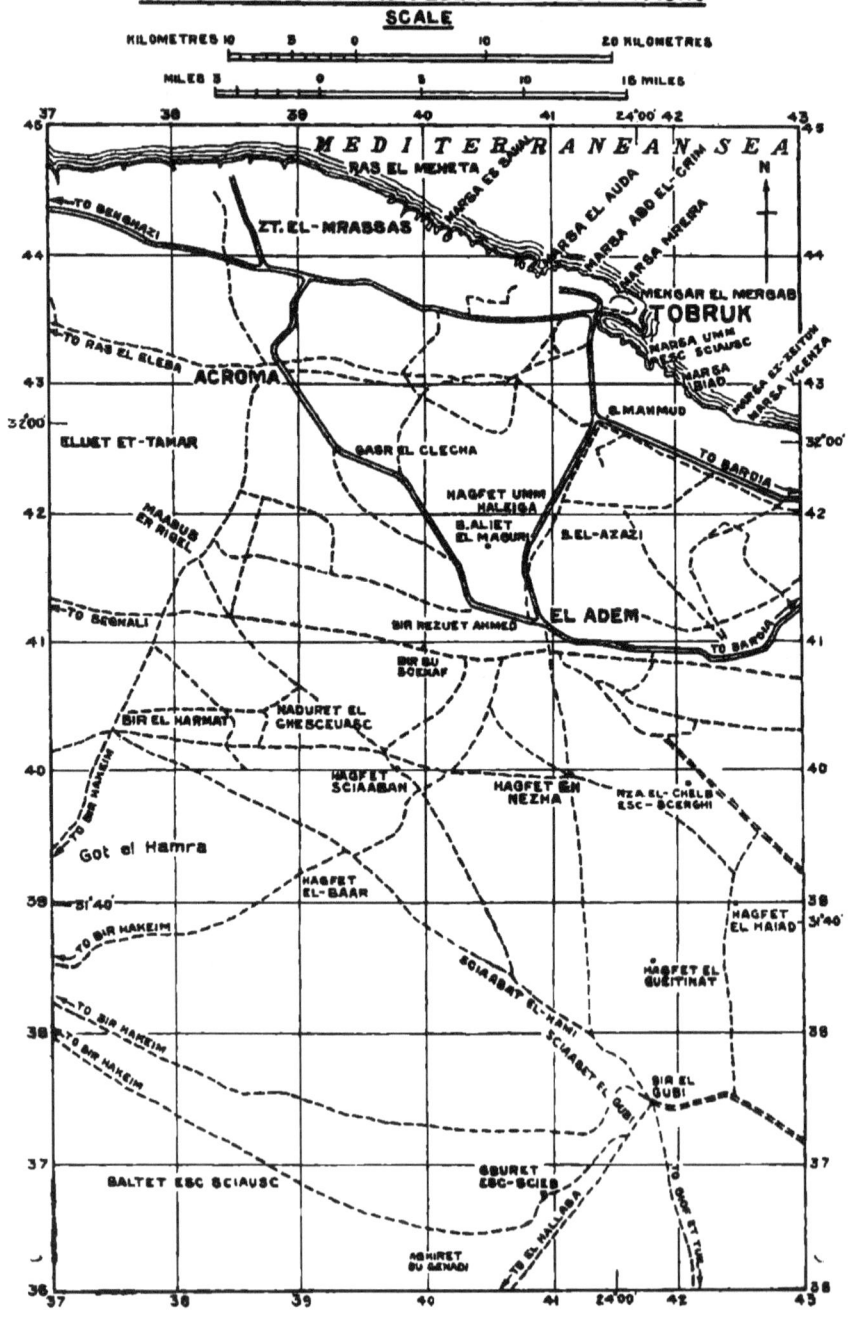

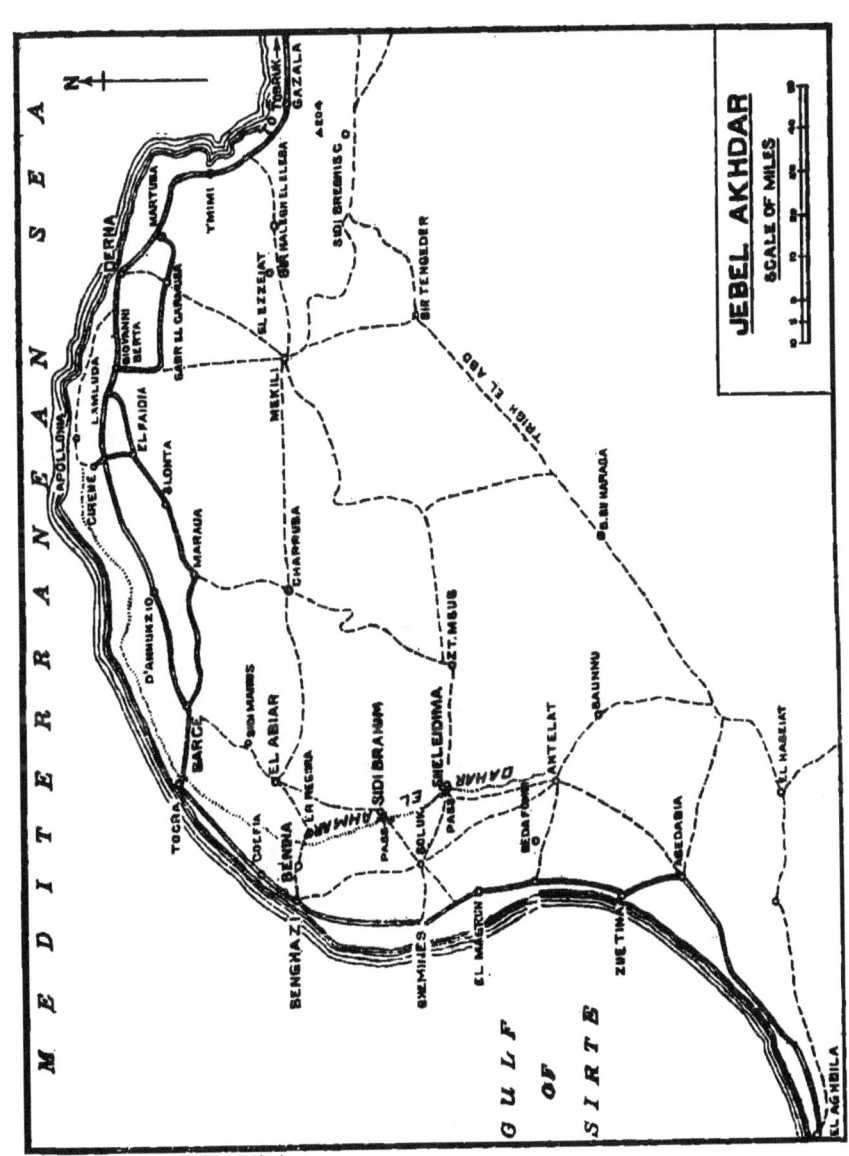

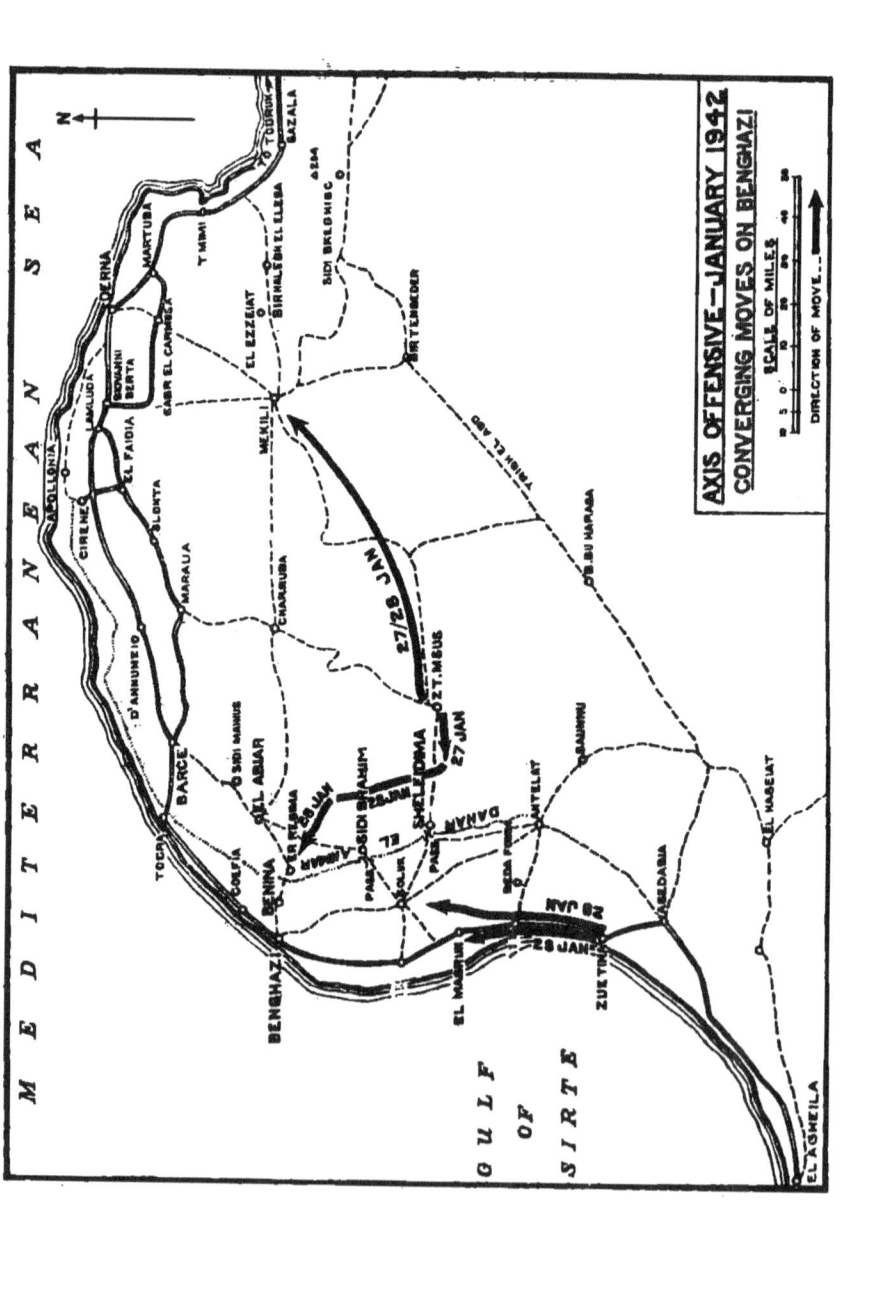

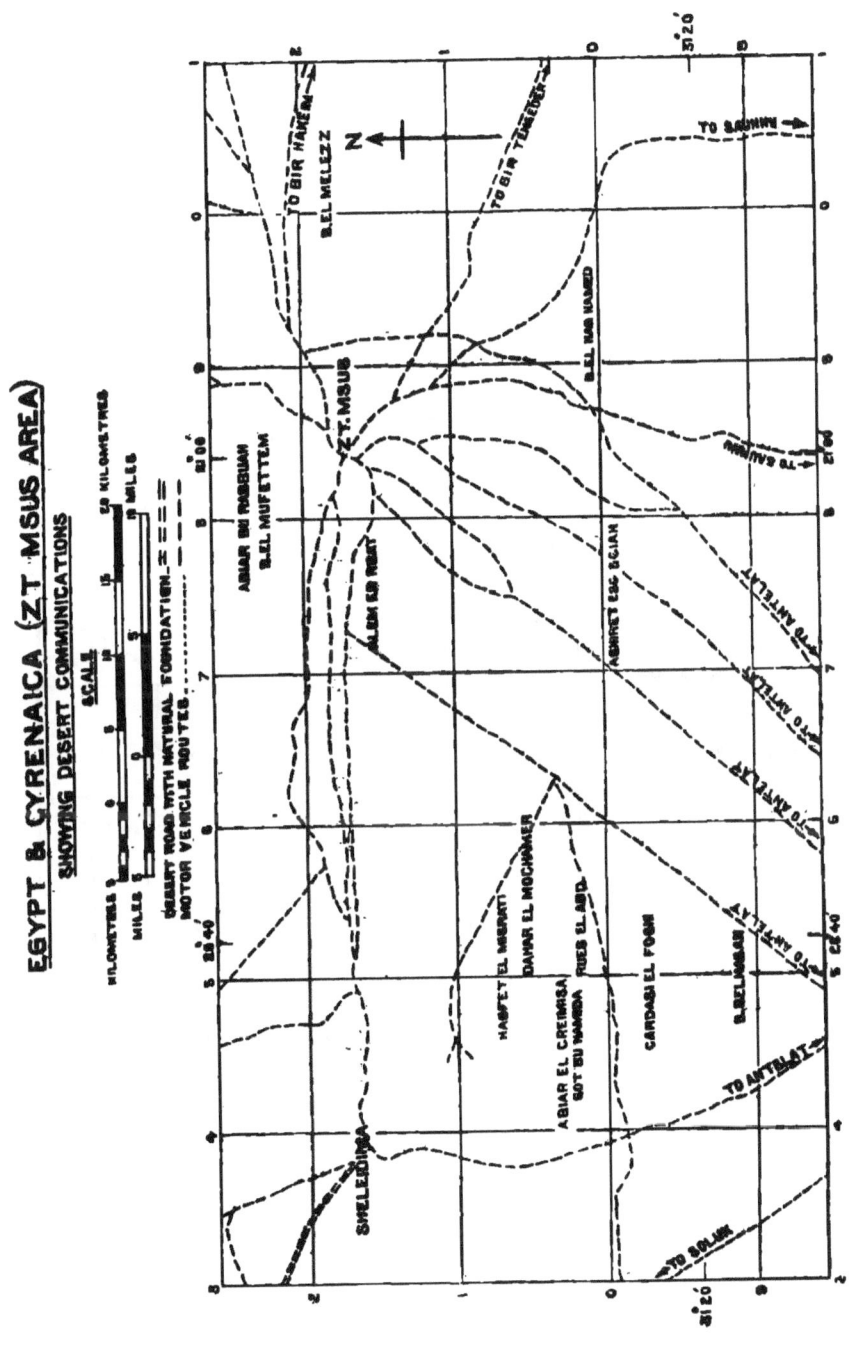

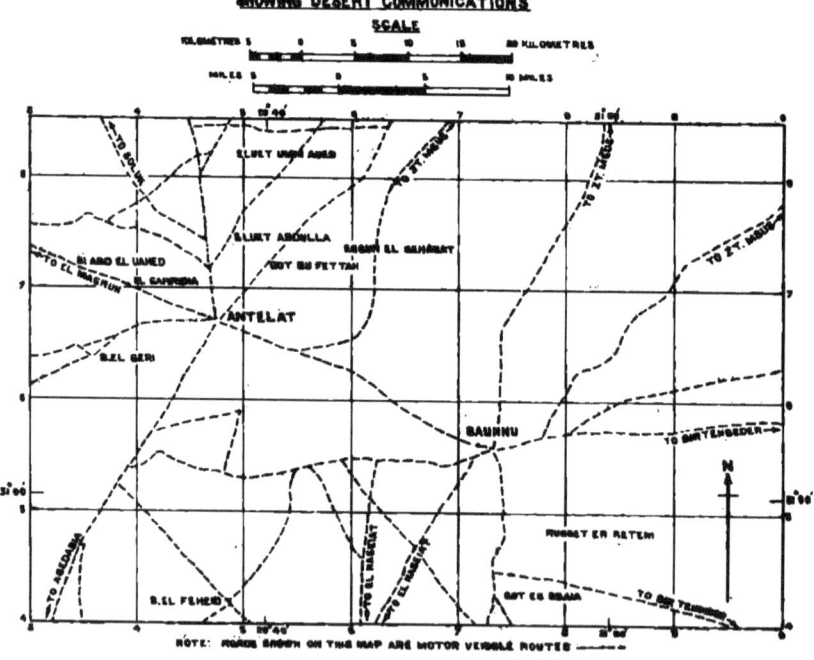

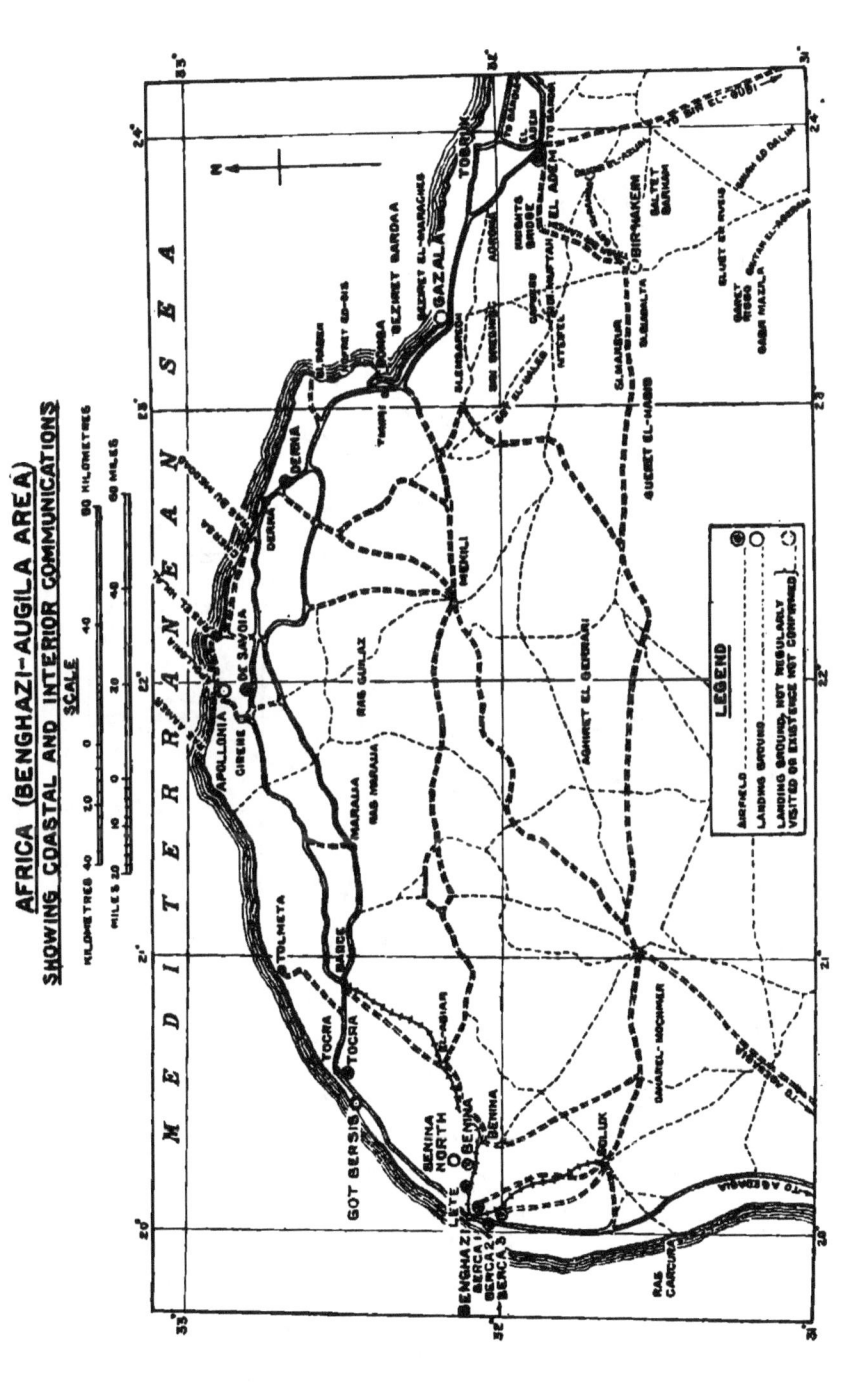

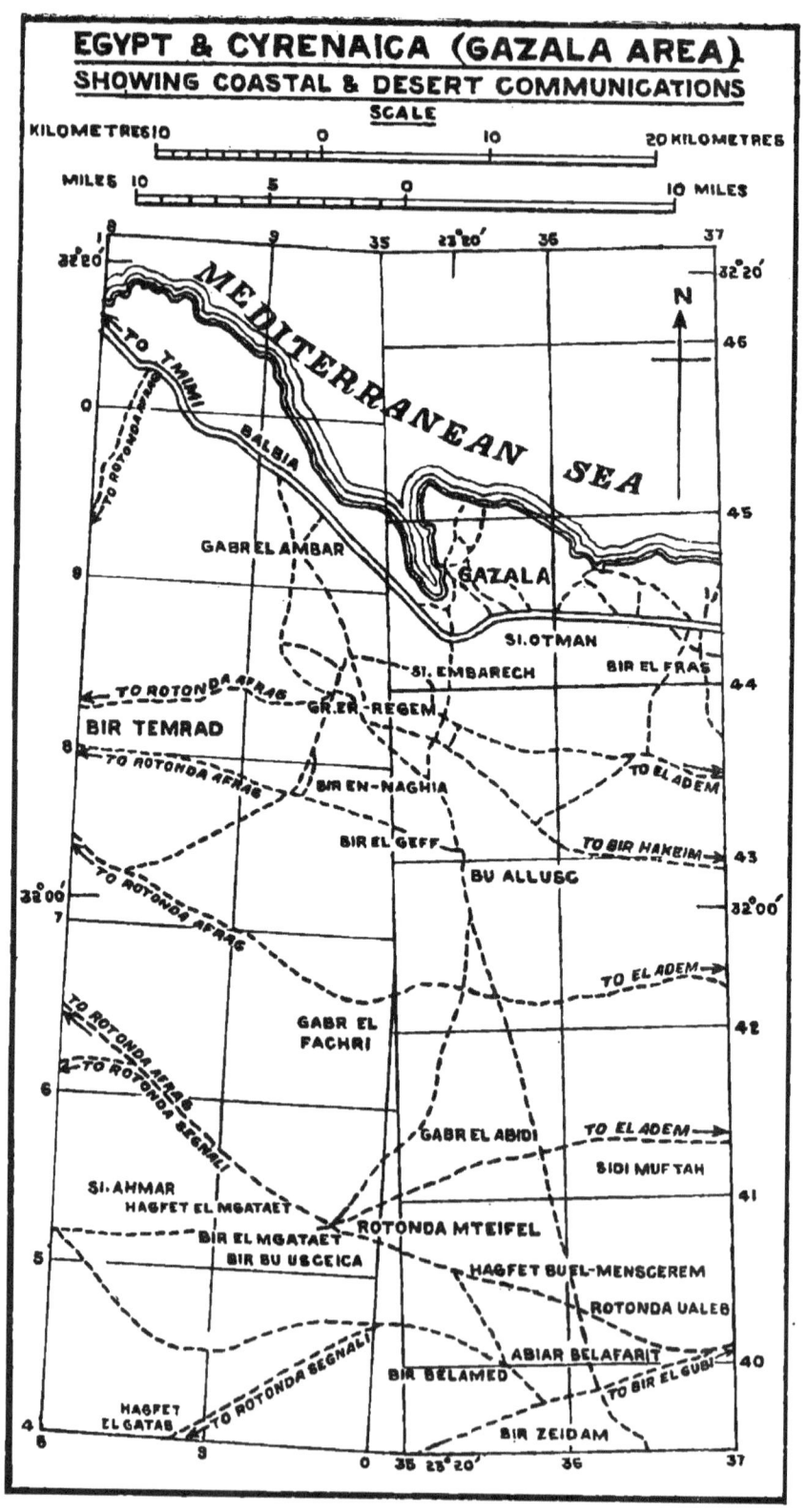

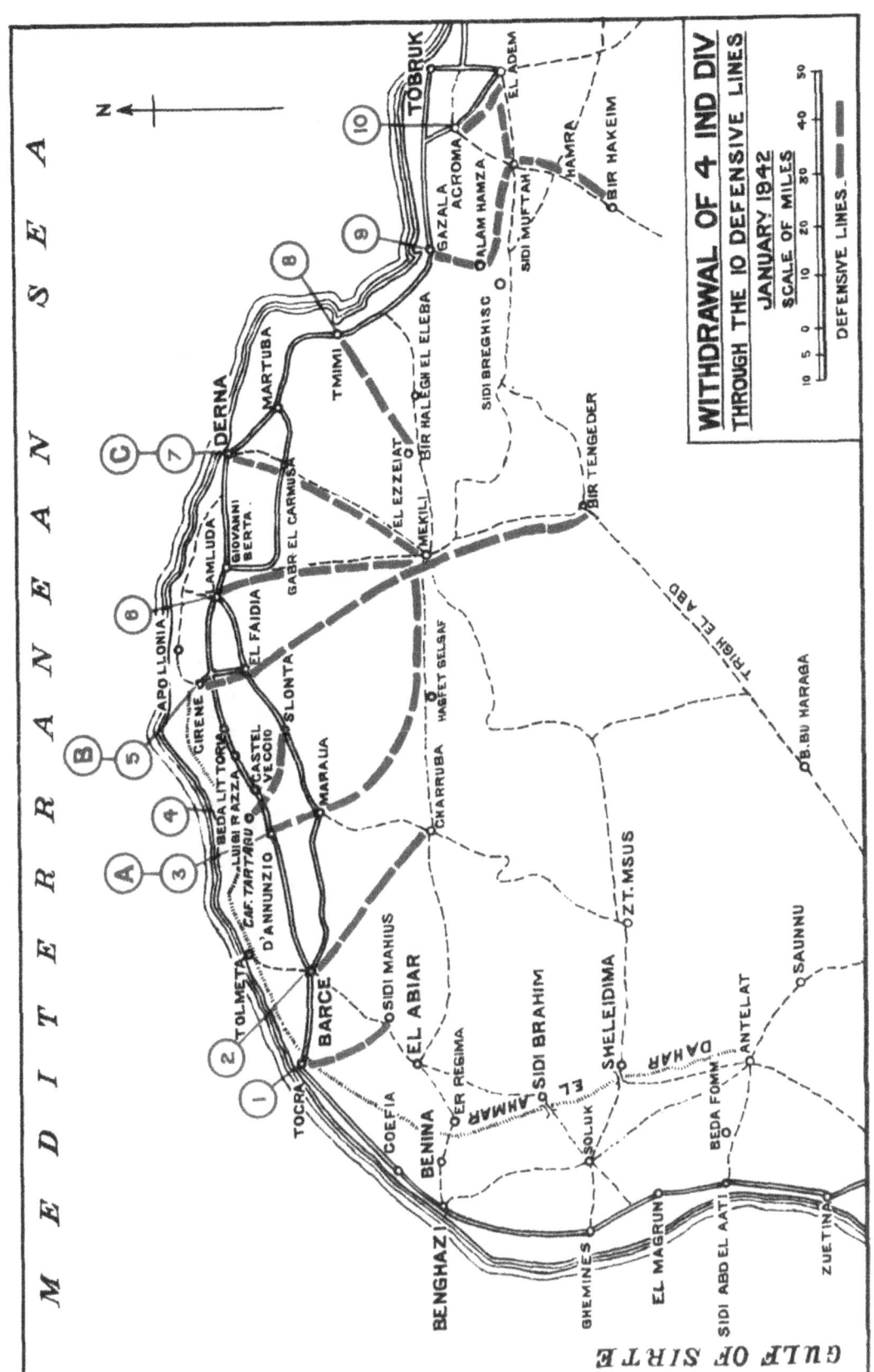

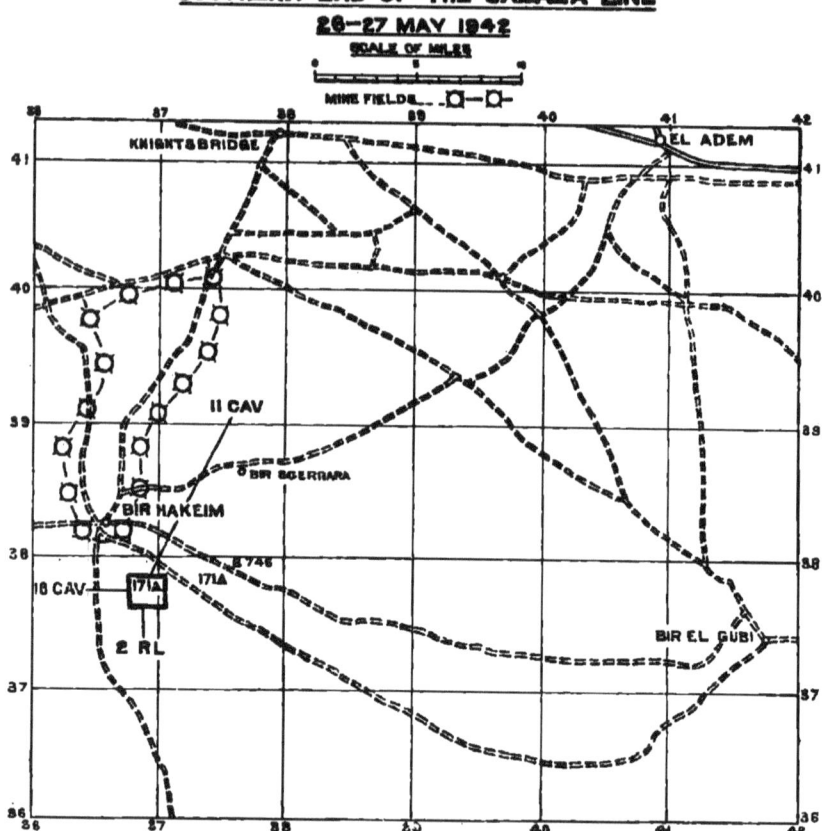

SKETCH No. 1

TOBRUK AXIS ASSAULT

20–21 JUNE 1942

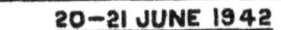

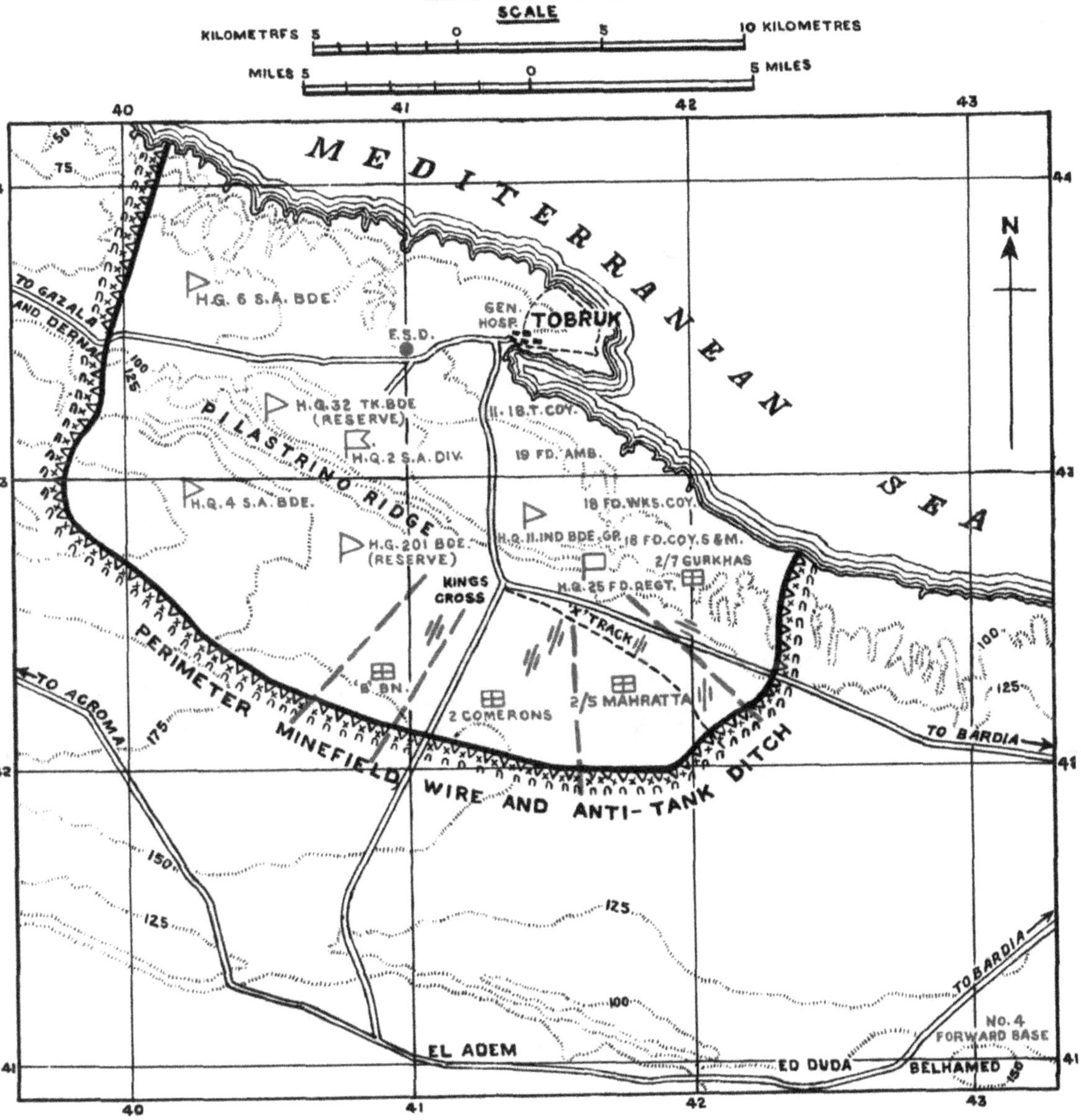

ALLIED DISPOSITIONS SHOWN IN RED.

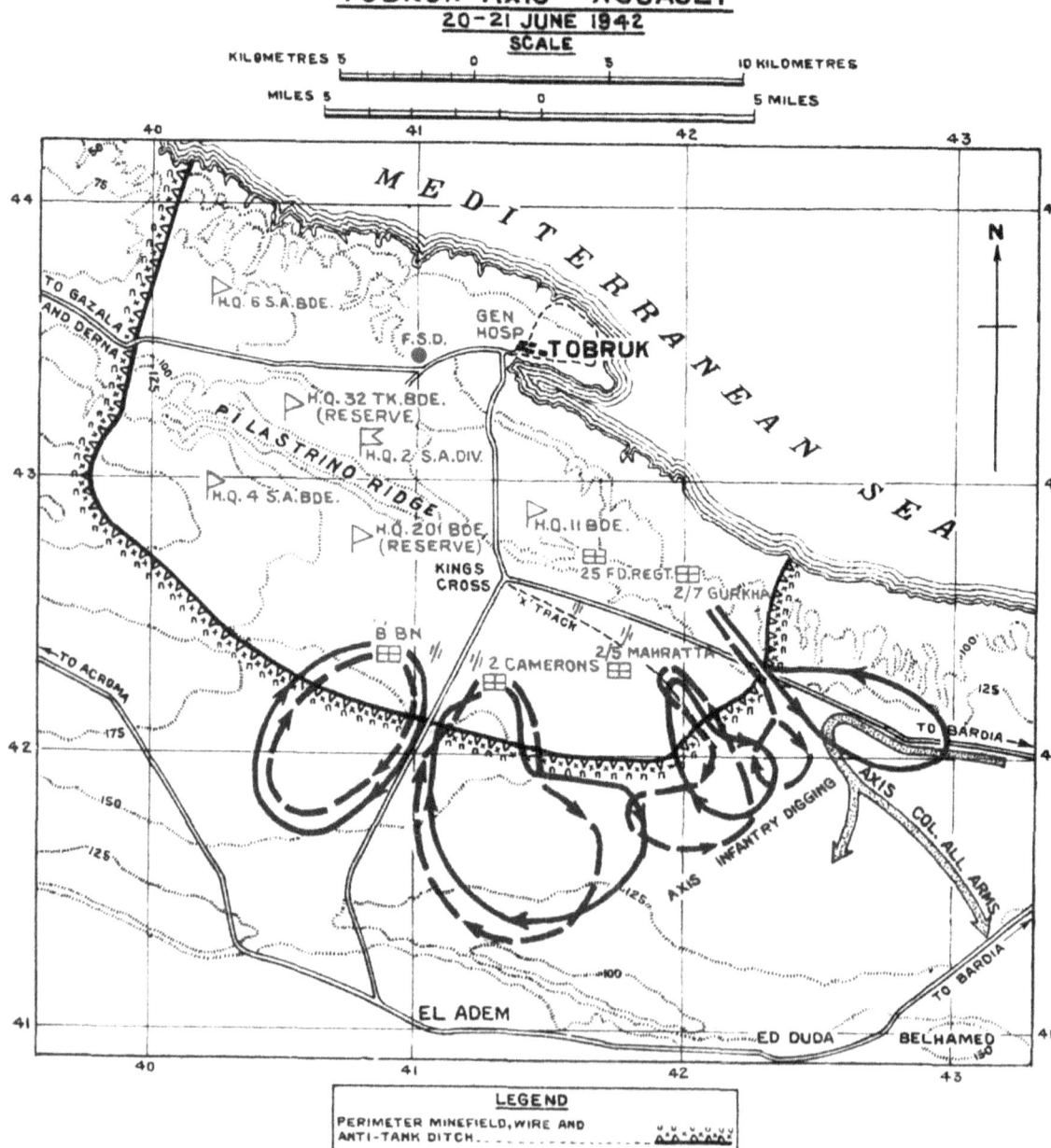

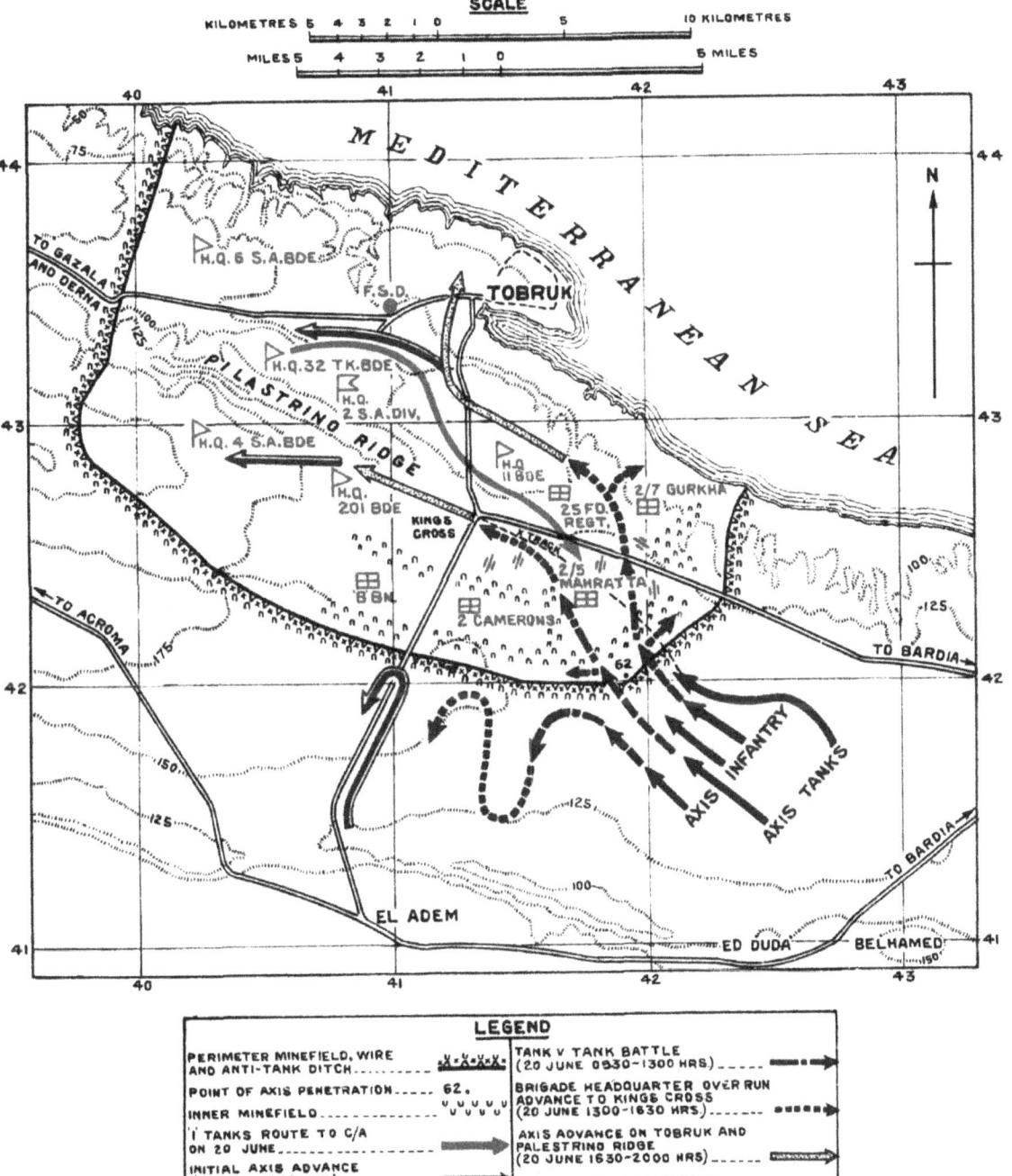

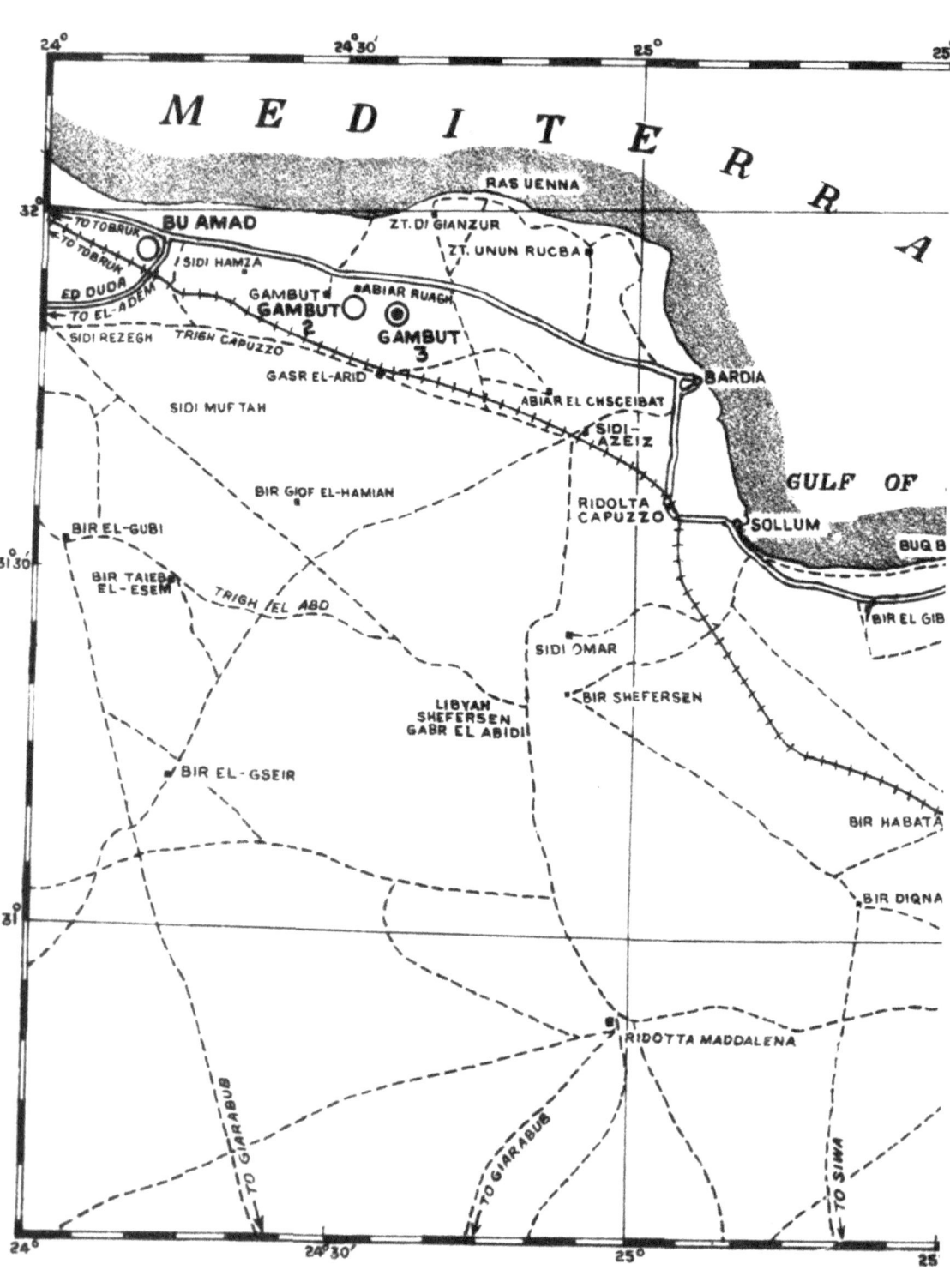

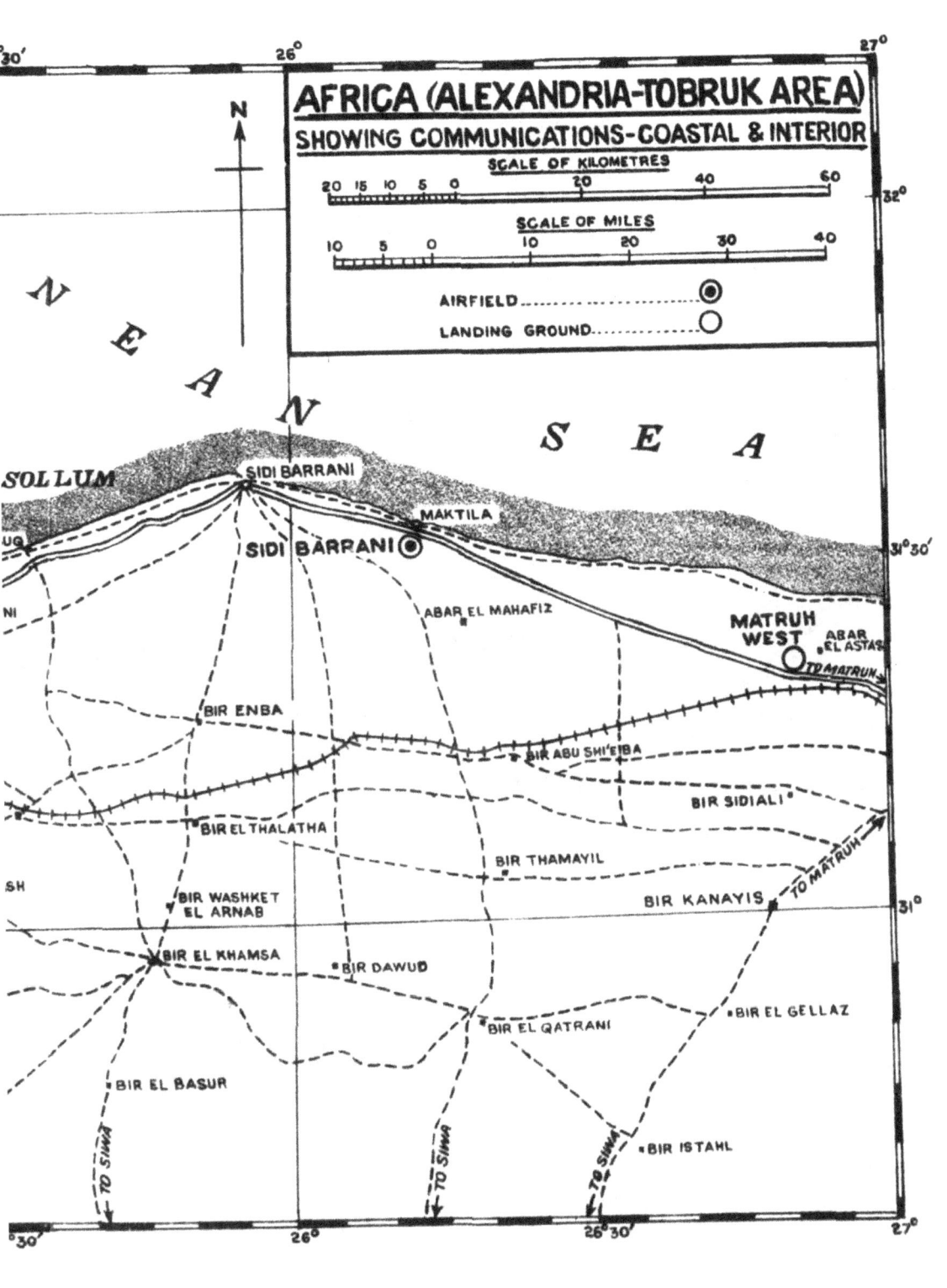

SKETCH No. 4
TOBRUK AXIS ASSAULT
20–21 JUNE 1942

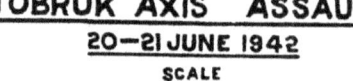

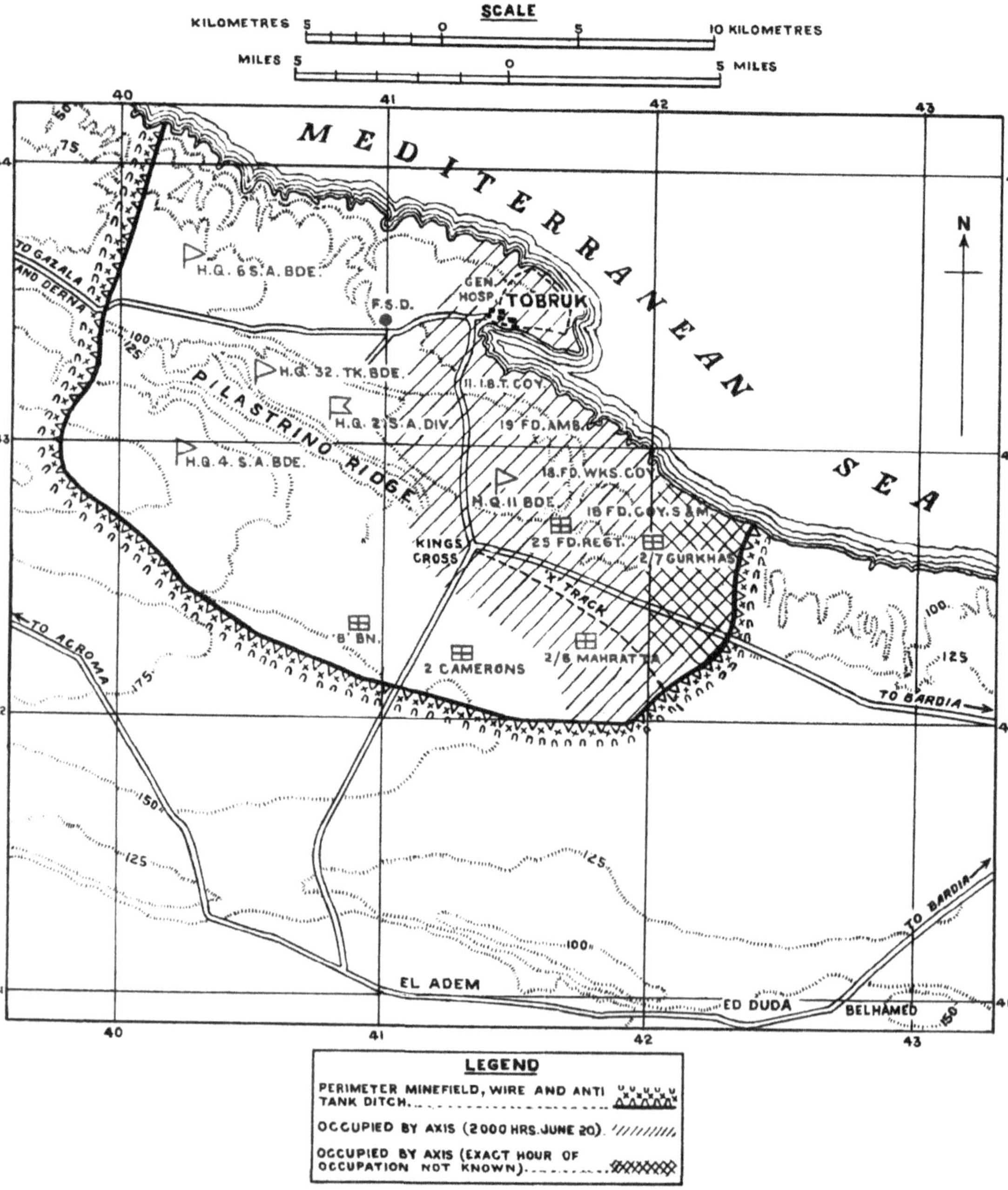

ALLIED DISPOSITIONS SHOWN IN RED.

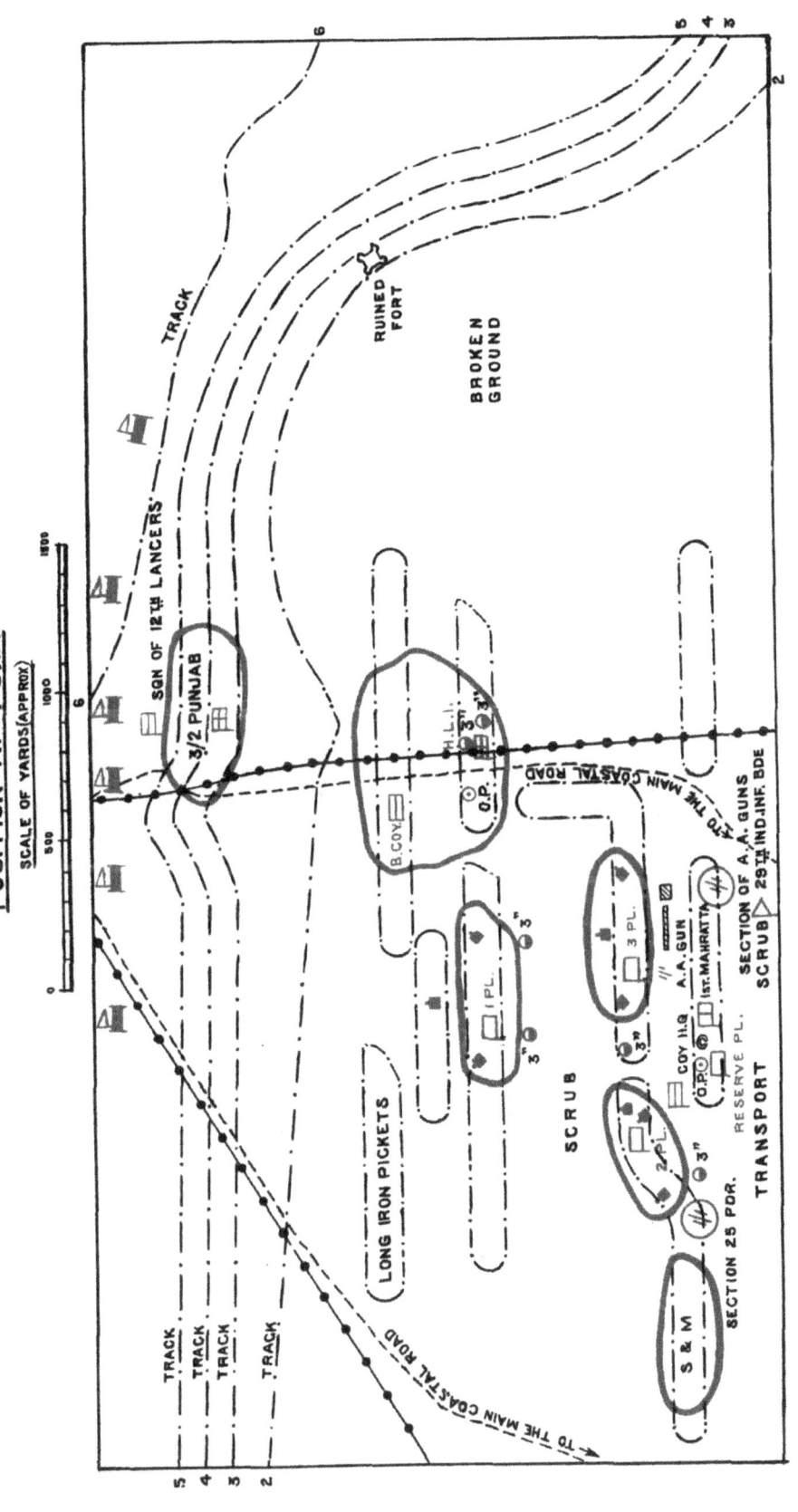

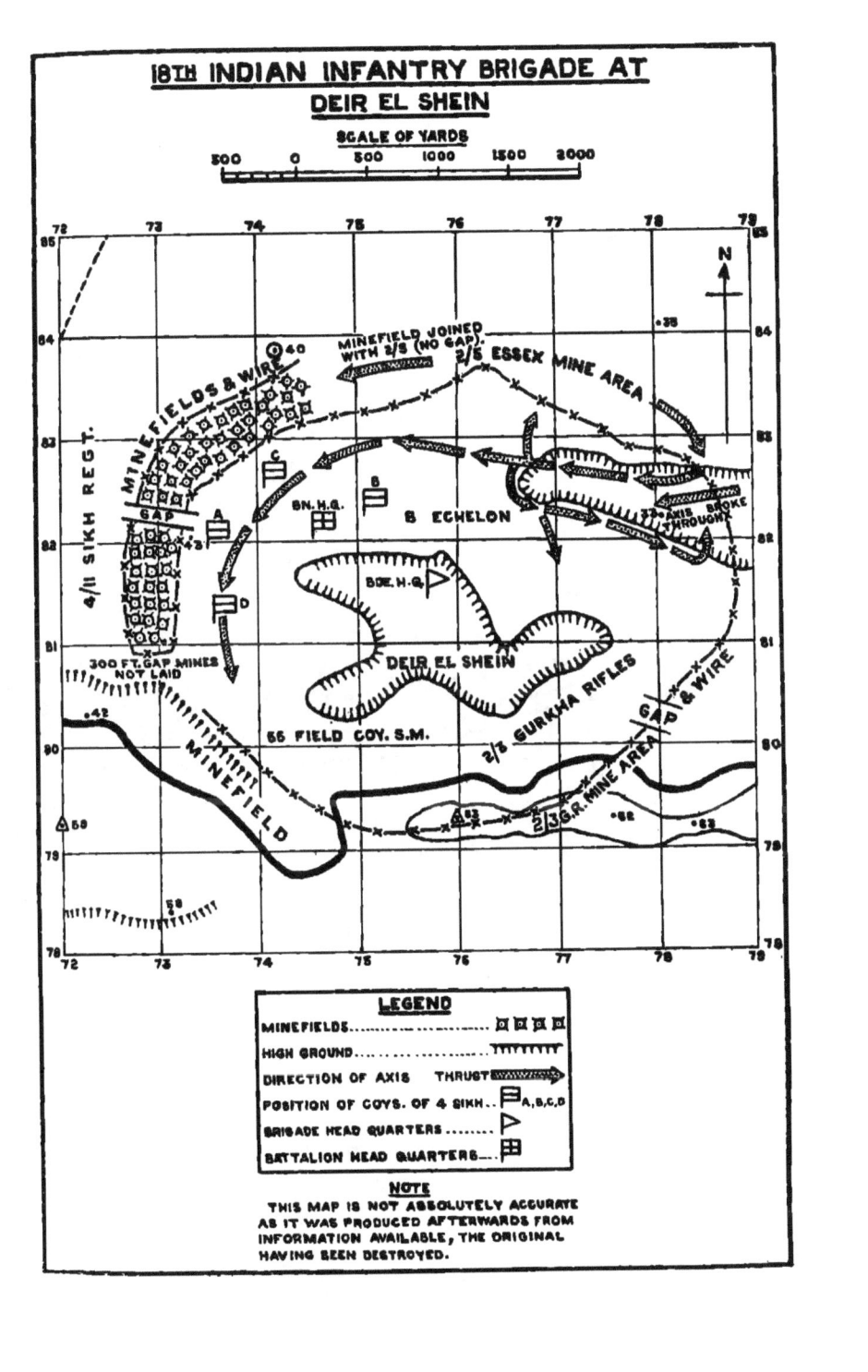

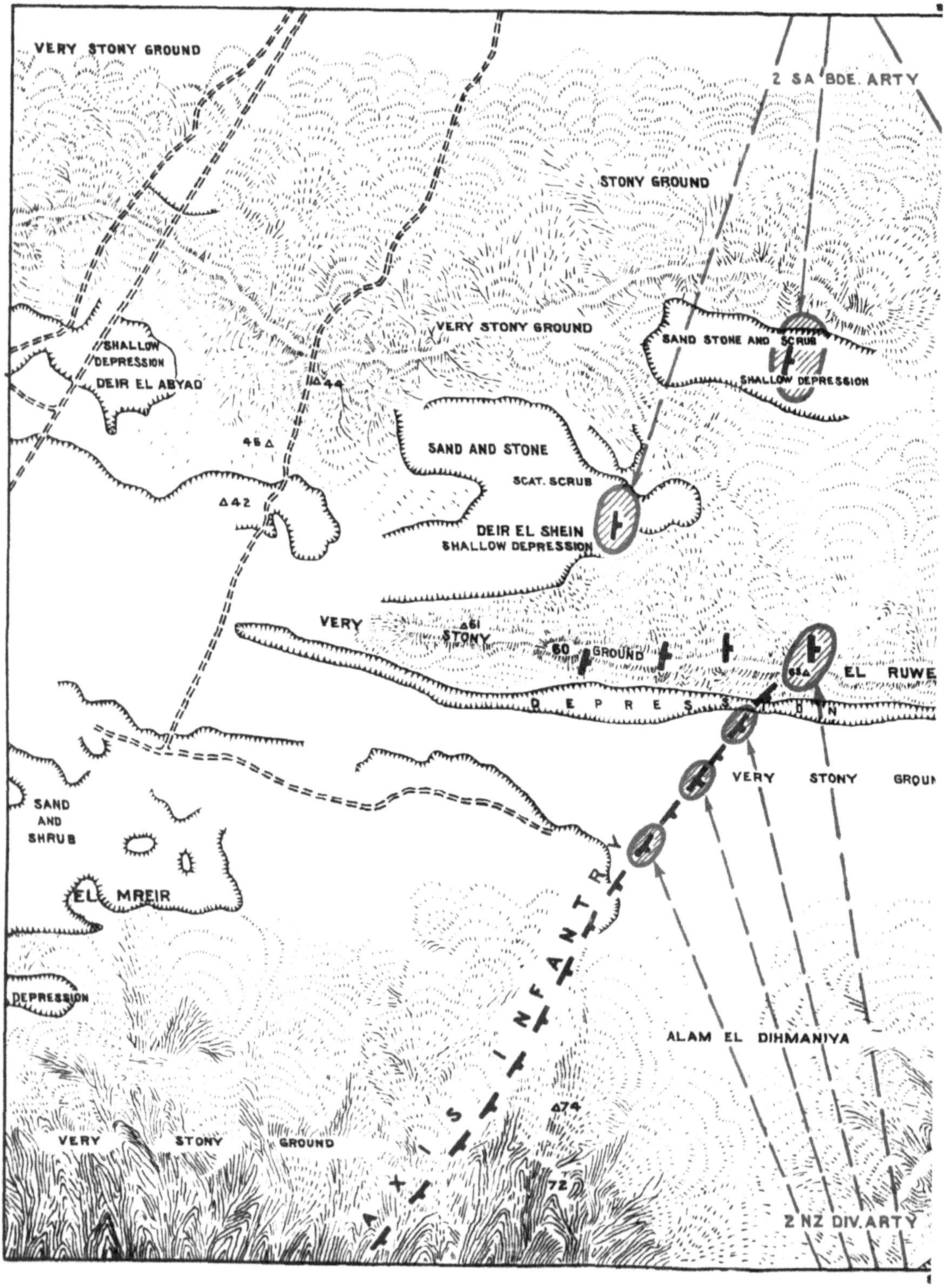

VERY STONY GROUND

2 SA BDE. ARTY

STONY GROUND

SHALLOW
DEPRESSION
DEIR EL ABYAD

VERY STONY GROUND

SAND STONE AND SCRUB

SHALLOW DEPRESSION

△44

45△

△42

SAND AND STONE
SCAT. SCRUB

DEIR EL SHEIN
SHALLOW DEPRESSION

VERY

△61

STONY

60

GROUND

65△ EL RUWE

D E P R E S S I O N

VERY STONY GROUN

SAND
AND
SHRUB

EL MREIR

I N F A N T R Y

DEPRESSION

ALAM EL DIHMANIYA

VERY STONY GROUND

△74

72

2 NZ DIV. ARTY

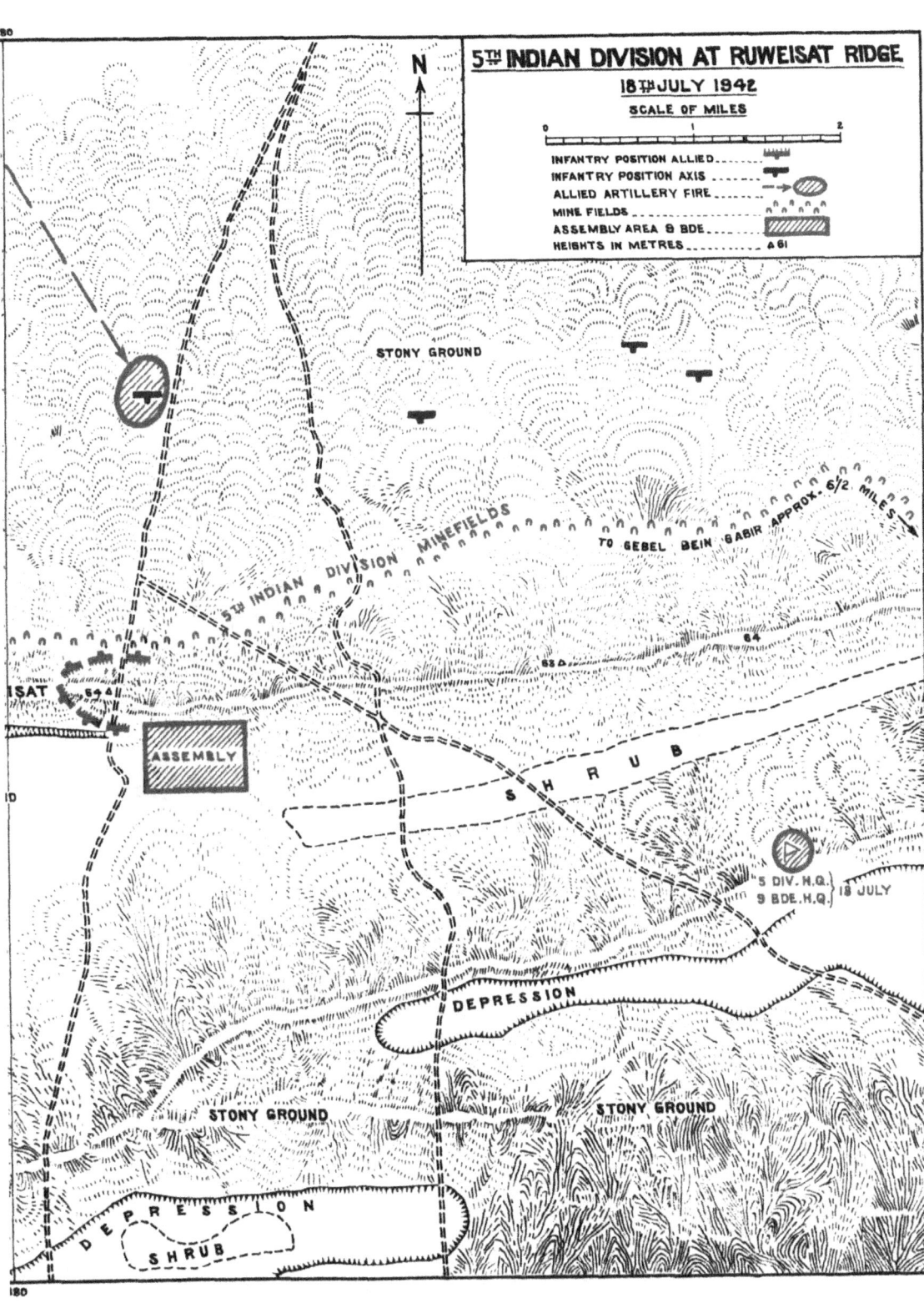

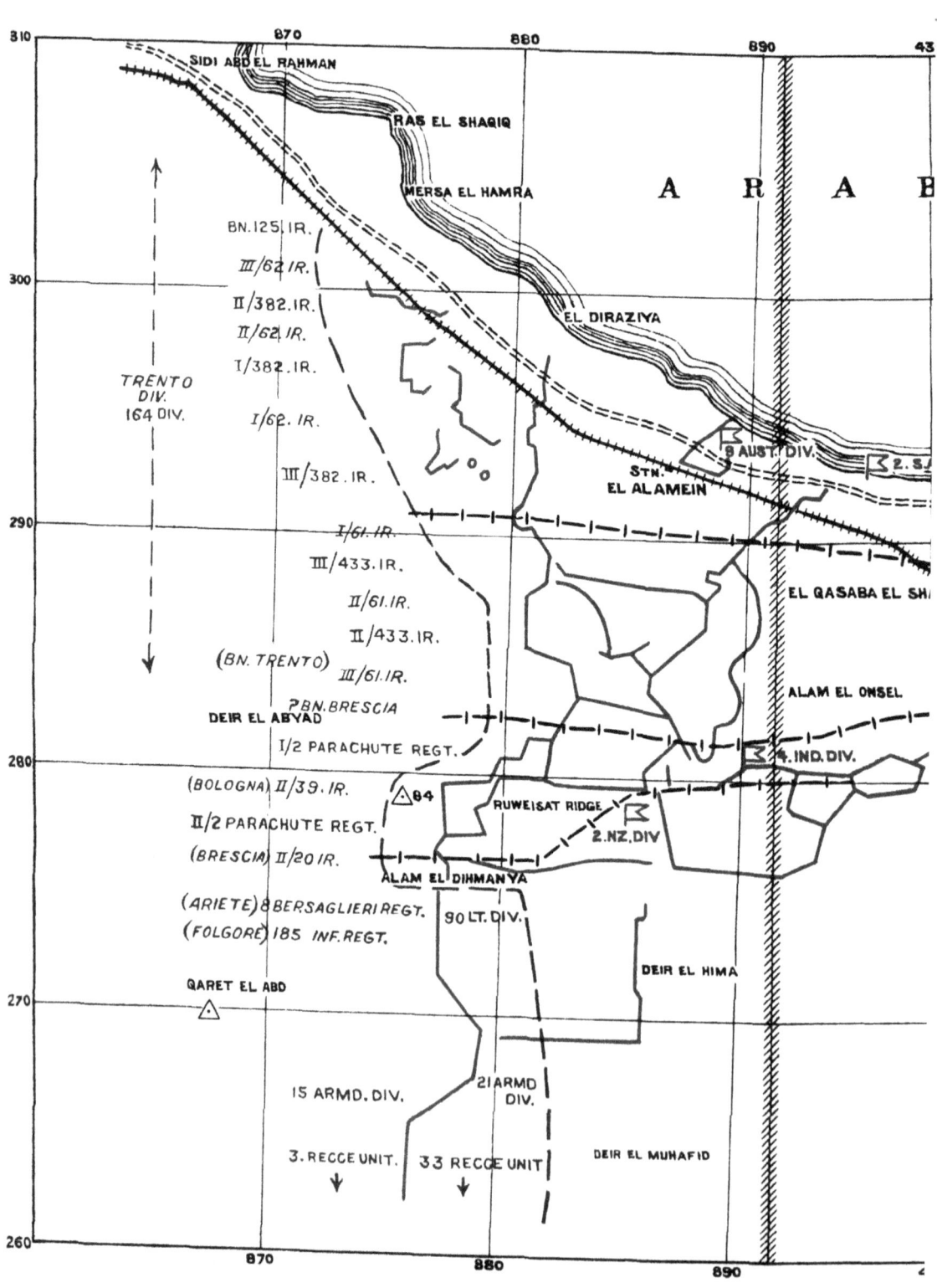

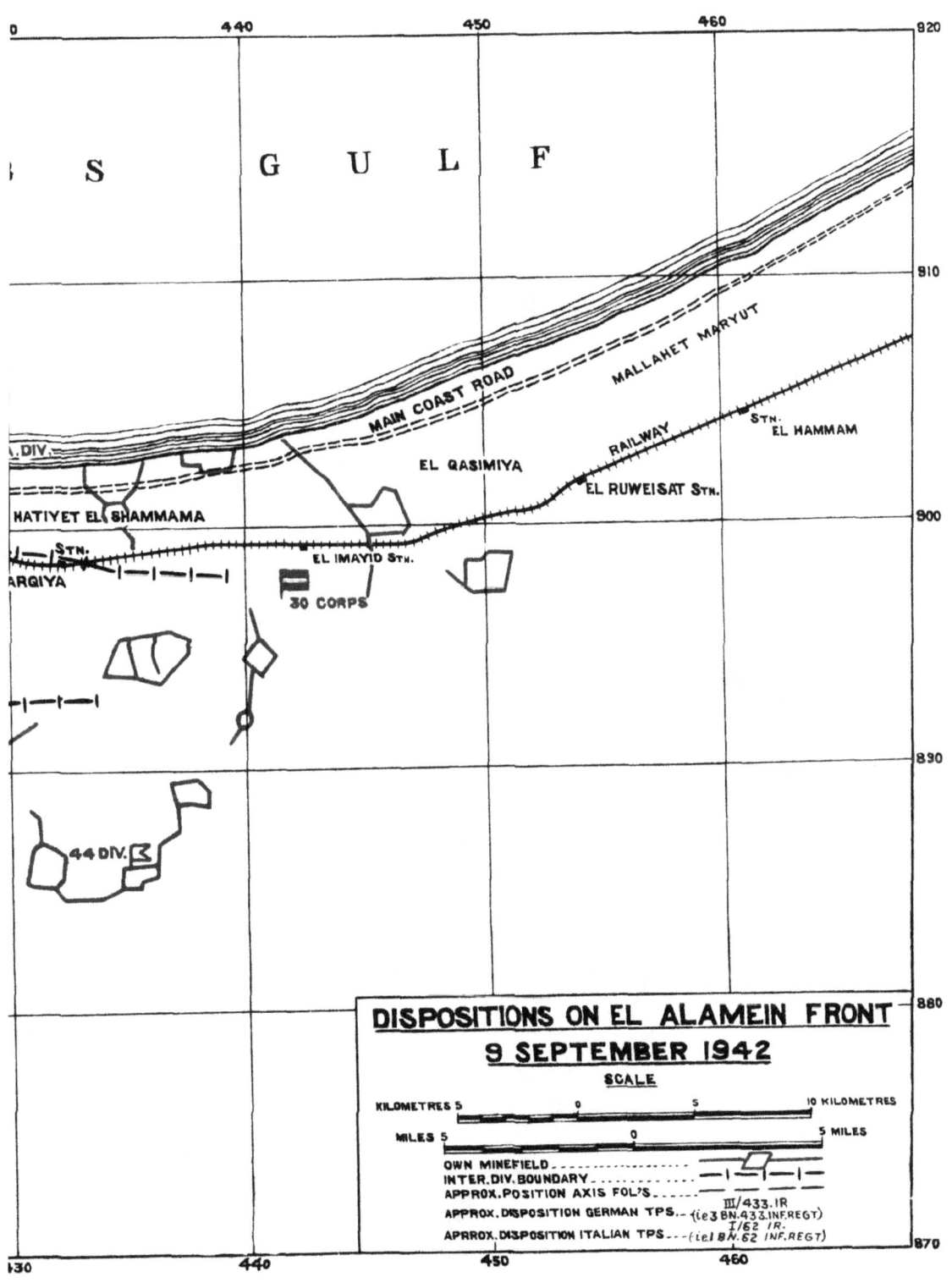

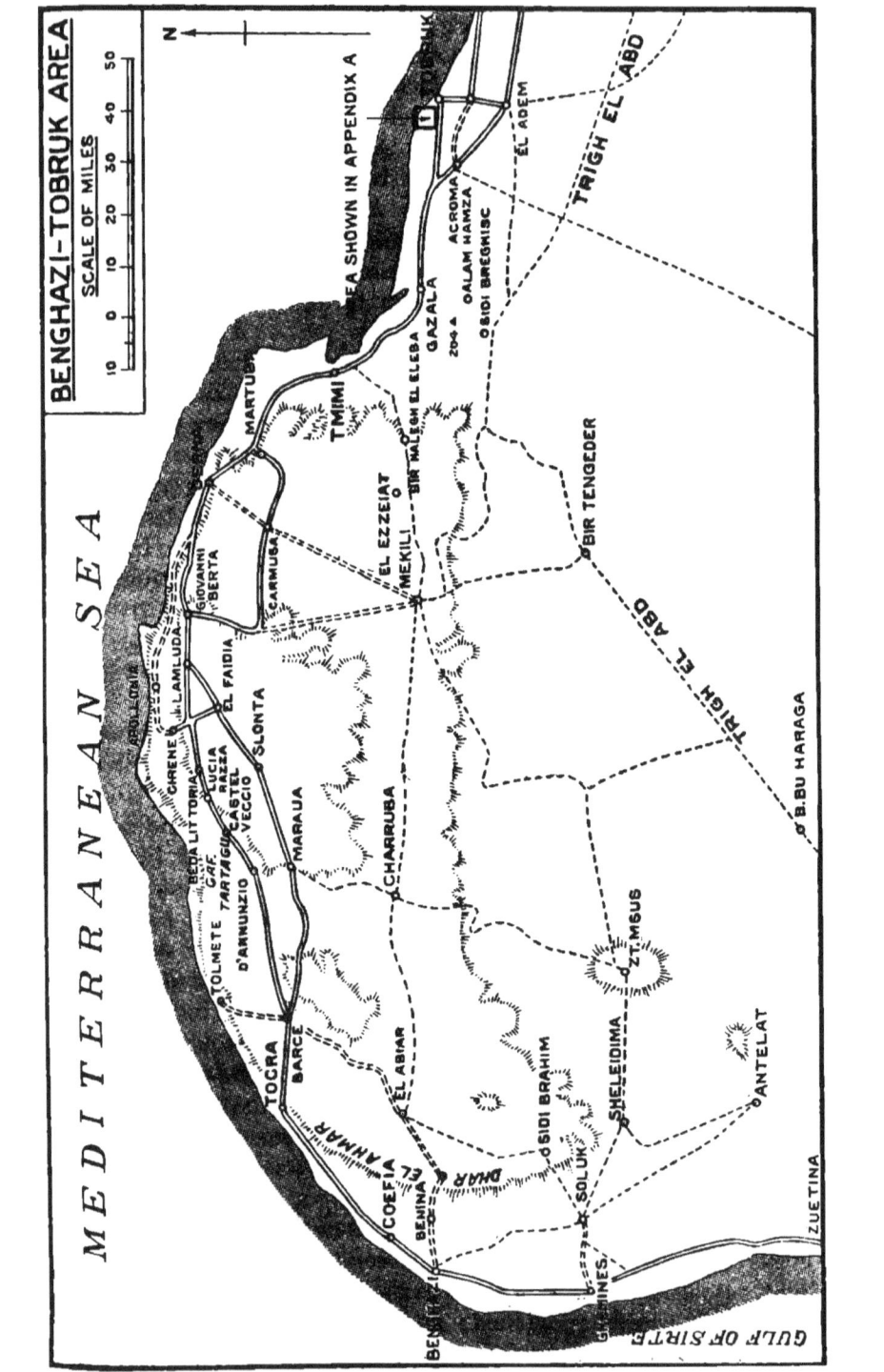

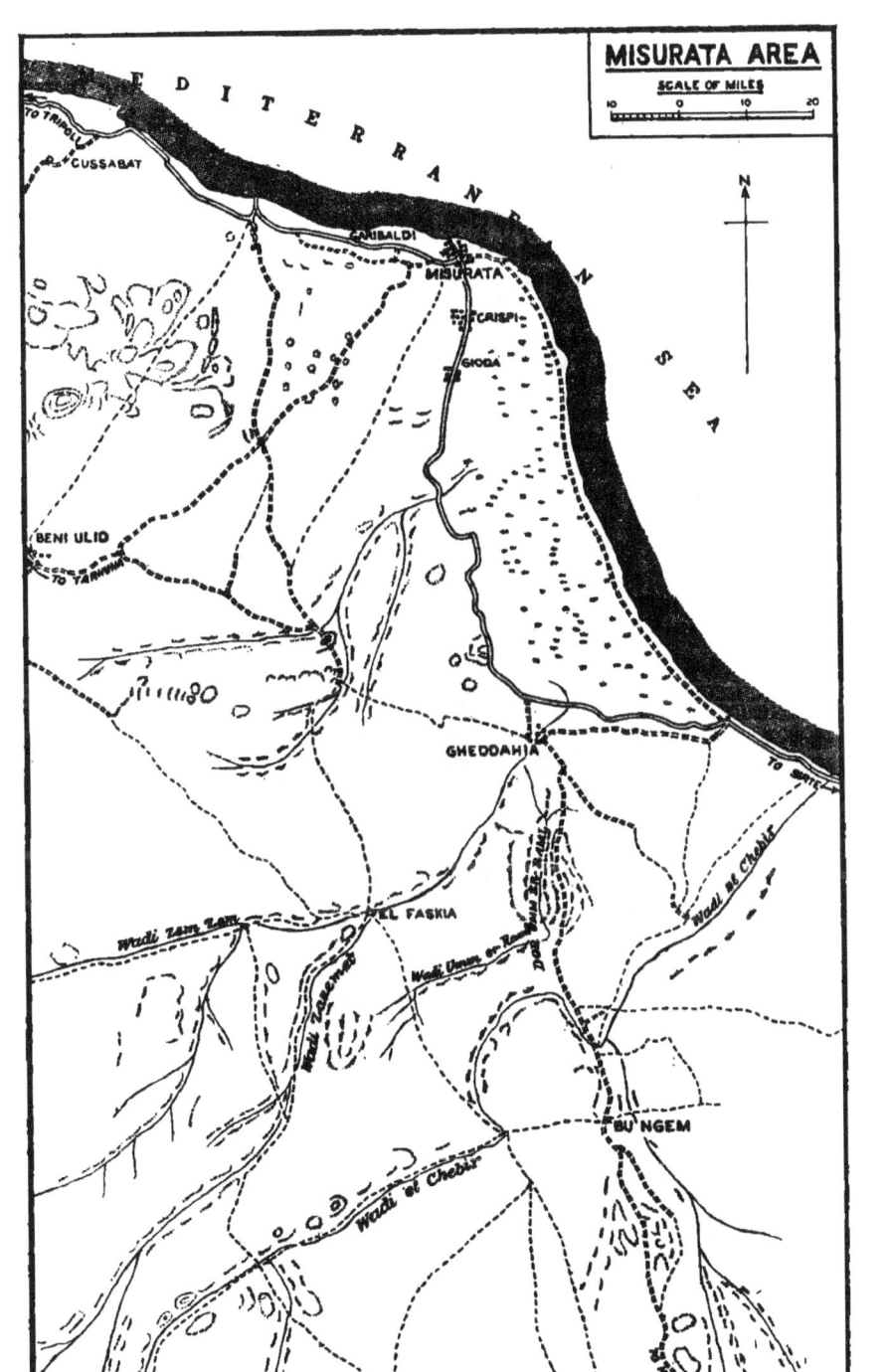

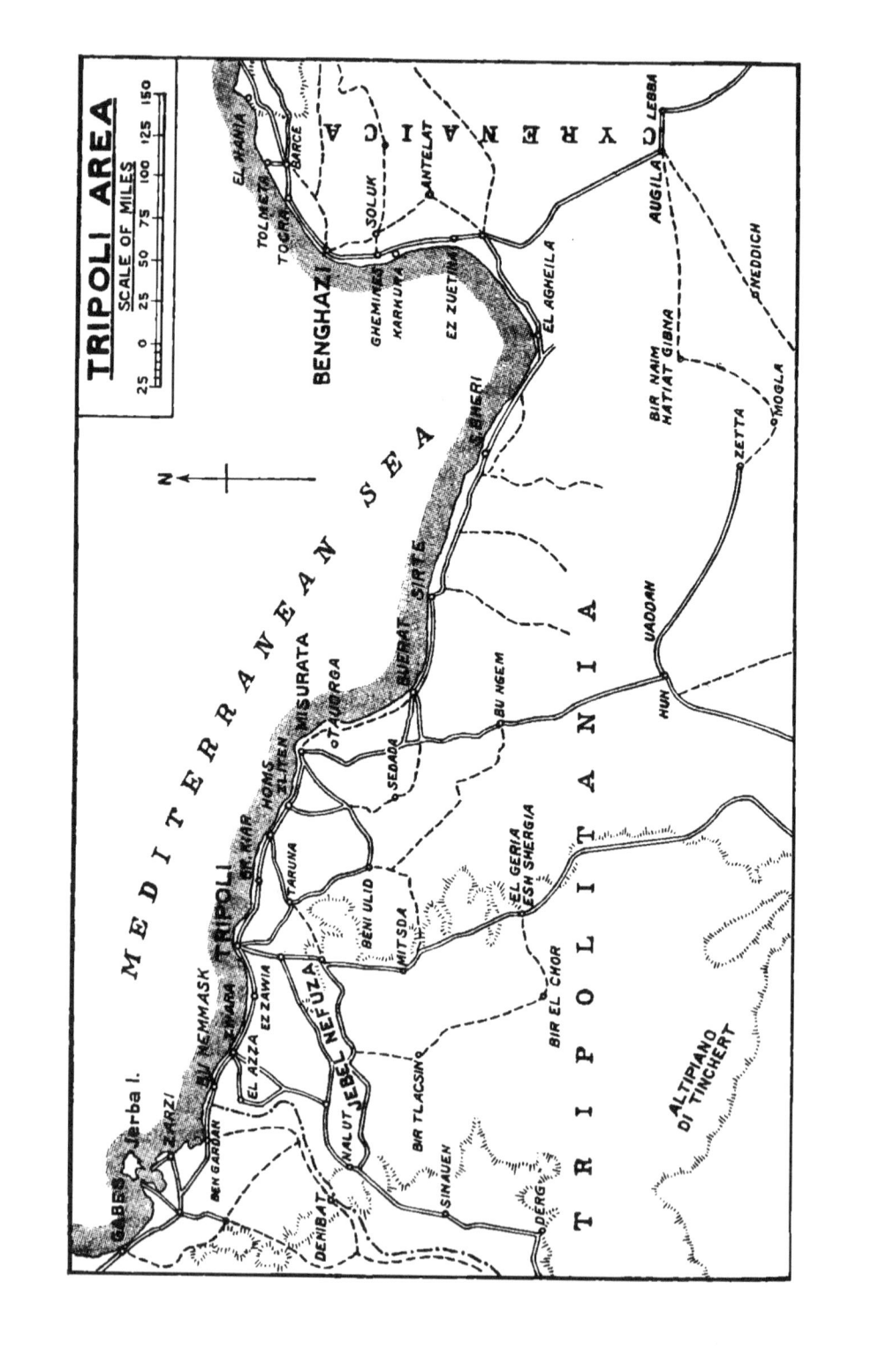

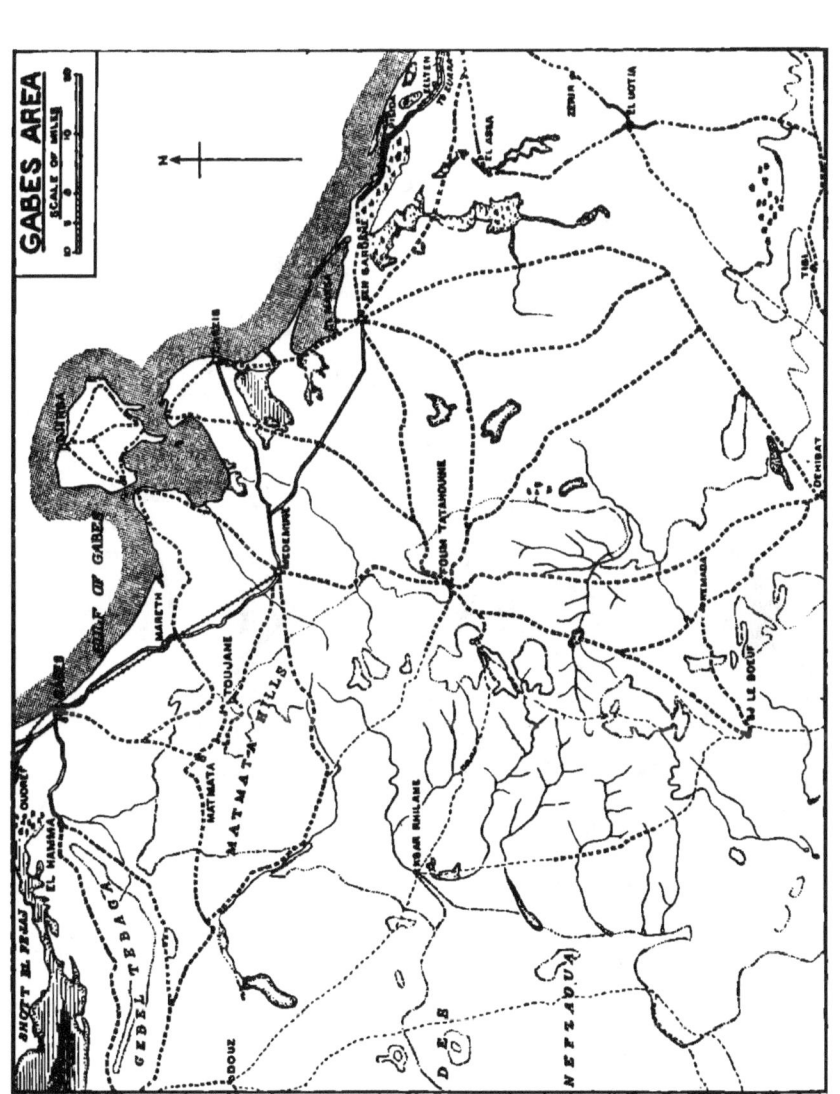

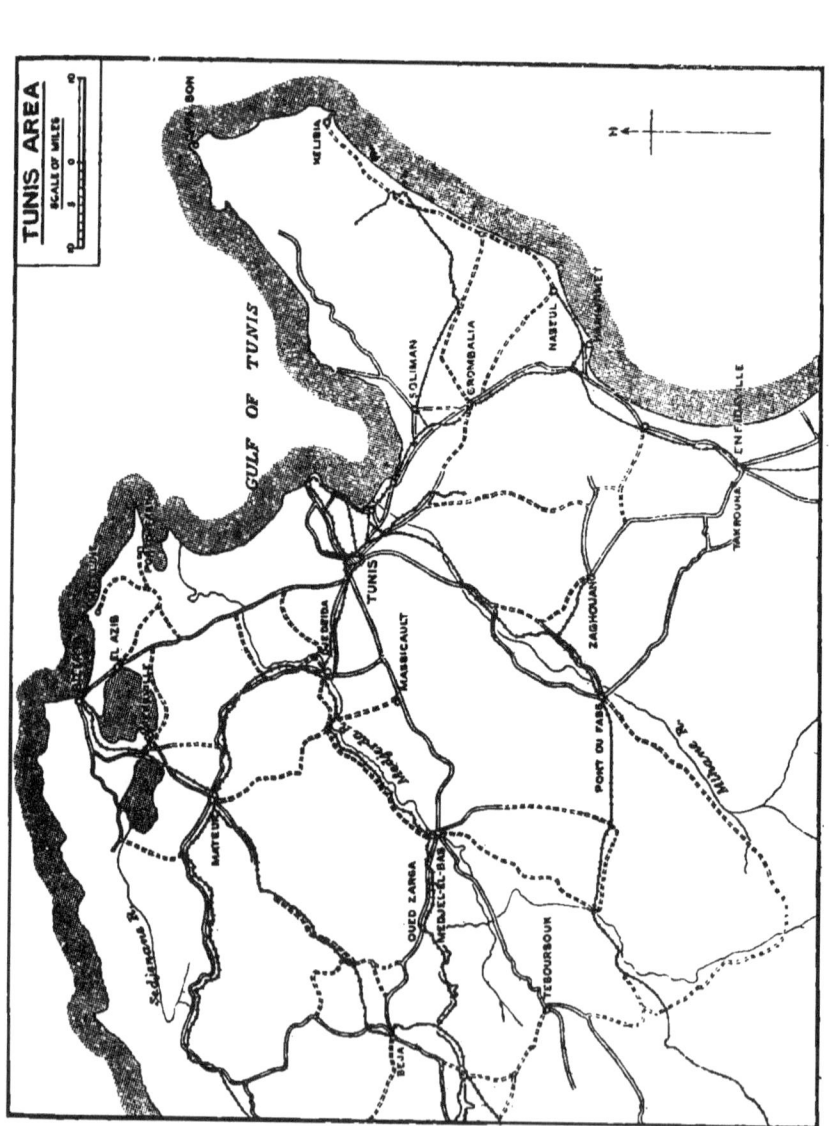

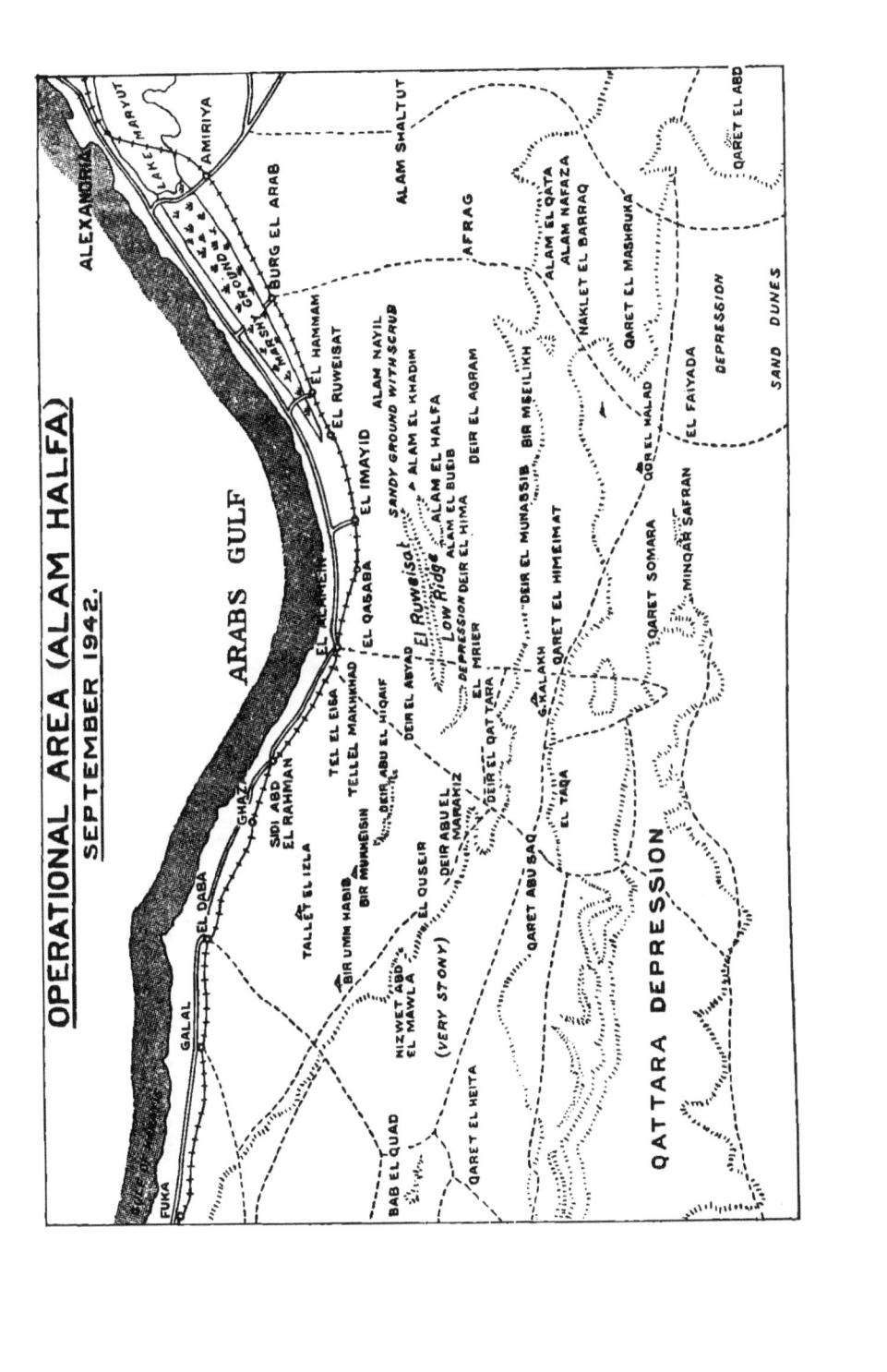

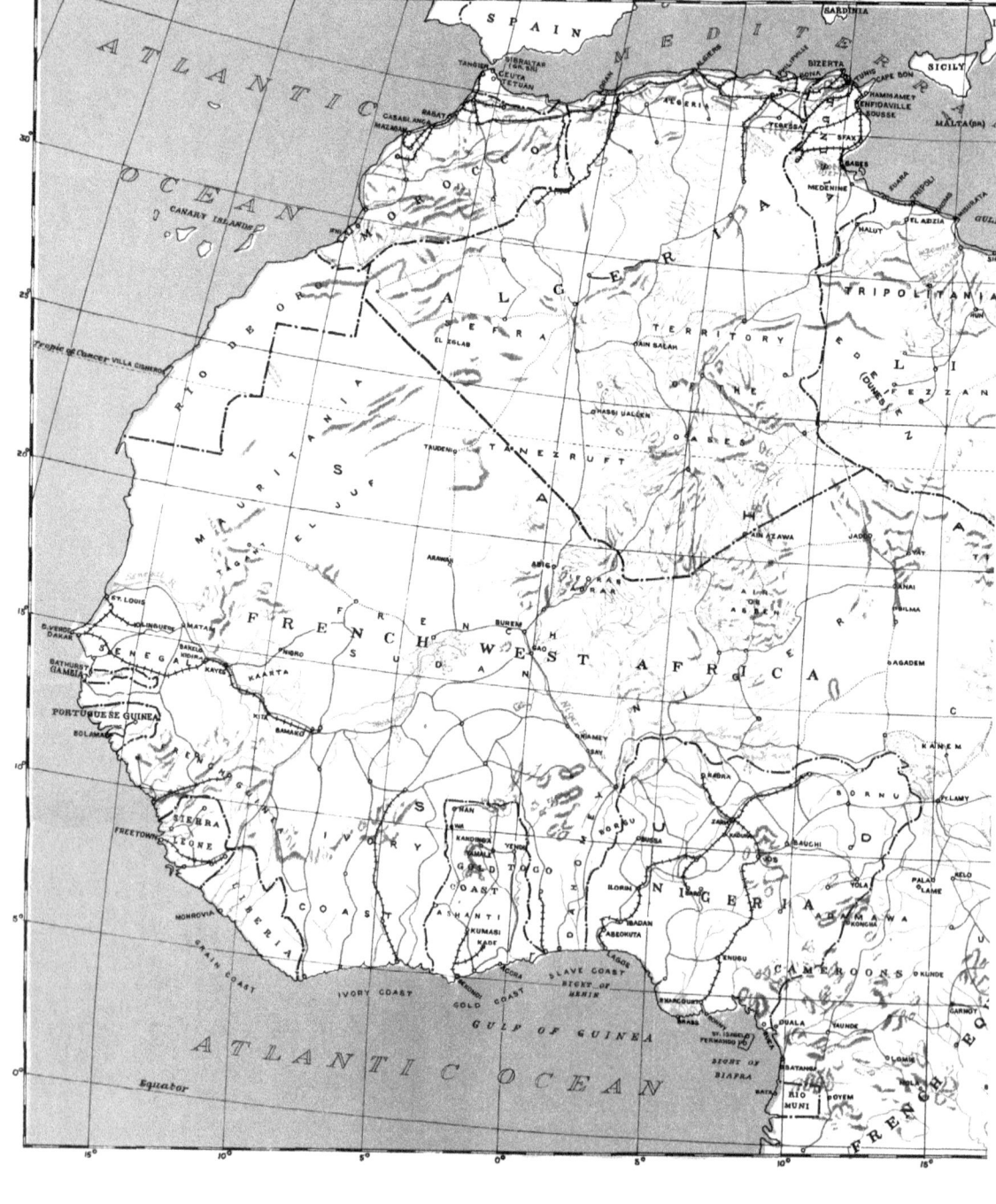

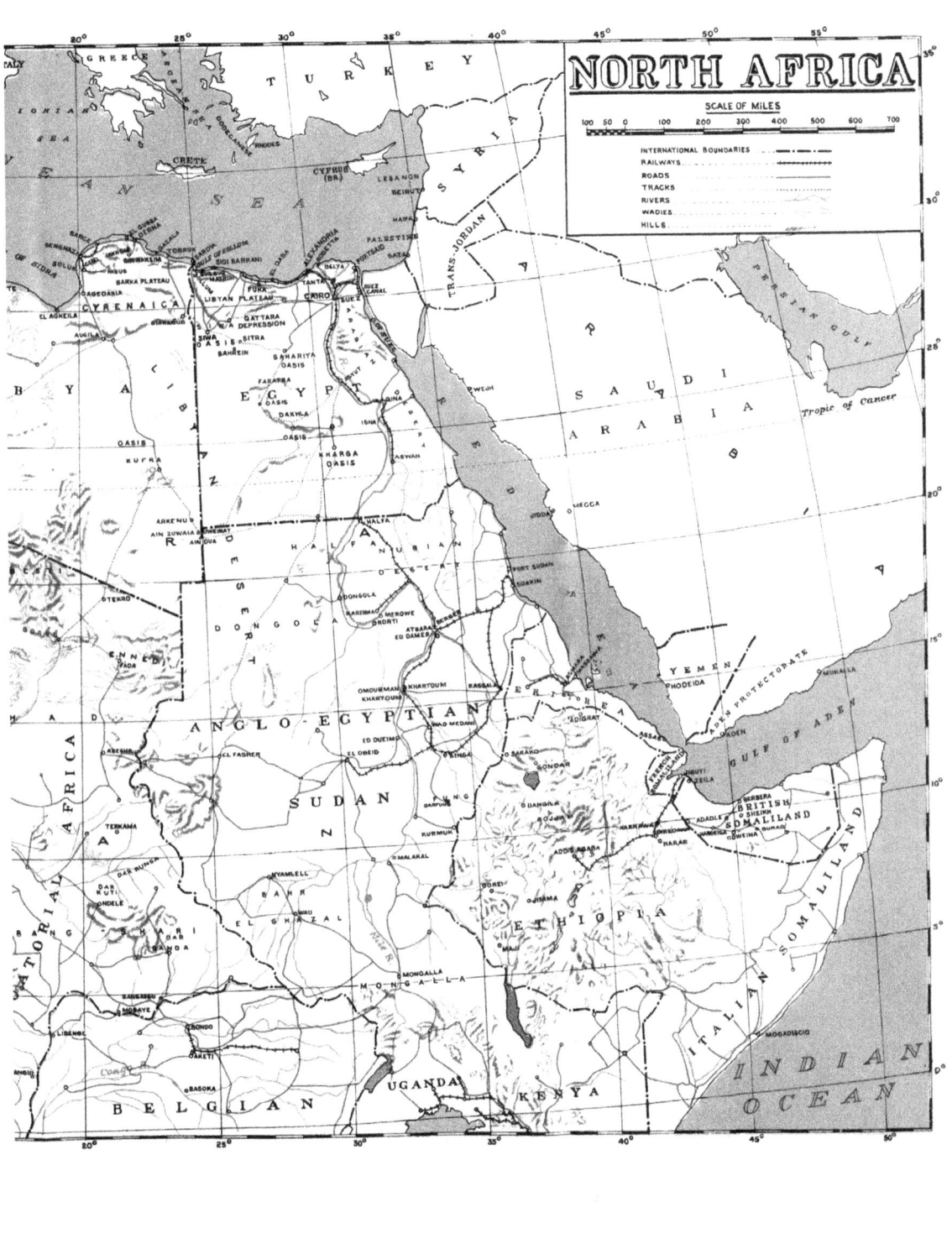

OFFICIAL HISTORY OF THE INDIAN ARMED FORCES
IN THE SECOND WORLD WAR
1939-45

CAMPAIGN IN WESTERN ASIA

Maps and Sketches

The Campaign in Western Asia
List of Maps

1. Example of a desert formation for an Infantry Brigade
2. Port of Basra
3. Projected Landings of Force "Trout"
4. Shuaiba Defences-May 1941
5. Basra Area
6. Attack on Habibshawi-24-May 1941
7. Mosul and Surrounding Area
8. Operations of 5 Indian Infantry Brigade in Syria, 8-9 June 1941
9. Kuneitra Defences
10. Damascus Area
11. Palmyra Area
12. 21 Indian Infantry Brig.ade Group's Advance to Tell Abiad, 30 June -9 July 1941
13. Sketch, Deir ez Zor, attaek by 4/13 F.F. Rifles, 3 July 1941
14. Raqqa—French counter-attack, 9-10 July 1941
15. Operations in N orth~East Syria, 2-11 July 1941
16. Iran-areas under the influence of Russia and Great Britain
17. Plan of Operations in South-West Iran—25 to 28 August 1941
18. Sketch map of Abadan
19. Advance into West Iran
20. Division of Military areas in Iraq and Iran
21. Iraq and Iran Transport in Aid to Russia
22. Iraq
23. Disposition of'lraqi ttoops at Habbaniya-1 May 1941
24. Occupation of Maqil-2 May 1941
25. Attack on Falluja-18-23 May 1941
26. Mosul aerodrome area Defences-29. June-1941
27. The Persian Gulf showing Defensive Layout
28. Defence of Iraq—1 September 1941–Plan
29. Plan 'Wonderful'—Proposed demolition zones and devastation areas in Iraq and Iran

30	Iraq and Iran, readjustment of Commands–23 July 1942
31	Syria
32	Deir'ez Zor—attack by 2/10 Gurkha Rifles 3 July 1941
33	Map of Iran
34	Khurramshahr
35	Attack on Qasr Shaikh
36	Plan Garment
37	Caucasia
38	Western Asia

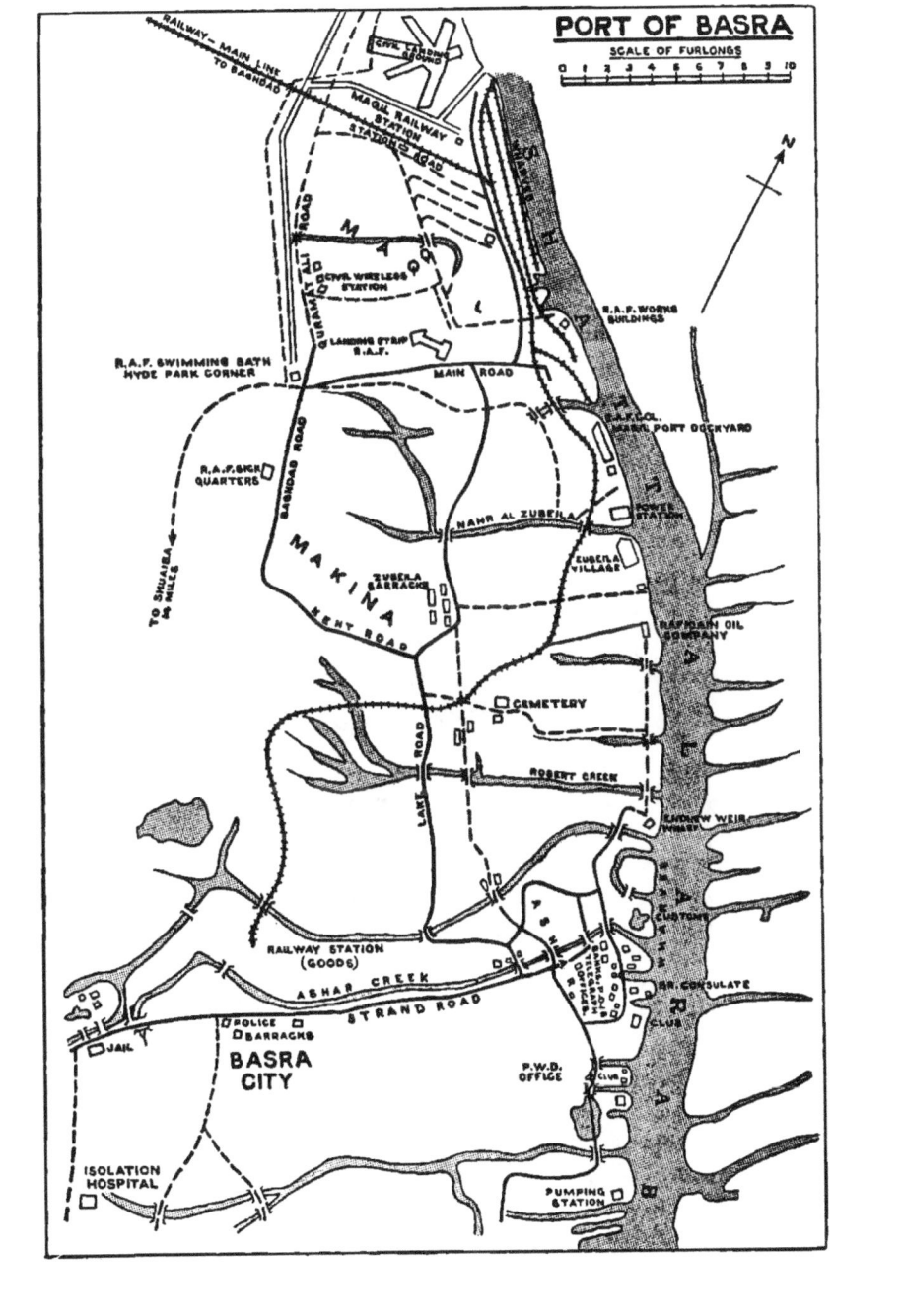

SKETCH MAP OF
PROJECTED LANDINGS OF FORCE "TROUT"

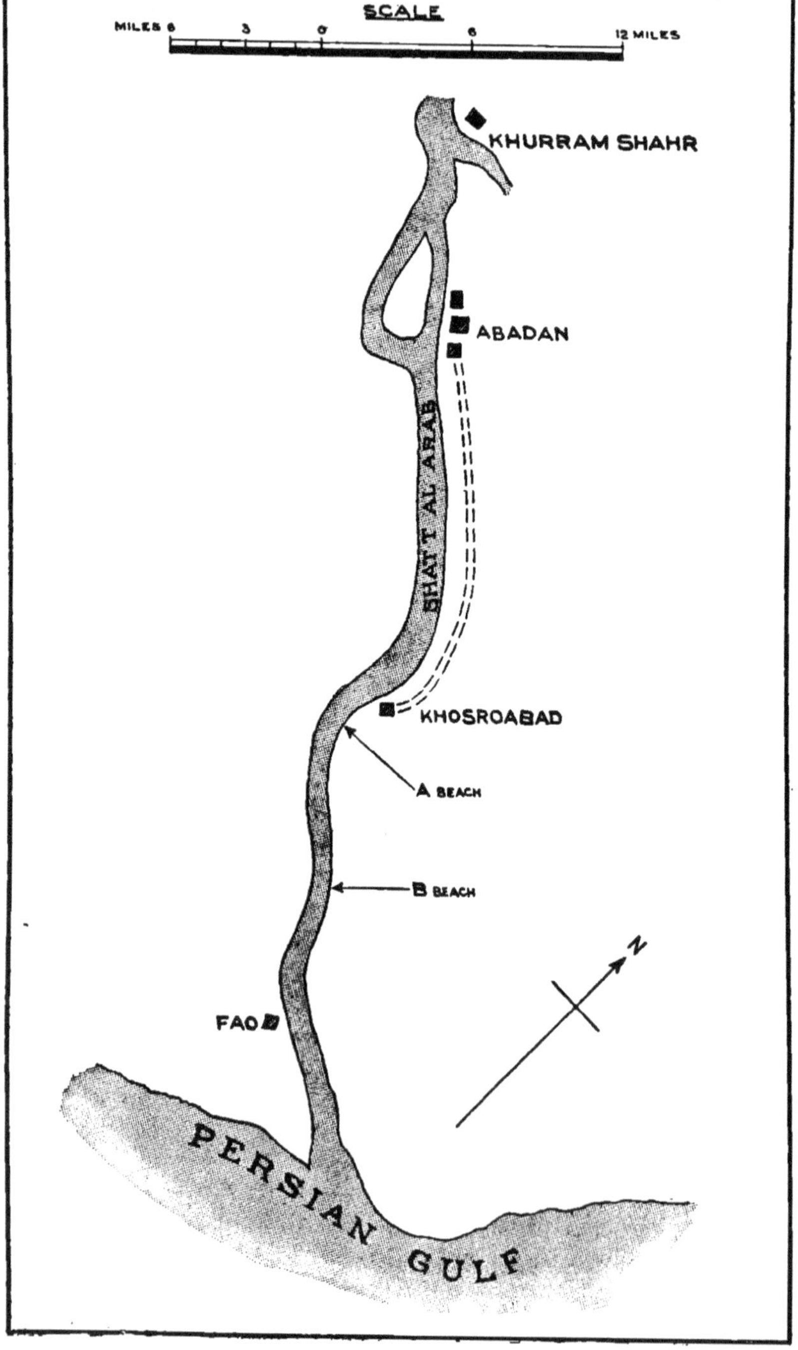

SCALE
MILES 6   3   0   6   12 MILES

- KHURRAM SHAHR
- ABADAN
- SHATT AL ARAB
- KHOSROABAD
- A BEACH
- B BEACH
- FAO
- PERSIAN GULF

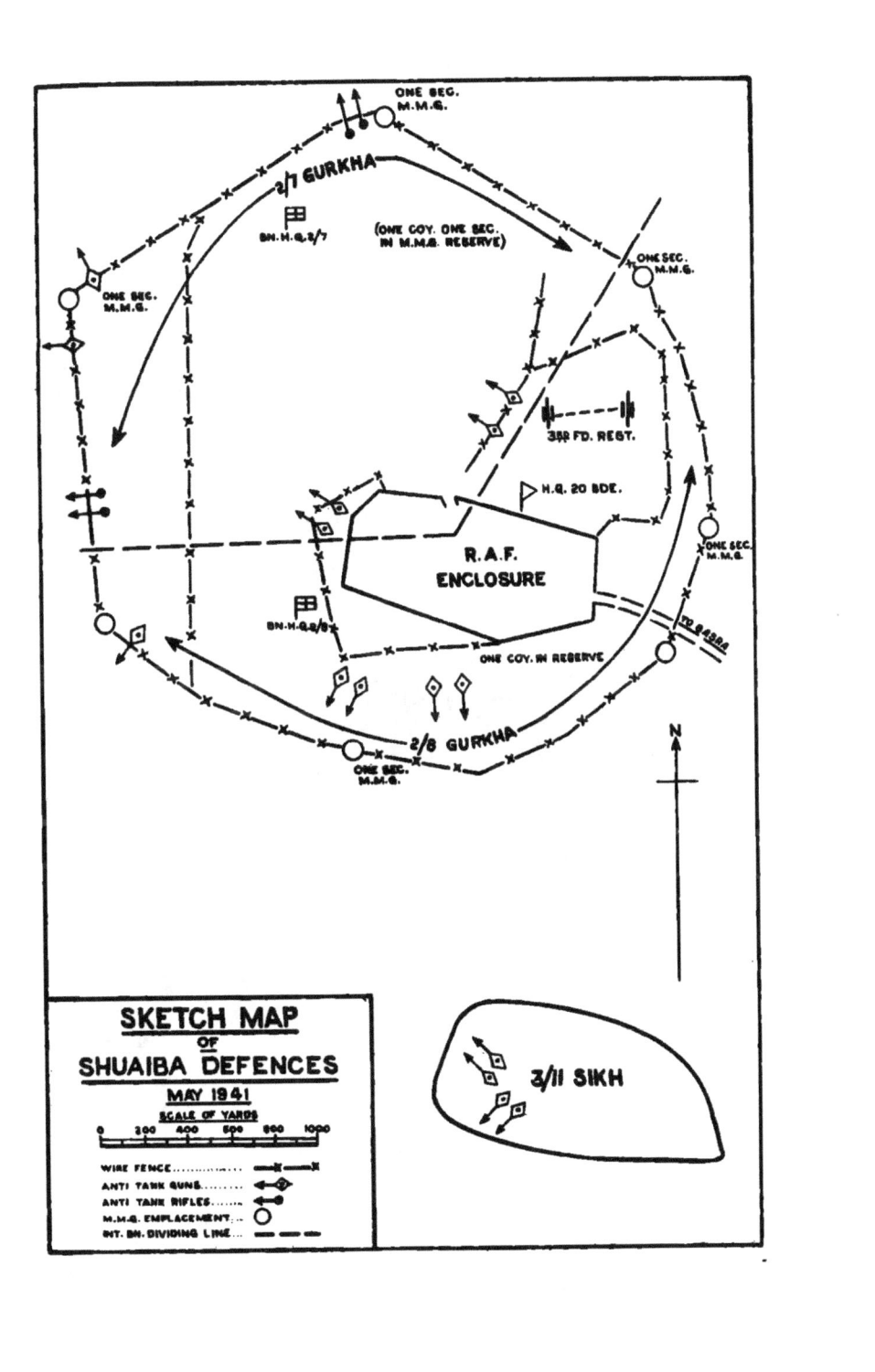

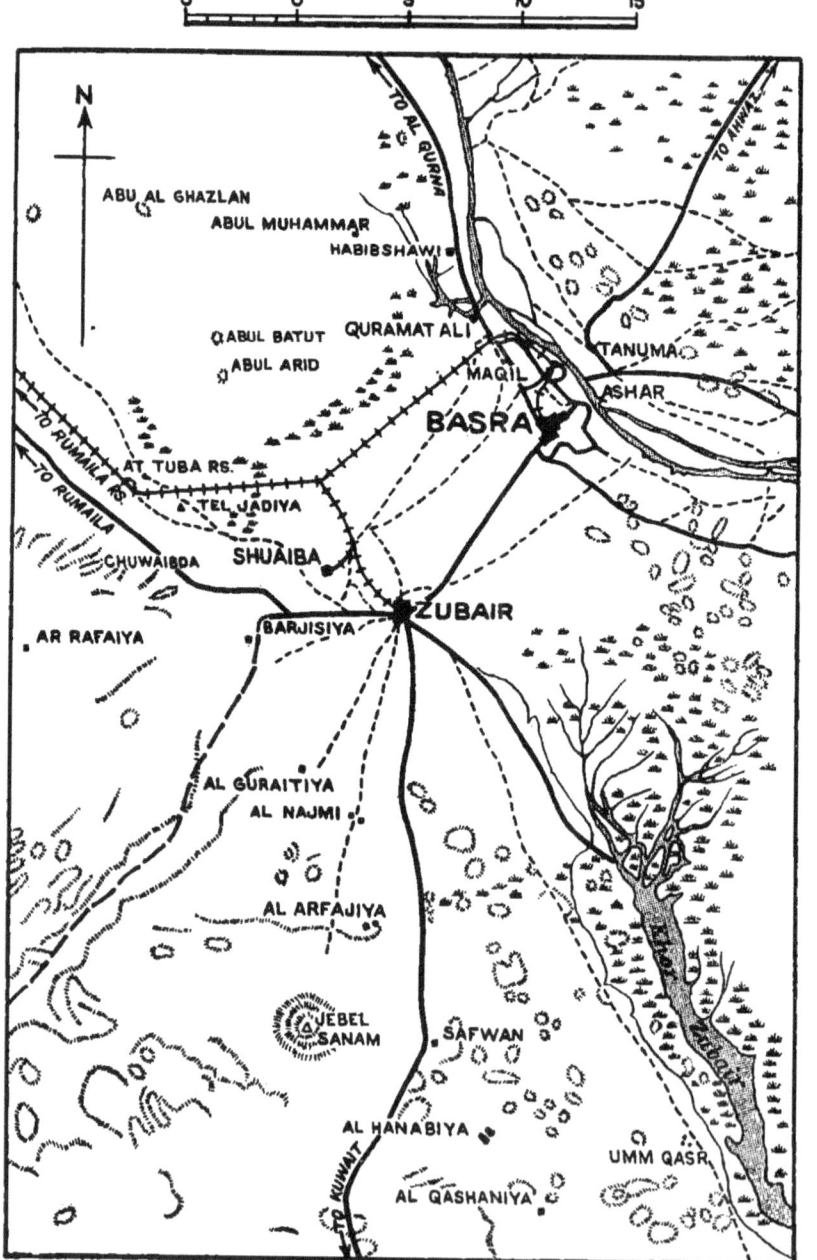

MOSUL AND SURROUNDING AREA

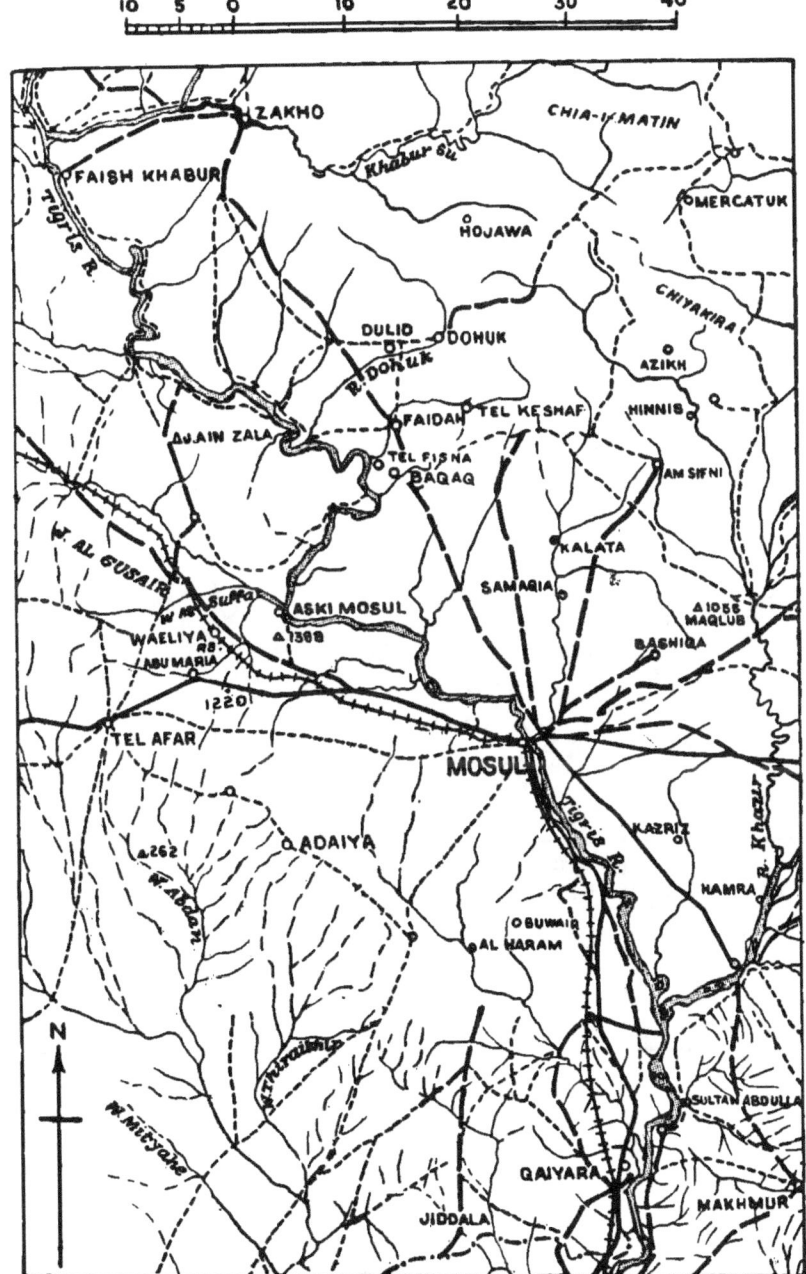

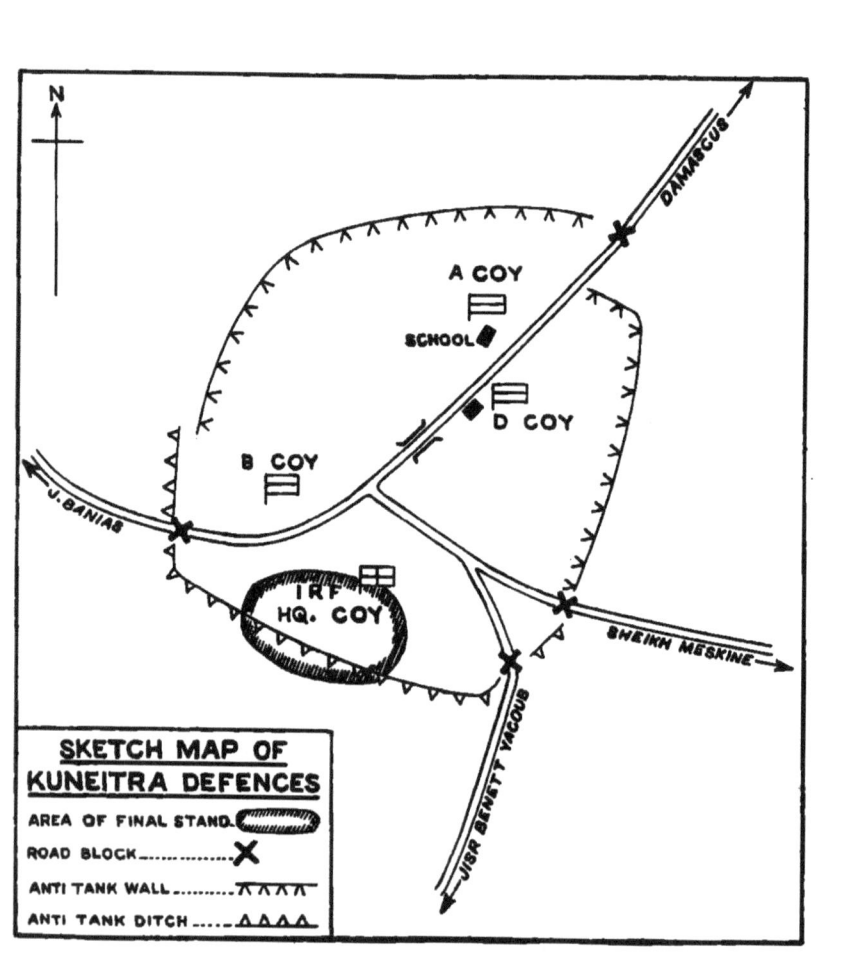

DAMASCUS AREA

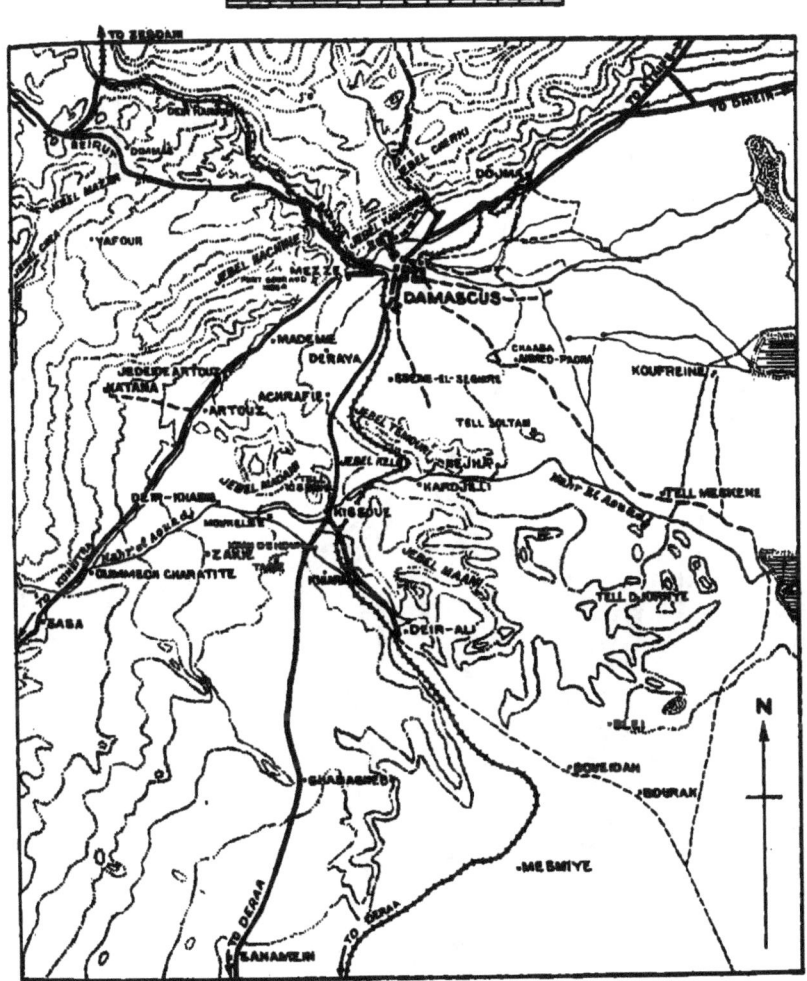

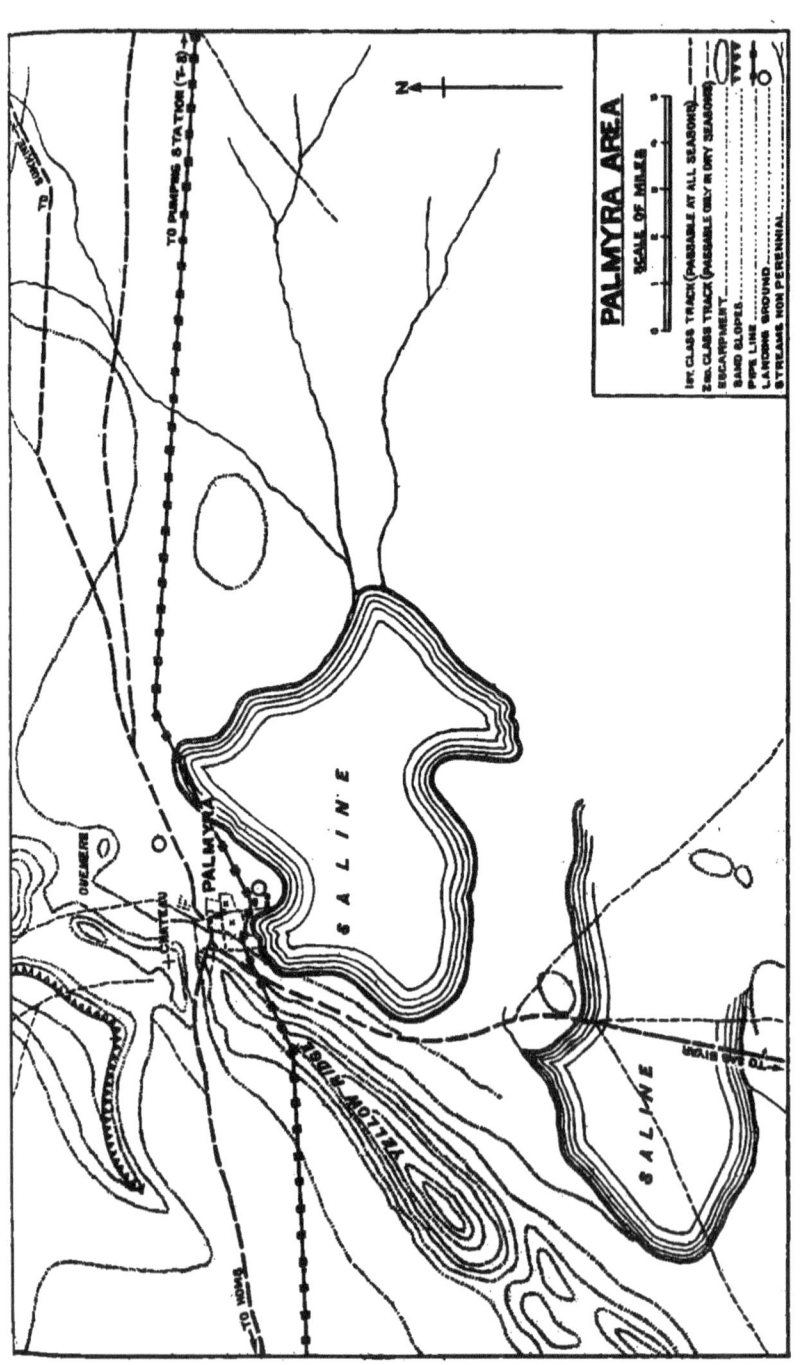

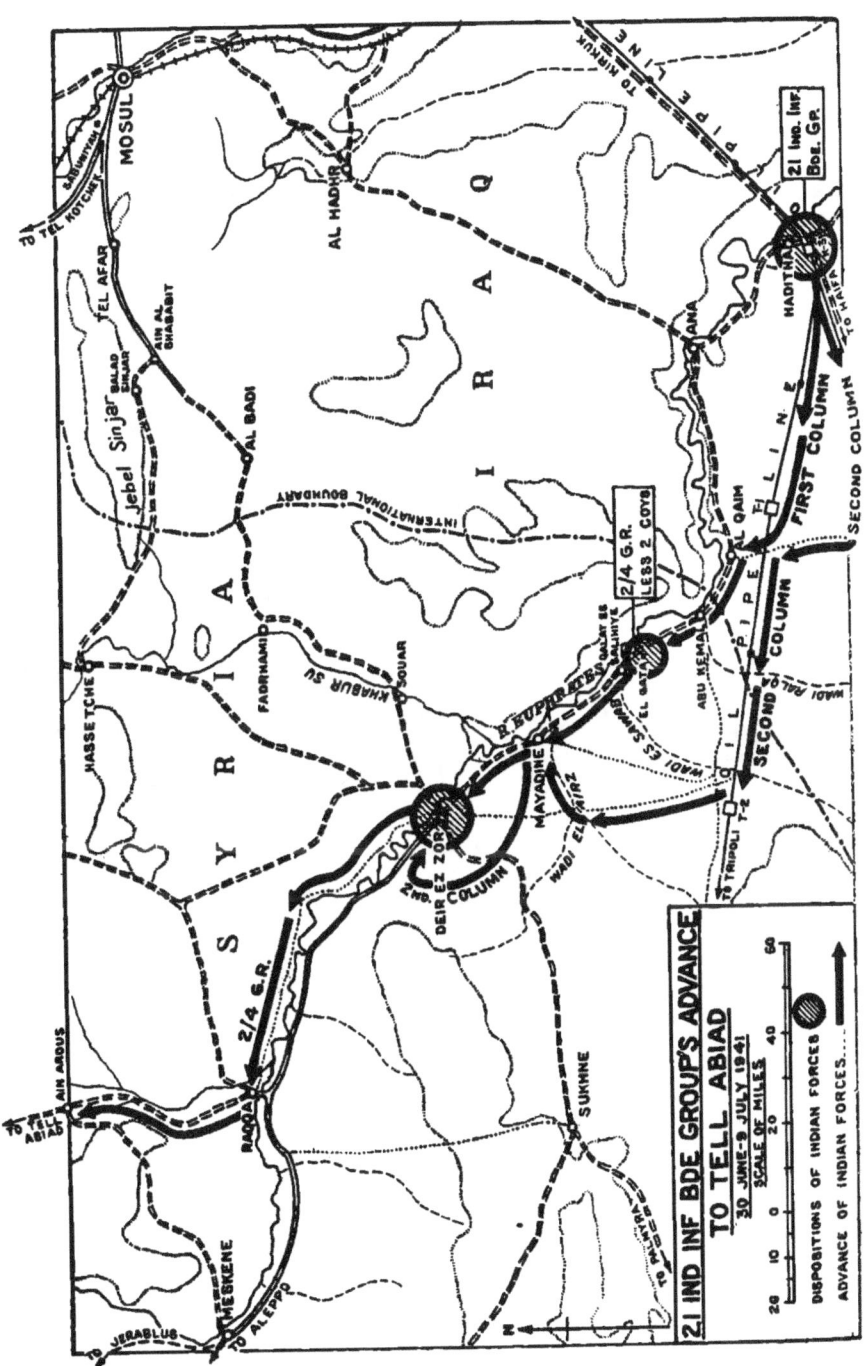

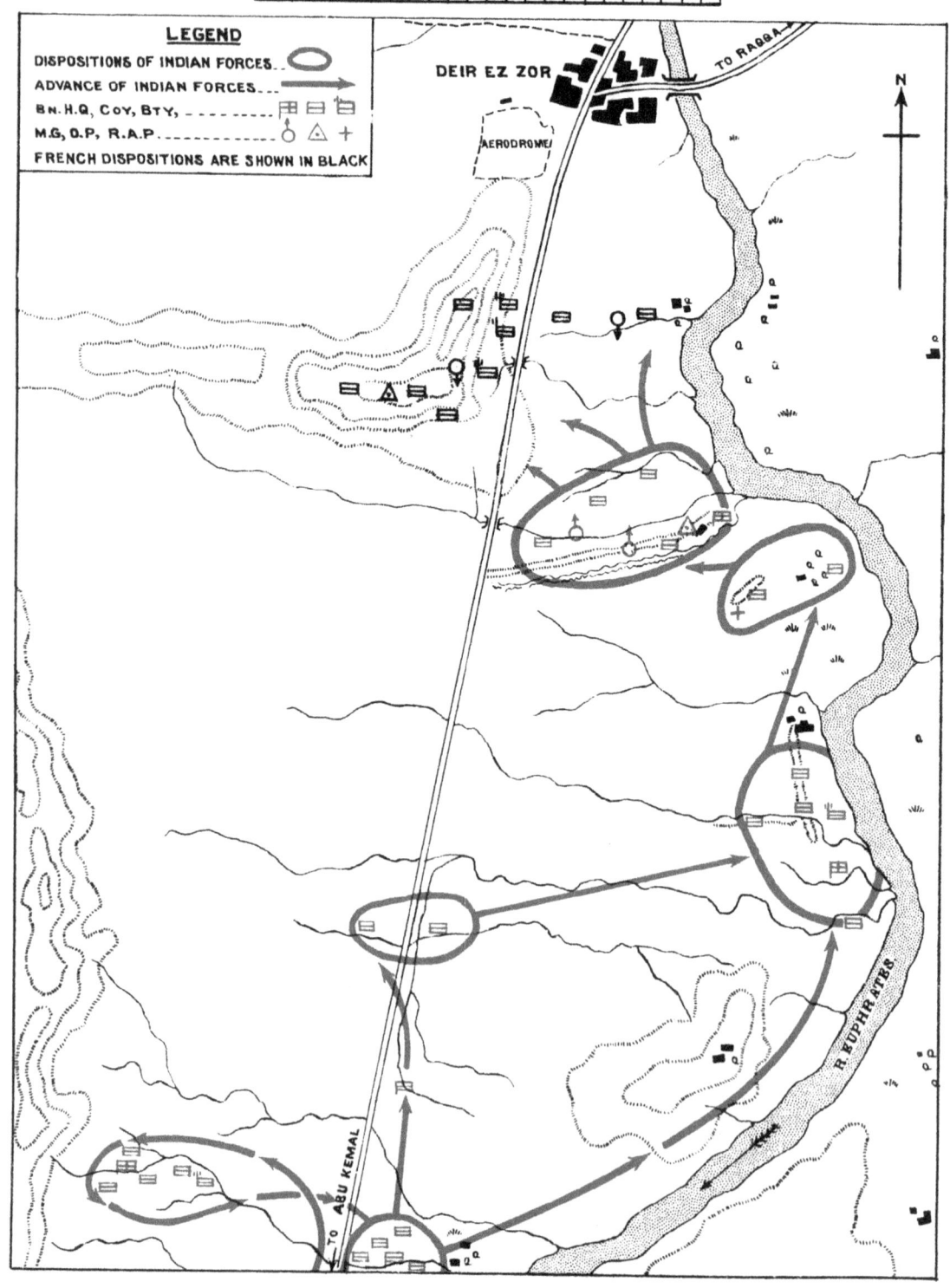

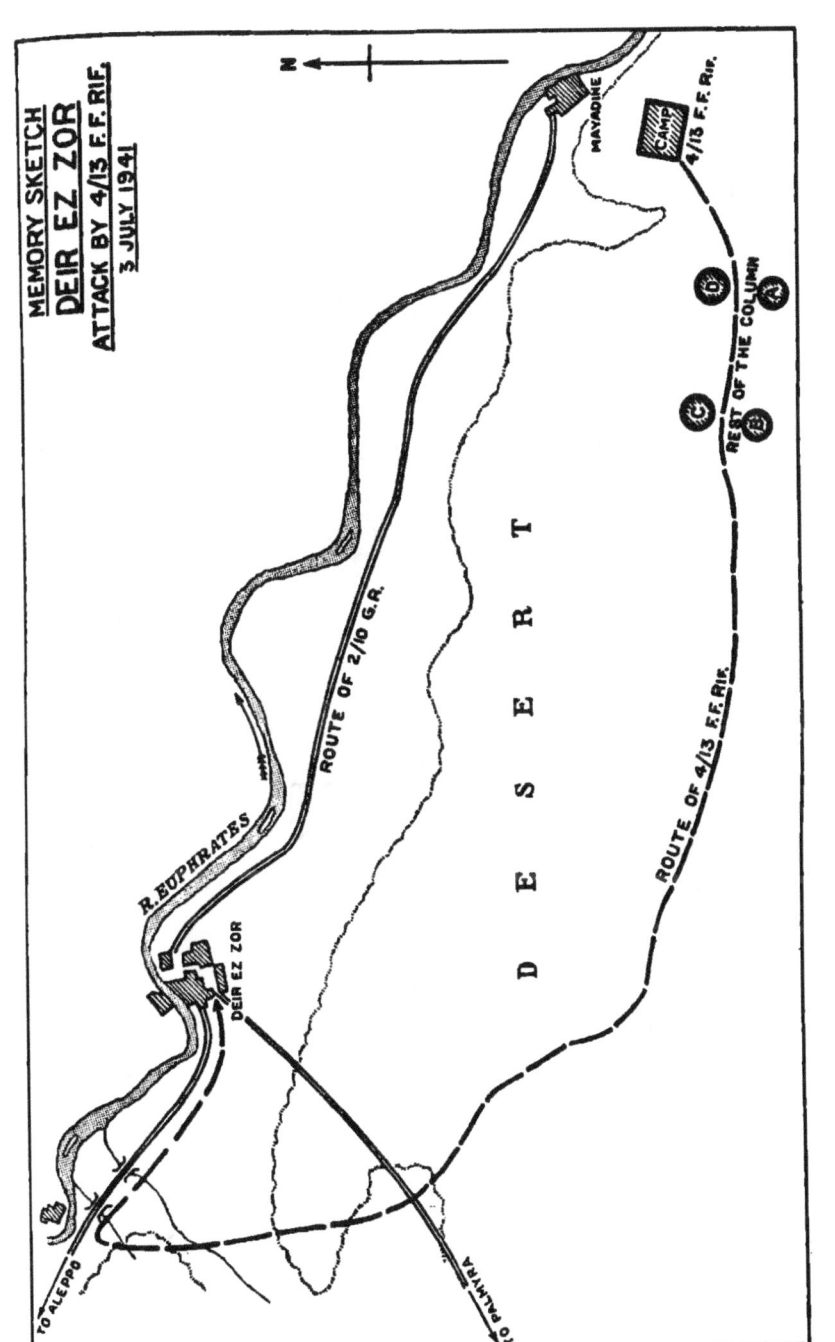

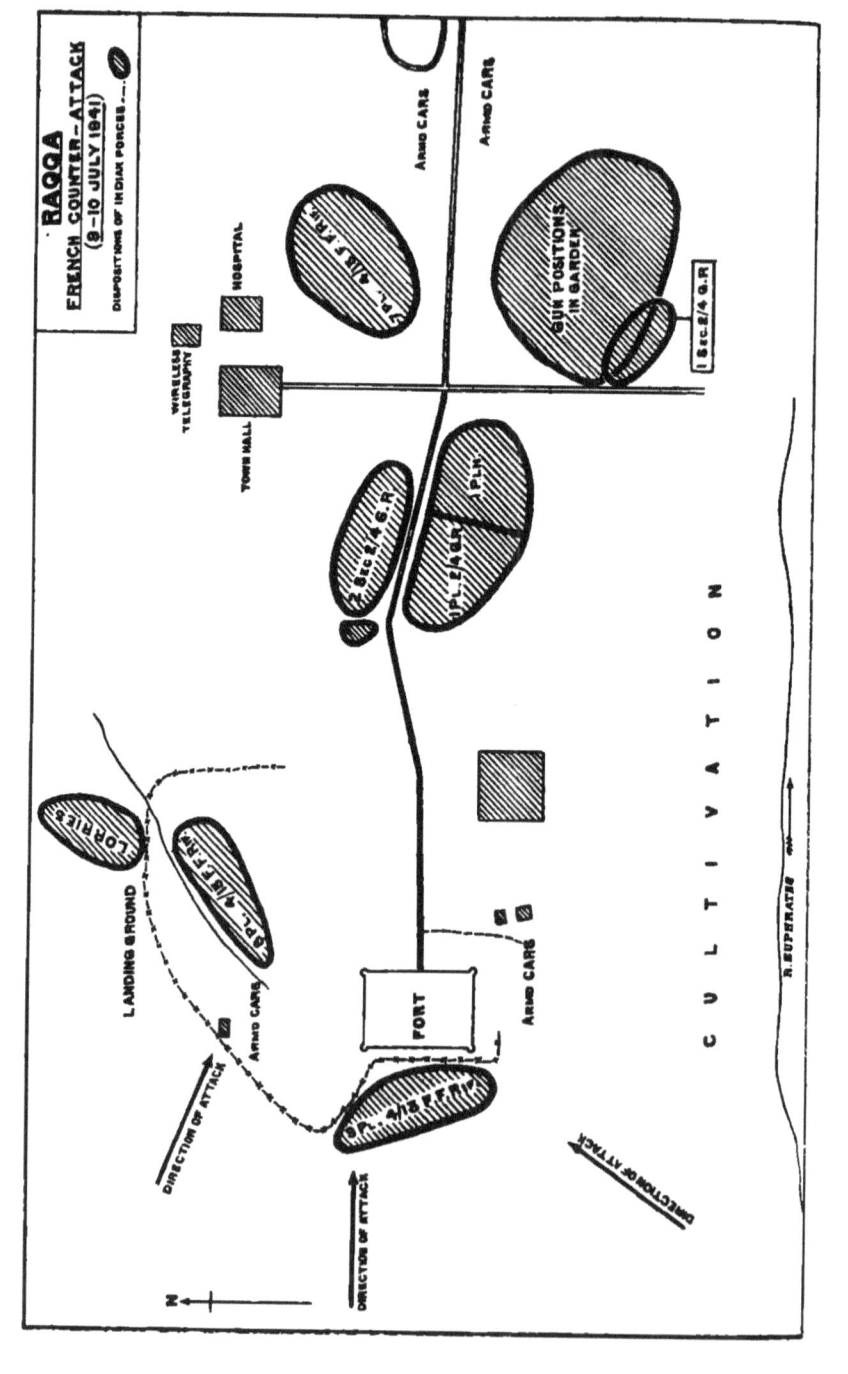

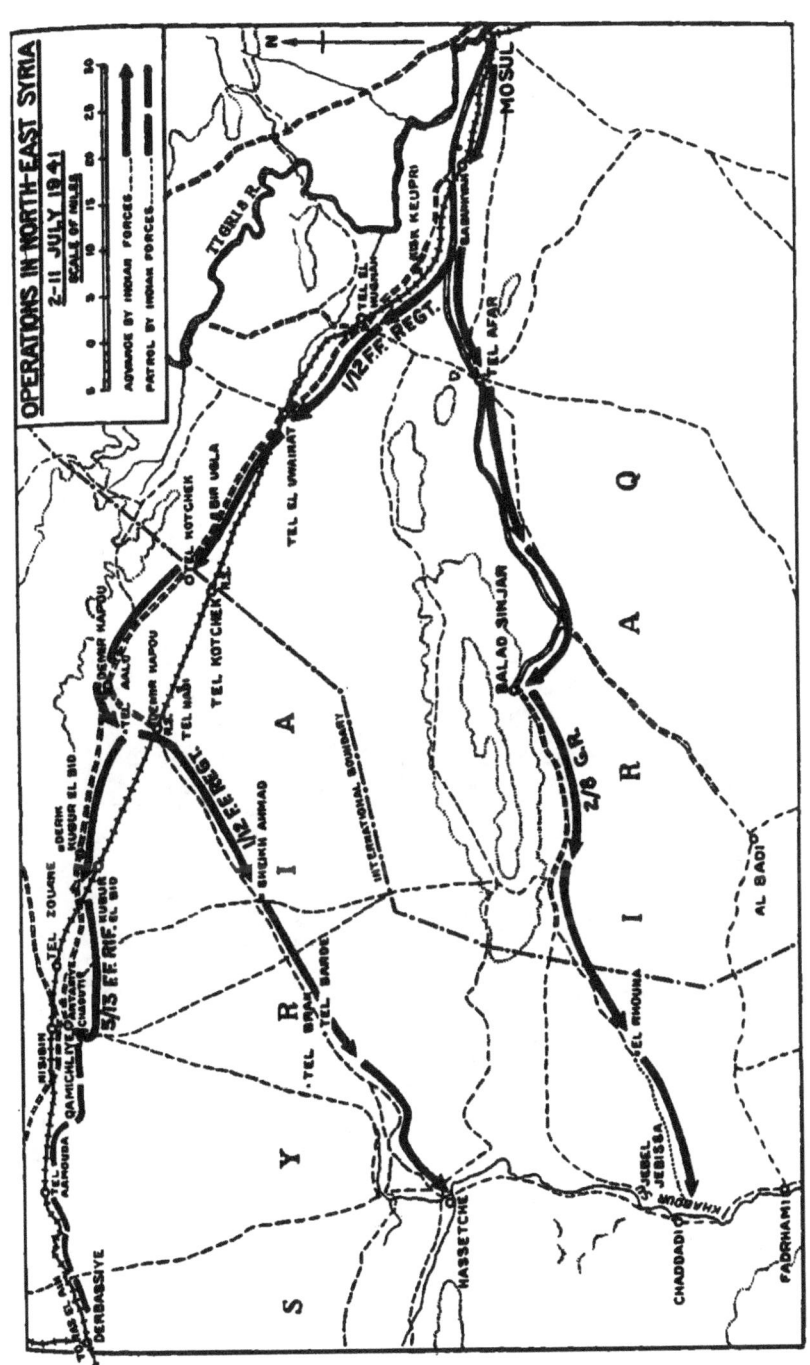

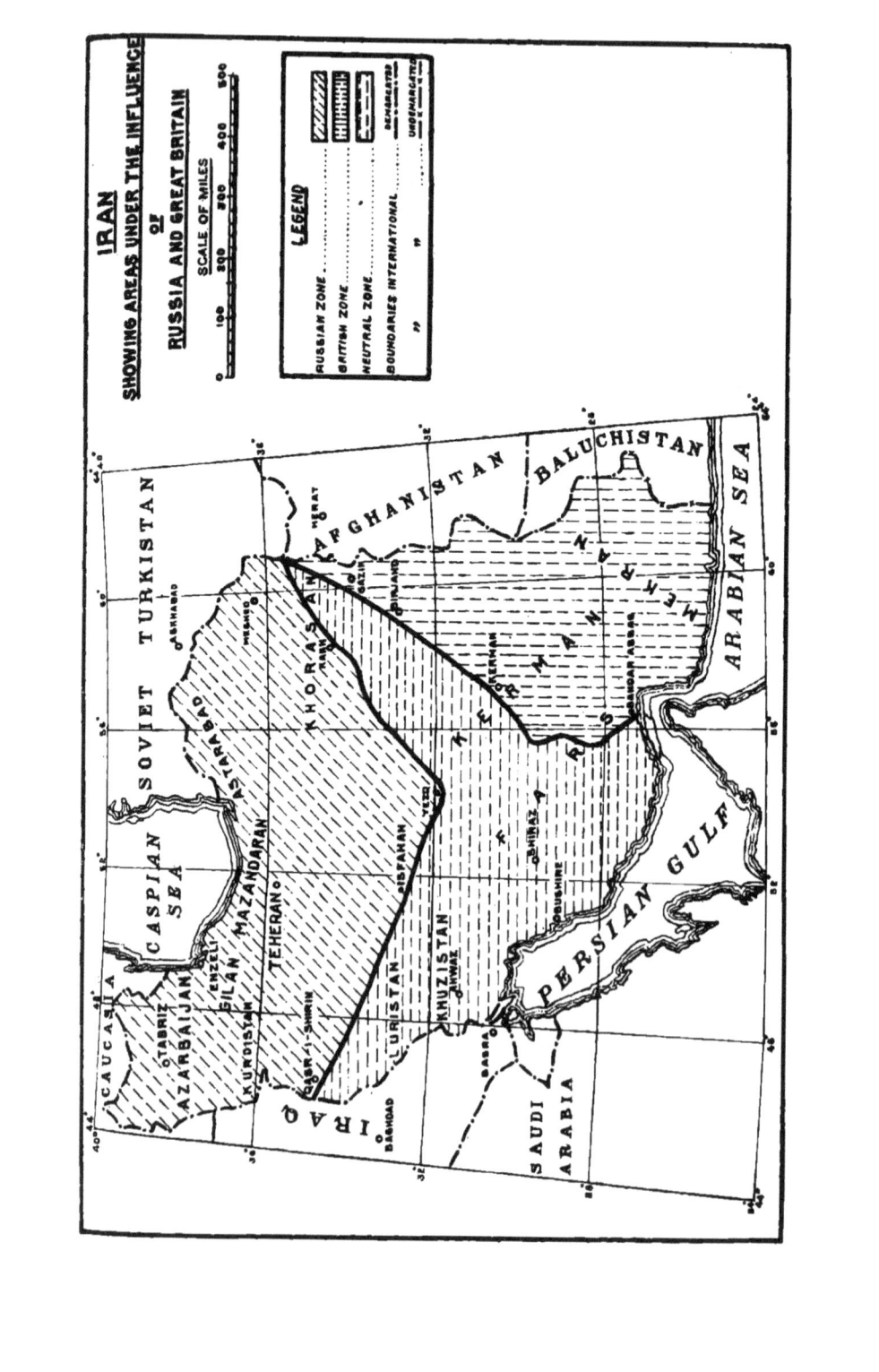

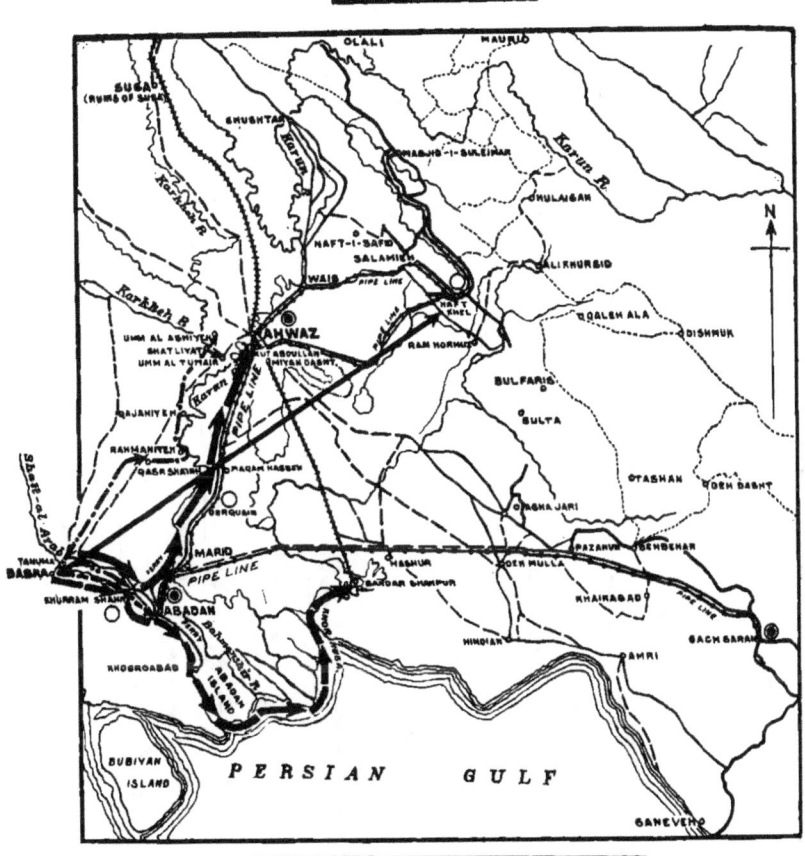

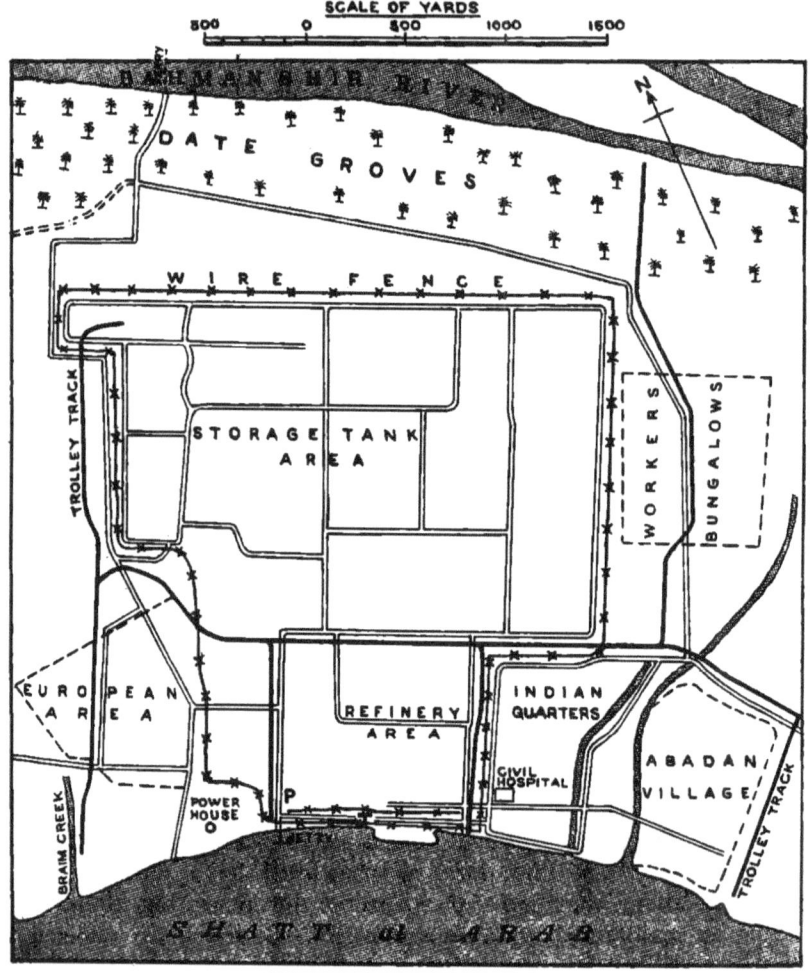

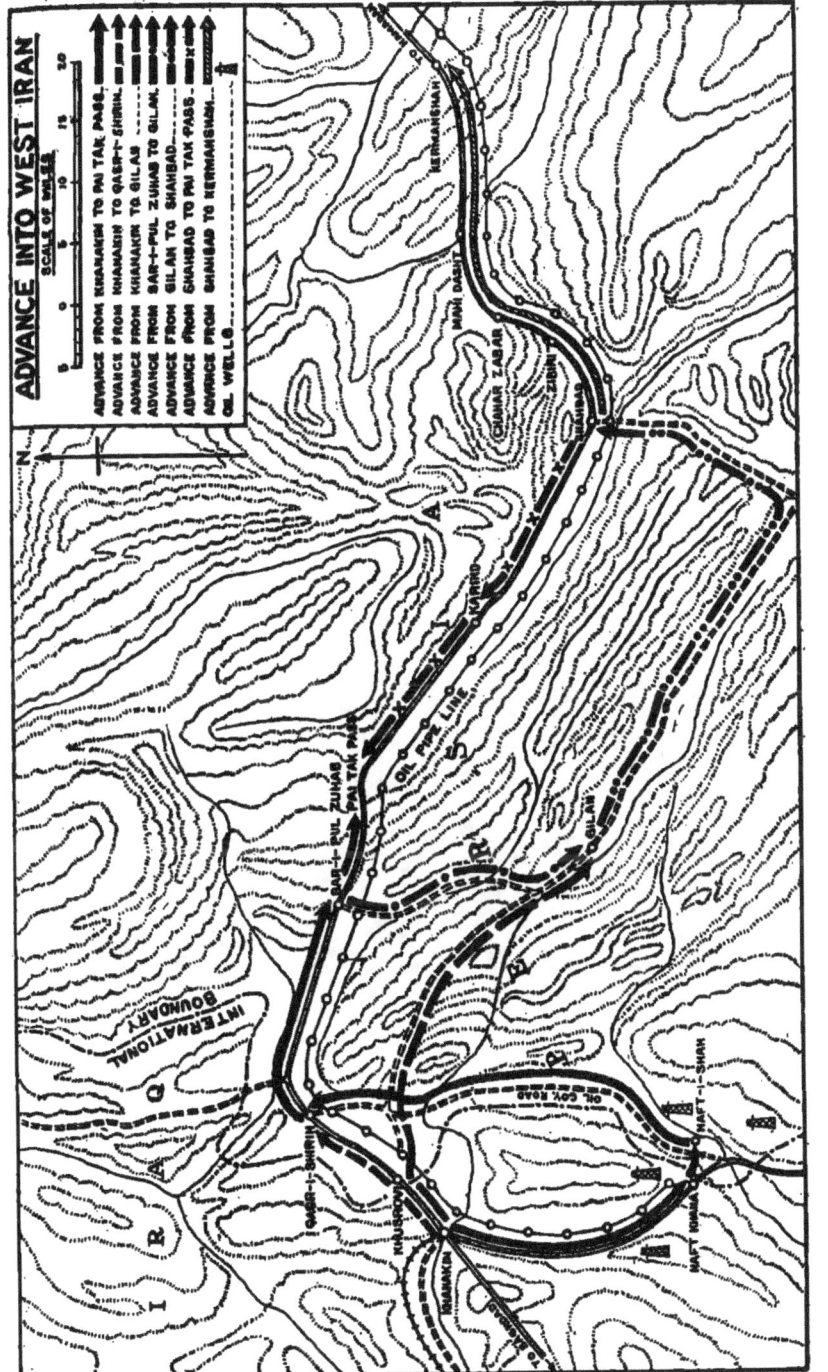

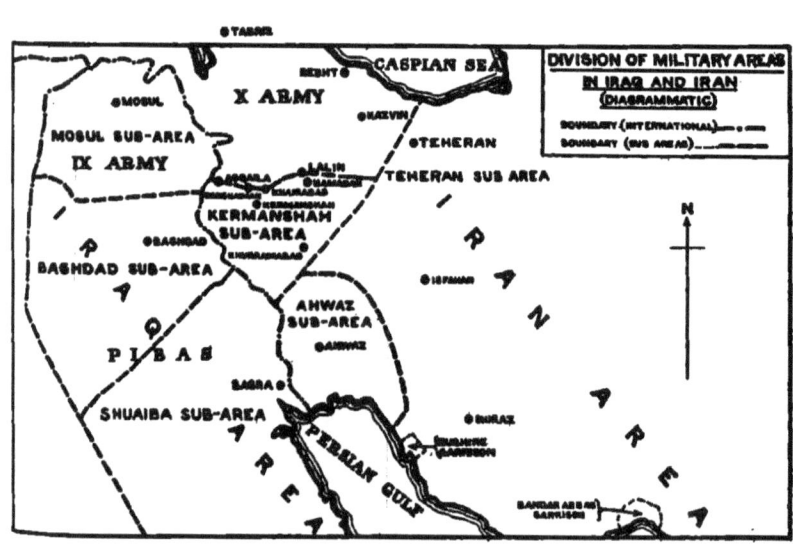

IRAQ AND IRAN
TRANSPORT IN AID TO RUSSIA
DIAGRAMMATIC

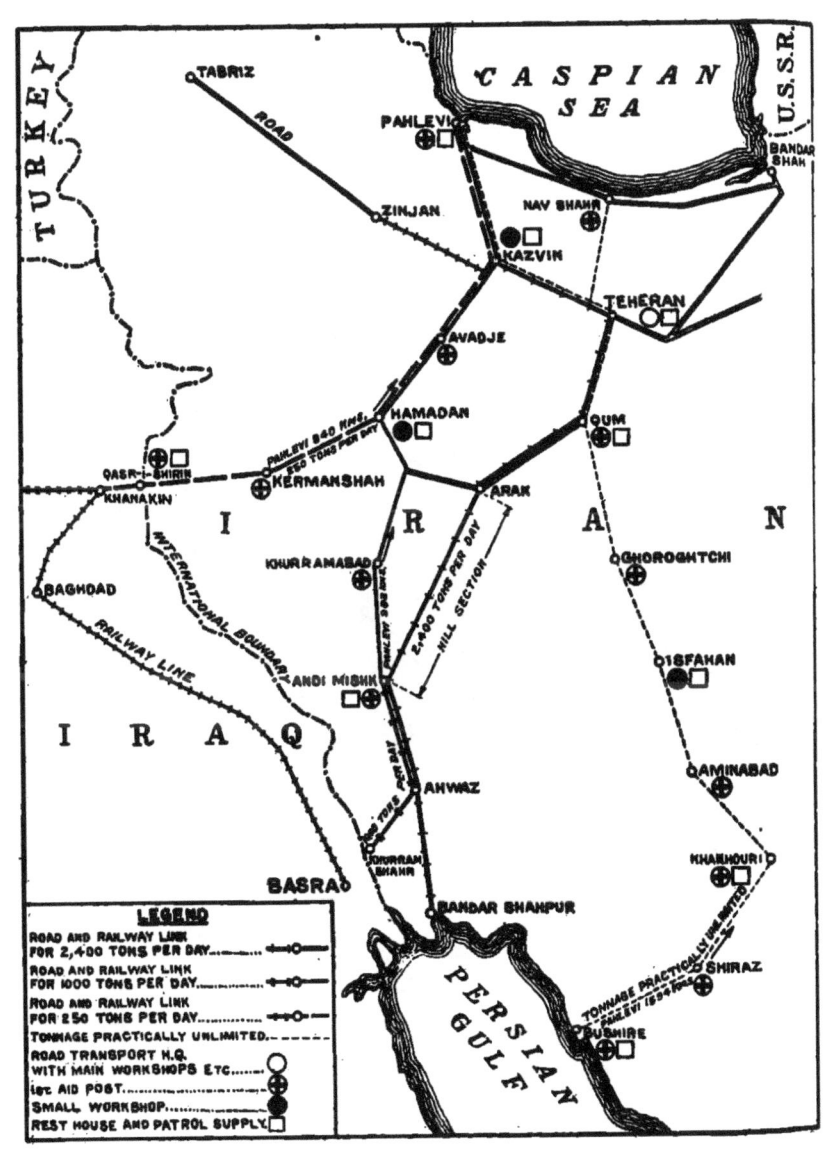

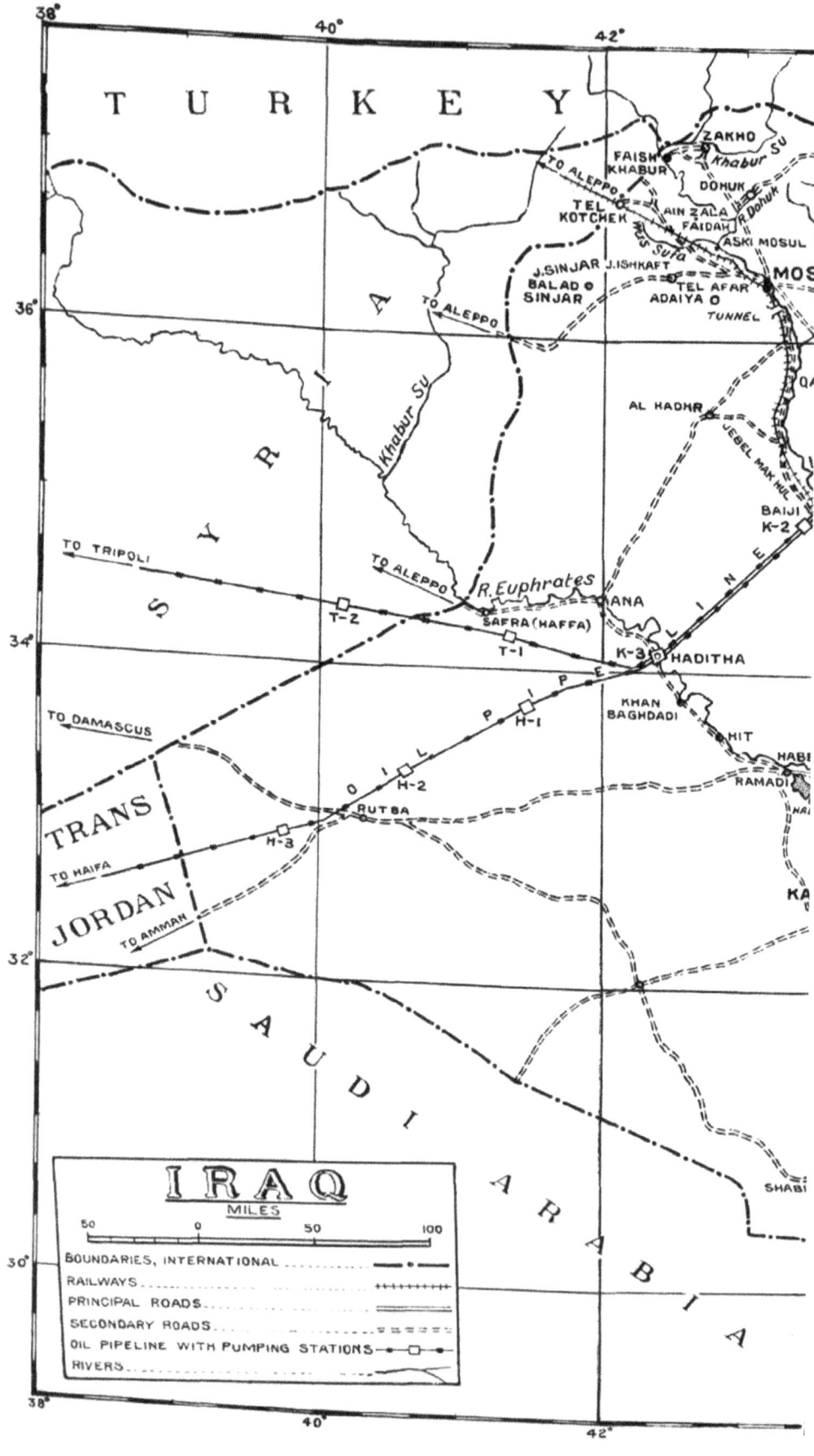

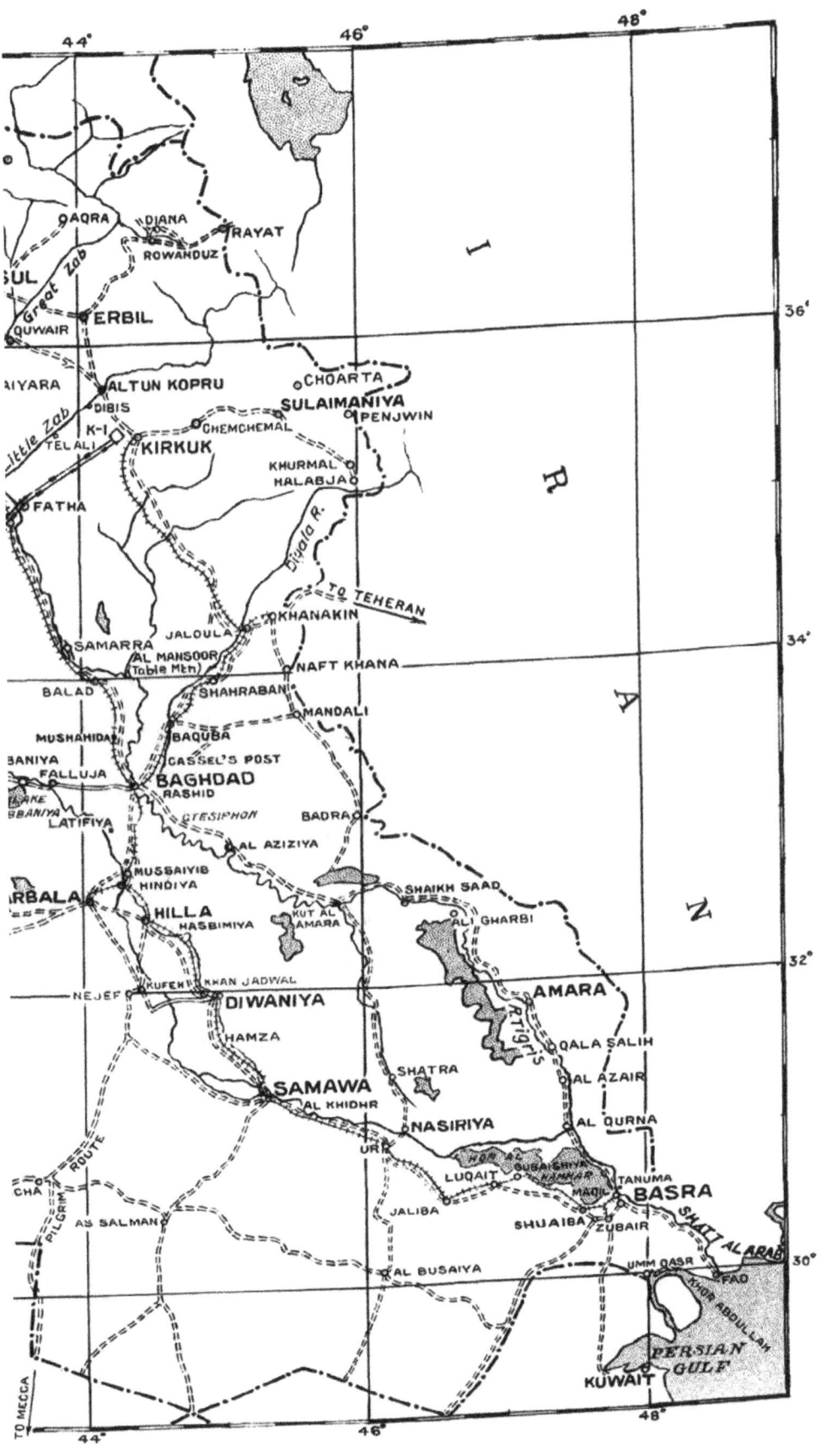

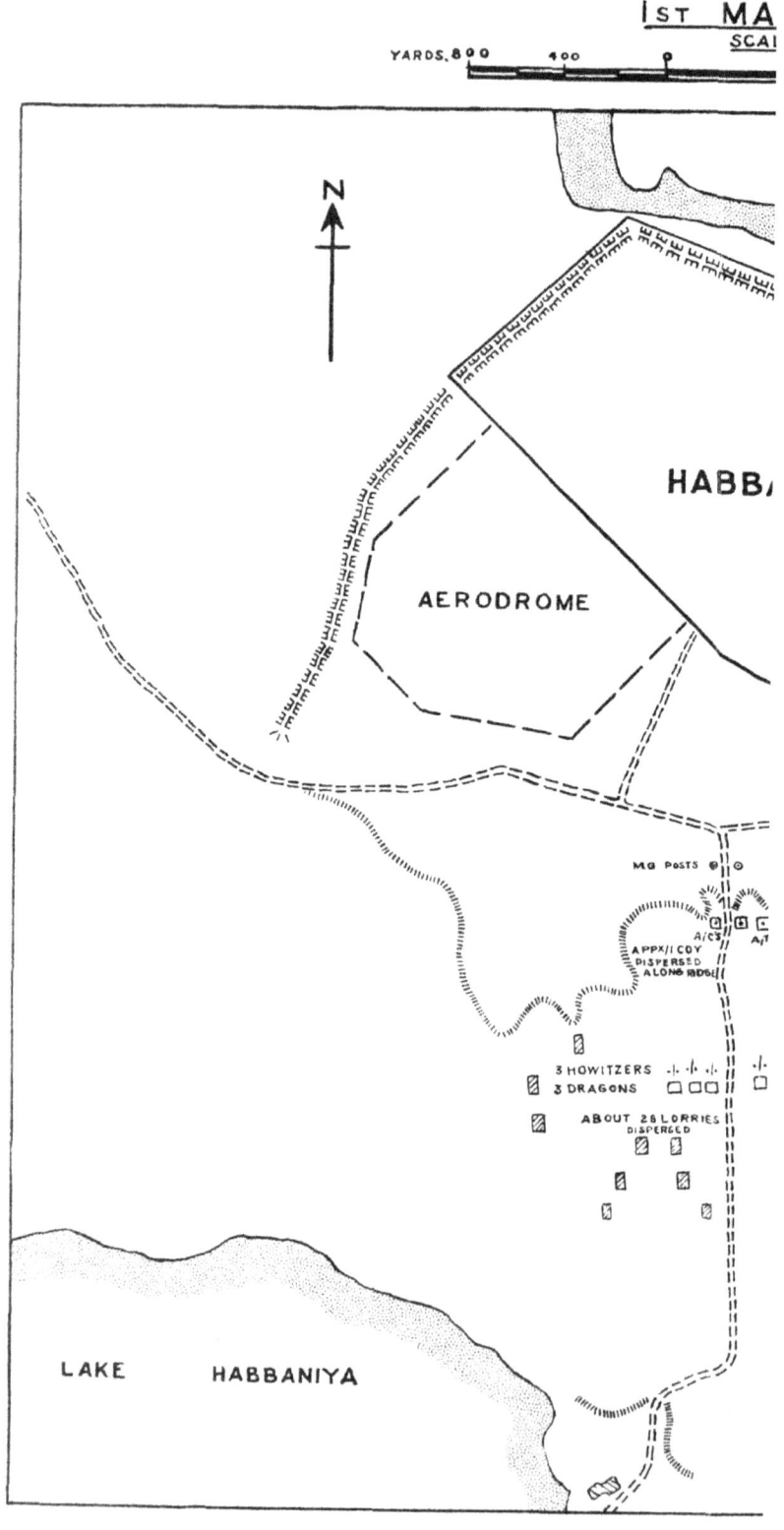

TROOPS AT HABBANIYA
Y 1941

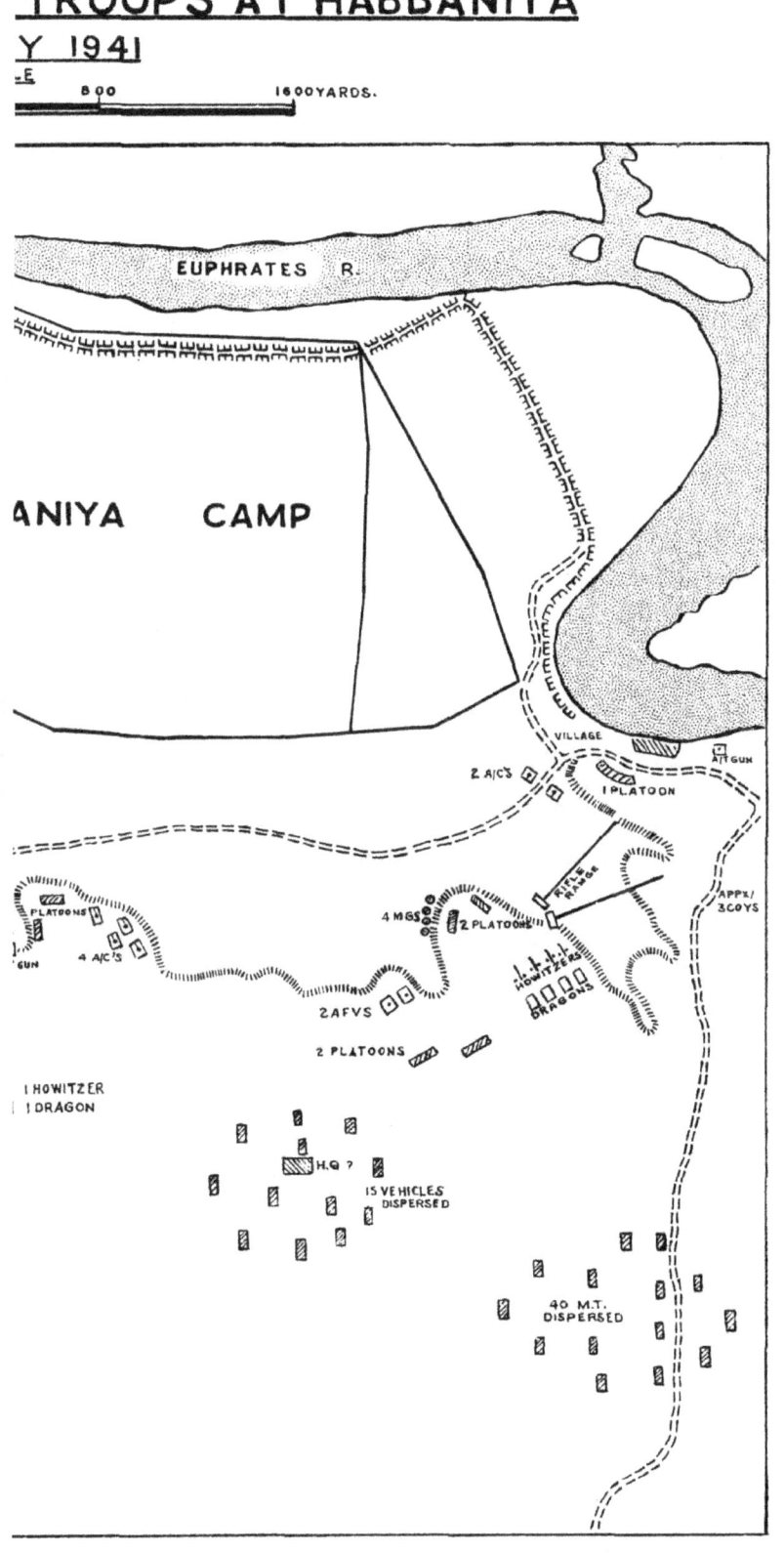

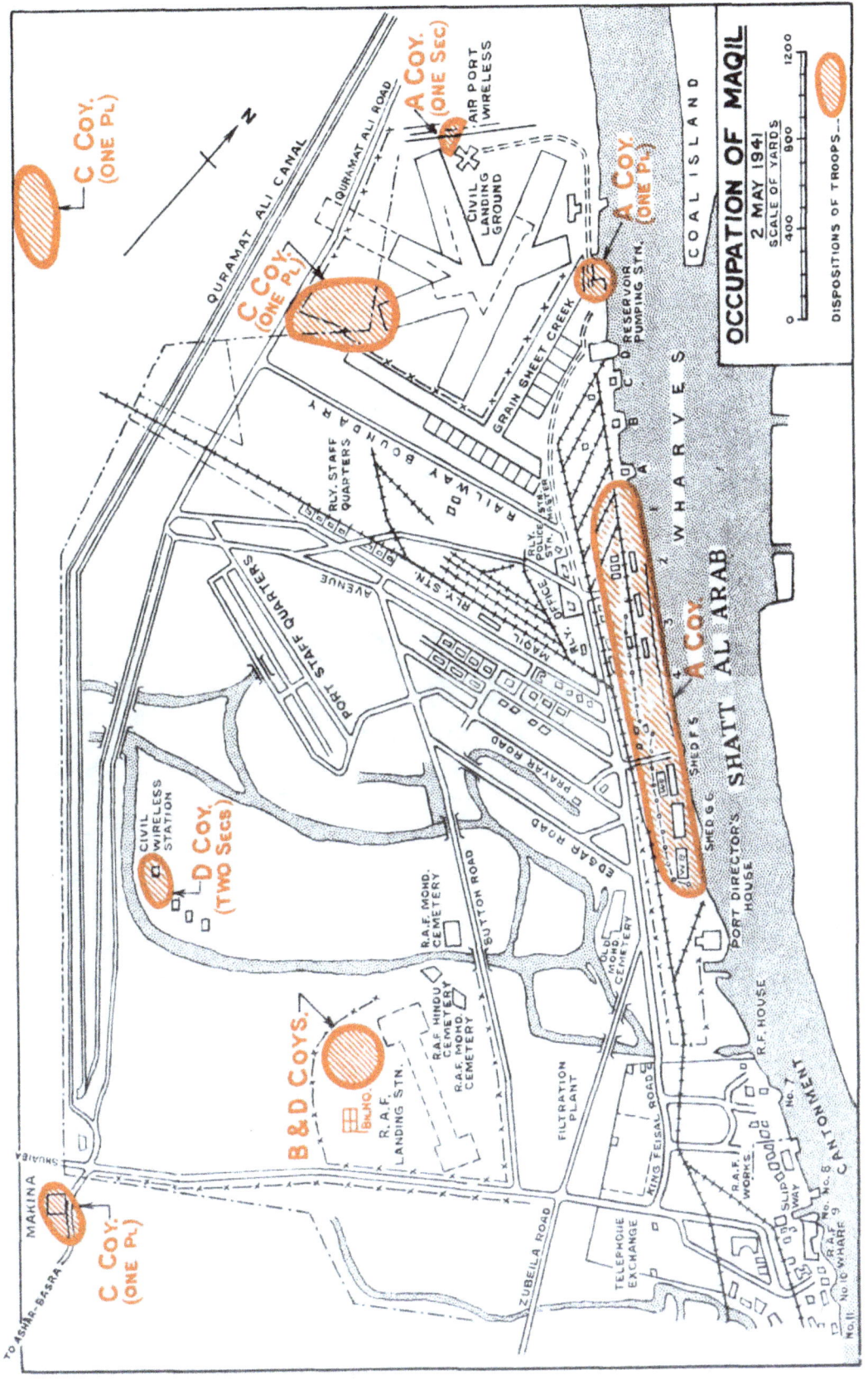

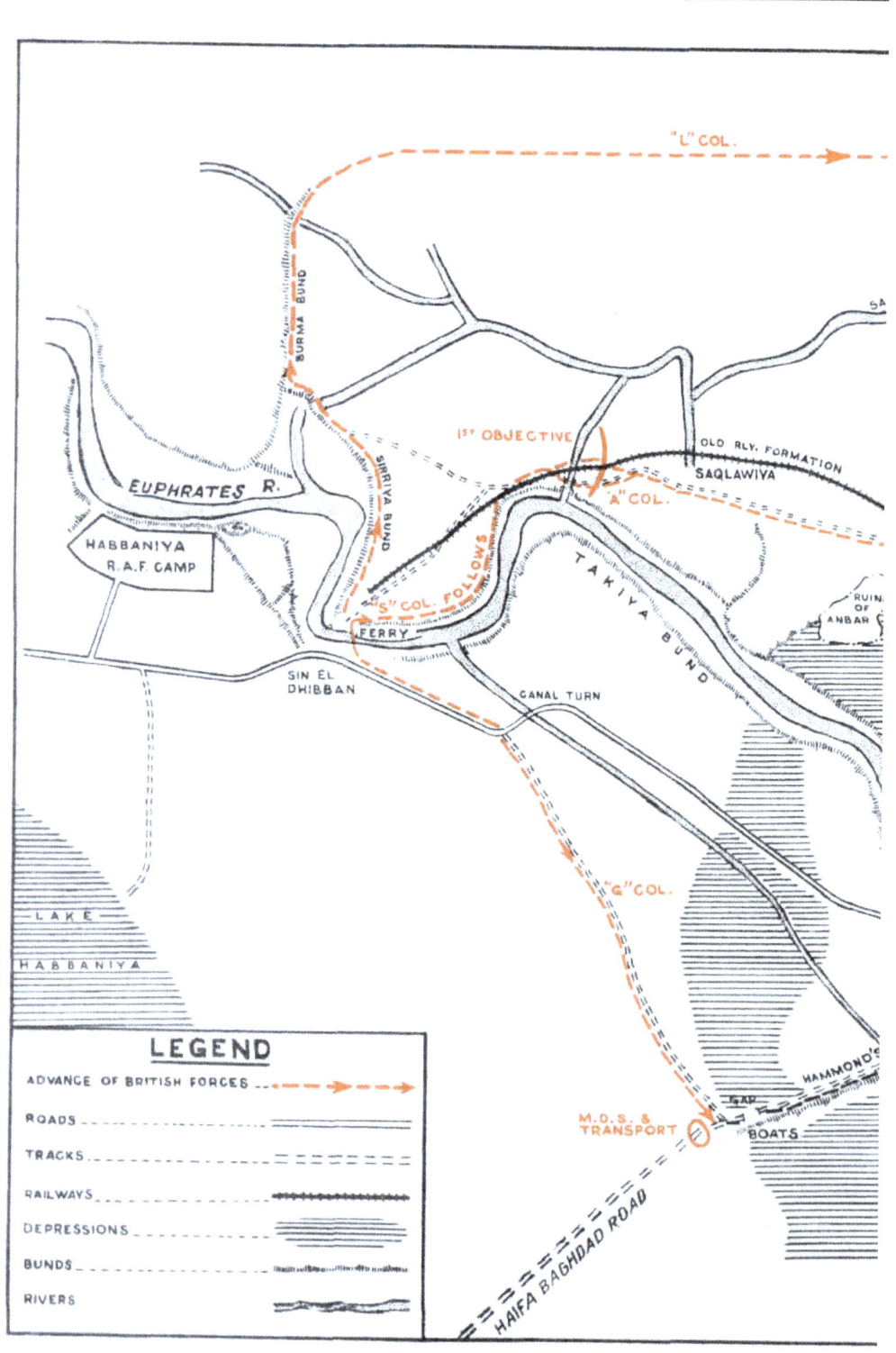

FALLUJA

Y 1941.

2   3 MILES

GLAWIYA CHANNEL
ALI SULAIMAN CANAL
IBRAHIM ALI CANAL
2ND OBJECTIVE
"V" COL.
FALLUJA
PALM GROVE
TROOPS IN POSITION
BUND
COY. H.Q.
EUPHRATES R.
ABU GHURAIB CANAL

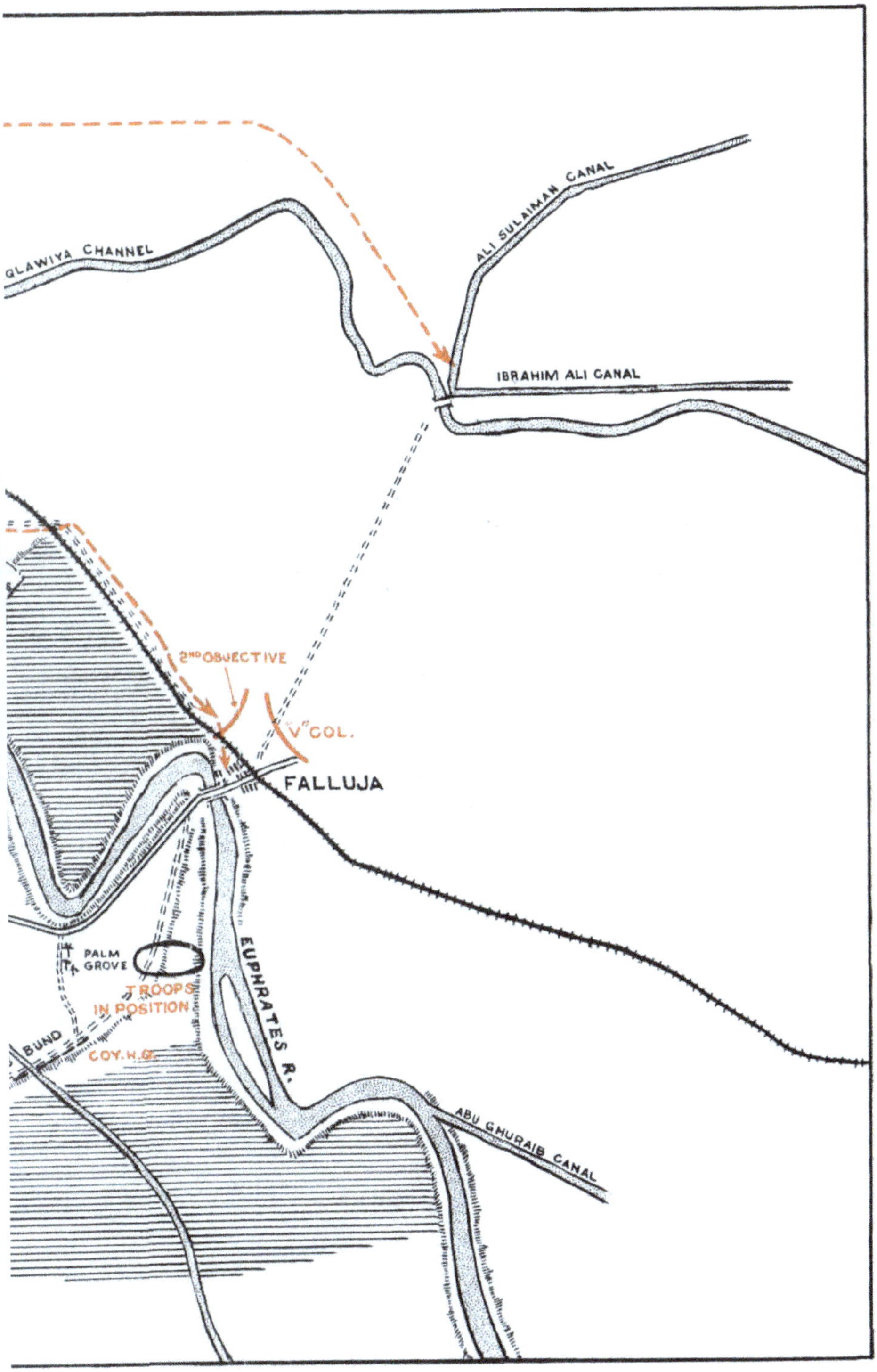

MOSUL AERODROME AREA DEFENCES
29 JUNE 1941

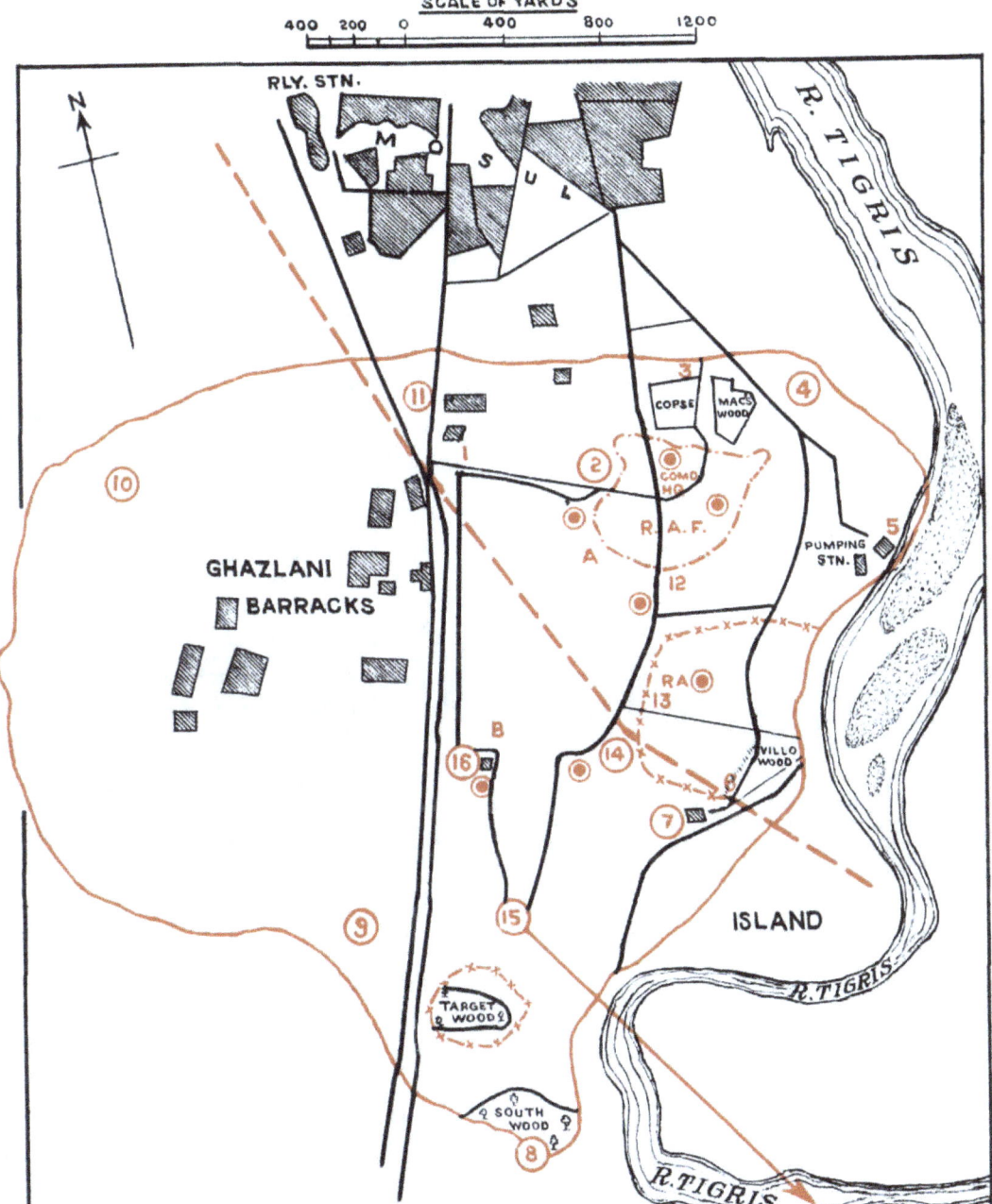

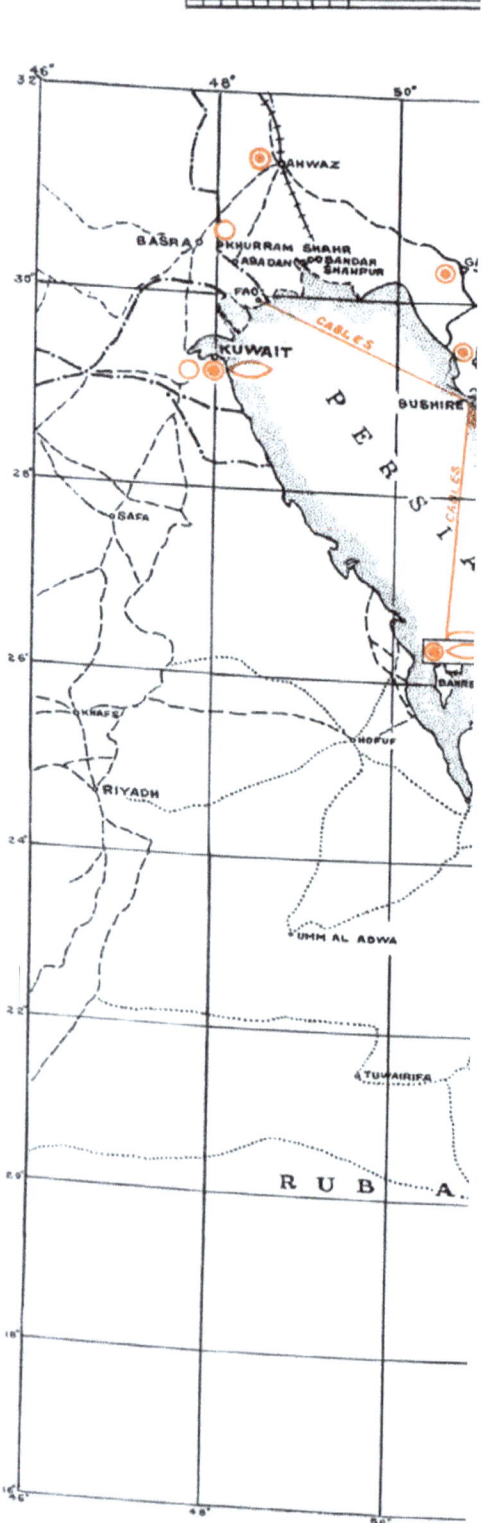

PERSIAN GULF
DEFENSIVE LAYOUT

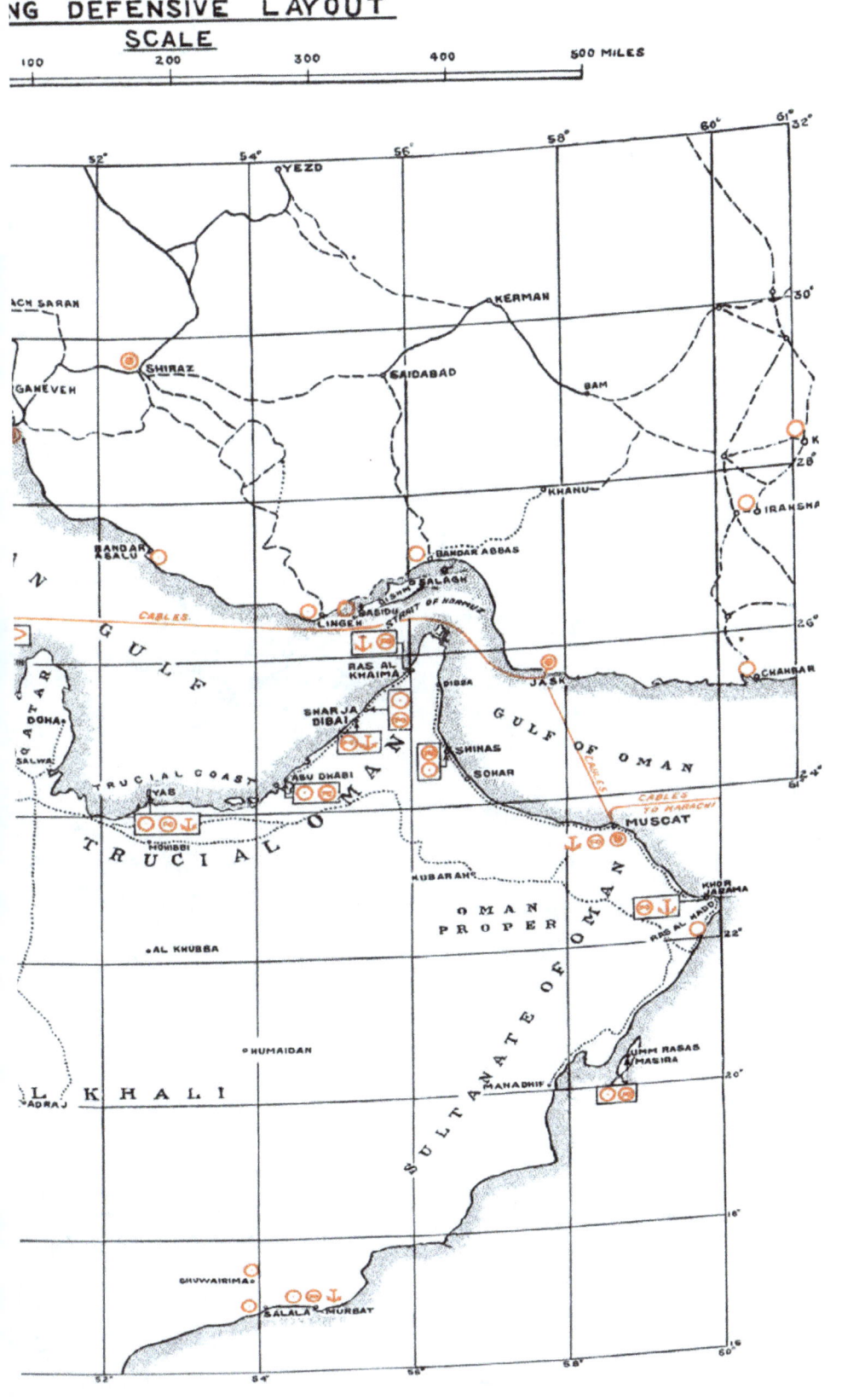

DEFENCE
1ST SEPTEMBER
SCALE O

PROPOSED DEFENSIVE

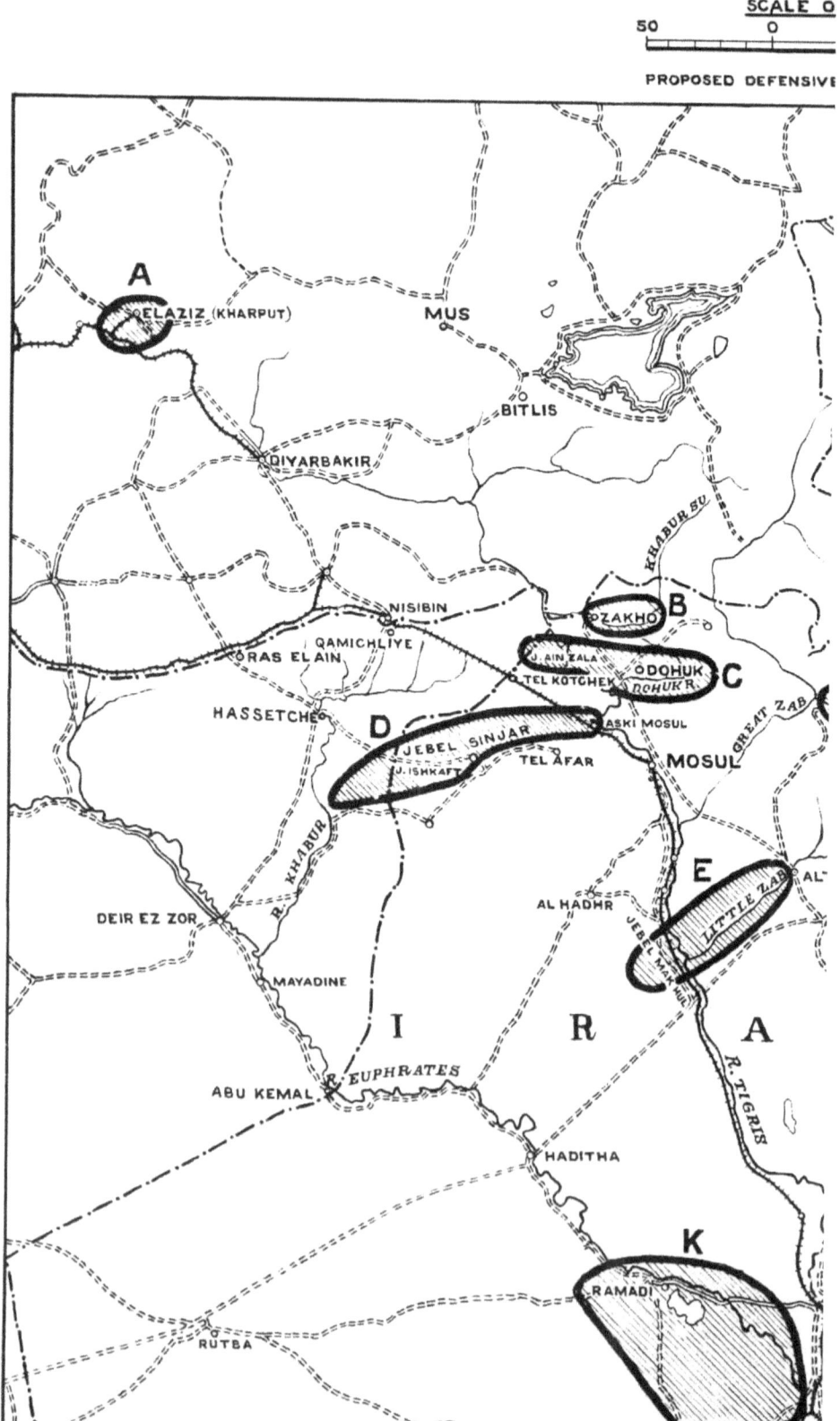

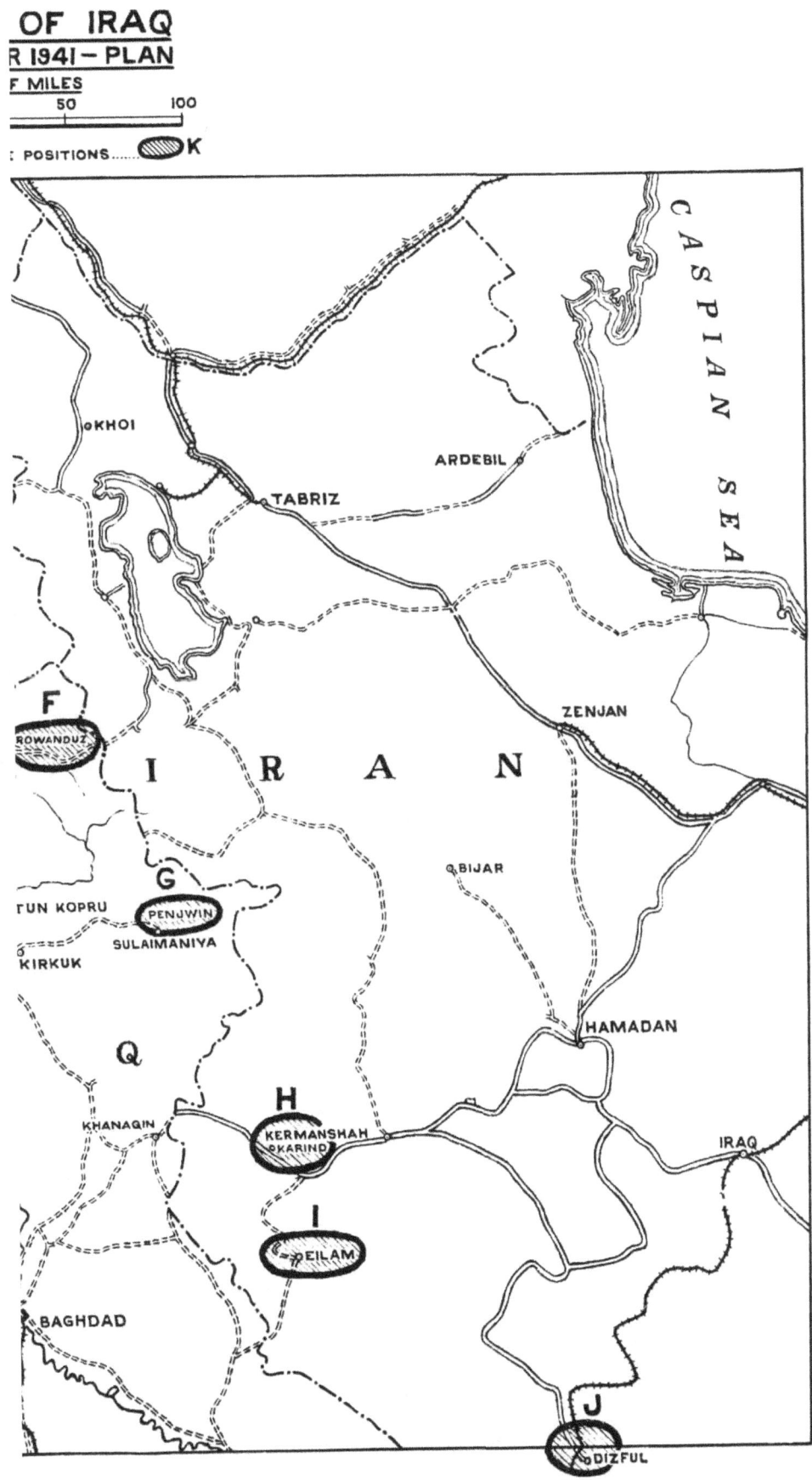

PLAN "WO[

PROPOSED DEMOLITION ZONES AND D[

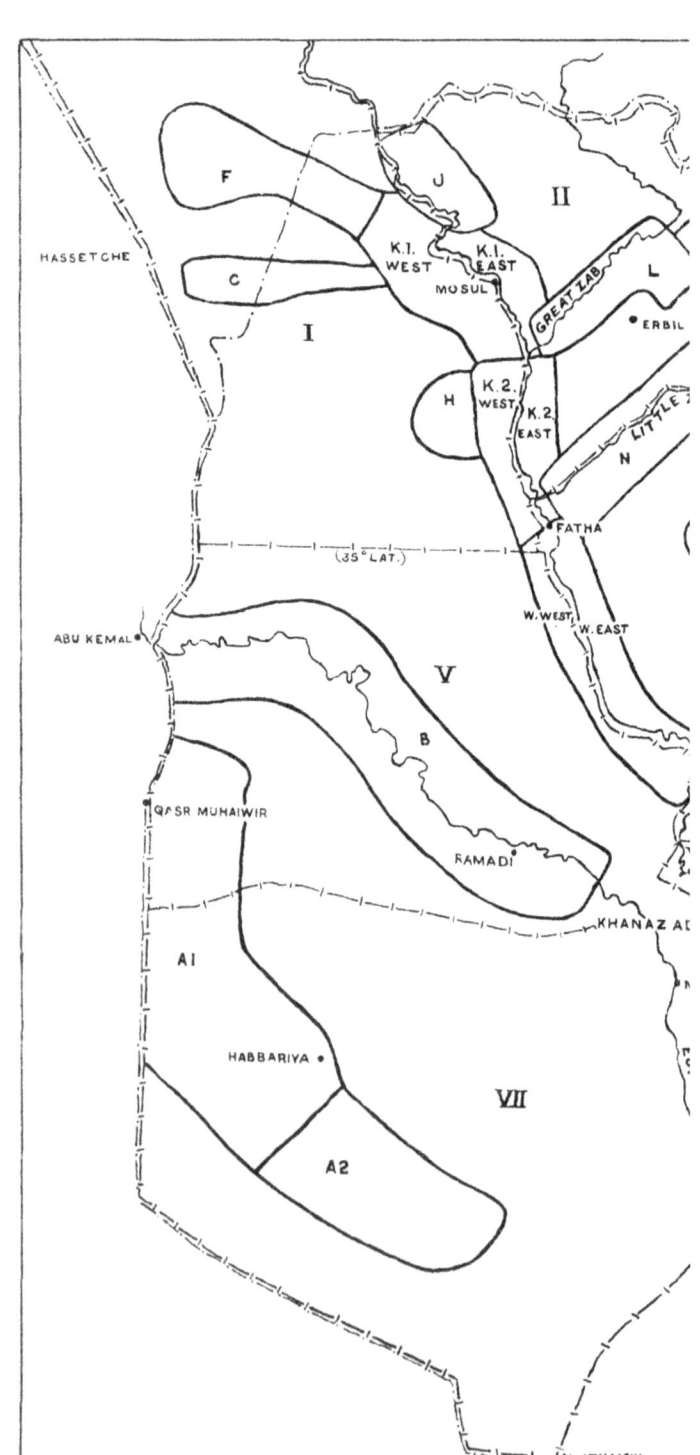

"NDERFUL"
DEVASTATION AREAS IN IRAQ & IRAN

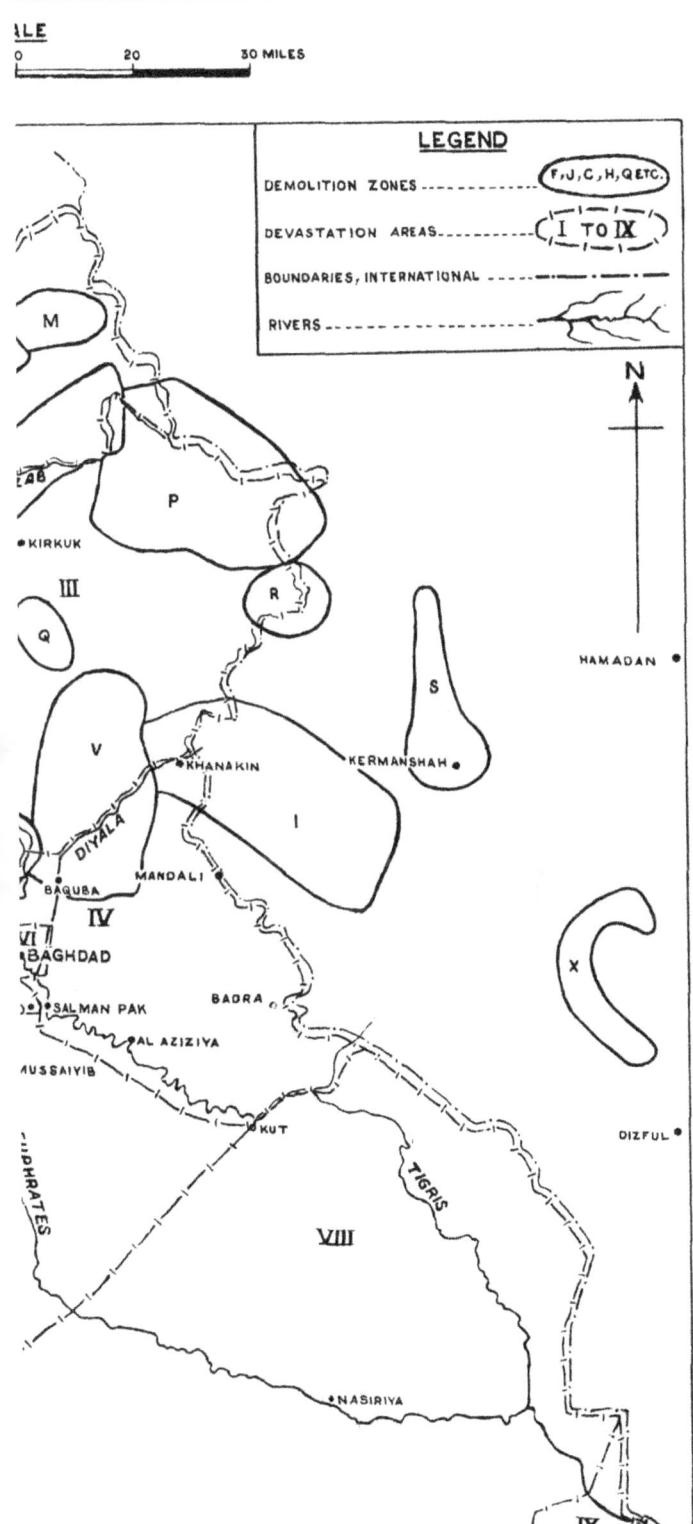

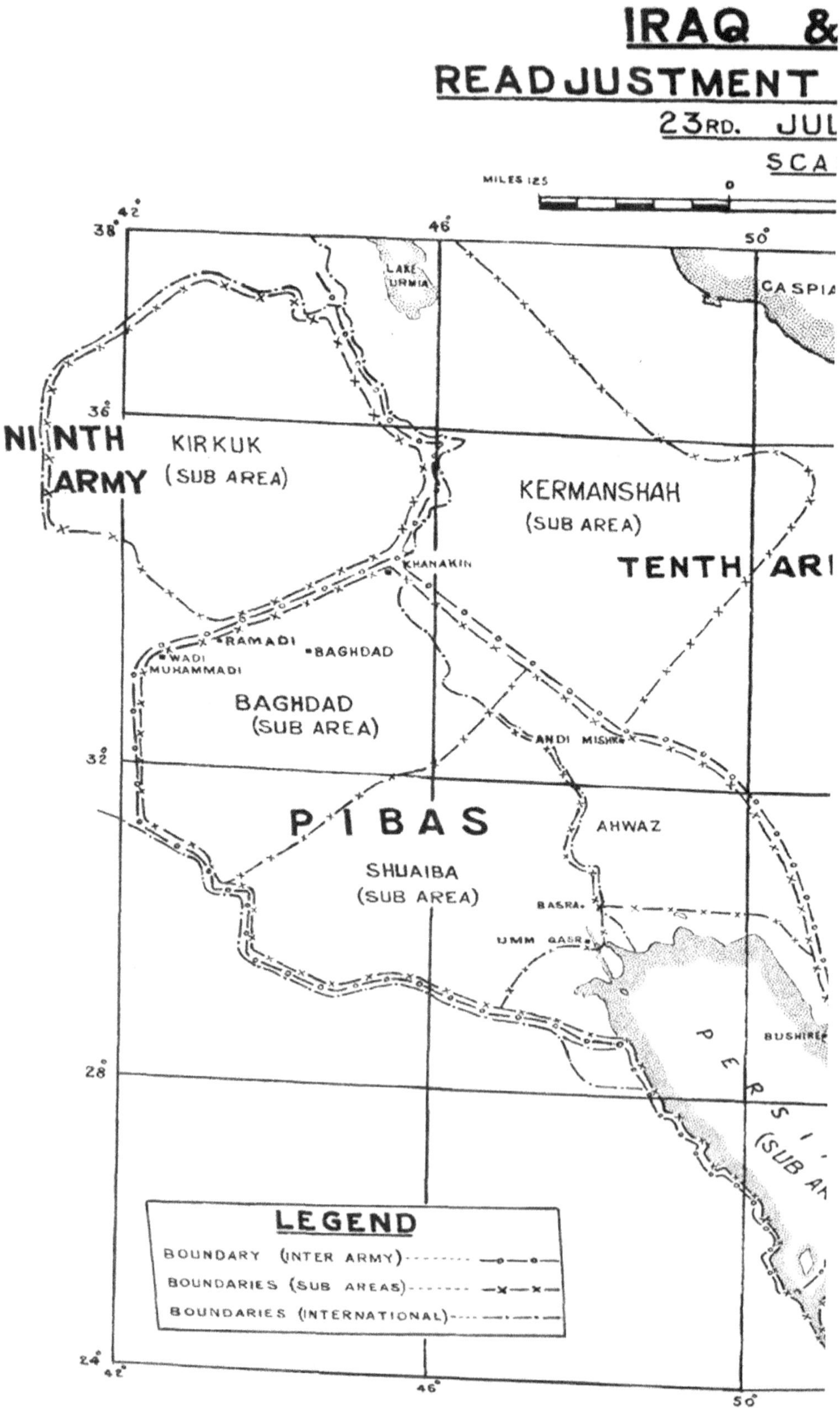

IRAQ &

READJUSTMENT
23RD. JUL
SCA

MILES 125

NINTH ARMY
KIRKUK (SUB AREA)

KERMANSHAH (SUB AREA)

TENTH AR

LAKE URMIA

CASPIA

KHANAKIN

RAMADI • BAGHDAD
• WADI MUHAMMADI

BAGHDAD (SUB AREA)

ANDI MISHK

PIBAS

AHWAZ

SHUAIBA (SUB AREA)

BASRA
UMM QASR

BUSHIRE

PER
(SUB A

LEGEND
BOUNDARY (INTER ARMY)	—o—o—
BOUNDARIES (SUB AREAS)	—x—x—
BOUNDARIES (INTERNATIONAL)	—·—·—

IRAN
OF COMMANDS
..Y 1942

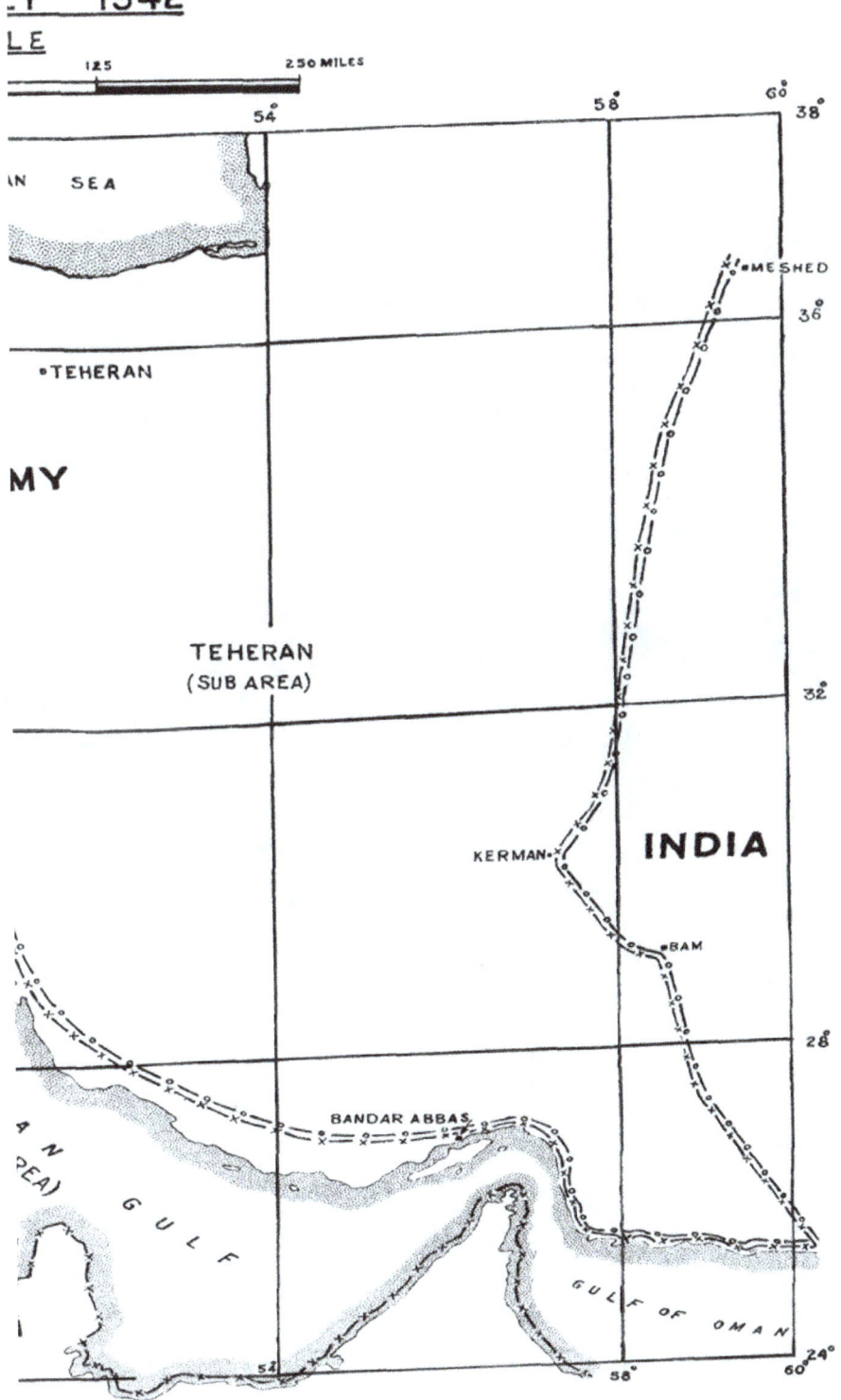

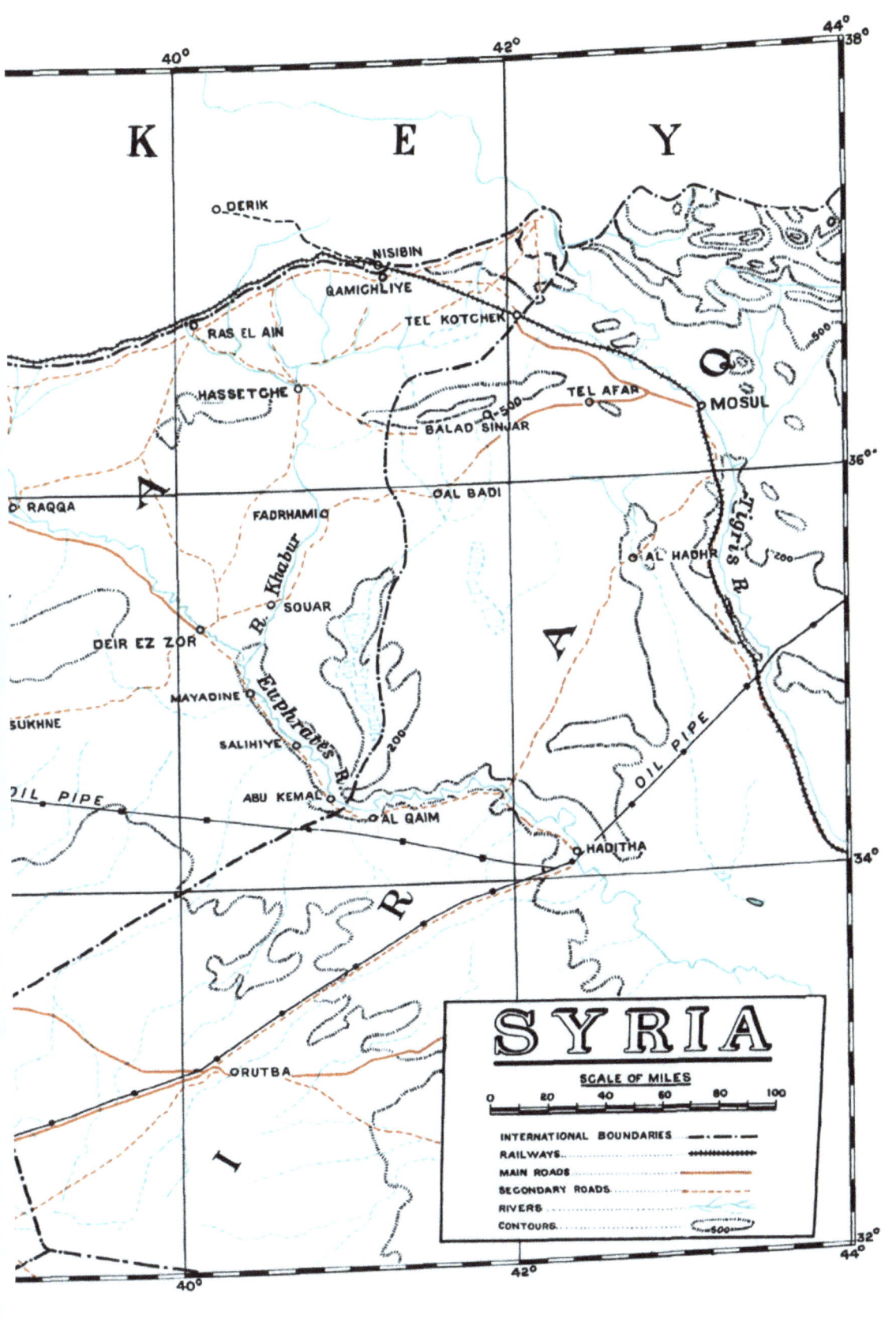

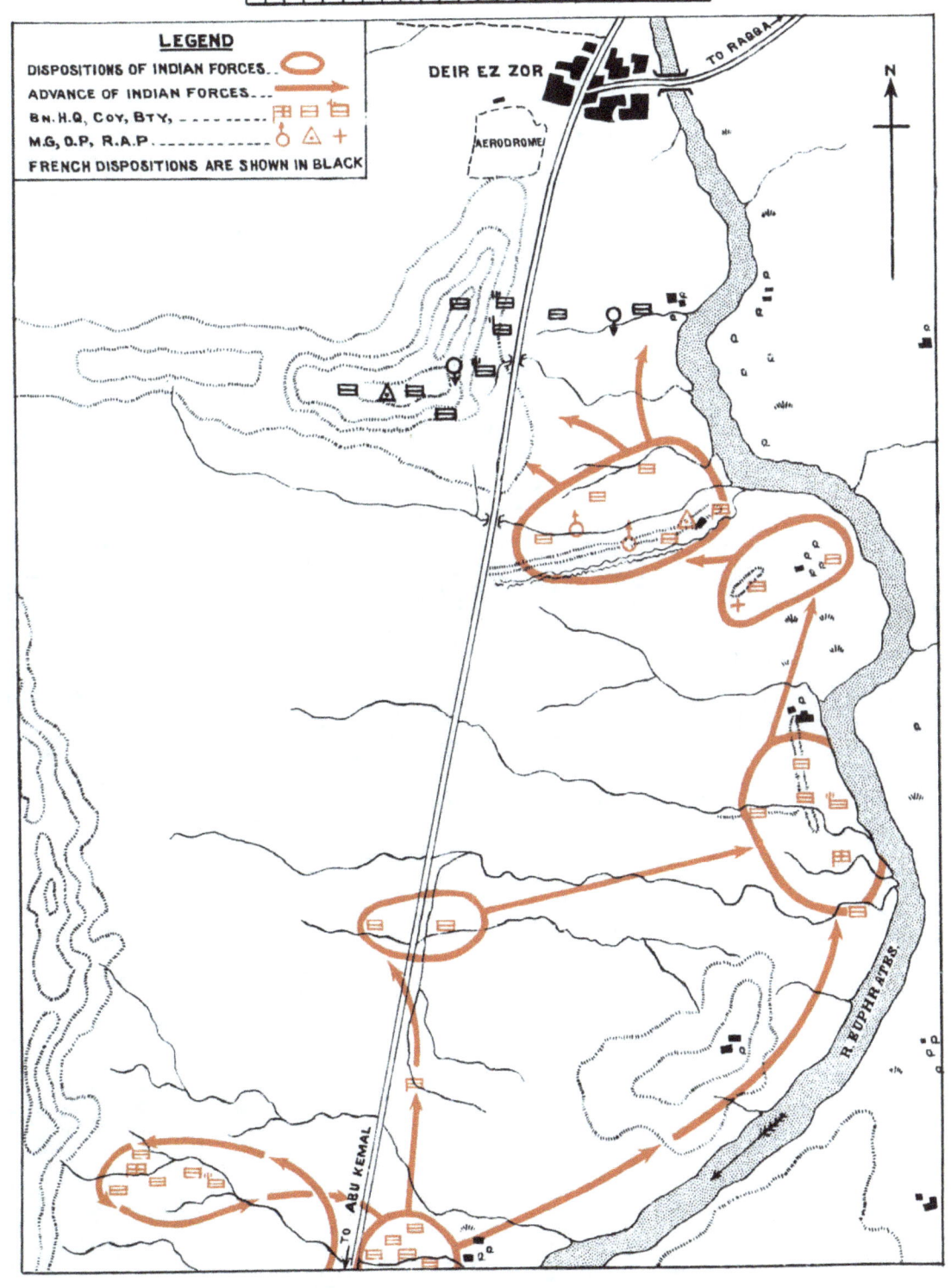

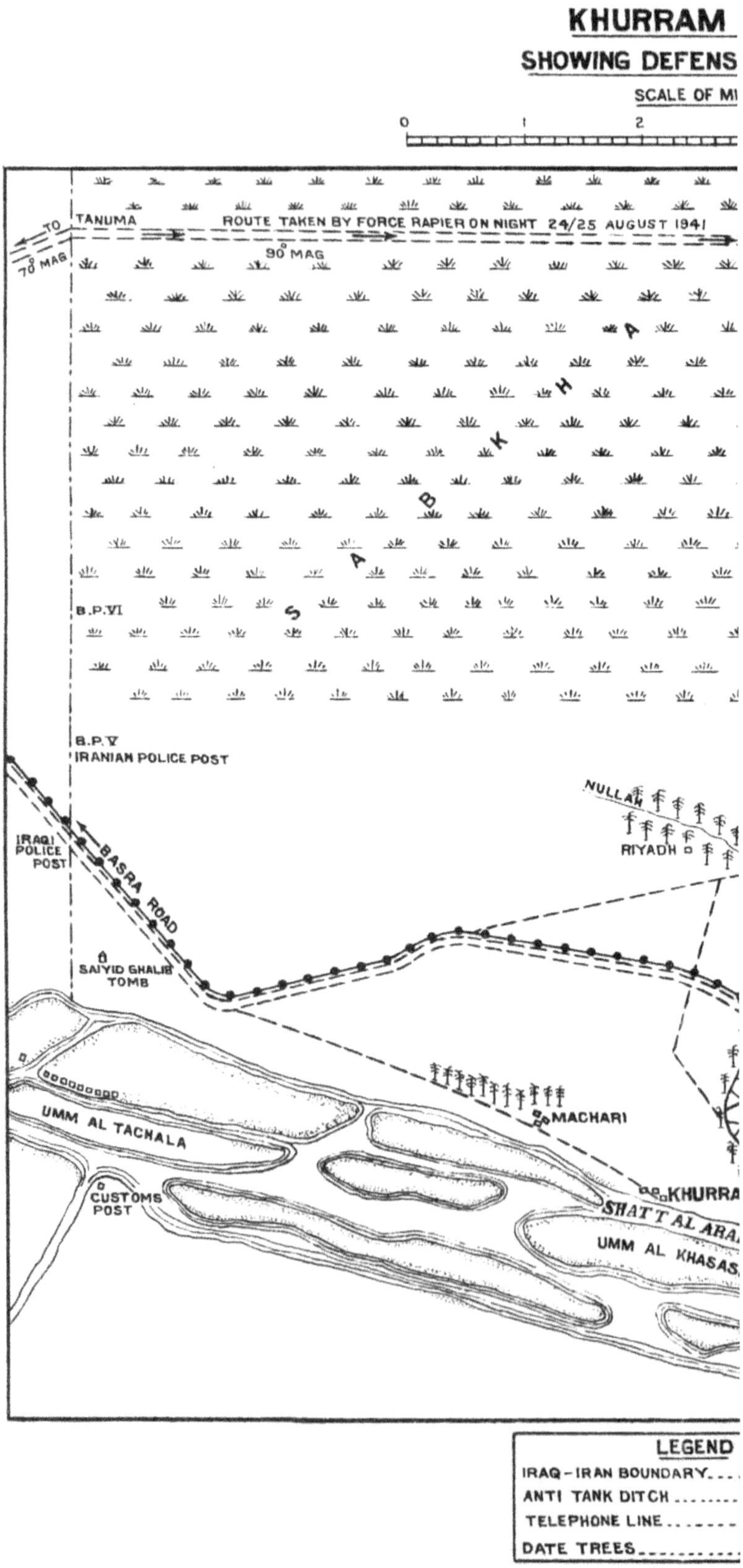

KHURRAM

SHOWING DEFENS[...]

SCALE OF M[...]

0　　1　　2

TO TANUMA
ROUTE TAKEN BY FORCE RAPIER ON NIGHT 24/25 AUGUST 1941
70° MAG
90° MAG

SABKAH

B.P.VI

B.P.V
IRANIAN POLICE POST

IRAQI POLICE POST

BASRA ROAD

SAIYID GHALIB TOMB

NULLAH
RIYADH

UMM AL TACHALA

CUSTOMS POST

MACHARI

KHURRA[M]
SHATT AL ARA[B]
UMM AL KHASAS

LEGEND
IRAQ-IRAN BOUNDARY....
ANTI TANK DITCH.........
TELEPHONE LINE........
DATE TREES............

SHAHR
IVE LAYOUT
LES

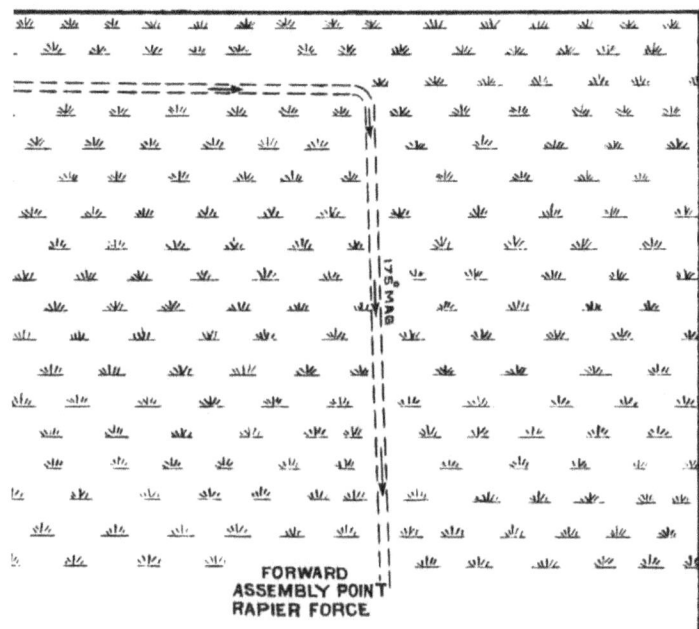
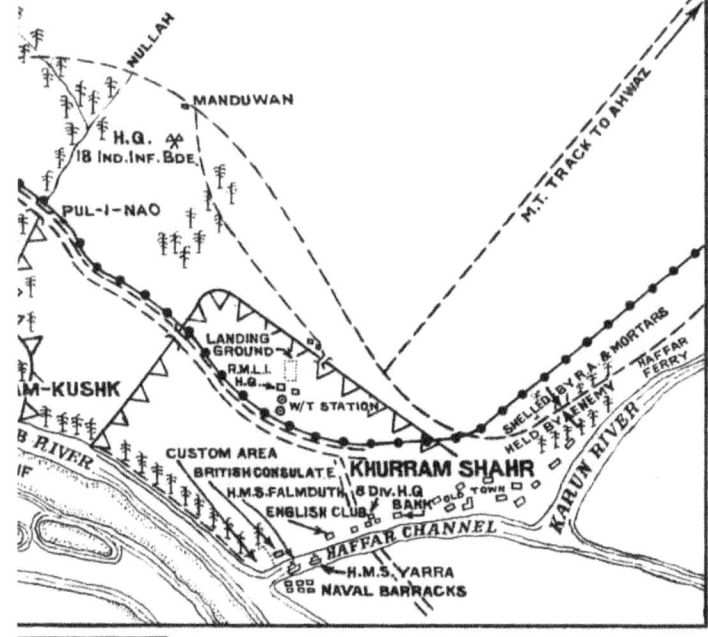

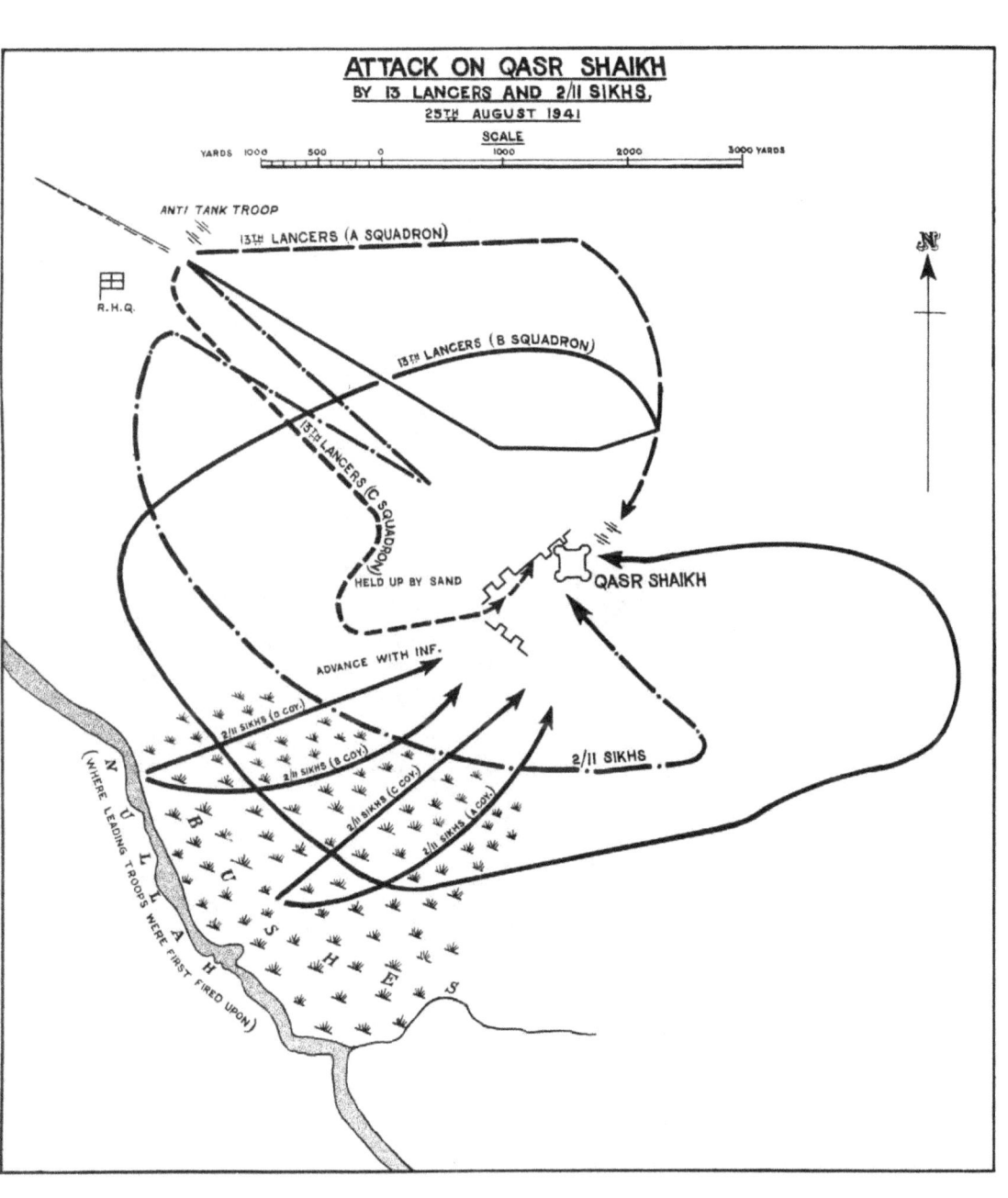

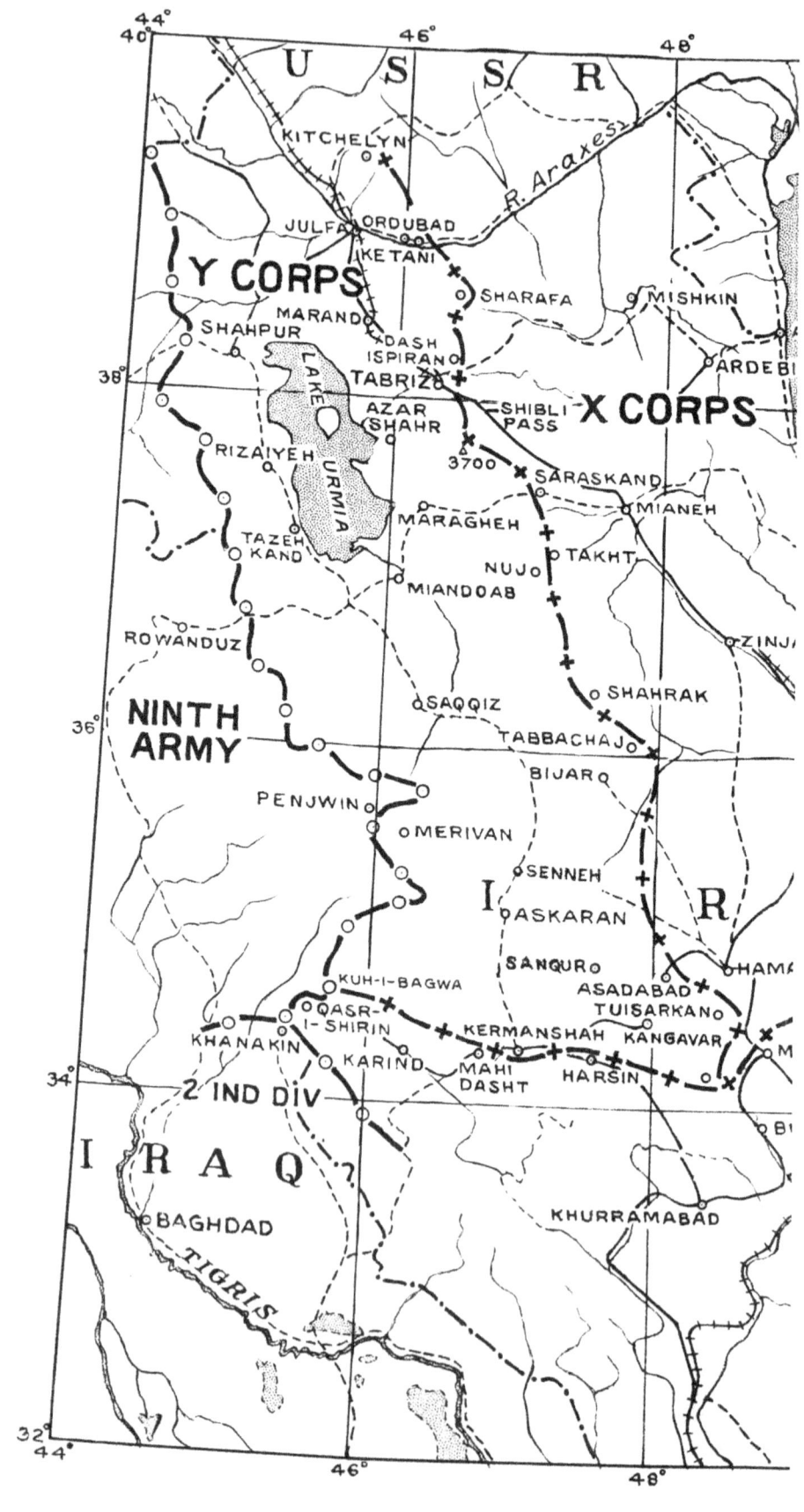

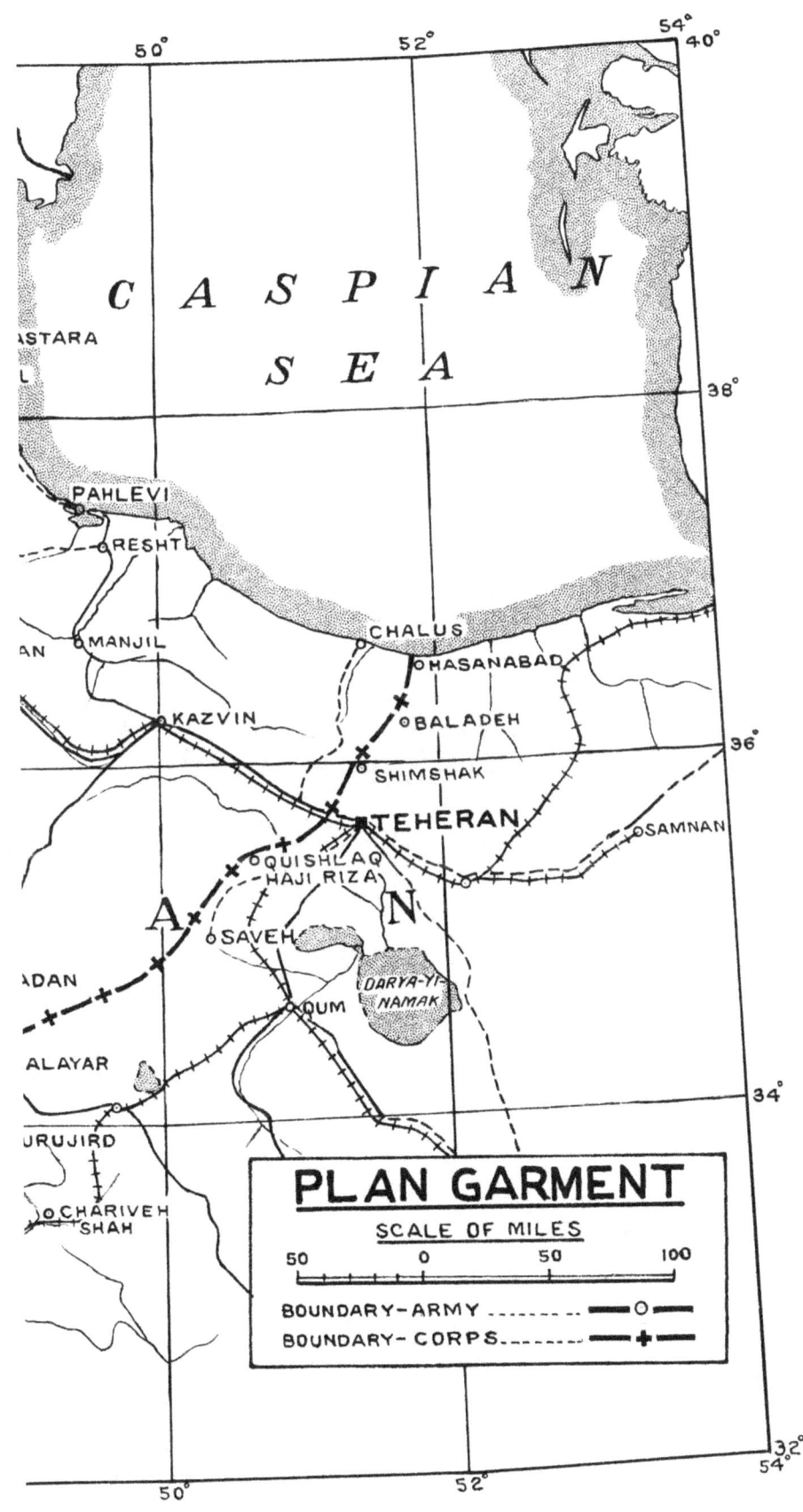

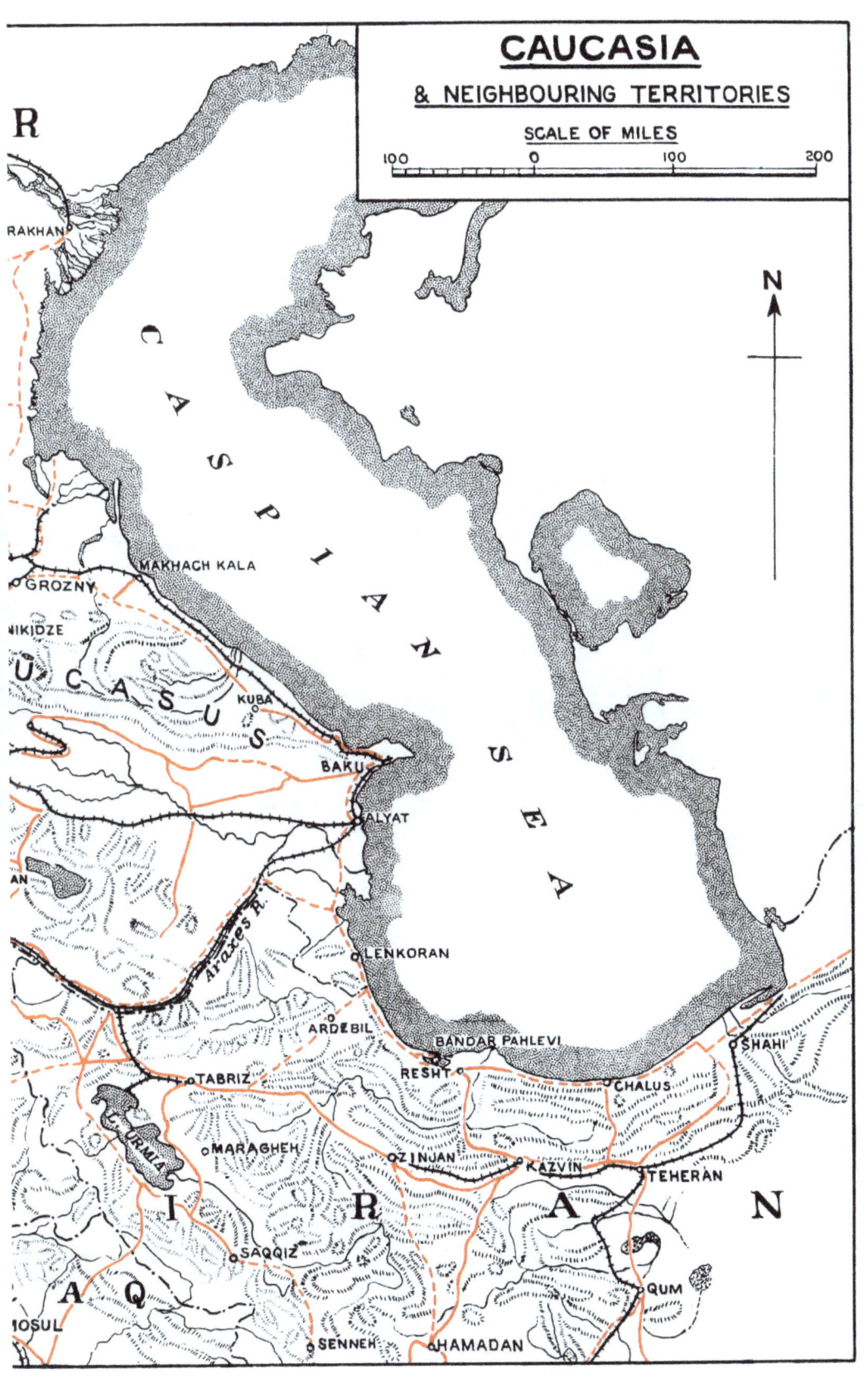

OFFICIAL HISTORY OF THE INDIAN ARMED FORCES
IN THE SECOND WORLD WAR
1939-45

EAST AFRICAN CAMPAIGN
1940-41

Maps and Sketches

The East African Campaign
List of Maps

1. East Africa
2. Eritrea (Communications)
3. Northern Ethiopia
4. Gallabat—Metemma Area
5. The Advance—Kassala to Keren, Part I
6. The Advance—Kassala to Keren, Part II
7. Operations in Om Ager Area
8. Keren—The First Attack, Part I
9. Keren—The First Attack, Part II
10. Operations by 7th Indian Infantry Brigade Part I
11. Operations by 7th Indian Infantry Brigade Part II
12. Operations by 7th Indian Infantry Brigade north of Keren
13. Keren—The Final Battle
14. The Pursuit by 5th Indian Division, Keren to Asmara
15. Advance to Massawa
16. Battle of Massawa
17. The Pursuit, southward from Asmara
18. The Area north of Amba Alagi
19. The Features north of the Falaga Pass
20. The Battle of Amba Alagi

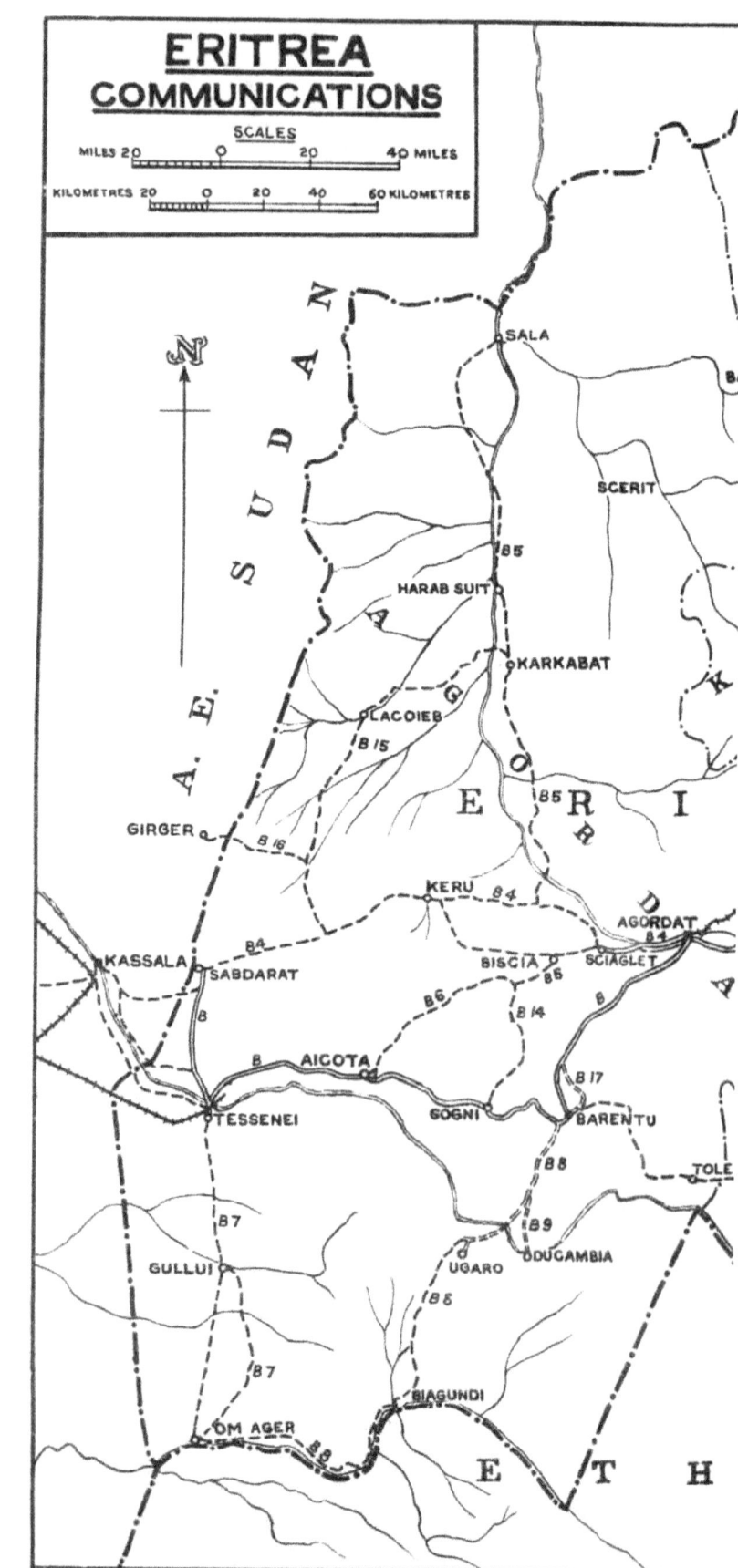

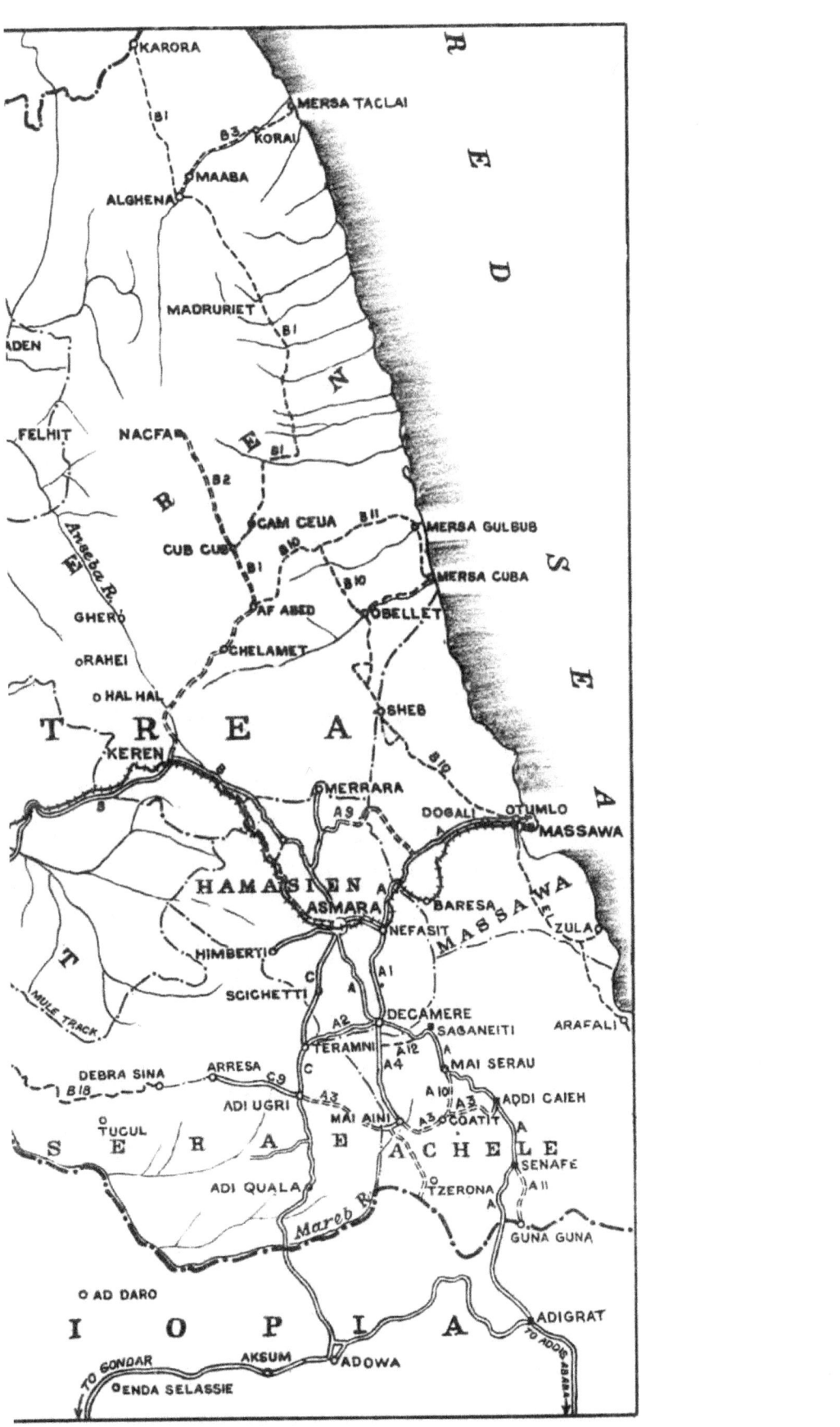

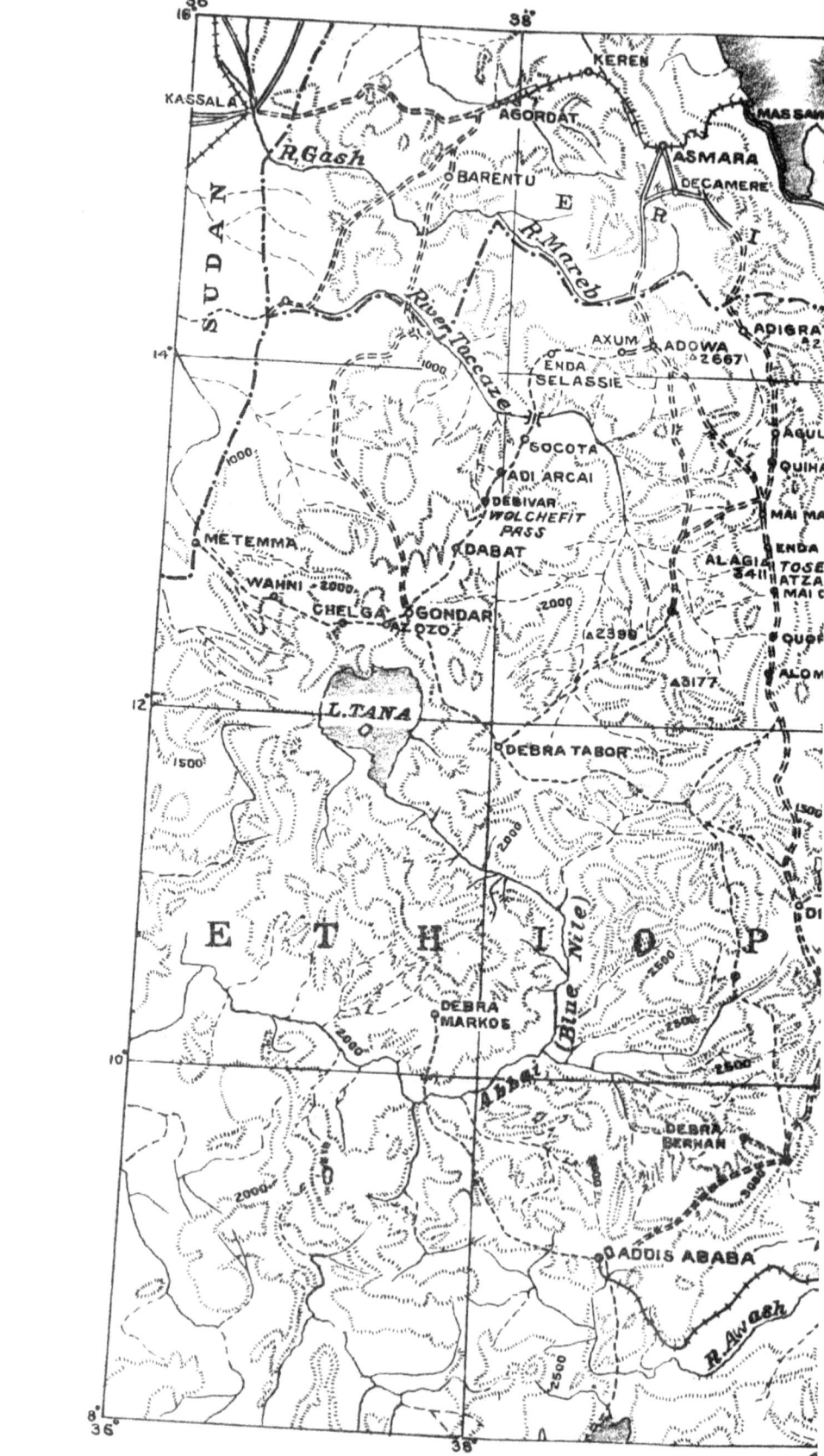

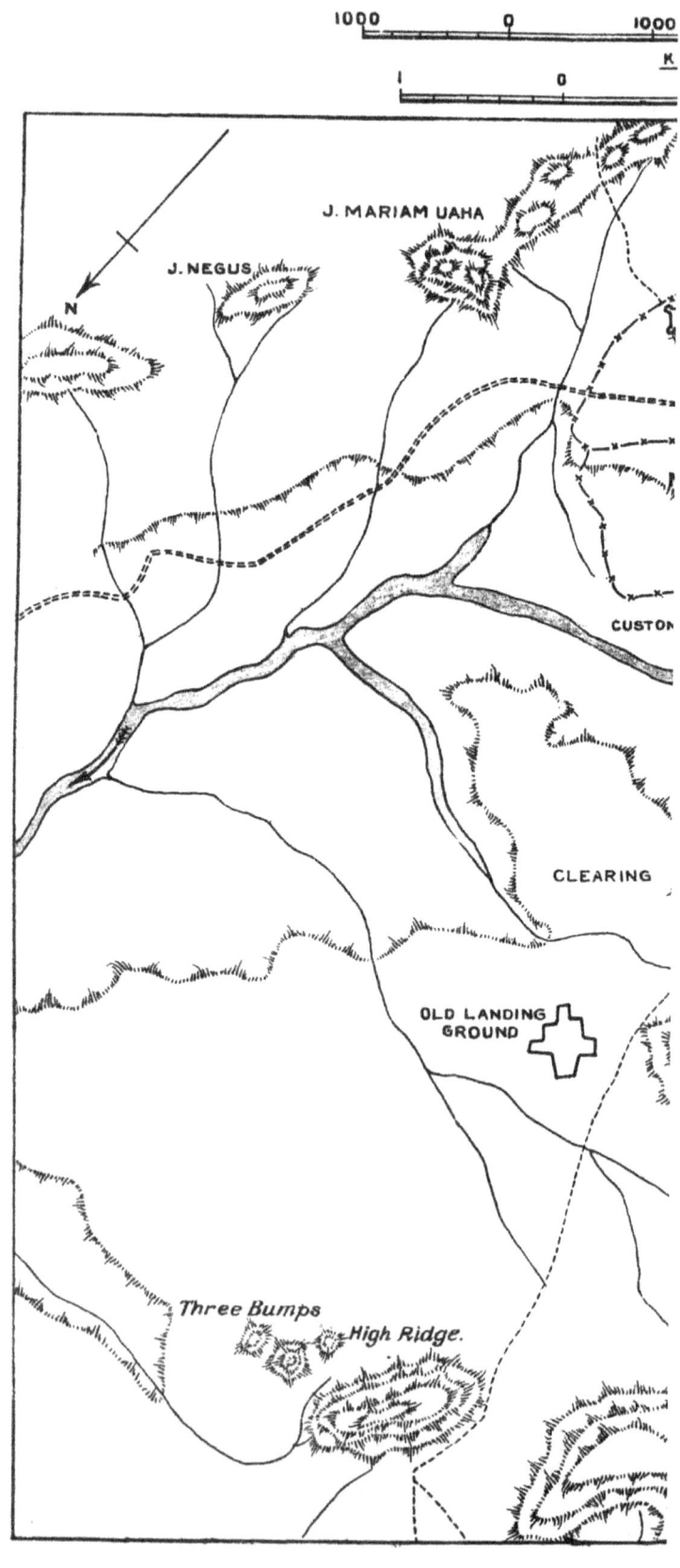

METEMMA AREA

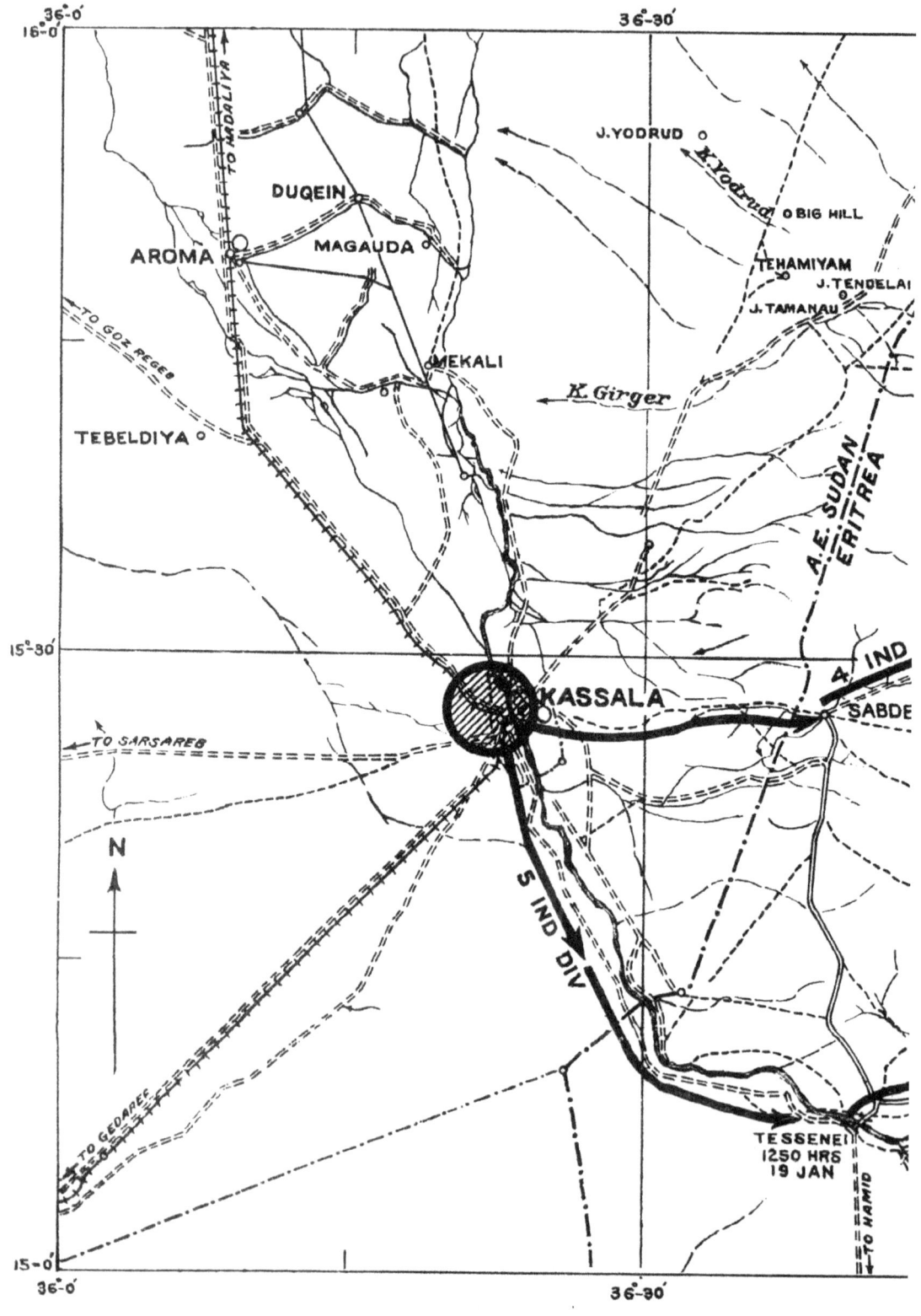

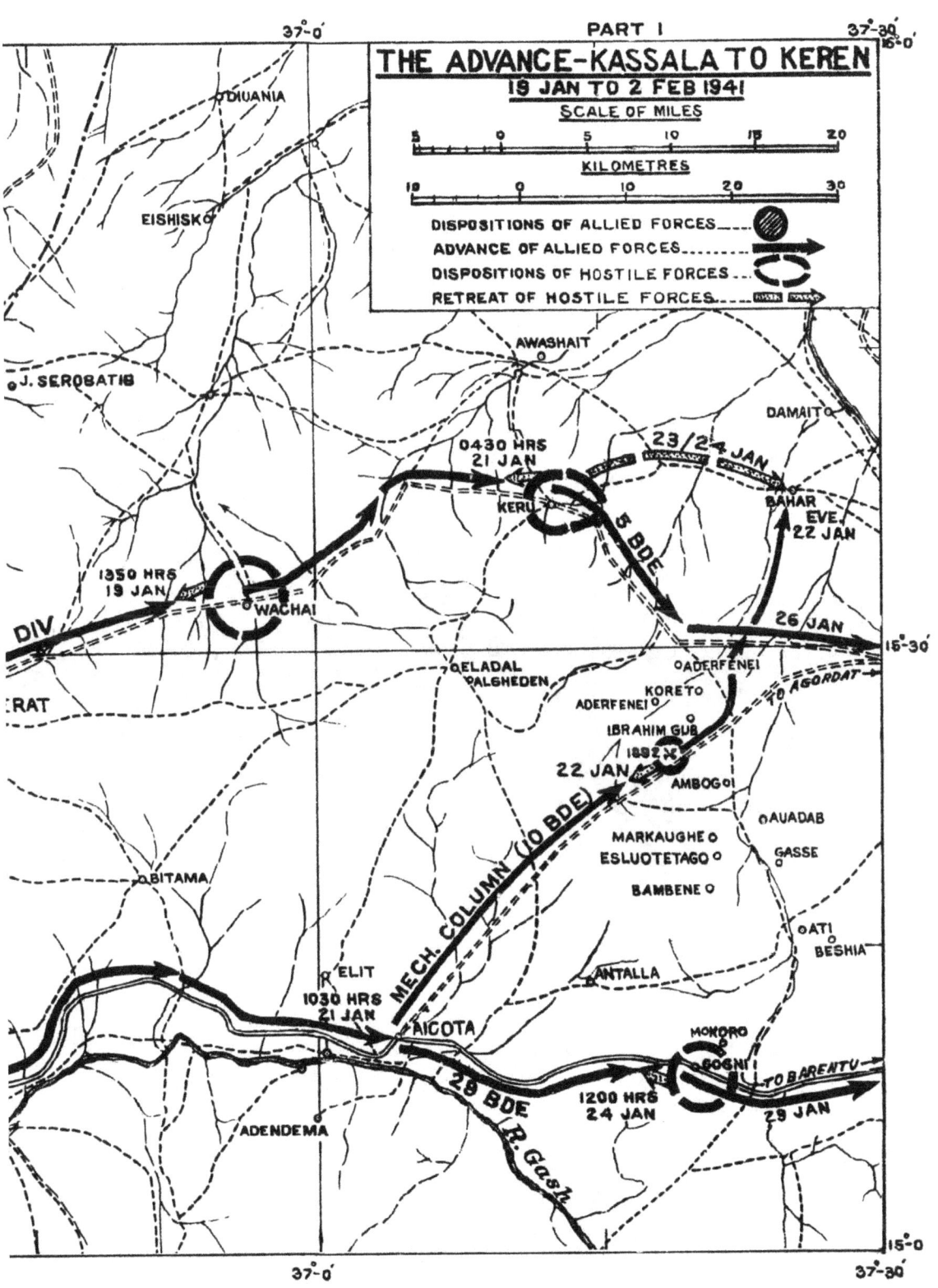

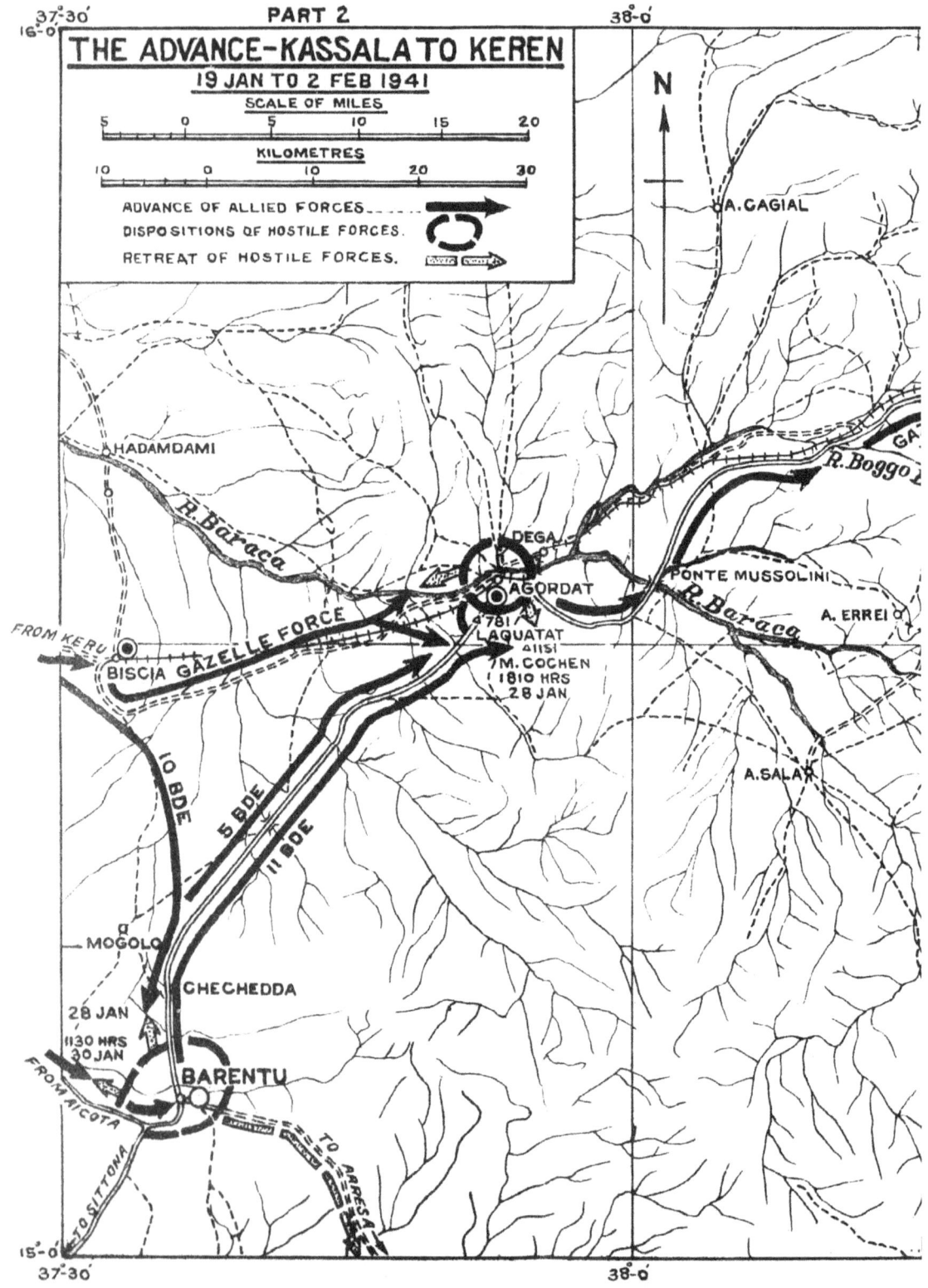

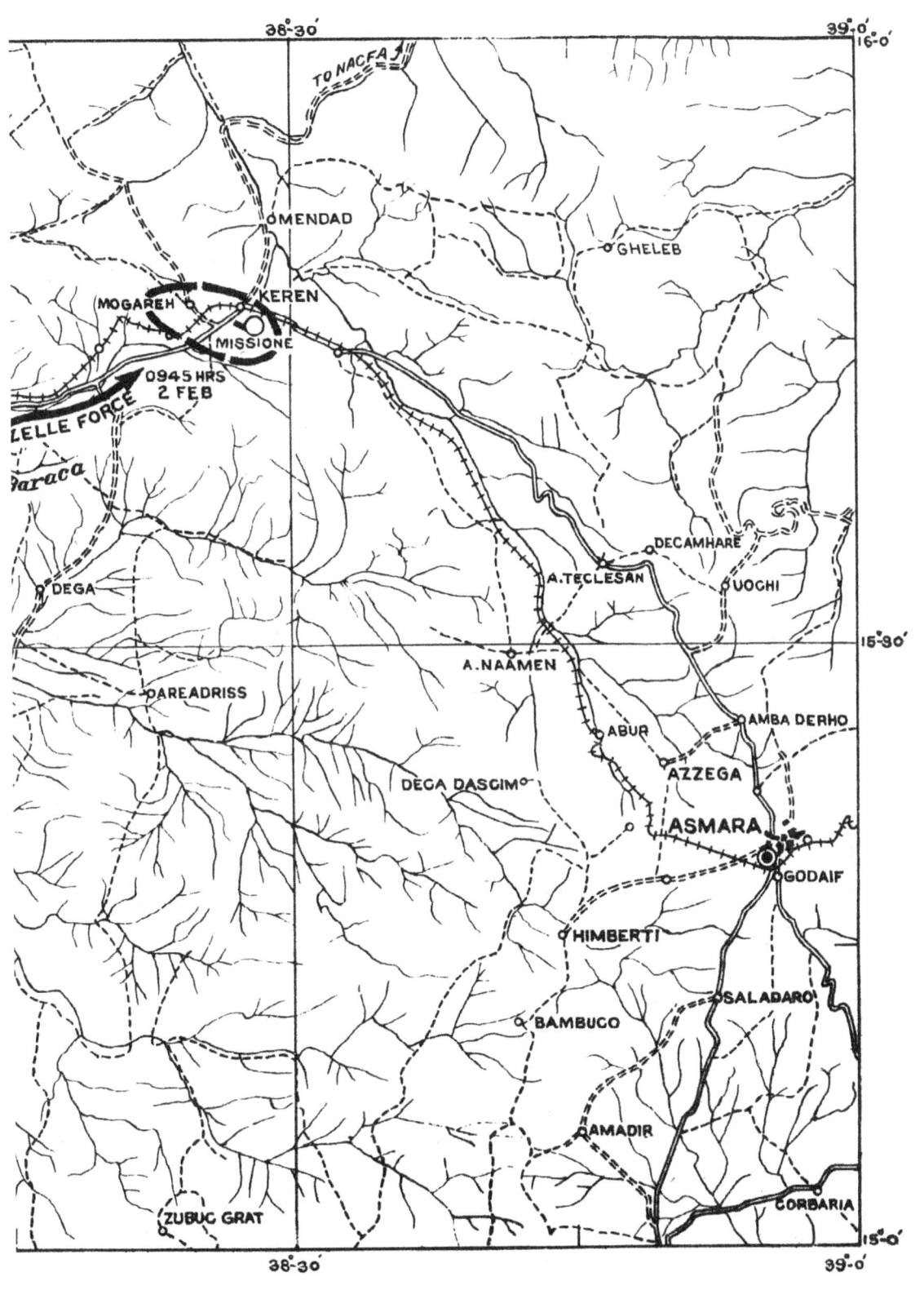

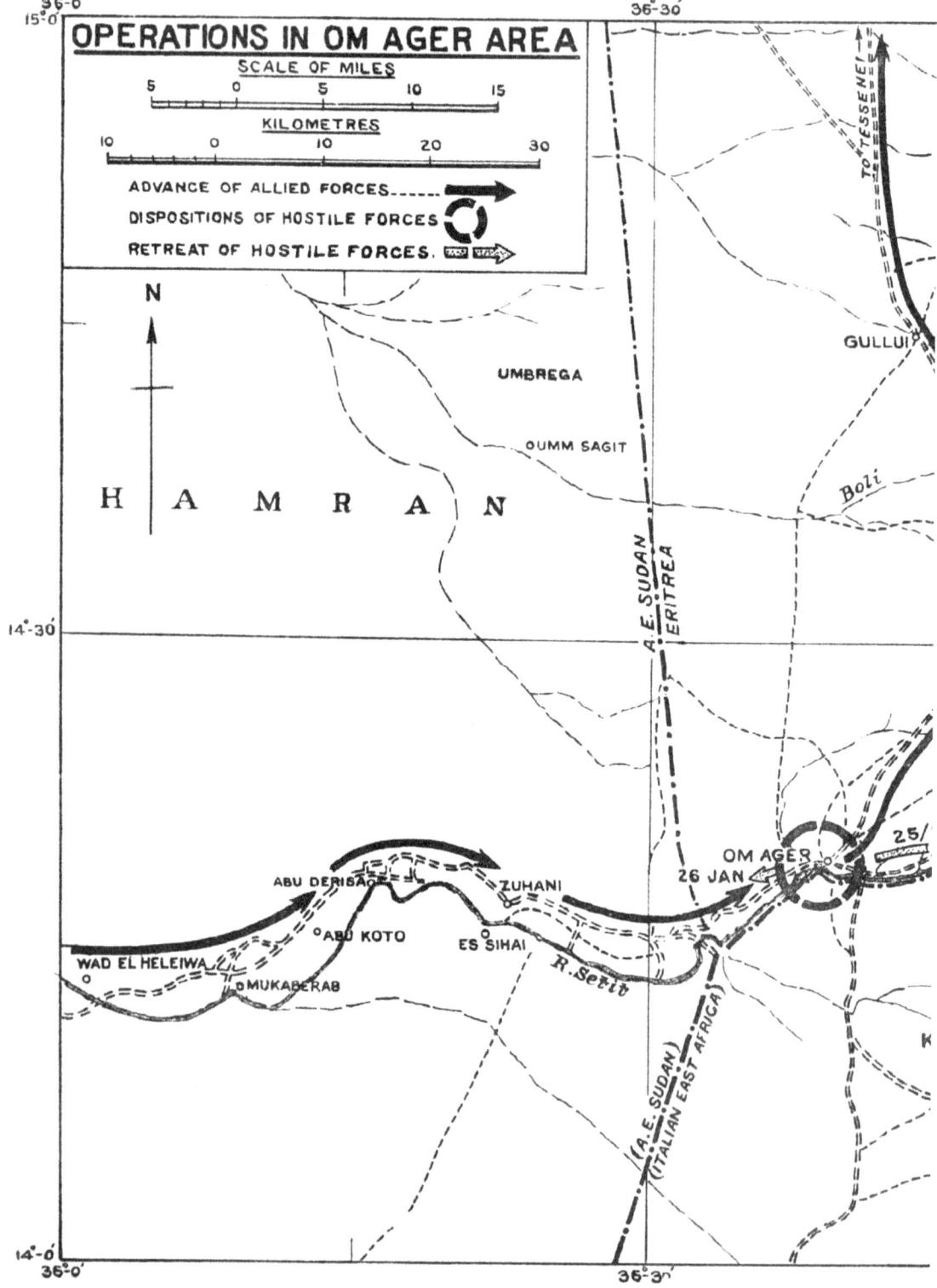

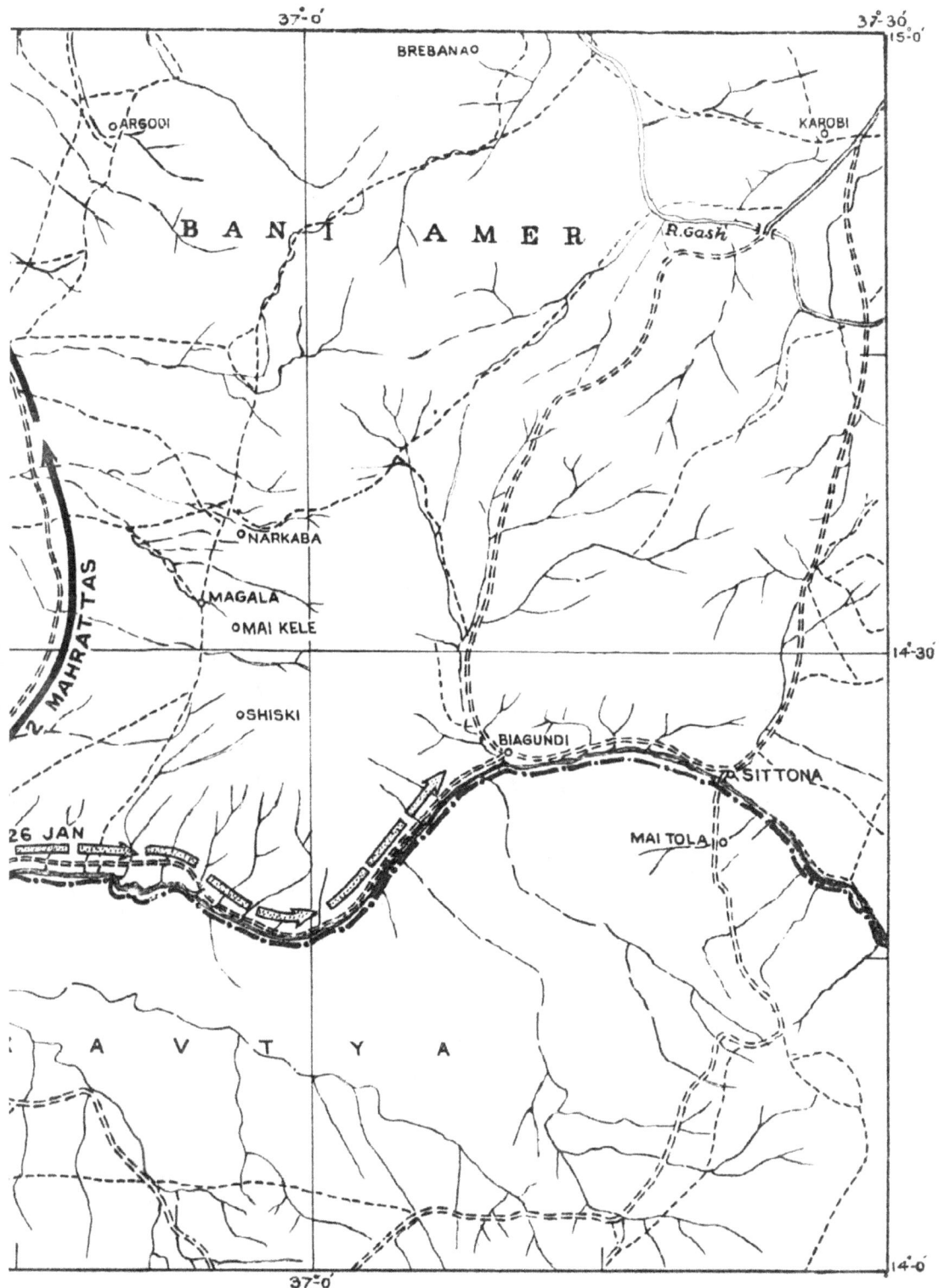

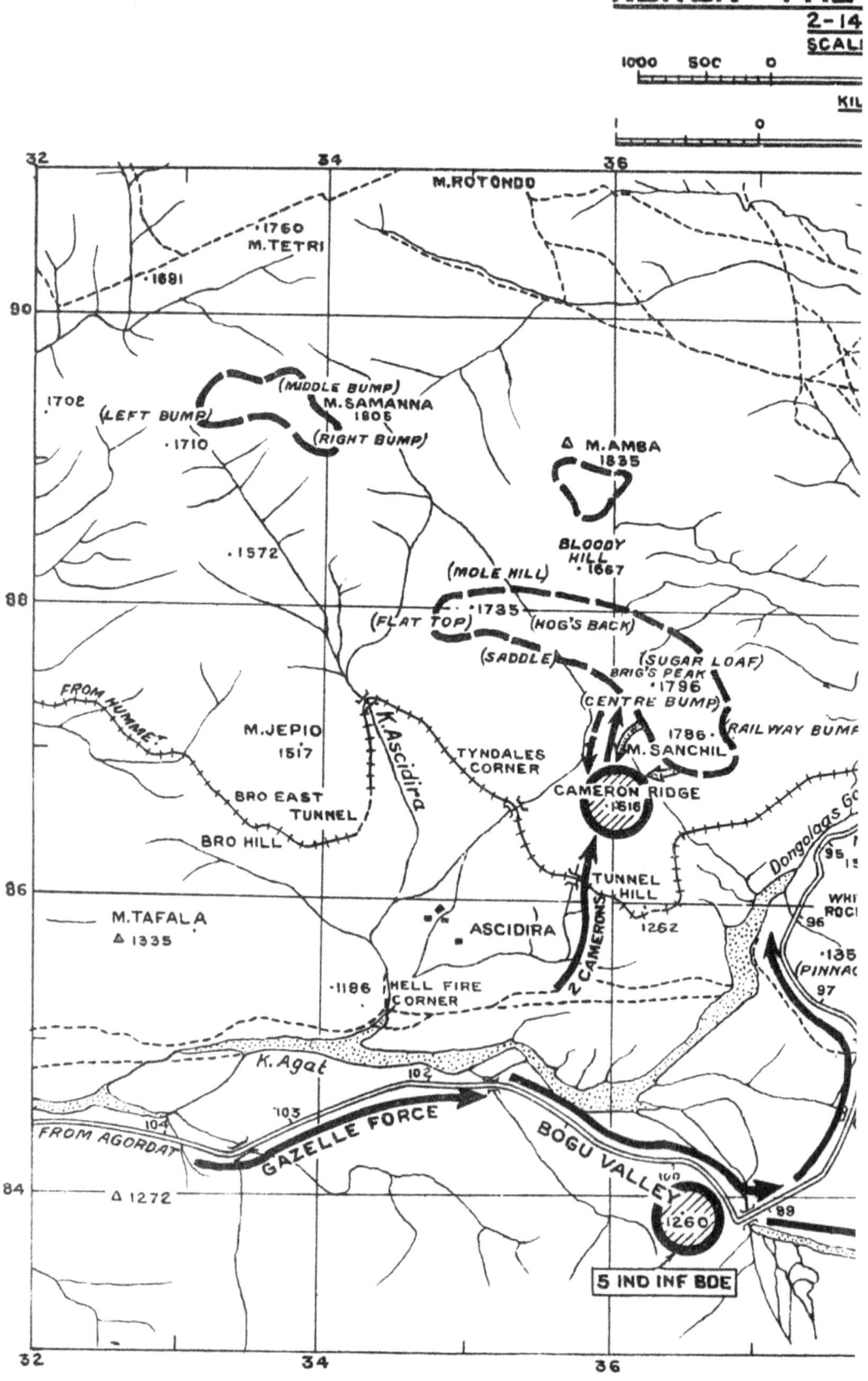

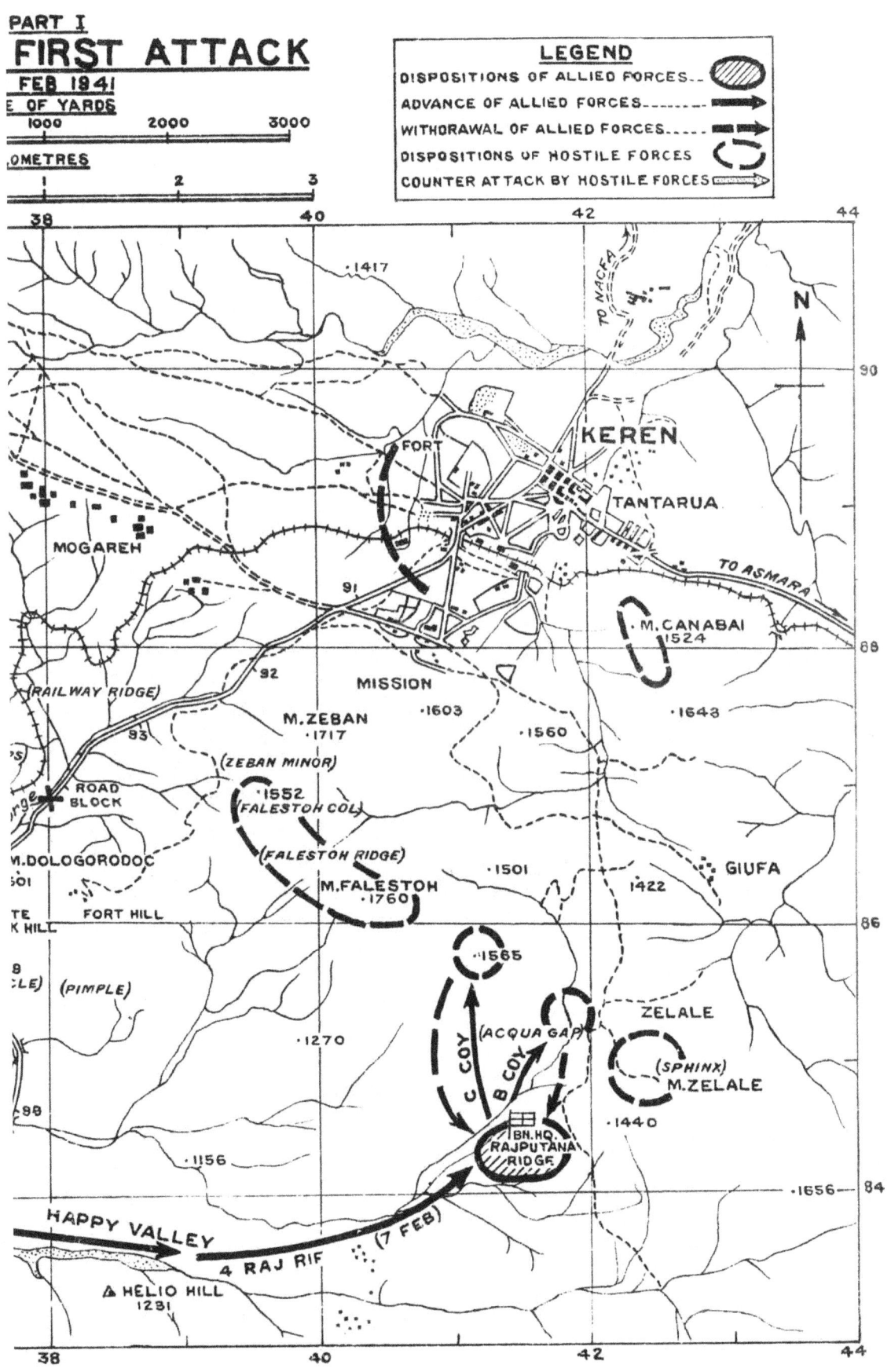

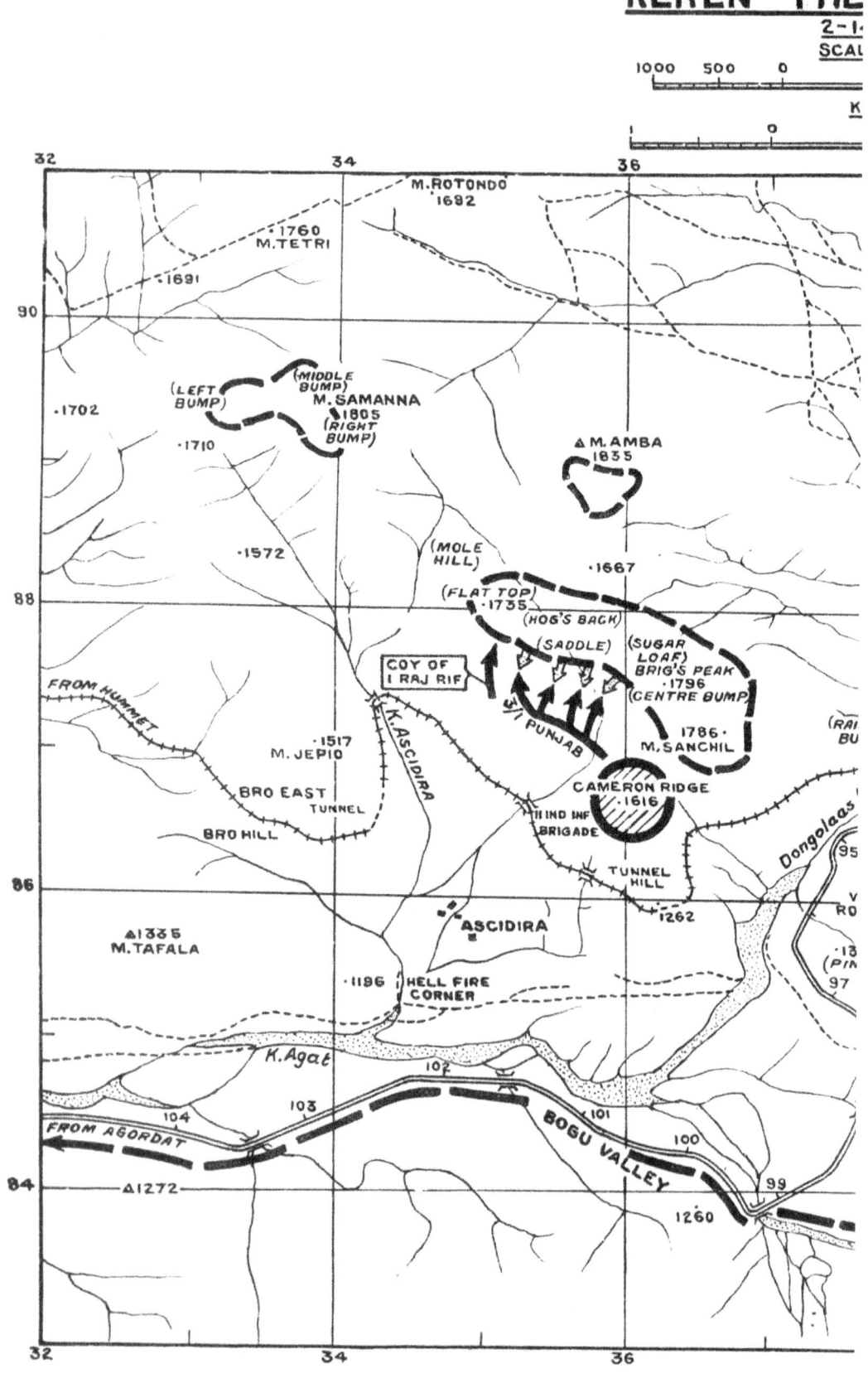

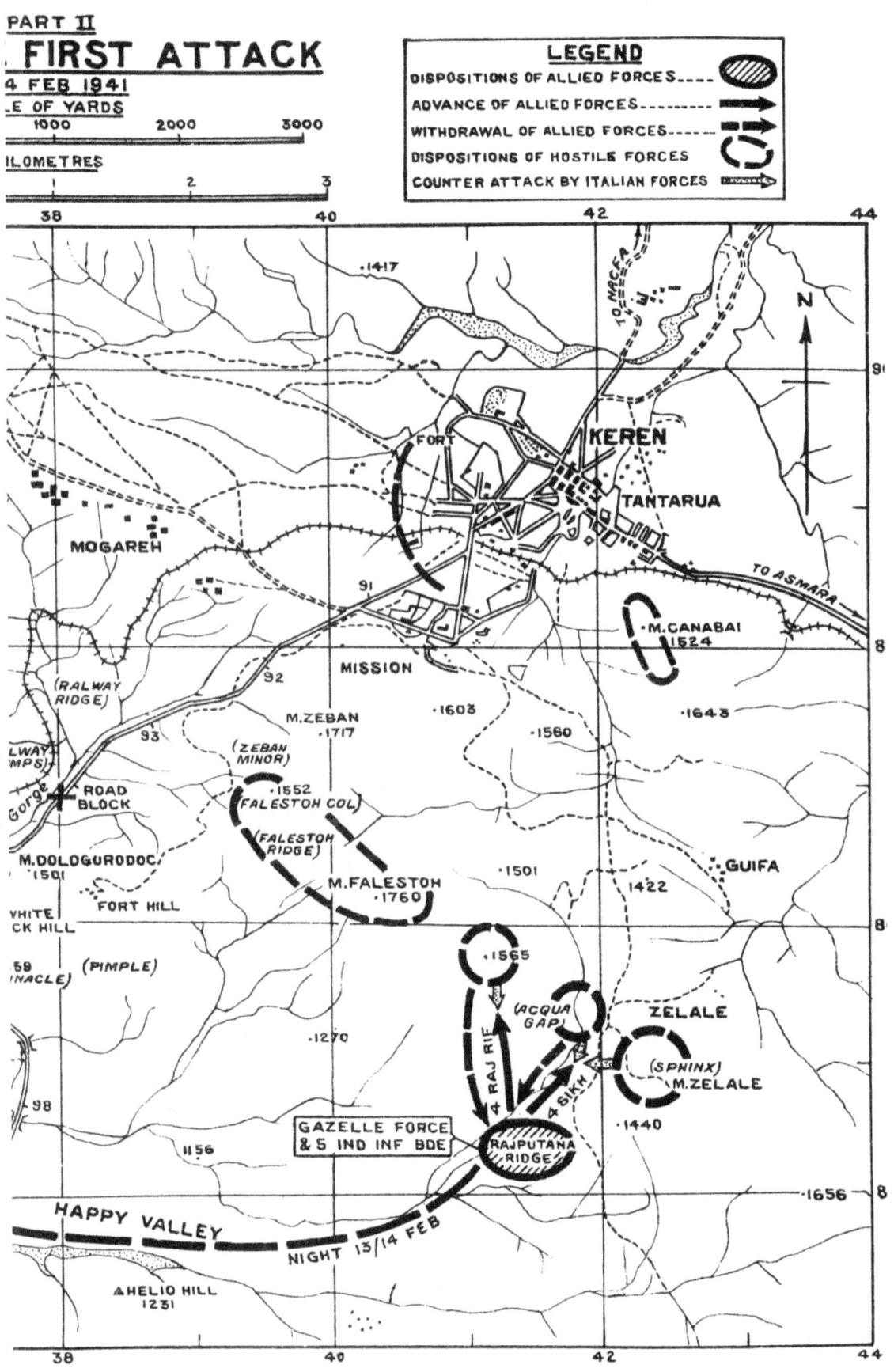

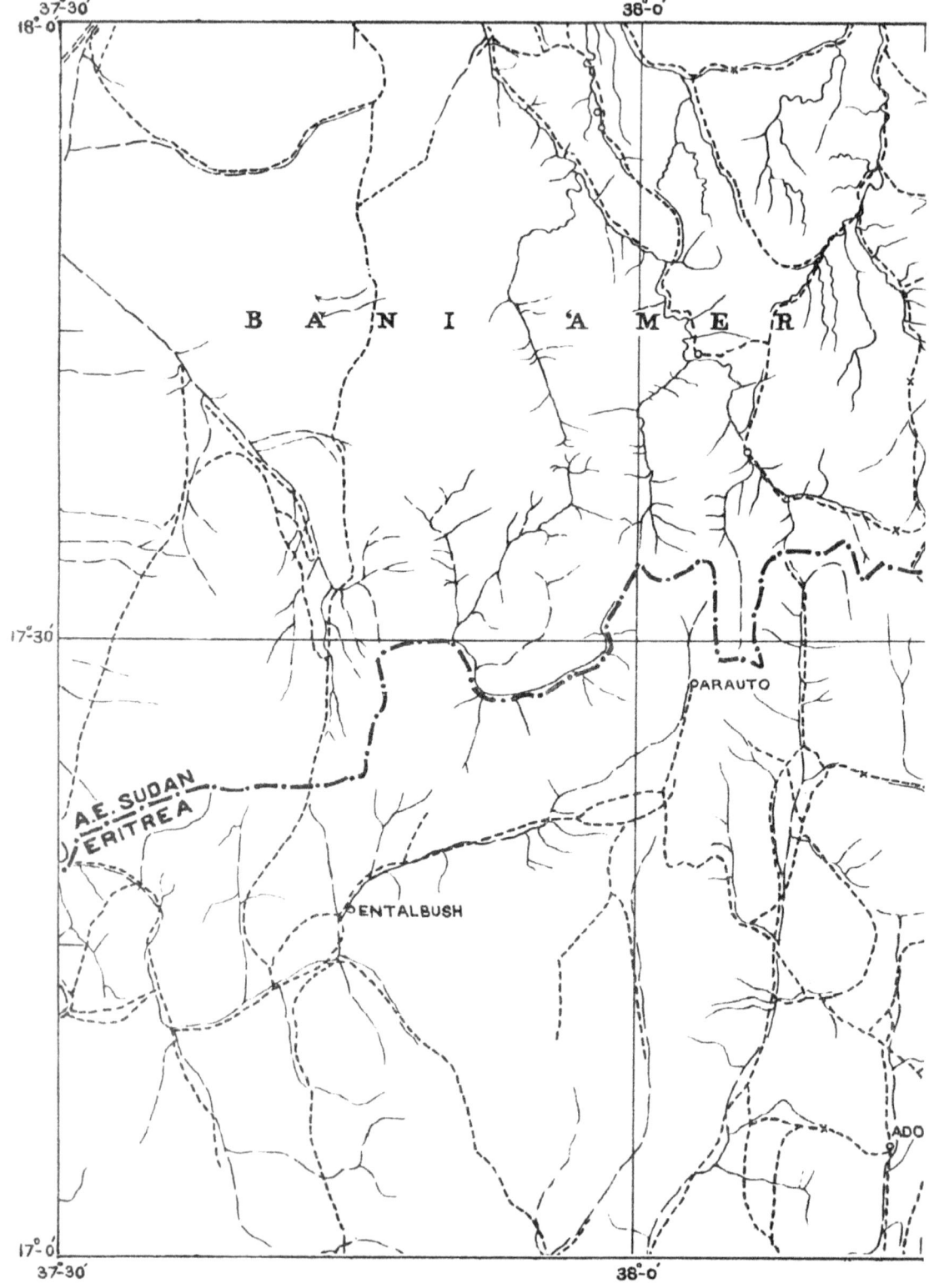

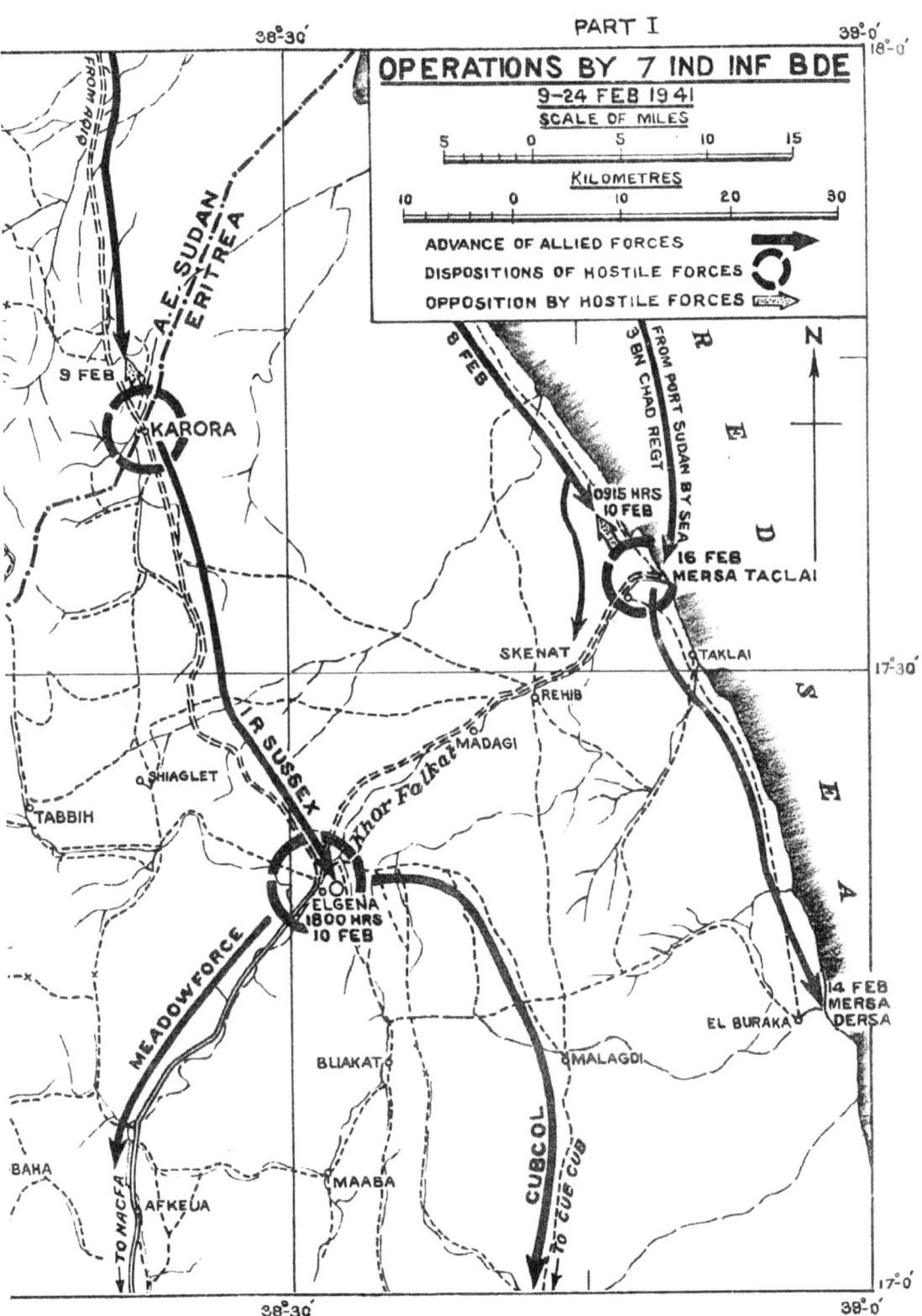

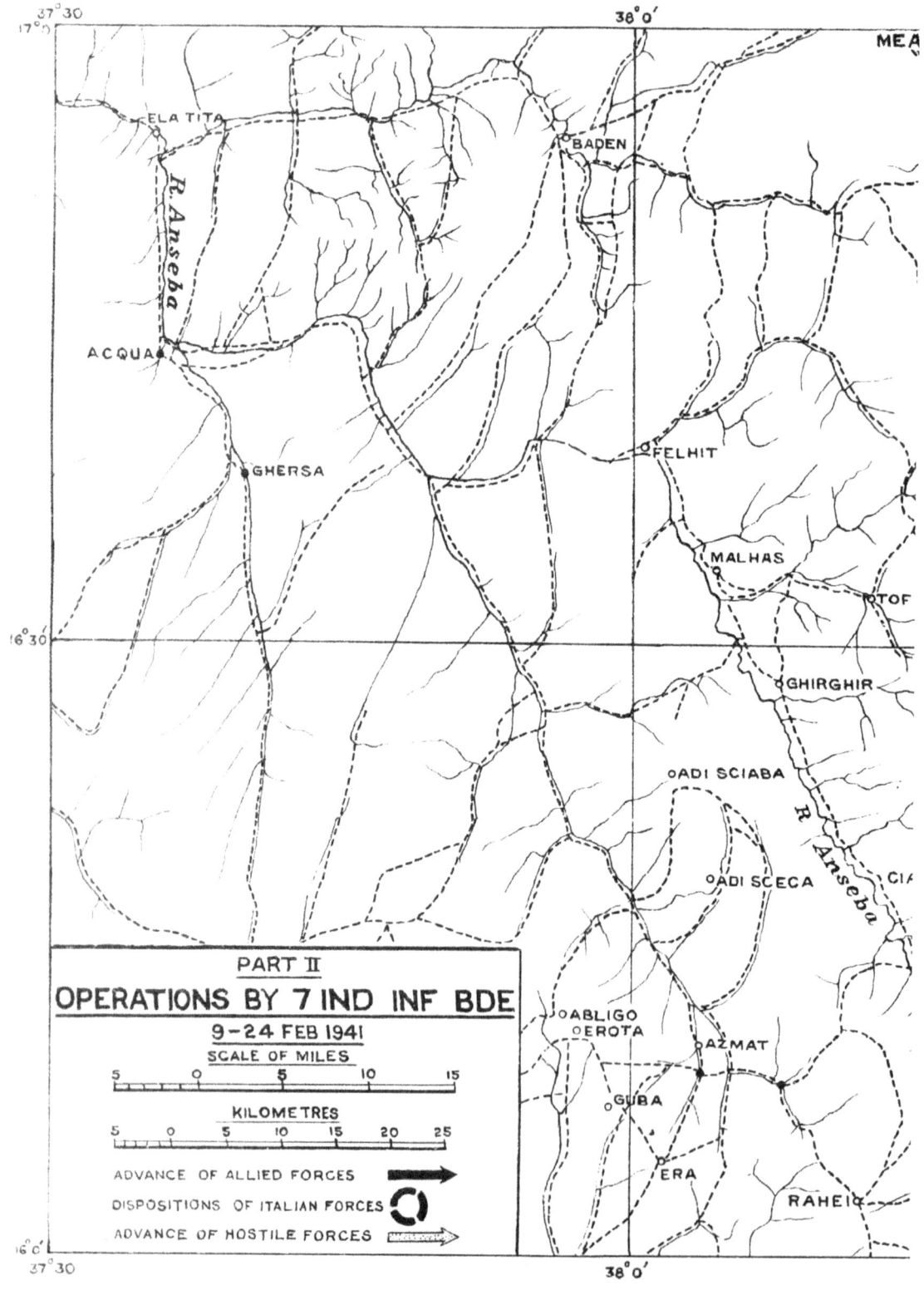

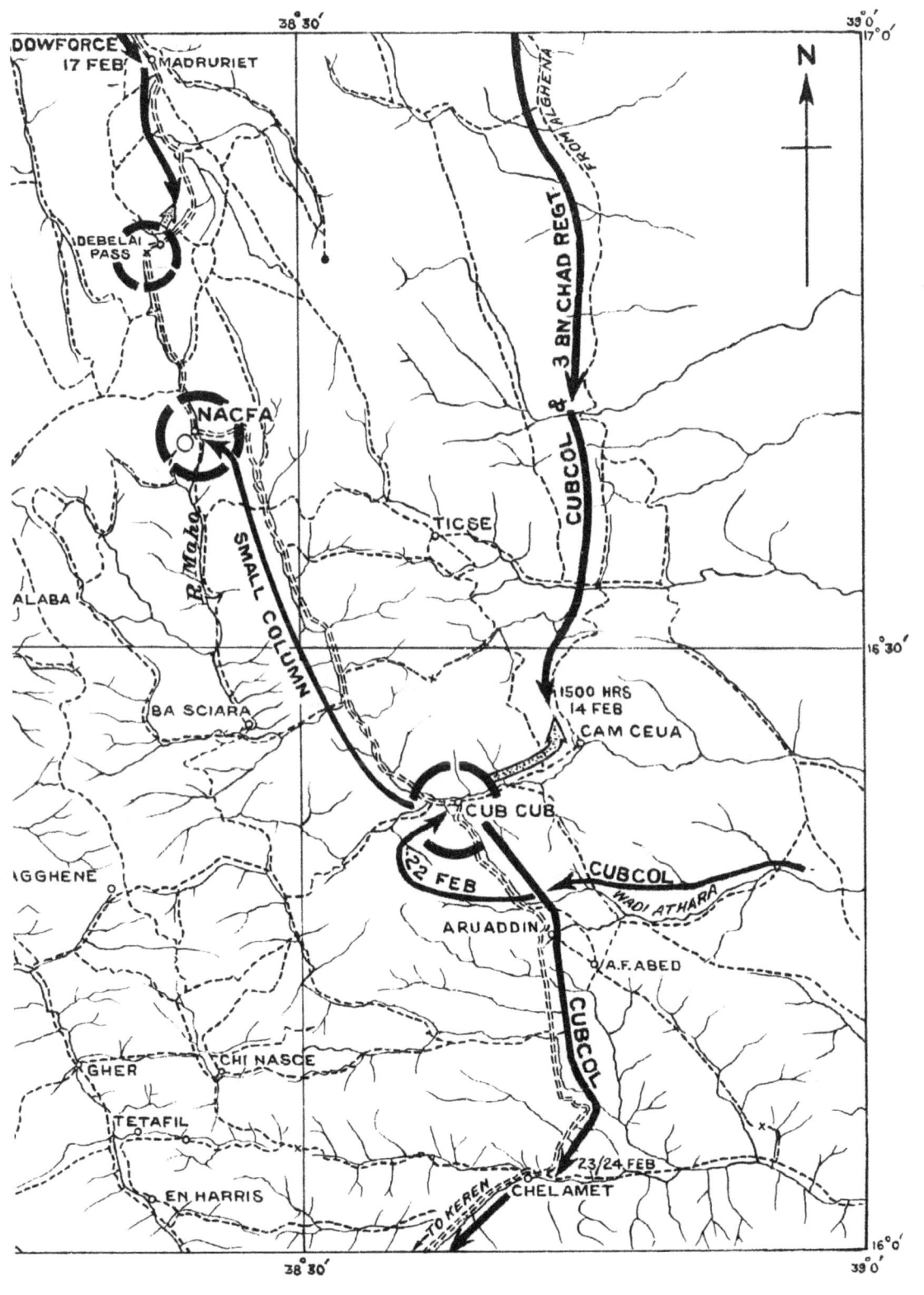

OPERATIONS OF 7 IND INF BDE NORTH OF KEREN
12–27 MARCH 1941

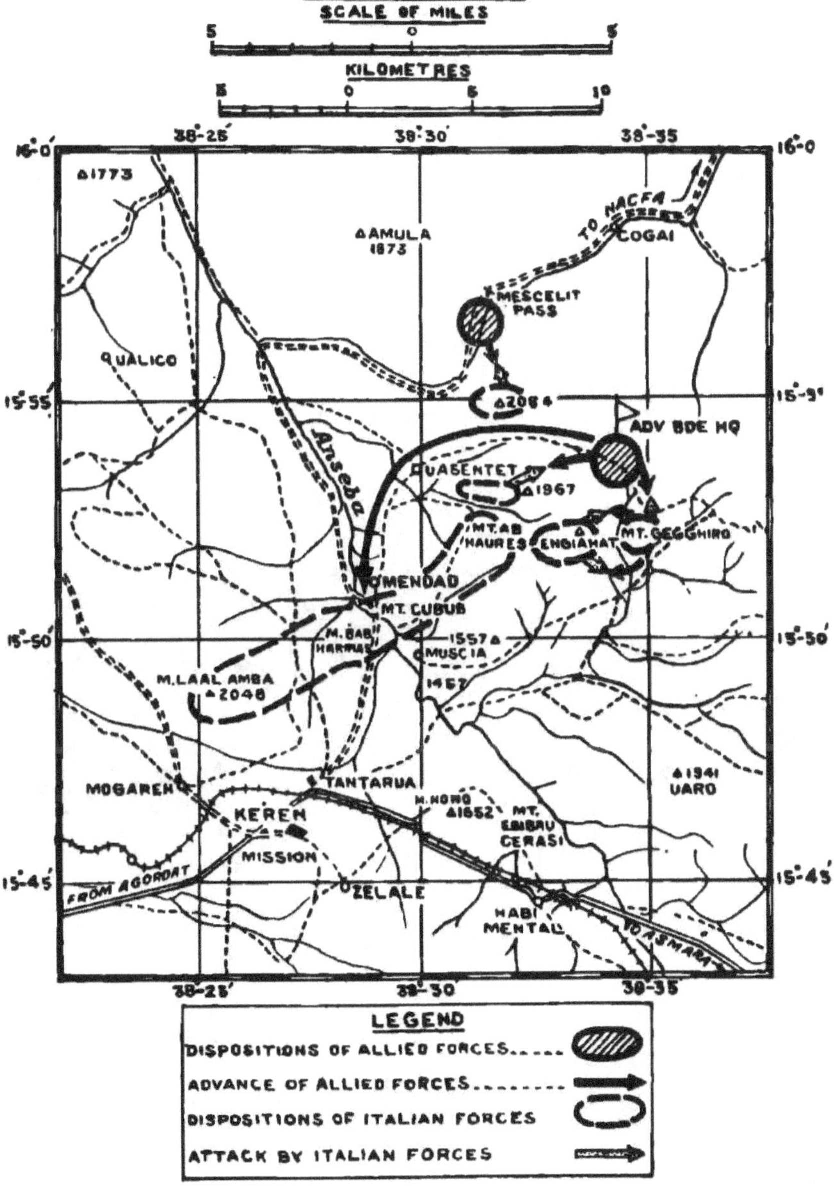

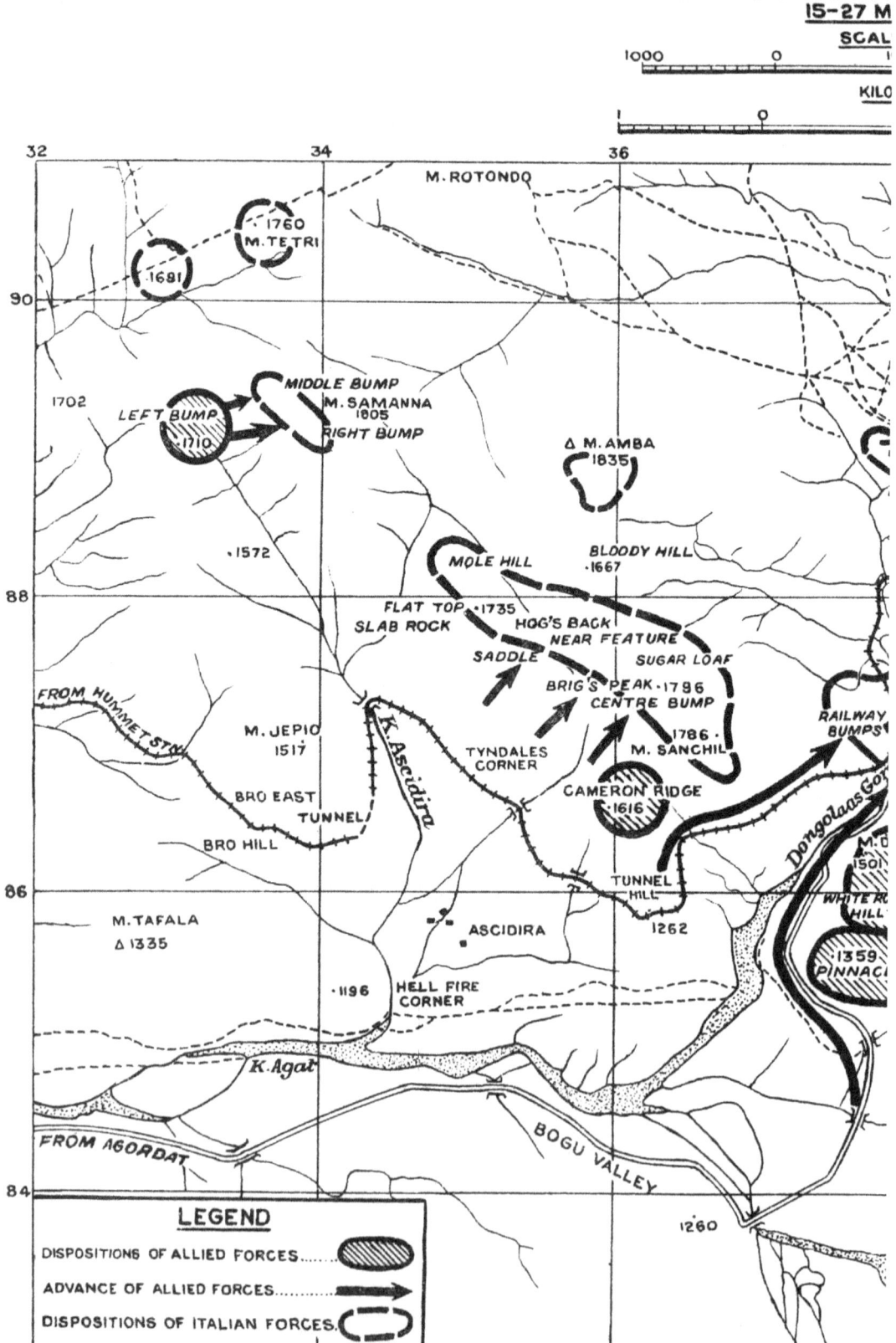

FINAL BATTLE
MARCH 1941

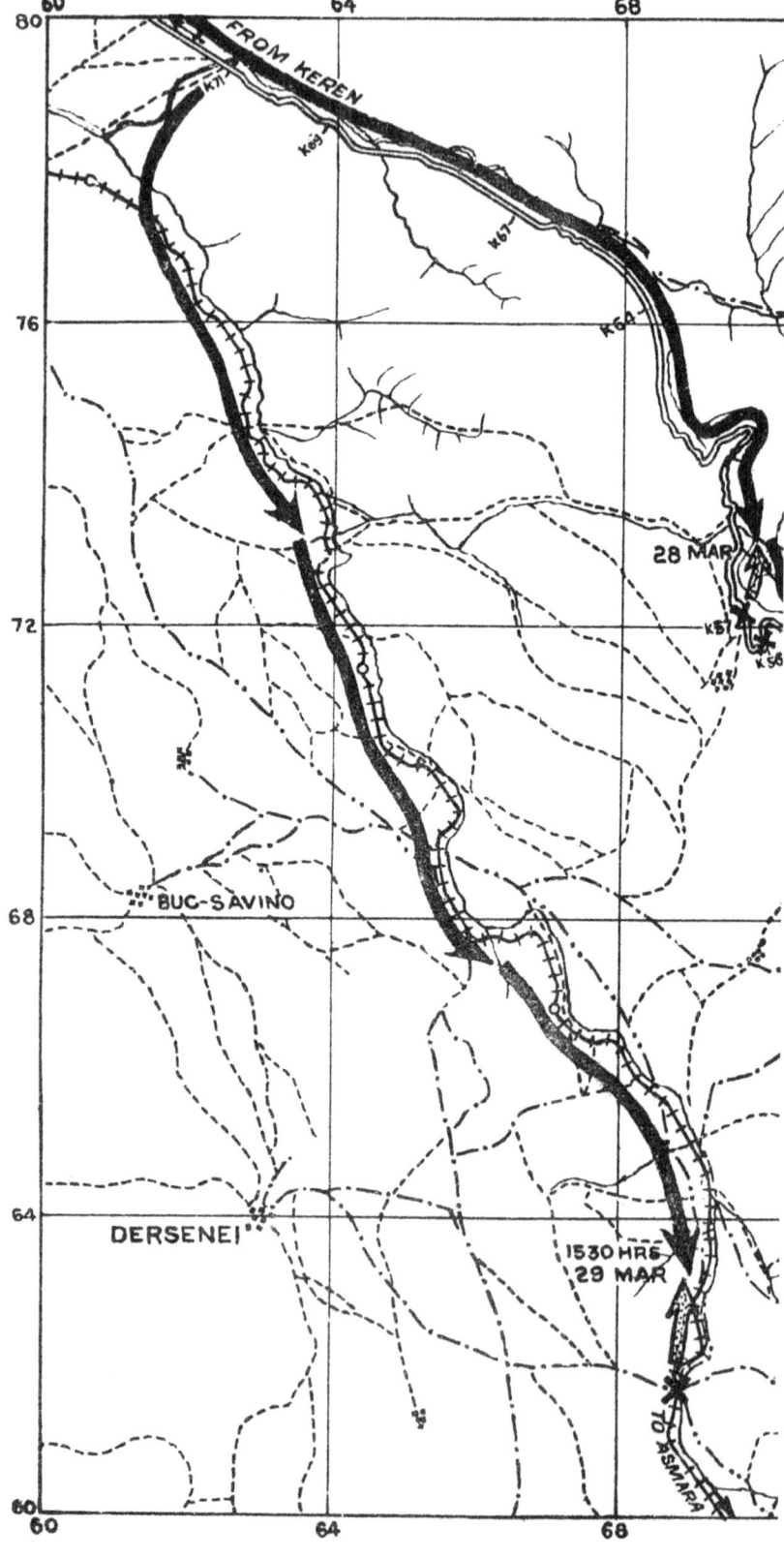

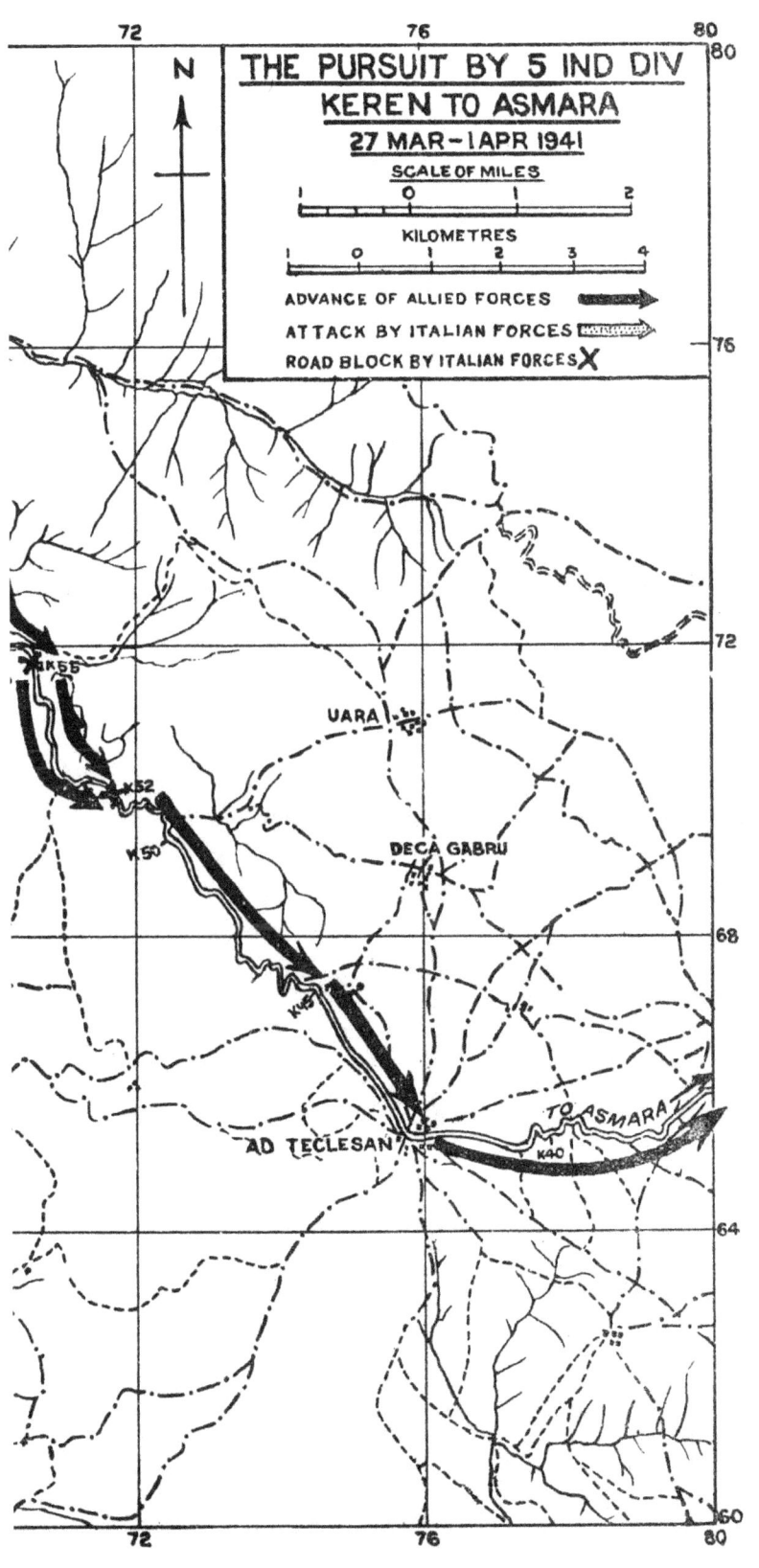

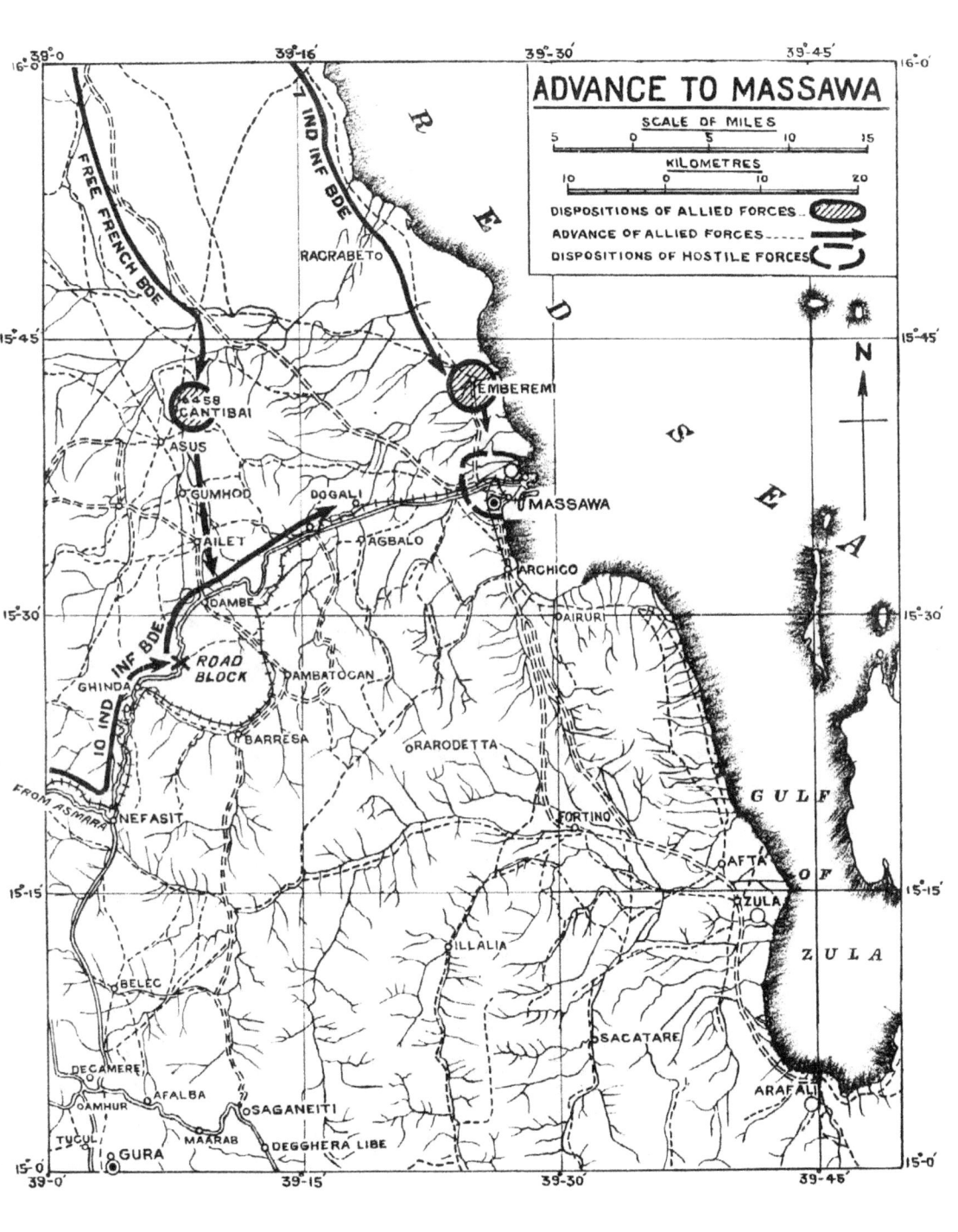

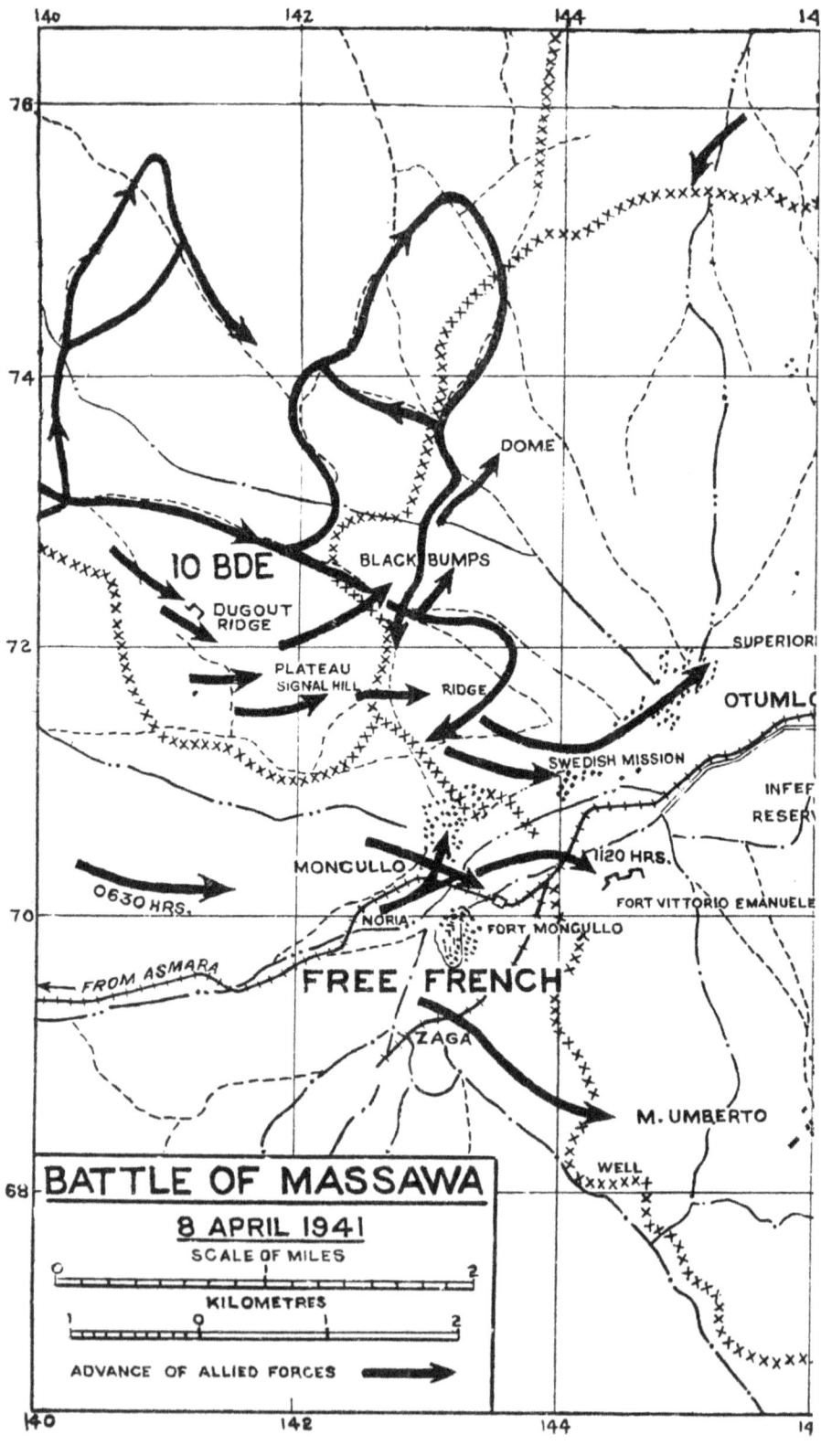

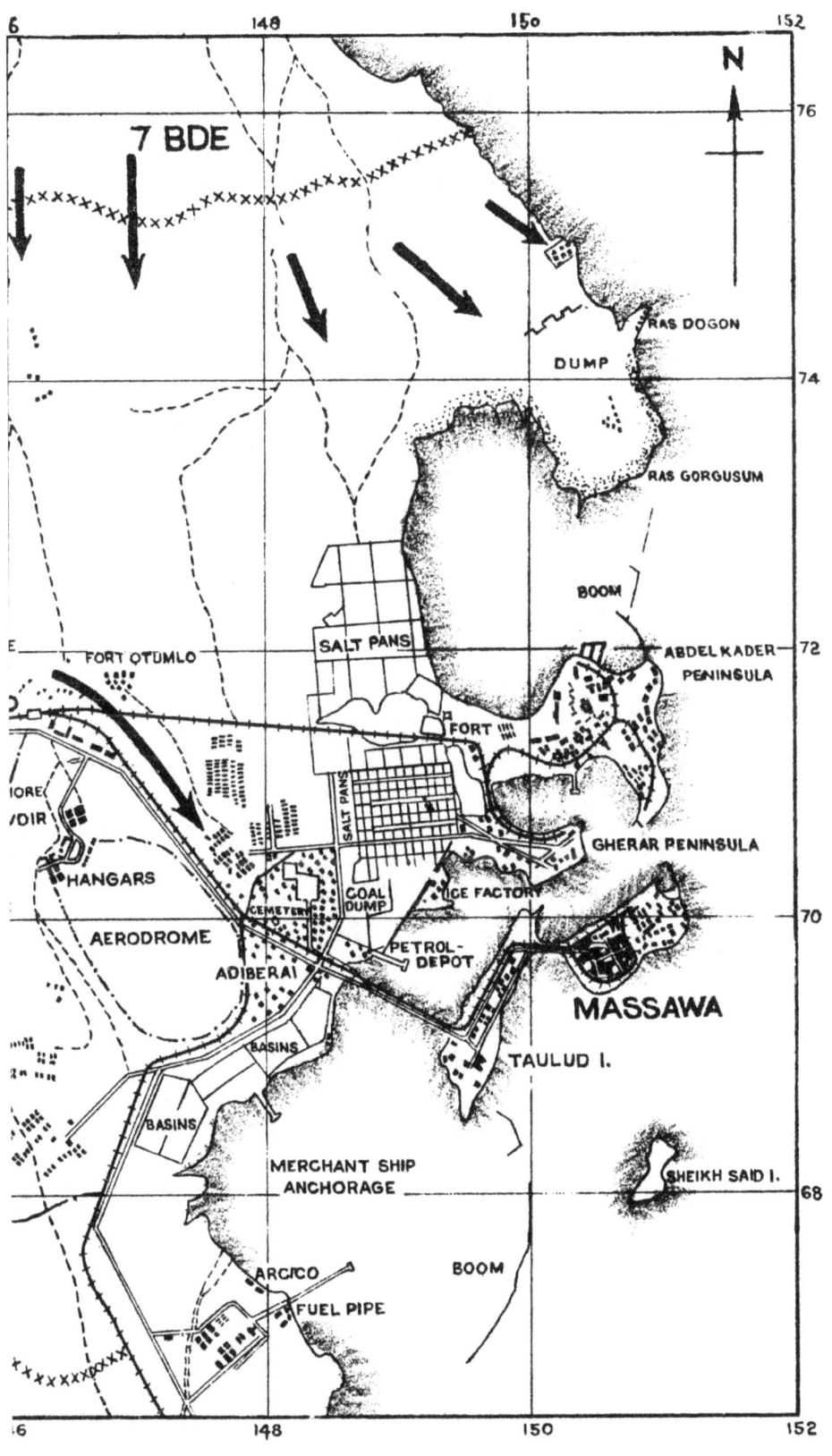

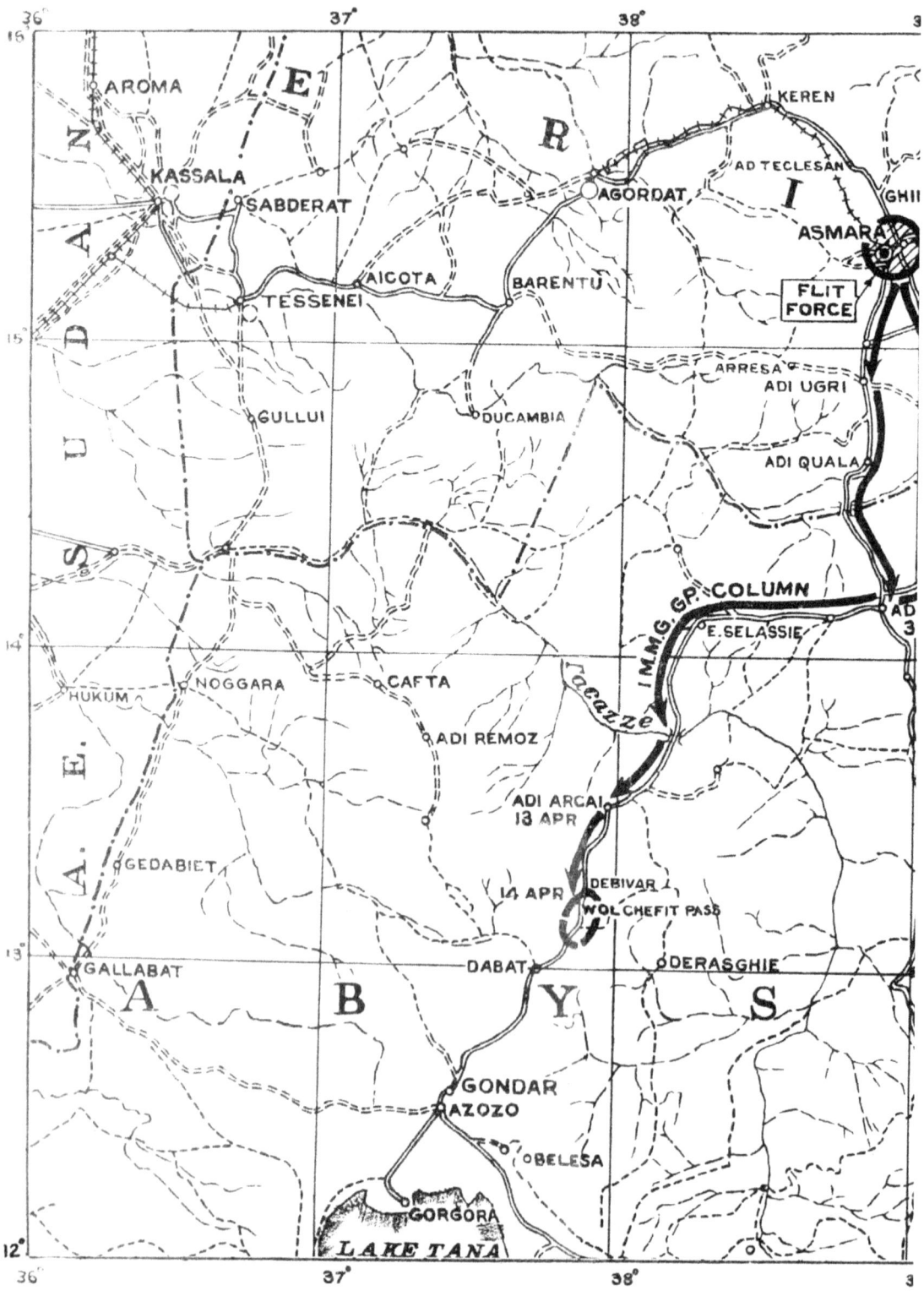

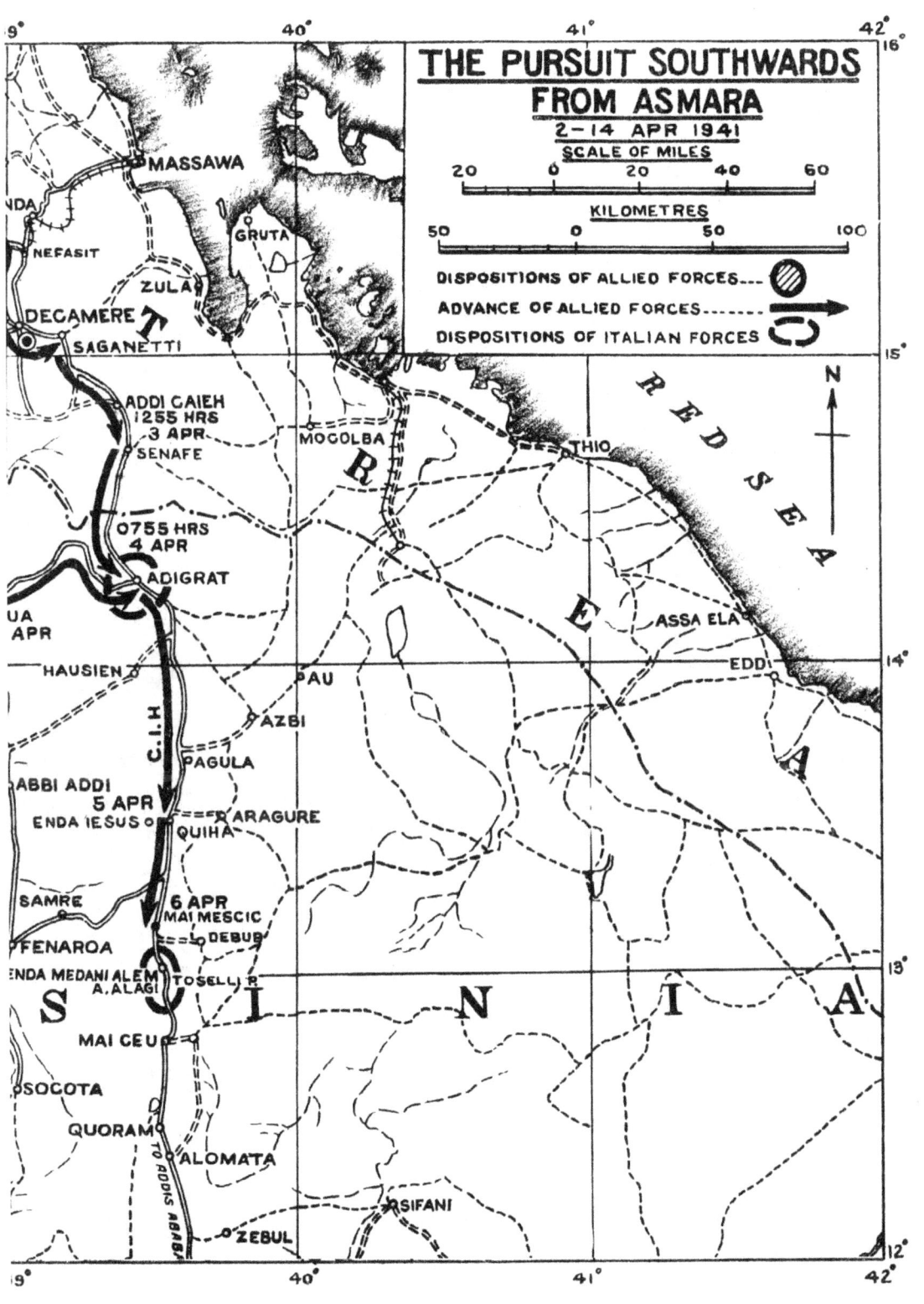

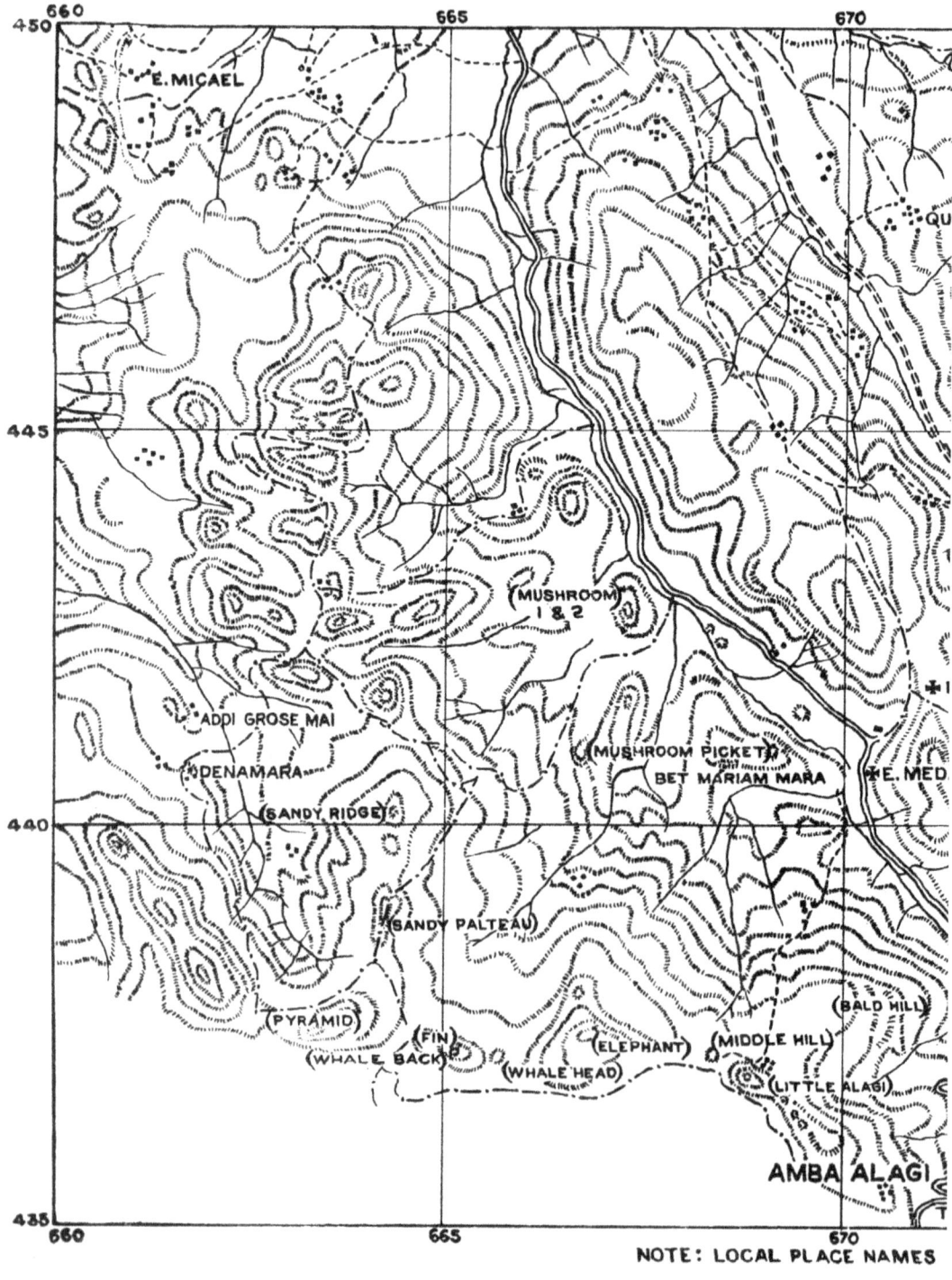
NOTE: LOCAL PLACE NAMES

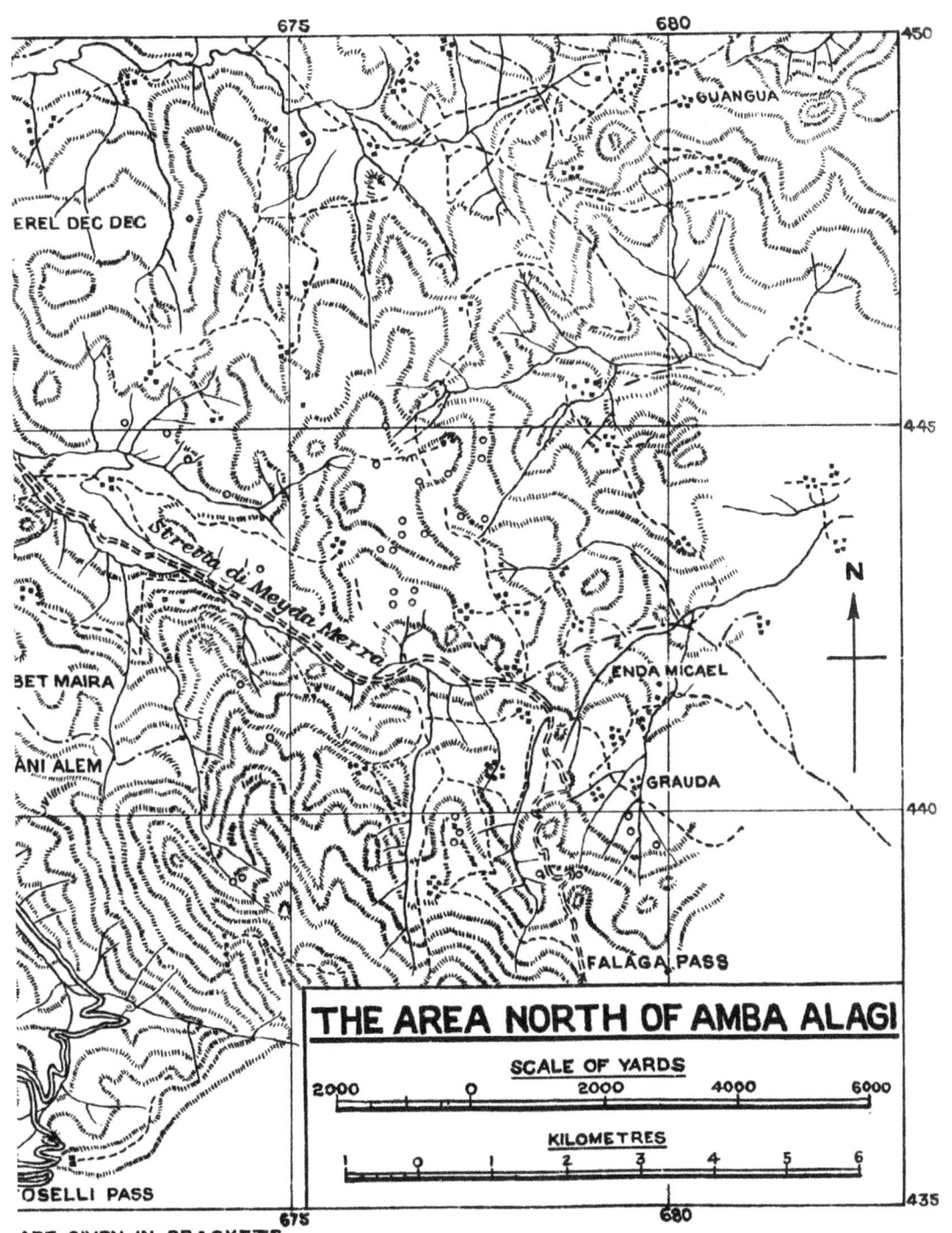

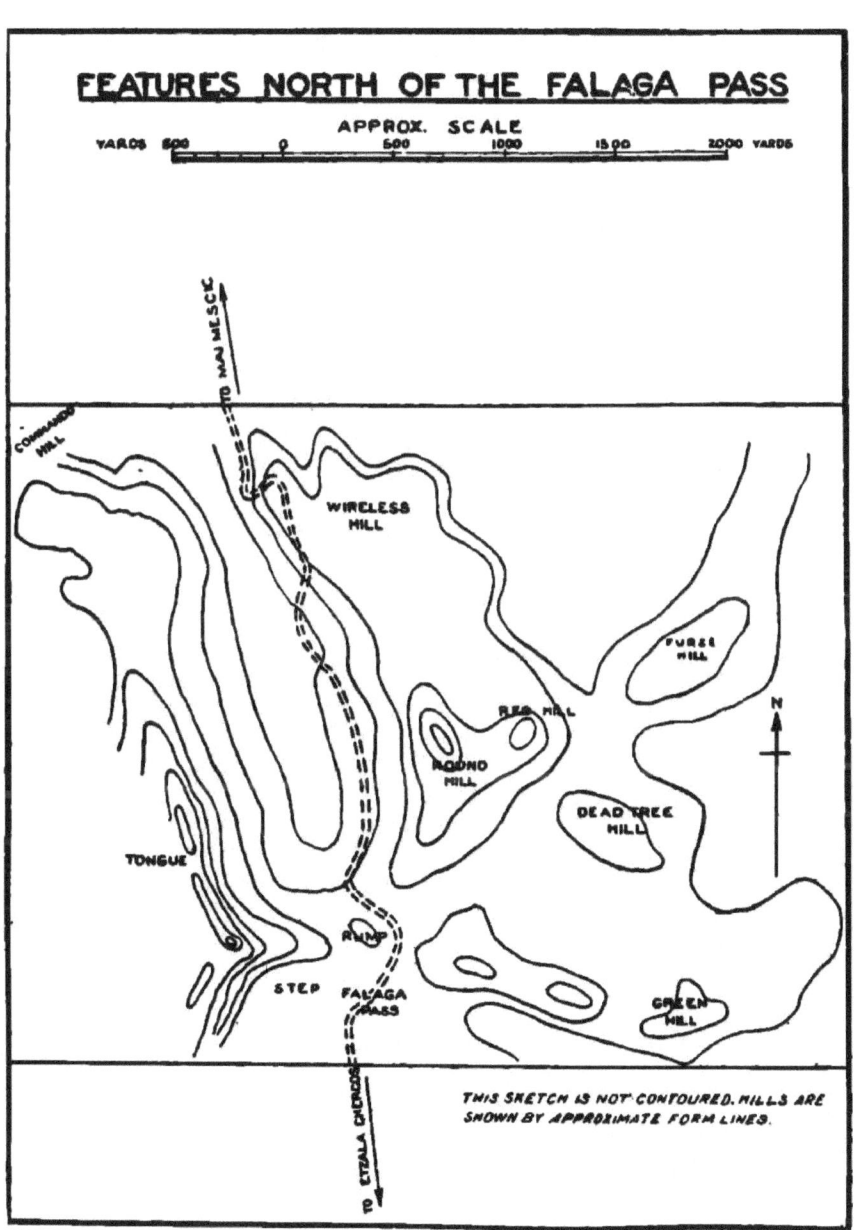

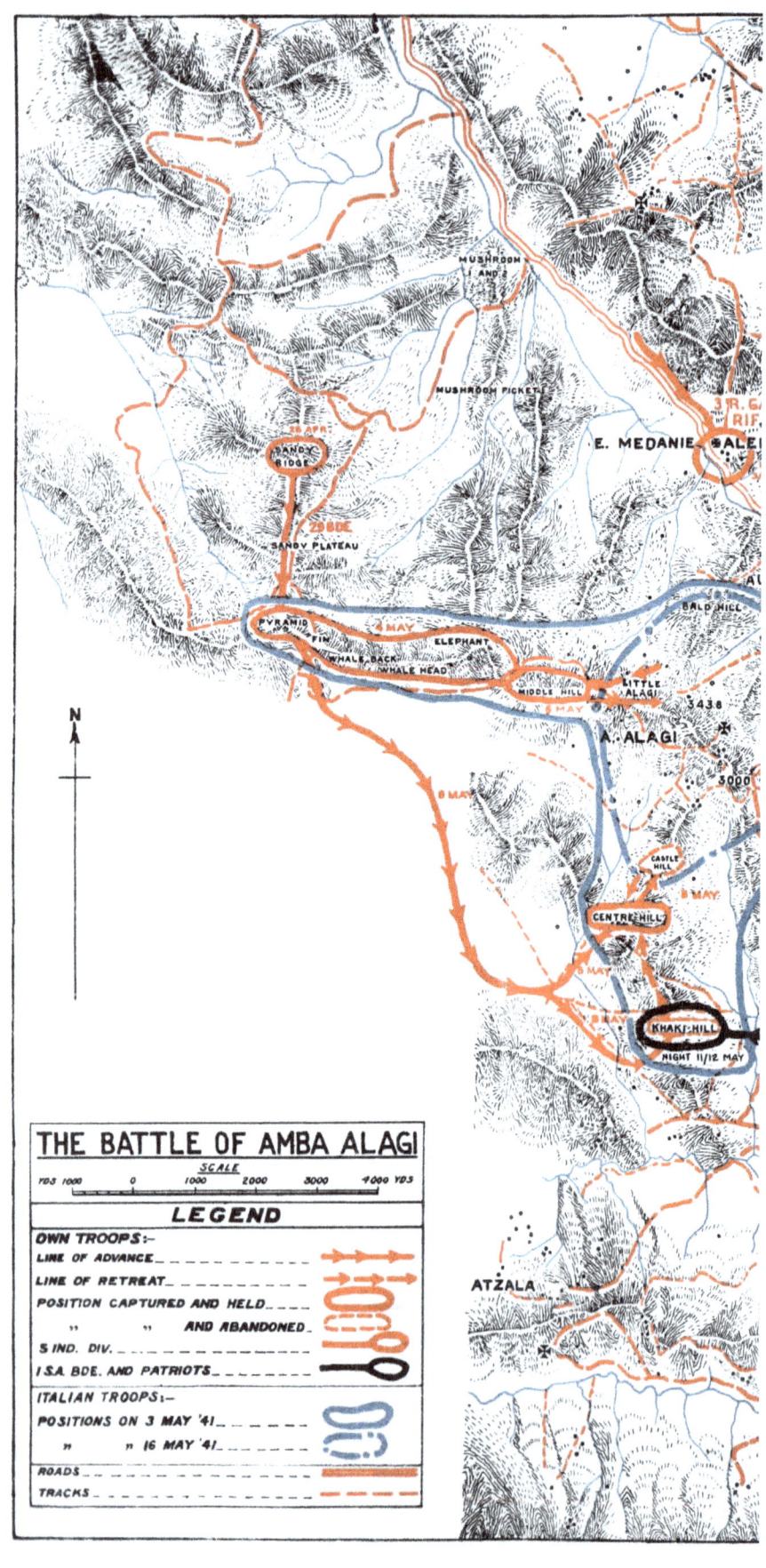

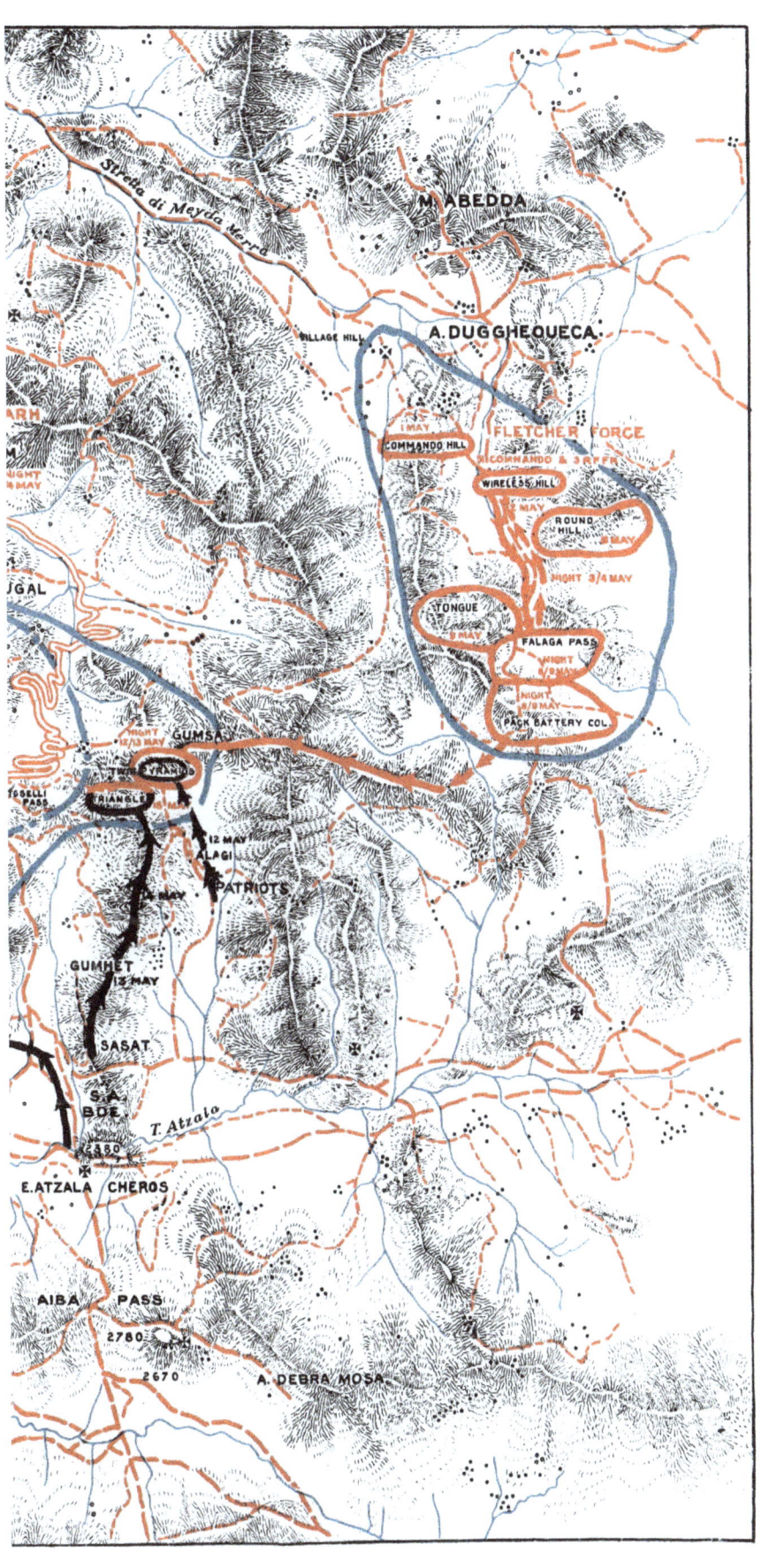

INDIAN DIVISIONS WON A FINE REPUTATION IN WORLD WAR TWO

Field Marshal Auchinleck, Commander-in-Chief of the British Indian Army from 1942, asserted that the British "*couldn't have come through both wars (World War I and II) if they hadn't had the British Indian Army*". British Prime Minister Winston Churchill also paid tribute to "*the unsurpassed bravery of Indian soldiers and officers*".

Between 1945 and 1947, the Director of Public Relations, War Department, Government of India, published a series of short publications covering the individual histories of the WWII Indian Divisions. They followed a consistent format, having between 44 and 48 pages within illustrated soft card covers. They have an average of 50 monochrome photographic illustrations, and each has a full colour centrespread depicting a scene from the Division's wartime operations (drawn by official war artists). They were printed at various presses in Bombay and New Delhi, and each contains at least one map.

As condensed histories they are useful – particularly those which relate to Divisions for which no other record was ever produced.

The British Indian Army during World War II began the war, in 1939, numbering just under 200,000 men. By the end of the war, it had become the largest volunteer army in history, rising to over 2.5 million men in August 1945. Serving in divisions of infantry, armour and a fledgling airborne force, they fought on three continents: in Africa, Europe and Asia.

This Army fought in Ethiopia against the Italian Army, in Egypt, Libya, Tunisia and Algeria against both the Italian and German Army and, after the Italian surrender, against the German Army in Italy. However, the bulk of the British Indian Army was committed to fighting the Japanese Army, first during the British defeats in Malaya and the retreat from Burma to the Indian border; later, after resting and refitting for the victorious advance back into Burma, as part of the largest British Empire army ever formed. These campaigns cost the lives of over 87,000 Indian service-men, while another 34,354 were wounded, and 67,340 became prisoners of war. Their valour was recognised with the award of some 4,000 decorations, and 18 members of the British Indian Army were awarded the Victoria Cross or the George Cross.

RED EAGLES
The Story of the 4th Indian Division
9781474537520

During the Second World War, the 4th Indian Division was in the vanguard of nine campaigns in the Mediterranean theatre, Egypt, Eritrea, Syria, Tunisia, Italy and Greece. The 4th Division captured 150,000 prisoners and suffered 25,000 casualties, more than the strength of a whole division. It won over 1,000 honours and awards, which included four Victoria Crosses and three George Crosses. Field Marshal Lord Wavell wrote: "The fame of this Division will surely go down as one of the greatest fighting formations in military history."

THE FIGHTING FIFTH
History of the 5th Indian Division
9781474537513

As described in much greater detail in Anthony Brett James's book 'The Ball of Fire', the division saw active service in East Africa, North Africa and Burma.

GOLDEN ARROW
The Story of the 7th Indian Division
9781474537506

The role of this division is also duplicated by a much larger work: the book by Brig. M. R. Roberts. However, this booklet gives a good account of Kohima and Imphal and the crossing of the Irrawaddy. In 1945, the division was flown into Siam, so becoming the first Allied formation to re-enter South East Asia.

BLACK CAT DIVISION
17th Indian Division
9781474537483

This formation was committed to Burma from the early days when the British were in full flight from the invading Japanese. It remained in Burma right through to the end, when the starving remnants of the Japanese Army were making their own desperate retreat.

ONE MORE RIVER
The Story of the 8th Indian Division
Biferno, Trigno, Sangro, Moro, Rapido, Arno, Senio, Santerno, Po, Adige

9781474537490

The 8th Indian Division started its overseas service in the Middle East in the garrisoning of Iraq and then the invasion of Persia to secure the oil fields of the area for the Allies, before moving to Italy in 1943. Landing at Taranto, it pushed up the length of the peninsula in a series of major battles: breaking the Sangro Line, forcing the Rapido and turning the defences at Cassino, breaking the stubborn German resistance at Monte Grande and, finally, forcing the Po River. It won four VCs, 26 DSOs and 149 MCs along the way. During the war the 8th Indian Division sustained casualties totalling 2,012 dead, 8,189 wounded and 749 missing.

TIGER HEAD
The Story of the 26th Indian Division
Arakan, Rangoon

9781474537452

This is a history of the division said later by the Japanese to have been the opponent which they most feared. The 26th held the Allied monsoon line in the Arakan during two such seasons, repulsing every attack launched against it. Later it made a series of leap-frog landings down the coast to clinch the issue in the Arakan. It was the first division to enter Rangoon, invading the city from the sea.

THE TWENTY THIRD INDIAN DIVISION
"The Fighting Cock Division"
Burma, Malaya, Java

9781474537469

The Fighting Cock Division is well recorded in the book by Doulton. This book gives coverage of the heavy fighting at the Kohima Battle, the capture of Tamu, the reoccupation of Malaya in August 1945, and then its strange role on the island of Java – concurrently disarming the Japanese garrison, fighting the insurgent Indonesian nationalists, and caring for 65,000 former internees pending the arrival of a new Dutch administration.

A HAPPY FAMILY
The Story of the Twentieth Indian Division,
9781474537476

One of the few Indian divisions in the 14th Army trained specifically for the war in Burma. Raised in Bangalore in 1942, it commenced active operations in late 1943 and served from Imphal through to the end. It established the 14th Army's first brigade-head across the Chindwin and its second such brigade-head across the Irrawaddy. Its final task was to round up the Japanese in French Indochina.

TEHERAN TO TRIESTE
The Story of the Tenth Indian Division
9781783317028

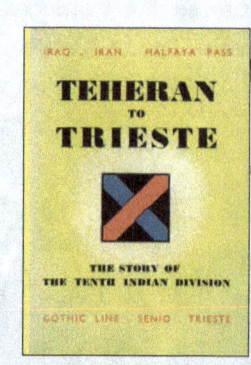

This History deals with the 10th Indian Div's exploits in Iraq (under Maj Gen "Bill" Slim) its role in the Libyan battles leading up to El Alamein, the following two years of garrison duties in Cyprus and Syria, and finally, its fighting services in the Italian campaign (from Ortona onwards).

THE STORY OF THE 25th INDIAN DIVISION
The Arakan Campaign
9781783317585

Formed in Southern India in August 1942 for defence of that area in case of Japanese invasion, the "Ace of Spades" Division had its baptism of fire in Arakan in February 1944. It served throughout the remainder of that campaign the climax being the battle of Tamandu. Its victorious fight for the Kangaw roadblock was considered by many to have been the fiercest battle of the entire Burma war, while its liberation of Akyab was the first convincing proof to the rest of the world that the tide had turned against the Japanese.

DAGGER DIVISION
The Story of the 19th Indian Division
9781783317035

Raised in the late 1941, the 19th was the first "standard" Indian Division. Its troops were the first to breach the Japanese defence line in Burma and to raise the flag at Fort Dufferin. It crossed the Chindwin in November 1944, driving on to Mandalay and Rangoon during seven months of continuous fighting. The 19th's exploits are graphically described also in John Masters' personal memoir, *The Road Past Mandalay*.